A Cultural History of Humour

From Antiquity to the Present Day

EDITED BY JAN BREMMER AND
HERMAN ROODENBURG

Polity Press

This collection © Polity Press 1997
Dutch language rights for this collection are retained by the editors.

Chapter 9 © Mariët Westermann. First published as Chapter 3 in *The Amusements of Jan Steen: Comic Painting of the Seventeenth Century*, Waanders Publishers, The Netherlands, 1996.

First published 1997 by Polity Press in association with Blackwell Publishers Ltd.

Reprinted 2005

2 4 6 8 10 9 7 5 3 1

Polity Press
65 Bridge Street
Cambridge CB2 1UR, UK

Polity Press
350 Main Street
Malden, MA 02148, USA

ISBN 0-7456-1535-X
ISBN 0-7456-1880-4 (pbk)

A CIP catalogue record for this book is available from the British Library and the Library of Congress.

Typeset in 10½ on 12 pt Sabon
by Ace Filmsetting Ltd, Frome, Somerset
Printed and bound in Great Britain by Marston Book Services Limited, Oxford

This book is printed on acid-free paper.

For further information on Polity, visit our website: www.polity.co.uk

Contents

List of Illustrations

Notes on Contributors

ANTOINE DE BAECQUE is Associate Professor of History at the Université de Versailles Saint-Quentin-en-Yvelines. He is the author of *La caricature révolutionnaire* (1988), *Le corps de l'histoire: métaphores et politique (1770–1800)* (1993) and *Les éclats du rire: essais sur la gaité française des Lumières au Romantisme* (1996).

JAN BREMMER is Professor of History of Religion at the University of Groningen. He is the author of *The Early Greek Concept of the Soul* (1983) and *Greek Religion* (1994), co-author of *Roman Myth and Mythography* (1987), editor of *Interpretations of Greek Mythology* (1987), *From Sappho to De Sade: moments in the history of sexuality* (1989), *The Apocryphal Acts of John* (1995) and *The Apocryphal Acts of Paul and Thecla* (1996), and co-editor of *A Cultural History of Gesture* (1991) and *Poverty and the Pyre: moments in the history of widowhood* (1995).

DEREK S. BREWER is Life-fellow and formerly Master of Emmanuel College, and Emeritus Professor of English, at the University of Cambridge. He is also part-founder and Director of the scholarly publishing firm, Boydell and Brewer. Among his many books and edited volumes are *Chaucer* (3rd edn, 1973), *Chaucer and his World* (1978), *Symbolic Stories* (1980), *English Gothic Literature* (1983), *An Introduction to Chaucer* (1984) and *Chaucer: the poet as storyteller* (1984).

PETER BURKE is Professor of Cultural History and Fellow of Emmanuel College at the University of Cambridge. Among his many books and edited volumes are *The Historical Anthropology of Early Modern Italy* (1987), *The French Historical Revolution* (1990), *The Fabrication of Louis XIV* (1992), *History and Social Theory* (1992), *The Art of Conversation* (1993), *Montaigne* (1994) and *The Fortunes of 'The Courtier': the European reception of Castiglione's 'Cortegiano'* (1995).

HENK DRIESSEN is Lecturer in Cultural Anthropology at the University of Nijmegen. He is the author of *Agro-Town and Urban Ethos in Andalusia* (1981) and *On the Spanish-Moroccan Frontier: a study in power, ritual and ethnicity* (1992), editor of *The Politics of Ethnographic Reading and Writing* (1993), and co-editor of *In de ban van betekenis: proeven van symbolische antropologie* (1994).

FRITZ GRAF is Professor of Latin and of Religions of the Mediterranean at the University of Basel. He is the author of *Eleusis und die orphische Dichtung Athens* (1974), *Nordionische Kulte* (1985), *Greek Mythology* (1993) and *Gottesnähe und Schadenzauber: Die Magie in der griechisch-römischen Antike* (1996), editor of *Klassische Antike und neue Wege der Kulturwissenschaften* (1992) and *Mythos in mythenloser Gesellschaft* (1993), and co-editor of *Wanderungen* (1995).

AARON J. GUREVICH is Professor Emeritus at the Institute of General History, Academy of Sciences, Moscow. Among his many books are *Categories of Medieval Culture* (1985), *Medieval Popular Culture* (1988) and *Historical Anthropology of the Middle Ages* (1992).

JACQUES LE GOFF was Director of Studies at the École des Hautes Études en Sciences Sociales. Among his many books and edited volumes are *Time, Work and Culture in the Middle Ages* (1980), *The Birth of Purgatory* (1984), *The Medieval Imagination* (1988), *History and Memory* (1992), *Intellectuals in the Middle Ages* (1993) and *Saint Louis* (1996).

HERMAN ROODENBURG is Research Fellow in Cultural History at the P. J. Meertens-Institute, Department of European Ethnology, Royal Netherlands Academy of Arts and Sciences, Amsterdam. He is the author of *Onder censuur* (1990) and *The Eloquence of the Body: walking, standing and sitting in the Dutch Republic* (1997), and co-editor of Aernout van Overbeke's *Anecdota sive historiae jocosae* (1991), *A Cultural History of Gesture* (1991) and *Image and Self-Image in Netherlandish Art, 1550–1750* (1995).

MARY LEE TOWNSEND is Associate Professor of History at the University of Tulsa. She is the author of *Humor als Hochverrat: Albert Hopf und die Revolution 1848* (1988) and *Forbidden Laughter: popular humor and the limits of repression in nineteenth-century Prussia* (1992).

JOHAN VERBERCKMOES is Lecturer and post-doctoral Research Fellow at the History Department, University of Louvain (KUL), Belgium. He is the author of *Laughter, Jestbooks and Society in the Spanish Netherlands* (1997).

MARIËT WESTERMANN is Assistant Professor of Art History at Rutgers University. She is the author of *A Wordly Art: the Dutch Republic, 1585–1718* (1996) and *The Amusements of Jan Steen: comic painting in the seventeenth century* (1996).

Preface

Humour has been studied since antiquity and from many different perspectives, but historians have mostly eschewed the subject. Traditionally, historical studies of humour have been written by literary historians and ethnologists, who tend to focus on problems of genre and literary tradition or those of type and motif. It is only recently that historians, seeing humour as a key to the cultural codes and sensibilities of the past, have become interested as well. This development and a growing interest among ethnologists and literary historians in a wider cultural perspective seemed an excellent opportunity to organize a colloquium on the subject, not only with historians but also with art historians, literary historians, classicists, ethnologists and anthropologists. The conference, which was held in Amsterdam in January 1994, proved to be highly stimulating.

We thank all those who made the event possible. The Royal Netherlands Academy of Arts and Sciences, the Faculty of Theology and Science of Religion of the Rijksuniversiteit Groningen, and the P. J. Meertens-Instituut, Amsterdam, supported the conference with generous contributions. Financial support was also received from the Oost-Europa Fonds of the Royal Academy and the M. A. O. C. Gravin van Bylandt Stichting in The Hague. Our friend Jan Gast made a donation towards the costs of the illustrations, as he had also done with our previous collection on gestures. The advice and enthusiasm of Peter Burke and Johan Verberckmoes were invaluable in helping us define the scope of the conference. We also profited greatly from the encouragement of Professor Jaap van Marle, director of the P. J. Meertens-Instituut, and from the assistance with the conference of Benjamin Bremmer, Rudi Künzel and Johannes Kolff. Ken Dowden, as always, Jennifer Kilian and Thomas McCreight skilfully revised the English of contributions to this volume at very short notice. Annabelle Mundy helpfully moved the book through the desk-editing process. We also would like to express our gratitude to Dr Elena Gurevich for kindly accompanying her father to Amsterdam.

Finally, we thank the contributors for their enthusiasm and interest in the colloquium. Without them we would have been unable to offer the reader this volume with its stimulating studies of life in the past. The book is dedicated to the memory of the German ethnologist Elfriede Moser-Rath, who at the time of the conference was already too ill to take part in it. Her fine studies on humour in early modern Germany remain an inspiration for us all.

Jan Bremmer, Herman Roodenburg

Introduction:
Humour and History

JAN BREMMER AND
HERMAN ROODENBURG

What is humour? In the title of this book we use it as the most general
and neutral notion available to cover a whole variety of behaviour:
from apophthegms to spoonerisms, practical jokes to puns, farce to
foolery. In other words, we see humour as any message – transmitted
in action, speech, writing, images or music – intended to produce a smile
or a laugh. This definition allows us not only to extend our investigations to antiquity, the Middle Ages and the beginning of the early
modern period, but also to pose questions of interest to cultural
historians: who transmits what humour in which way to whom, where
and when?

Strictly speaking, the notion of 'humour' is relatively young.[1] In its
modern meaning it is first attested in England in 1682, whereas before
that it used to signify mental disposition or temperament. Lord
Shaftesbury's famous *Sensus communis: an essay on the freedom of wit
and humour* (1709) was one of the earliest writings to use it in the sense
familiar to moderns as defined by the *Concise Oxford Dictionary*,
which characterizes humour as 'facetiousness, comicality' and considers it 'less intellectual and more sympathetic than wit'. Voltaire, in
contrast, proposed a French origin for the term. He claimed that
humour in the new English sense, meaning 'plaisanterie naturelle', was
derived from the French *humeur* as employed by Corneille in his first
comedies.[2] It is true that the English originally derived '*humour*' from
the French in the meaning of one of the four chief fluids of the body
(blood, phlegm, bile and black bile), but it is more than doubtful
whether the contemporary English meaning was also derived from
France. In fact, from 1725 onwards the French invariably characterize
the term as an English borrowing – a usage for which Voltaire is, of
course, an indirect witness.[3] In 1862 Victor Hugo still spoke about 'that
English thing they call humour', and it was only in the early 1870s that
some Frenchmen started pronouncing it in the French way.[4]

A similar development may be traced in other countries. In the Dutch

Republic, in 1765, English humour was still seen as something 'which they virtually find only on their isle'.⁵ In Germany, too, the word was an English 'import', as Lessing explicitly states. In fact, he first translated 'humour' as 'Laune', taking it in its older sense, although he corrected himself afterwards.⁶ And still in 1810 an early German biographer of Joseph Haydn noted that 'a sort of innocent mischievousness, or what the British call humour', had been a principal trait of the composer's character.⁷

Yet the first mention of a new term does not always imply the rise of a new phenomenon, as is illustrated by the German *Witz* or the Dutch *mop*. These two relatively late words describe a phenomenon that far antedates them, namely the short joke, which rushes headlong to its punch line. Such narratives were already present in the seventeenth century, but *Witz* first appears at the end of the eighteenth and its equivalent *mop* at the end of the nineteenth century. These examples also show that specific terms, such as joke, gag or *blague*, all have their own history and may differ more from one another than is usually realized.

It would be fascinating to follow the meanderings of the notion of humour and all the other humorous terms handed down from antiquity or coined in later times. As part of such an undertaking the topic of 'national styles' could be addressed.⁸ What does it mean, for example, when Robert's standard French dictionary defines humour as 'Forme d'esprit qui consiste à présenter ou à deformer la réalité de manière à en dégager les aspects plaisants et insolites', whereas its German counterpart, the Duden, defines it as the 'Gabe eines Menschen, der Unzulänglichkeit der Welt und der Menschen, den Schwierigkeiten und Missgeschicken des Alltags mit heiterer Gelassenheit zu begegnen'? Part of this national style is also the tendency to deny a sense of humour to others, as when a character in one of André Maurois's novels claims that their lack of a sense of humour was the sole reason that the Germans started the Great War.⁹

Although humour should produce laughter, not all laughter is the fruit of humour. Laughter can be threatening and, indeed, ethologists have suggested that laughter originated in an aggressive display of teeth. On the other hand, humour and its corresponding laughter can also be highly liberating. We all know how a flash of humour can suddenly dissolve a tense atmosphere. In a wider context, carnival and comparable festivities can temporarily dissolve the rigid social rules with which we all have to comply, although often with low rather than high humour. Considering this diversity, it is not surprising that in his contribution to this book Jacques Le Goff observes that, until now, it has been impossible to establish coherence in the various words, concepts and practices of laughter.

Scholars have certainly tried to find such coherence. From Freud and Bergson to Mary Douglas, psychologists, philosophers, sociologists and anthropologists have endeavoured to find an all-encompassing theory of humour and laughter.[10] A mistake common to all these attempts is the tacit presupposition that there exists something like an 'ontology of humour', that humour and laughter are transcultural and ahistorical. However, laughter is just as much a culturally determined phenomenon as humour. As Henk Driessen notes in the final chapter, fieldwork experience documents the richness of comic expression around the world: some tribes laugh easily, whereas others are said to be dour and sombre. Similar variations can be noted in the history of Europe: the ancient Anglo-Saxons found it normal to roll over the floor with laughter, but modern man often expresses his appreciation of humour with a civilized chuckle.[11]

Until now, scholarly attention to humour has usually concentrated on works of literature or folk narratives. Typical examples are studies of humour in Shakespeare or jest-books from the early modern period. The more interesting of such studies try to relate the contents of humorous texts to particular literary traditions or to a specific type or motif, as classified in the motif indexes drawn up by ethnologists or literary historians. Unfortunately, it is only rarely that these studies clearly situate such texts within the group or culture in which they must have circulated. The authors of this volume aim at a wider application. In their different ways, they are interested in humour as a key to specific cultures (such as Renaissance Italy and nineteenth-century Germany), religions (such as early or post-Reformation Christianity) and professional groups (such as the laughter of politicians, as studied by Antoine de Baecque). This variety implies that they draw on a much wider range of source material than is normally taken into account. From philosophers and orators, from Church Fathers and manuals of civility, from practical jokes and jest-books, from parliamentary records and diaries, from paintings and collections of anecdotes – the contributors to this volume open up new vistas in cultural history by their use of uncommon or rarely exploited sources. Not that every possible source has been exhausted: lovers of Beethoven's *Diabelli Variations*, Ives's songs or Ligeti's *Aventures* and *Nouvelles aventures* will immediately note the absence of any reference to humour in music. An admirer of the folly in the shape of a pepperpot in Dublin's Power Court will ponder the absence of architecture, and the study of satiric journals, such as by Mary Lee Townsend, has certainly revealed only the tip of the iceberg. The mere mention of *Punch*, *Private Eye* or the *National Lampoon* strongly suggests that the printing press in this respect has perhaps opened up more fields than most historians would want.

Humour was studied systematically first in antiquity. Unfortunately, it is not possible to trace satisfactorily the ancient theories of humour, since the second book of Aristotle's *Poetics*, which concentrated on comedy, has been irretrievably lost – a theme brilliantly exploited in Umberto Eco's *The Name of the Rose* – as have *On Comedy* and *On the Ludicrous* (fragments 709–10) by his pupil Theophrastus. Quotations and fragments of these and other works of Aristotle and his school, the Peripatetics, show that in his discussion of humour in *De oratore* (2.216–90) Cicero used this tradition, although certainly indirectly and transformed by Roman ideas. His is our first extant systematic analysis, and the next elaborate discussion, a century later by Quintilian, is heavily indebted to him.

Cicero is also an important source for the Roman vocabulary of humour. Although the Romans used their various terms without much consistency, some differentiation can be made. For example, *facetiae*, 'wittiness' or 'joke', is usually contrasted with *gravitas*, 'seriousness, respectability' (2.262, 3.30), whereas the less elegant *iocus*, which Quintilian contrasts with *serium* (6.3.21), means 'joke' but also 'banter'. Cicero also distinguished between 'wit of matter', telling anecdotes or entertaining stories, and 'wit of form', the making of humorous remarks and puns (2.239–47). Good humour knows its bounds and avoids at all costs mimicry and the postures of mimes and buffoons (2.244, 247). As Fritz Graf demonstrates, Cicero discussed humour for an upper-class readership, which had to amuse the public without losing its dignity.[12]

It is important to note that Cicero's treatise was very much alive in the Renaissance and early modern period. In his *Libro del cortegiano* of 1528 Castiglione made the same distinction between wit of matter and wit of form, but added a third type of humour, the *burla* or mild practical joke; as wit in action it combined the two other types. He equally warned that crying and laughing or miming the gestures and postures of other people were deemed indecorous and so were coarseness in words and deeds.[13]

Castiglione also cautioned his readers not to make fun of men and women from a good background. It was a truth already recognized by Cicero, when he advised his colleagues of the senatorial order not to make fun of one another, and a similar concern for the status of one's own group was found among the Spartans and the Athenian aristocracy, as Jan Bremmer demonstrates. This concern for the status of the group did not necessarily exclude poking fun at others outside one's own circle, however high their rank might be. At the end of her life, Sophia (1630–1714), electress of Hanover and mother of George I, remembered her youth at the court in The Hague. She tells how she loved to mock everybody (*à railler tout le monde*), to the pleasure of the *gens d'esprit* but the chagrin of others. One of her favourite victims was a complete outsider, the prince of Talmont, who came to ask the hand of one of the princesses of Orange and was therefore hardly in the position to offer repartee.[14] In other words, where so many manuals on civility cautioned their readers that their mockery should be innocent, 'like the bites of lambkins', as Della Casa phrased it, the ridiculing of those outside one's own group may still have been 'like the bites of dogs'.[15] In the art of joking, considerations of rank and class often outweighed those of decorum and good form.

In fact, Sophia is one of the few women whose (merciless) wit was recorded. In antiquity, women were probably allowed to be present at performances of Greek comedies (although even this remains debated), but in general their social place, certainly for elite women, was inside the house rather than in the public sphere. It is therefore not surprising that for observations on female wit we have to go to a female anthropologist in modern Greece.[16] Due to the nature of our male-dominated sources, humour between women is also difficult to find in the Middle Ages. Moreover, feminist scholars have not failed to point out how misogynistic much male humour is in these periods, and how often male historians have failed to see this.[17] In the early modern period women took a more active part in public life, certainly in Northern Europe, but it is probably safe to say that, although women and the lower classes are represented in the sources, their voices are mostly faked, functioning as a vehicle to bolster existing hierarchies.

Although laughter is often associated with the lower classes or with popular culture, this volume hardly supports such a view. Aaron Gurevich takes a critical look at Bakhtin's famous study of Rabelais and his interpretation of popular culture as a culture of laughter. He accepts neither Bakhtin's suggestion of a clear opposition between learned and popular culture nor his characterization of the culture of the illiterati as based on laughter, even to the exclusion of fear and anxiety. Indeed, in recent years scholars have increasingly realized that much of the humorous material was thoroughly enjoyed by the elite. Although many intellectuals condemned jest-books, by doing so they often betrayed an intimate knowledge of the genre. Several chapters in this volume, all dealing with the early modern period, discuss the significance of the upper classes at length. Derek Brewer reminds us that 'popular culture includes gentlemen'; Mariët Westermann sees the boisterous paintings of Jan Steen as 'sublimated transgressions', constituting 'the private, perhaps nostalgic pleasures of an urban élite'; and Herman Roodenburg relates a Dutch manuscript containing some 2500 jokes, many of them far from purified, to the art of conversation cherished by the Dutch upper classes. Indeed, the appreciation of (low) humour by the elite has become so obvious that a recent study of Dutch seventeenth-century farce chides those scholars in the 1980s who cautiously suggested this relish.[18] It should not be forgotten, however, that the present stress on elite humour may well be the outcome of a certain slant in our sources, which are, after all, rarely the product of the lower strata. A fresh look at the old sources may perhaps redress the imbalance in this respect.[19]

Bakhtin's idea of a pernicious influence on laughter by the Church is similarly unacceptable. The *risus monasticus*, as studied by Jacques le Goff, the *risus paschalis* or the well-known *exempla* belie this picture. After the Middle Ages, Catholics and Protestants did not ban all humour from the pulpit either. It remained a salient ingredient of the German *Barockpredigt*,[20] and in the Spanish Netherlands, as Johan Verberckmoes tells us, the Counter-Reformation produced its own jokes and anecdotes in combating the Protestants. Even the churches of Dutch Calvinism knew their mirth and laughter: an Amsterdam professor of rhetoric reproachfully noted that the ministers vented jokes and witticisms that would not do in the theatre, let alone in church.[21]

One may wonder why the behaviour of ministers would worry a professor of rhetoric, but when Erasmus, in his *Ecclesiastes* of 1535, opined that good preachers should eschew such habits as distorting their faces or gesticulating like buffoons, he was more or less quoting Cicero. Just as there was an art of conversation, so there was an art of joking, both relying heavily on ancient rhetoric. In the early modern period many boys went to schools where Latin was taught,[22] and in this way they learned, directly or indirectly, the prescriptions of ancient rhetoric, which, moreover, were often translated. Perhaps the enormous impact of these influences, not only on late medieval and early modern rhetoric but on the culture in its entirety (ranging from the codes of civility to the requirements of decorum in contemporary painting, acting and dancing), has only recently been fully realized.[23]

Let us conclude these introductory remarks with three observations on the development in humour through time. First, it is striking how the ruling discourse changes in the different periods. Whereas in antiquity philosophers and rhetoricians are the main authors of leading handbooks and discussions, in the Middle Ages monks and other theologians lay down the law; they retained their leading position in post-Tridentine Flanders, as Johan Verberckmoes shows. On the other hand, in the areas influenced by the Reformation, manuals of civility and the writings of essayists, such as Joseph Addison and Richard Steele, now set the tone. It is hardly surprising that in modern times psychologists and sociologists have come to the fore, the study of Freud being the most widely acknowledged example of this trend.[24]

Secondly, there is a continuous turnover in the producers of humour. Greece and Rome show that moderate humour became the domain of the social elite, whereas buffoons and mimes gradually lost official approval. Our term 'scurrilous' still shows something of the deprecia-tion of the *scurra*, the late antique and medieval professional jester, who in the times of Plautus and Cicero was a malicious gossip but still a man-about-town. In the Middle Ages he is usually classified with actors, jongleurs and mimes, people with a low social standing, and it is only the court fool who rises to social prominence. After the Middle Ages the collecting and telling of jokes became widely spread over the social spectrum, and it is clear that the telling of jokes even became part and parcel of the art of conversation among gentlemen. The gradual disappearance of this ideal and the rise of the modern professional jester, such as the clown, the comedian and the satirist, still remain largely uncharted.

Our third and final point is the development of humour itself. To what extent did humour change over the centuries? Did our ancestors laugh at the same jokes as we do, or was their sense of humour radically different from our own? Those who have read some of the humorous texts of the past may have found that some jokes are not bad at all, others distinctly unfunny and several even incomprehensible. In other words, these texts appear both familiar and unfamiliar to us. We may appreciate the wit of Erasmus, but the practical jokes relished by the English aristocracy, as related by Samuel Pepys, nowadays appear rather silly.

In his contribution to this volume, Peter Burke notes some important changes. He speaks of a 'disintegration' of traditional humour, which began in the later sixteenth century: there was a reduction of comic domains, occasions and locales; moreover, the clergy, ladies and gentlemen no longer participated in certain kinds of humour, at least not in public. This shifting of the 'frontiers' of the comic well fits Norbert Elias's study of the rise of 'civilization', which after nearly half a century still remains the central point of reference for the study of such developments.[25]

In his classic study on humour in Tudor and Stuart England Keith Thomas identified more or less the same development, emphasizing in particular the areas into which laughter was no longer allowed to penetrate.[26] Quoting Francis Bacon, who felt that 'there be certain things' which had to be protected from jest, Thomas pointed to the domains of Church and state, where a 'cult of decorum' cherishing values of sobriety and gravity gradually gained the upper hand. As we saw above, although after the Reformation priests and ministers may have been less austere in their sermons than is usually assumed, the early modern period clearly witnessed some important changes. Most of them are related to a strengthening of hierarchy, which culminated at the end of the seventeenth century in a general, neoclassical disdain of all sorts of lower humour. It was also this preoccupation with decorum, as Thomas notes, which made the Augustan literary critics write so much on the topic of humour and laughter.[27] The coining of our modern concept of humour seems to have been a by-product of these larger social developments.

It was also in this period that the court fool finally made his exit. Charles II seems to have been the last king who took his court jester seriously. Such inversionary laughter, which ridiculed those in power and did not differ much from the laughter elicited by lords of misrule, still popular in the English countryside, or similar licensed buffoons, no longer fitted the new social structures. By this time, in England but also elsewhere in Europe, polite and folk humour had grown apart. It was a legacy that would persist for a long time. When the brothers Grimm rediscovered the 'people' and started to collect folk tales, they deliberately omitted jests and comic stories, concentrating instead on the more innocent genre of legends and fairy tales. We are still trying to fill that gap.

NOTES

1 The standard study of the term 'humour' still remains F. Baldensperger, *Études d'histoire littéraire* (Paris, 1907), pp. 176–222.
2 *Oeuvres complètes de Voltaire*, ed. L. Moland (54 vols, Paris, 1877–85), vol. 19, pp. 552–4: 'Les anglais ont pris leur *humour*, qui signifie chez eux plaisanterie naturelle, de notre mot *humeur* employé en ce sens dans les premières comédies de Corneille; et dans toutes les comédies antérieures' (from *Questions sur l'encyclopédie*). We are most grateful to Dr Robert McNamee from the Voltaire Foundation for his help in identifying quotations from Voltaire.
3 W. von Wartburg, *Französisches etymologisches Wörterbuch*, vol. 4 (Basel, 1952), p. 514.
4 V. Hugo, *Les Misérables*, vol. 1 (Paris, 1862), p. 800: 'cette chose anglaise qu'on appelle l'humour'; E. Littré, *Dictionnaire de la langue française* (4 vols, Paris, 1873–4), s.v.
5 As is observed by Belle van Zuylen in a letter to her brother describing the contacts with the English general Eliot, the later Lord Heathfield, and his wife, quoted by P. Godet, *Madame de Charrière et ses amis (1740–1805)* (Lausanne, 1947), p. 69; 'J'ai dans mes folies de cet *humour* qui'ils ne trouvent guère que dans leur île'.
6 C. G. Lessing, *Sämmtliche Schriften*, ed. K. Lachmann (13 vols, Berlin, 1838–40), vol. 4, p. 399 and vol. 7, p. 414: 'von dem was die Engländer humor nennen'.
7 The quotation derives from a fine essay by Alfred Brendel, 'Must classical music be entirely serious?', in his *Music Sounded Out: essays, lectures, interviews, afterthoughts* (London, 1990), pp. 12–53, esp. p. 14.

8 For an exploration of the subject, see A. Ziv (ed.), *National Styles of Humor* (New York, 1988).

9 A. Maurois, *Les silences du colonel Bramble* (Paris, 1918), p. 139: 'La seule cause de cette guerre, c'est que les Allemands n'ont pas le sens de l'humour'.

10 For the various titles, see the bibliography at the end of this volume.

11 G. Blaicher, 'Über das Lachen im englischen Mittelalter', *Deutsche Vierteljahrsschrift für Literaturwissenschaft und Geistesgeschichte*, 44 (1970), pp. 508–29; M. Douglas, *Implicit Meanings* (London, 1975), pp. 83–9.

12 For a detailed commentary on Cicero, see A. D. Leeman, H. Pinkster and E. Rabbie (eds), *M. Tullius Cicero. De oratore libri III*, vol. 3 (Heidelberg, 1989), pp. 172–333. Cicero is only marginally shorter than Quintilian's *Institutio oratoria* 3.6, on which see most recently T. Viljamaa, 'Quintilian's theory of wit', in S. Jäkel and A. Timonen (eds), *Laughter down the Centuries*, vol. 1 (Turku, 1994), pp. 85–93.

13 On Castiglione's discussion of humour, see J. R. Woodhouse, *Baldesar Castiglione. A Reassessment of The Courtier* (Edinburgh, 1978), pp. 101–8.

14 Quoted in S. van Zuylen van Nyevelt, *Court Life in the Dutch Republic 1638–1689* (London and New York, n.d.), p. 67.

15 Giovanni della Casa, *Il galateo*, ed. M. Rumpf ([Florence, 1558] Heidelberg, 1988), p. 66.

16 J. du Boulay, *Portrait of a Greek Mountain Village* (Oxford, 1974), pp. 46–7.

17 See, e.g., B. Zweig, 'The mute nude female characters in Aristophanes' plays', in A. Richlin (ed.), *Pornography and Representation in Greece and Rome* (New York and Oxford, 1992), pp. 72–89; M. H. Caviness, 'Patron or matron? A Capetian bride and a vade mecum for her marriage bed', *Speculum*, 68 (1993), pp. 333–62, esp. 357–62.

18 R. van Stipriaan, *Leugens en vermaak. Boccaccio's novellen in de kluchtcultuur van de Nederlandse renaissance* (Amsterdam, 1996), p. 235, n. 7.

19 See, for example, N. Schindler, *Widerspenstige Leute. Studien zur Volkskultur in der frühen Neuzeit* (Frankfurt, 1992), pp. 151–74 ('Körpergroteske und Lachkultur im 16. Jahrhundert').

20 E. Moser-Rath, *Predigtmärlein der Barockzeit: Exempel, Sage, Schwank und Fabel* (Berlin, 1984).

21 Petrus Francius, *Posthuma: quibus accedunt illustrium eruditorum ad eundem epistolae* (Amsterdam, 1706), Oratio III (*De usu eloquentiae in sacris*), pp. 213–14; see lso H. Roodenburg, 'Predikanten op de kansel: een verkenning van hun "eioquentia corporis"', in *Mensen van de nieuwe tijd: een liber amicorum voor A. Th. van Deursen* (Amsterdam, 1996), pp. 324–8.

22 For the knowledge of Latin in the early modern period, see the splendid chapter in P. Burke, *The Art of Conversation* (Cambridge, 1993), pp. 34–65.

23 See the excellent introduction by Brian Vickers, *In Defence of Rhetoric* (Oxford, 1988).

24 S. Freud, *Der Witz und seine Bedeutung zum Unbewussten* (Leipzig and Vienna, 1905), Eng. trans. J. Strachey as *Jokes and their Relation to the Unconscious* (London, 1960); A. C. Zijderveld, *Reality in a Looking-Glass: rationality through an analysis of traditional folly* (London, 1982) and 'The sociology of humour and laughter', *Current sociology – La sociologie contemporaine*, 31–3 (1983), pp. 1–103.

25 N. Elias, *Über den Prozess der Zivilisation* (2 vols, Basel, 1939).

26 K. Thomas, 'The place of laughter in Tudor and Stuart England', *Times Literary Supplement*, 21 January 1977, pp. 77–81.

27 It will be hardly chance that the words 'pun' and 'joke' are also attested first in 1670 (*Oxford English Dictionary*, 2nd edn).

1

Jokes, Jokers and Jokebooks in Ancient Greek Culture

Jan Bremmer

It was a warm summer evening in 422 BC. Young Autolycus had just gained a victory in the pancratium, the annual 'all in' boxing and wrestling contest, and his uncle, the wealthy Callias, had taken him and his father Lykon to the horse-races. On their way home to his villa in the Piraeus, where they would conclude the day with a banquet, Callias suddenly caught sight of Socrates and a group of friends. He walked over to the philosopher and invited him to the banquet too on the grounds that the evening's entertainment would be even more brilliant if graced by his presence. Socrates accepted, and when all the guests had lain down they were strangely fascinated by the victorious boy's beauty and so influenced by Eros that they grew totally quiet and feasted in silence.

With this intriguing scene Xenophon (c.430–350 BC) opens his *Symposion*, which he composed after 380 BC in order to give his own picture of his revered master Socrates, only a few years after Plato's brilliantly evocative *Symposium*.[1] Having thus set the scene, Xenophon applied a well-known literary device by introducing a stranger.[2] After a sudden knock on the door the porter announced the arrival of Philip the *gelotopoios*, literally the 'laughter-producer' (but henceforth, for lack of a better English equivalent, 'buffoon'). Having been permitted to enter, he stood on the threshold and stated: 'you all know that I am a buffoon; and so I have come here on purpose, thinking it more of a joke to come to your dinner uninvited than to come by invitation.' 'Well then', said the host, 'take a place, for the guests though well fed, as you observe, on seriousness, are perhaps rather ill supplied with laughter.' The buffoon immediately attempted a joke and failed miserably. When his second joke was not well received either, he stopped eating, wrapped himself in his cloak, lay down on a couch and started to groan. Only after the other guests promised to laugh next time, and one of them burst out in loud laughter at the buffoon's misery, did he resume his dinner (1.11–16).

When the tables had been removed, a professional entertainer from

Syracuse entered the room with a flute girl, a dancing girl and a beautiful boy, who was expert at playing the cither and at dancing. After the dancing girl had performed various acrobatic tricks, such as juggling twelve hoops and turning somersaults into a hoop with upright swords, Philip the buffoon must have felt that her successful performance challenged his own status as an entertainer. So he got up and, mimicking in detail the dancing of both the boy and the girl, made a burlesque out of their performance 'by rendering every moving part of his body more grotesque than it naturally was'. This, at long last, produced the so much desired laughter (2.22–3). After these light intermezzos, a serious discussion arose in which Philip intervened a few times. During a debate about everybody's most valuable possession he confirmed that his pride lay in jesting (3.11), and, later, he explained the reason for his pride: 'whenever people have a bit of good fortune, [they] give me hearty invitations to come and join them, but when suffering some reverse they run from me with never a glance behind, fearing that they may be forced to laugh in spite of themselves' (4.50).

Finally, towards the end of the evening, one of the guests praised Philip's skill 'at hitting off a person's likeness'. The buffoon jumped at the possibility of demonstrating his art, but Socrates admonished him that he would be a valuable asset to the diners only if he would be 'reticent on matters that should not be talked about', and 'thus was quenched this bit of convivial unpleasantness' (6.8–10).

Xenophon's description of Callias' dinner is a fairly realistic picture of the entertainment enjoyed by the rich and famous in late fifth-century Athens, although he was probably too young to have been present on such occasions. It is also our most extensive description of a 'professional' jester, since other notices do not provide much more than a name or a detail.[3] It raises a number of questions. Was it normal for buffoons to intrude into a banquet – and why there? Who were they and what was their repertory? Did they use jokebooks? Why was Philip not allowed to draw certain comparisons? Was humour perhaps considered dangerous? The last point leads us finally to those who attempted to 'tame' laughter or even opposed witticisms and laughter altogether: conservative philosophers, Spartans and the early Christians.

BUFFOONS

It is rather striking that Philip's performance did not take place in public space, as is the case with most modern entertainers. On the contrary, he performed during a *symposion*, in the safe surroundings of the most distinctive room in the Greek house, the so-called *andron* (1.13), which was the one room in the house to which male non-family members had access.[4] It was typical of Greek civilization that the occasions for laughter and mockery were not those of everyday life but those of conviviality and festivity. The great religious festivals, especially, allowed the Greeks to relax the usual standards of behaviour and to indulge in legitimate laughter and ribald humour.[5] As the philosopher Democritus said, 'A life without festivals is like a road without inns' (fragment 230). The great comedies of Aristophanes were never performed on just any odd day in the year but only at the Dionysia (both urban and rural) and Lenaea. Both at the Lenaea and another Dionysiac Athenian festival, the Anthesteria, men stood on waggons and made mocking remarks at passers-by.[6] Another occasion for mocking people was the procession of the Athenians to Eleusis in order to be initiated in the Mysteries of Demeter. When this procession passed the bridge over the River Kephisos on their way out of Athens, a veiled prostitute (or a male) mocked the most prominent citizens by name.[7] Both Dionysos and Demeter were gods closely associated with reversals of the social order and both occupied an 'eccentric' position in the Greek pantheon.[8] Humour could be dangerous, and its place in culture had to be limited to strictly defined occasions.[9] The Greeks were only too well aware that laughter could have a very unpleasant side.[10]

One of these occasions, then, was the *symposion*, the banquet, which in the archaic age (*c*.800–500 BC) had been the stage where the elite demonstrated its superiority. Here the aristocrats discussed politics, made alliances and, last but not least, entertained themselves with dice and games, by telling anecdotes and by singing songs.[11] When, towards the end of the sixth century, politics started to develop into a separate sphere, which was no longer the monopoly of the aristocracy, the symposion gradually lost its central position and became part of a more private personal sphere.[12] Aristocrats now started to show the typical characteristics of a leisure class with its stress on displaying wealth and passive entertainment. It was not, though, until the middle of the fifth century that Athenian aristocrats could afford to invite all kinds of people to their tables.[13] Their guests soon included a particular type, the flatterer (*kolax*), who, evidently, in order 'to pay' for his food flattered his host, whom he called *ho trephon* ('the feeder').[14] As the chorus says in *Flatterers*, a comedy of 421 by Aristophanes' contemporary Eupolis:

> I go out to the market. And when I spy a sucker who is rich, I fasten upon him at once. And if the rich fool happens to say something, I loudly praise him and express my amazement, pretending delight in his words. Then we go to dinner, one of us in one direction, another in another – all to get a barley-cake not our own.[15] There the flatterer must at once begin his witty chatter or be chucked out at the door.[16]

Jokes, then, were the expected contribution of the uninvited,[17] as also appears from the words of another parasite in a comedy by the Sicilian Epicharmus, who lived in the first half of the fifth century: 'Dining with him who desires me (he needs only to ask me), and alike with him who desires me not (and there is no need to ask); at dinner there I am a wit, and cause much laughter and praise my host.'[18] Originally, a *parasitos*, literally 'one who eats at the table of another', had been a religious official of the Attic demes,[19] but towards the middle of the fourth century BC, although for obscure reasons, the term gradually developed into the more modern sense and became synonymous with *kolax*.[20] In the fifth century we also find the term *bomolochos*, literally 'he who lays an ambush at altars', namely to beg food, as a late lexicon explains. The particular place may look strange at first sight, but is to be expected because the Greeks consumed meat mainly through sacrifice.[21] The custom of exchanging food for jokes was probably old because the related verb *bomolocheuo* means 'to play the buffoon' or 'to indulge in ribaldry', but in the course of time successful buffoons had evidently moved from the altars of the pious to the more extragavant dining rooms of the Athenian elite.

Like jokes, parodic imitations such as Philip's burlesquing of the dancing boy and girl were probably the stock-in-trade of buffoons, since we also hear of a different fourth-century *gelotopoios*, Eudikos, who imitated boxers and wrestlers, whereas others imitated dithyrambs and songs to the harp. The tyrant of Syracuse, Agathocles (*c*.300 BC), 'who was by nature a buffoon and a mimic', even made himself highly popular with the people by mimicking some of those present at the meetings of the popular assembly.[22]

In addition to jokes and imitations, the jokers also made comparisons, a popular feature of weddings and symposia.[23] We find these comparisons in Aristophanes' *Wasps*, but they also occur in Plato's *Symposion*, where Alcibiades compares Socrates to 'one of those little sileni that you see on the statuaries' stalls . . . and then again . . . of Marsyas the satyr' (215A). It is not surprising that the comparison is hardly flattering: comparisons seem to have focused especially on physical peculiarities, since in Plato's *Meno* Socrates observes that all good-looking people enjoy a game of comparisons because 'they get the best of it, for naturally handsome folk provoke handsome similes' (80C).[24] Apparently, these comparisons were also collected into books (for use at banquets?). A papyrus of the late third century BC contains an enumeration of abusive sentences, which were divided in various sections and directed against people with physical peculiarities. One of the sections concerned the redhead, who would be made fun of by feeble statements such as 'you do not have a face but an evening-sun', another the bald, who would be mocked by 'you do not have a head but . . .', at which point the papyrus, perhaps fortunately, breaks off. Most likely, the book was owned by a professional joker, such as we encountered in Xenophon's *Symposion*.[25] But, if these comparisons were completely normal, why then did Socrates object to Philip making them? Was everybody not perhaps happy with humour?

Before we turn to this question, let us first look at the problem of where exactly in the social spectra we should situate these buffoons. From comedy we know the names of various buffoons and parasites, which shows that they were well known in Athens (Athenaeus 240–6). The activity may have run in families because, during the wedding of the Macedonian Karanos, 'the clown Mandrogenes had come in, a descendant, so they say, of the celebrated Athenian clown Straton. He caused many a laugh among us by his jokes, and afterwards danced with his wife, who was over eighty years old' (Athenaeus 130c). Jokers may even have achieved a certain reputation through their wit, since comedy invented a pair of mythological inventors for jesting: Rhadamanthys and Palamedes. The former was one of the best-known residents of the carefree Isles of the Blest, where food was abundant, the latter Greece's most ingenious mythological inventor, witticisms being among his inventions.[26]

In Athens, in the second half of the fourth century, there even existed a club of buffoons, called 'the sixty', who regularly met in the sanctuary of Heracles in Diomeia, one of Athens' suburbs.[27] They were so well known that sayings circulated, such as 'I have just come from the sixty' and 'The sixty said so-and-so'. These jokers must even have been famous outside Athens, since Philip II of Macedonia, who was fond of all kinds of entertainment, sent them a talent in return for their jokes. The members of the 'club' were evidently amateurs not professionals, since their names show them to have belonged to the Athenian upper class; one of them, the cross-eyed Callimedon, was even a renowned politician.[28] Considering that buffoonery seems to have become less and less acceptable in the fourth century, the club may well point to a group of citizens wanting to shock the existing social order.[29]

Outside Athens buffoons were welcome guests at the courts of the neighbouring kings of Thrace and Macedonia and the successors of Alexander the Great.[30] Yet it seems that among the urban elite clowning strongly diminished in status. An indication may be the end of Dionysius the Second, tyrant of Syracuse. The contemporary historian Theopompus (*c*.377–320) relates that he was gradually losing the sight of his eyes. For a while his parasites behaved as if they also suffered from bad eyesight, and they would feel for the food put in front of them, pretending not to see it, until Dionysius guided their hands towards the dishes – a behaviour which earnt them the nickname 'Dionysius-fawners' (*Dionysokolakes*). It is hardly strange that Dionysius eventually lost his position and ended up, as Theopompus states, not necessarily reliably, 'sitting in barbershops and playing the buffoon.'[31] The barbershop was of course the place of male gossip *par excellence*, not least by the barber himself – witness the request of his client, when asked how to be shaved: 'in silence'.[32] In other words, Dionysius fell from the height of society to its very bottom. This negative view of buffoonery accelerated in the course of time, and in the Roman period buffoons were often closely associated with performers in mimes and, therefore, pretty low on the social scale.[33] According to the second-century *Dreambook* of Artemidorus, dreaming of buffoons now meant 'cheating and trickeries' (1.76).

JOKERS AND THEIR BOOKS

It is clear that Philip's skills only partially approached those of modern entertainers. Cracking jokes and impersonating are the hallmark of many a modern comedian, but Philip also did comparisons, an art which is not typical of modern entertainment. Unfortunately, Xenophon does not supply any examples of the jokes, and neither do other authors. We do not know, therefore, either the nature of these jokes or their origin. Did buffoons also make use of jokebooks? One of our sources for 'the sixty' says that Philip asked for the jokes to be copied out, which would suggest a kind of jokebook, but another source mentions that he merely asked for them to be written down. We cannot be absolutely certain, then, about the existence of jokebooks in the later half of the fourth century, but they are attested in the Roman comedian Plautus, who used Greek comedy as his source. In his *Stichus*, produced in 200 BC, the parasite Gelasimus (significantly a Greek name meaning 'Laughter man' and suggestive of the *gelotopoios*) is reduced to such straits that he intends to hold an auction and sell his jokebooks, which consist of jests, flattering remarks and small-scale lies.[34] And in Plautus' *Persa* the joker Satyrio considers giving his jokebooks to his daughter for her dowry (vv. 389–96). It is clear, then, that these jokers possessed jokebooks to help them make a living, whereas some early modern diners, such as Aernout van Overbeke, collected jokes in notebooks to be a social success among their peers.[35] Like Xenophon, Plautus gives no example of these jokes, but we are lucky that in late antiquity an anonymous author composed a jokebook that has survived.

A series of manuscripts, none older than the tenth century, called *Philogelos*, or 'Laughter-lover', contains a collection of 265 jokes.[36] Its author and purpose are, unfortunately, unknown, and only one joke refers to an event that can be dated, namely the games celebrating Rome's millennium on 21 April 248 AD. The collection was probably put together in the third century, but the late nature of its vocabulary strongly suggests that the final edition was made only in early Byzantine times, probably not later than the sixth century.[37] One source was clearly Plutarch's collection of *apophthegmata*, which here regularly appear in 'diluted' form as a joke.[38] Obviously, space prevents us from analysing its content in depth, but we will briefly discuss some of its main targets.[39]

From the 265 jokes, 110 concern the *scholastikos*, literally 'somebody who gives or follows lectures' *(scholas)*.[40] It is the pedantic student, the lawyer, but also the professor – in short, in Barry Baldwin's happy translation, 'the egghead'. The jokes may suggest a certain wittiness as in no. 55: 'A witty young *scholastikos* sold his books when short of money. He then wrote to his father, "Congratulate me, father, I am already making money from my studies!"' But mostly they focus on his stupidity or social ineptness, as in the following example, which at the same time illustrates the gruesome realities of ancient slave-society:[41] 'When a *scholastikos* had a child by a slave girl, his father advised him to kill it. But he replied, "First, you bury your own children, then advise me to kill mine!"' (no. 57).

Some sixty jokes concern cities in the ancient world which were famous for their stupidity: Cyme (on the western coast of modern Turkey), Sidon (in modern Lebanon) and Abdera (on the coast of Thrace). These jokes rarely rise above the normal level of jokes celebrating the stupidity of neighbouring cities: 'An inhabitant of Cyme brought his father's body to the mummifiers after the latter's death in Alexandria. When he returned later to fetch it, the man had several bodies present and asked him the mark of his father's case. He answered: "He coughed"' (no. 171). The reason why the first two cities figured in these jokes is totally obscure, but Abdera was well known for its 'laughing philosopher' Democritus, who seems to have received his name for laughing at the stupidity of his fellow citizens, and who became a popular figure in philosophical and moralizing treatises from late Hellenistic and Roman times.[42]

In some thirty jokes doctors are the object or play a supporting role. Some of these jokes even combined the reference to doctors with the already mentioned *scholastikoi* or cities famous for their stupidity: 'When somebody came to a *scholastikos* doctor and said: "Doctor, when I wake up I am dizzy for half an hour before I start feeling better," the doctor said: "Wake up half an hour later!"' (no. 3). 'When his patient suffered and cried loudly, a doctor from Cyme exchanged his knife for a more blunt one' (no. 177). It is hardly surprising that in a time in which medical care was still highly undeveloped, individual doctors or the medical profession as a whole were the butt of lay derision. In addition to the fact that doctors were intellectuals, it was probably also

significant that they frequently advertised their skills and even undertook surgery on street corners or in the theatre.[43]

There are some seven jokes regarding seers and astrologers. Seers had
already been a favourite target of ancient comedy, and Roman satirists
had made fun of astrologers and fortune-tellers, but both categories
managed to maintain their influence through the whole of antiquity,
despite the scepticism which these jokes attest.[44] Finally, there are small
sections of jokes about the lazy, the greedy, cowards, gluttons, alcohol-
ics, people with bad breath and misogynists. Given that misogyny was
widespread in antiquity, it is striking that so few jokes are obscene or
concern women. Still, they are not totally absent: 'Said a young man to
his randy wife, "Wife, what shall we do, eat or make love?" "Whichever
you like; there's no bread"' (no. 244). Or, 'The wife of a misogynist,
who was so ill that he was expected to die, swore that she would hang
herself if anything happened to him. Perking up, he asked, "Will you do
the same if I recover?"' (no. 248).

The prominence of eggheads and doctors in the collection probably
points to a specific social milieu. In Aristophanes' *Clouds*, Socrates
enumerates his guardian gods: sophists, who were in fact quacks, seers,
poets and jugglers (vv. 332–3). In other words, these were mainly the
intellectuals of his time, who were not engaged in any kind of manual
work. The same prejudice seems to be in operation here, and it would
fit this disdain for intellectuals that many jokes celebrate the common
sense of the man in the street. Consequently, the origin of the collection
is probably the lower urban classes, even though it remains obscure for
what reason this jokebook had been composed.

THE TAMING OF BUFFOONERY AND LAUGHTER

The objections of Socrates could have fitted the fictional time of
Xenophon's *Symposion*, since a late anthology ascribed the following
quotation to Socrates: 'One ought to use laughter as one uses salt –
sparingly' (Stobaeus 3.34.18). If the ascription is correct, Socrates
would have been one of various philosophers who were reputed never
or only rarely to have laughed, such as Pythagoras, Anaxagoras and the
wise king Anacharsis.[45] On the other hand, around 420 there was still
a robust sense of humour prevailing in Athens, and the absence of
laughter was thought to be characteristic of a misanthrope,[46] even
though Aristophanes regularly, if disingenuously, claimed that he did
not use the coarse comic tricks normally employed by Old Comedy;[47]
in his last comedies, however, he employed less and less personal
invective and buffoonery.[48] Evidently the tide had turned, and the more
refined manners which were gradually developing among Athenian

aristocrats must have started to make personal attacks and less refined humour gradually unacceptable.

The first element of this development is also visible in Xenophon's treatise on the education of the Persian king Cyrus, the *Cyropaedia*, which often indirectly discusses Greek customs and probably has to be dated to the first half of the fourth century. Here Cyrus remarks that the Persians ask each other only those questions which could be easily answered and made only those jokes which did not hurt anybody (5.2.18). We are here confronted with the negative power of jokes, which can hurt us and, by implication, still more those who live in a real shame culture. This power of jokes can still be observed in contemporary Crete. Michael Herzfeld, the best contemporary ethnographer of Greece, recently noted an incident in which Cretan villagers would ask permission to recite satiric songs in order not to be blamed for offending anybody's dignity.[49] This concern with the power of jokes to hurt seems to have become more pronounced in the course of the fourth century.

The growing unacceptability of less refined humour becomes clearly apparent in various works of Isocrates in the 350s. In his *Antidosis* this conservative orator, who frequently idealized the past, disapprovingly notes that nowadays 'they speak of men who play the buffoon and have a talent for mocking and mimicking as "gifted" – an appellation which should be reserved for men endowed with the highest excellence' (284, trans. G. Norlin). And in his *Areopagiticus* he notes that previous generations 'cultivated the manner of a gentleman, not those of a buffoon; and as for those who had a turn for jesting (*eutrapelous*) and playing the clown, who we today speak of as clever wits, they were then looked upon as sorry fools' (49, trans. Norlin).

In fact, both Plato and Aristotle, the major philosophers of the fourth century, opposed coarse humour and ribaldry and stressed the need for restrained, inoffensive laughter. In the *Republic* Plato states that the guardians of the ideal state are forbidden to indulge in laughter because excessive laughter is usually followed by a violent reaction (388). This stress on moderation in laughter also comes to the fore somewhat later in the *Republic* in the discussion of poetry (606). Here Plato rejects buffoonery in comedy because it may make people imitate it in private. And in the *Laws*, admittedly a very conservative work, Plato even wants to abolish comedy altogether and leave buffoonery to slaves or hired aliens (816–17). It fits with Plato's opposition to laughter that in his school, the Academy, laughter was forbidden, and he himself was represented in Athenian comedy as a grouch.[50]

Unlike wealthy Callias and his friends, Plato also completely rejected the presence of hired entertainment at the symposion:

the wine-parties of second-rate and commonplace people. Such men, being too uneducated to entertain themselves as they drink by using their own voices and conversational resources, put up the price of female musicians . . . and find their entertainment in its warblings. But where the drinkers are men of worth and culture, you will find no girls piping or dancing or harping. They are quite capable of enjoying their own company without such frivolous nonsense, using their own voices in sober discussion and each taking his turn to speak or listen – even if the drinking is really heavy.

(*Protagoras* 347CD, trans. W. K. C. Guthrie)

It fits with Plato's description that the host in Xenophon's *Symposion*, Callias, was not particularly ascetic and managed to squander his considerable inheritance quickly by his extragavant life style.[51]

Aristotle's *On Comedy* has unfortunately not survived,[52] but he presents a systematic analysis of jests and laughter in his *Nicomachean Ethics* (4.8). In Aristotle we can see the tendency in Plato fully elaborated, since he considers as vulgar buffoons those who carry humour to excess and aim at raising a laugh rather than saying something flattering and avoiding hurting the object of their fun. Those, on the other hand, who joke in a tasteful way are called ready-witted (*eutrapeloi*). They are the men who observe the mean, whereas the buffoon is the slave of his sense of humour, and spares neither himself nor others if he can raise a laugh. Naturally, in his ideal state the young should not be exposed to indecent talk – the law-giver should even banish it from the state altogether (*Politics* 7.15.7). Aristotle summarizes his views in the *Rhetoric* as follows: 'Some jokes are becoming to a gentleman, others are not; see that you choose such as become you. Irony better befits a gentleman than buffoonery; the ironical man jokes to amuse himself, the buffoon to amuse other people' (3.18).[53]

In the fourth century, then, two developments regarding humour at the symposion are noticeable. First, buffoonery became less and less acceptable to the upper class as an expression of humour. Secondly, as the reaction of Socrates showed, insulting others with jokes also became less acceptable at the symposion, although quarrels and verbal offences had always been an integral part of the sympotic tradition; like early Ireland, early Greece had a lively tradition of blame poetry.[54] These developments were also reflected in performances of comedy where the element of buffoonery diminished and personal insults disappeared from the comic repertory.

How can this development, which has more often been observed regarding comedy than for the symposion be explained? Clearly, important changes were taking place in Athenian society in these days. The fourth century showed all the traces of a growing 'embourgeoisement' with the corresponding refinement of morals: telling jokes made way for wittiness. It is significant that the noun 'wittiness' (*eutrapelia*) is not found before Plato's *Republic* but is often discussed in Aristotle; *eutrapelos* ('witty') now also started to lose the negative connotation which, for example, it still had in the passage of Isocrates quoted above.[55] At the same time, perspectives developed by Norbert Elias and Pierre Bourdieu may perhaps be applied here. As the aristocracy started to withdraw from public life and to concentrate more on the symposion, disagreements and internal quarrels became less acceptable. Moreover, as they had little to gain by being active in public life, they had to distinguish themselves in different ways. And just as they started to move in a more controlled manner, so they also developed a more urbane style in their sympotic behaviour.[56]

OPPOSING HUMOUR AND LAUGHTER

We need not assume that the growing refinement in Greek culture actually became the rule. The fact that four centuries later Plutarch (*c*.40–120) still thought it necessary to repeat the plea for the painless jest (*Moralia* 629E) suggests that the habit of insulting was deeply rooted in the world of the ancient symposion. However, others went further and opposed humour and laughter altogether.

The first group known to have opposed laughter were the Pythagoreans. Around 530 BC Pythagoras left the island of Samos and settled in South-Italian Croton, where he founded a movement based on numerous ascetic prescriptions. Although the figure of Pythagoras is surrounded with legends and the lack of early written sources makes it very difficult to reconstruct this phase of Pythagoreanism, one of these prescriptions evidently concerned laughter: the master himself reputedly never laughed, as was reported of the Pythagorizing tyrant of Syracuse, Dionysius II, and the fullest source for ancient Pythagoreanism, the fourth-century philosopher Aristoxenus; Pythagoras' followers were mocked by Athenian comedy for their joyless facial expressions.[57]

Considering that we have identified the symposion and the festivals of Dionysos as the scenes for humour, it is worth observing that in Plato's *Laws* the Spartan remarks that his state has forbidden festive indulgence at these occasions (637B). Xenophon, too, mentions in his booklet on the Spartan constitution that their symposia lacked hybris, drunkenness and foul language (5.6), and Plutarch stresses that the young could attend the Spartan messes in order to get accustomed to mocking without buffoonery and to endure being mocked. However, when a Spartan could no longer tolerate being mocked, he could ask the mocker to stop, which he immediately did, according to Plutarch in his idealizing biography of Lycurgus (12.6–7). The strong pressures on Spartan life to close ranks in the face of the threat of the subject population, the Helots, had probably made festivity and mockery intolerable.[58]

But some went even further. In the New Testament Epistle to the Ephesians, the author (probably not St Paul) states that *eutrapelia*, 'wit', had no place in the Christian community (5.4). It has been suggested that *eutrapelia* here means something like 'suggestive language',[59] but wit is condemned by somewhat later Christian authors such as Ignatius, Clement of Alexandria, Origen, and, in literally dozens of passages, Basil and John Chrysostom. The last two even went so far as to condemn laughter too, which in fact many Church Fathers did.[60] Clement of Alexandria (*c.*150–215), who wrote a book, the *Paedagogus*, in order to instruct upper-class Christian youths, dedicated a special section to the problem of laughter. He wished to banish buffoons from Christian society,[61] but he did not aim at abolishing laughter altogether. It would be unnatural to suppress laughter, according to Clement, but the Christian had to display moderation, as in all things. A smile should be sufficient for the Christian, whereas women and young men should be very careful not to laugh; a similar rule was laid down by Basil of Caesarea (*c.*330–79) in one of the first monastic *Rules*, the so-called *Regulae fusius tractatae*. In this respect, as in several others, these Church Fathers followed the tradition of the more conservative philosophers. Their Christian life style was in many ways still a pagan one.[62]

Enjoying humour and boisterous laughter is eminently opposed to striving to keep all of life under control, which can be observed among the Pythagoreans, the Spartans and, to a much more marked degree, the ascetic Christians. It should be no surprise that a social group which attempted to keep in check all sorts of physical expression, such as eating, sleeping and sexuality, also objected to laughter. To enjoy humour and laughter freely is the mark of a relaxed, open community, not of an ascetic ideology or tense society.

It must have been the similarities between Pythagoreans, Spartans and Christians which led to a mutual influence in late antiquity. According to the pagan philosopher Iamblichus in his *On the Pythagorean Way of Life* (25), Pythagoras had visited Sparta in order to study its laws, and the passage in Athanasius' *Life of Antony* (14), in which he observed that the saint never laughed or grieved, was taken almost word-for-word from the pagan Porphyry's *Life of Pythagoras* (25). In fact, both in practices and hagiography Pythagoreans and early Christians were much more interrelated than they themselves would have liked to admit.[63] Regarding laughter, this combined heritage would prove to have a long tradition in the Western Church – witness the prohibitions and restrictions of laughter in the medieval monastic *Rules*.[64] Moreover, in addition to this heritage from late antiquity, Thomas Aquinas would again take up the ideas of Aristotle on *eutrapelia* and interpret them as a plea for restrained laughter, a plea which was followed by Pascal.[65] And so the echo of ancient laughter would be audible – albeit moderately for many centuries.

NOTES

I am most grateful to André Lardinois for comments and to Robert Parker for his skilful correction of my English.

1 For a full study of Xenophon's dialogue see G. J. Woldinga, *Xenophons Symposium* (Diss., University of Amsterdam, 1938). In my quotations and summary I have used the translation by O. J. Todd in the Loeb *Xenophon*, vol. 4 (Cambridge and London, 1923).
2 The same device occurs in Plato, *Symposium* 174A, cf. Woldinga, *Xenophons Symposium*, p. 141.
3 For a good survey of the ancient buffoons, see P. Maas, '*Gelotopoioí*', in *Pauly's Realencyclopädie der classischen Altertumswissenschaft*, vol. 7 (Stuttgart, 1912), pp. 1019–21.
4 Cf. M. Jameson, 'Private space and the Greek city', in O. Murray and S. Price (eds), *The Greek City from Homer to Alexander* (Oxford, 1990), pp. 170–95; idem, 'Domestic space in the Greek City-state', in S. Kent (ed.), *Domestic Architecture and the Use of Space* (Cambridge, 1990), pp. 92–113.
5 For a good survey of ancient festivities, see C. Calame, 'La festa', in M. Vegetti (ed.), *Introduzione alle culture antiche*, vol. 3 (Turin, 1992), pp. 29–54.
6 W. Burkert, *Homo necans* (Berkeley, 1983), p. 229.
7 F. Graf, *Eleusis und die orphische Dichtung Athens in vorhellenistischer Zeit* (Berlin and New York, 1974), pp. 45–6; Burkert, *Homo necans*, p. 278; A. M. Bowie, *Aristophanic Comedy* (Cambridge, 1993), pp. 239–40.
8 J. Bremmer, *Greek Religion* (Oxford, 1994), pp. 18–20.
9 This is rightly stressed by S. Halliwell, 'The uses of laughter in Greek culture', *Classical Quarterly*, 41 (1991), pp. 279–96.
10 D. Lateiner, 'No laughing matter: a literary tactic in Herodotus', *Transactions of the American Philological Association*, 107 (1977), pp. 173–82. For laughter in Greek culture the best study remains L. Woodbury, *Quo modo risu ridiculoque Graeci usi sint* (Diss., Harvard University, 1944); see also S. Milanezi, 'Le rire d'Hadès', *Dialogues d'histoire ancienne*, 21 (1995), pp. 231–45.
11 On the *symposion*, see most recently O. Murray (ed.), *Sympotica* (Oxford, 1990); K. Vierneisel and B. Kaeser (eds), *Kunst der Schale – Kultur des*

Trinkens (Munich, 1990); W. J. Slater (ed.), *Dining in a Classical Context* (Ann Arbor, 1991).

12 E. Stein-Hölkeskamp, 'Lebensstil als Selbstdarstellung: Aristokraten beim Symposium', in *Euphronios und seine Zeit* (Berlin, 1991), pp. 39–48; B. Seidensticker, 'Dichtung und Gesellschaft im 4. Jahrhundert. Versuch eines Überblicks', in W. Eder (ed.), *Die athenische Demokratie im 4. Jahrhundert v. Chr.* (Stuttgart, 1995), pp. 175–98.

13 E. Pellizer, 'Outlines of a morphology of sympotic entertainment', in Murray, *Sympotica*, pp. 177–84.

14 Timocles, fr. 8.8; R. Kassel and C. Austin, *Poetae comici Graeci* (Berlin and New York, 1983–), from which excellent edition I quote all the fragments of ancient Greek comedy; Macho *apud* Athenaeus 579b; Nicocles *apud* Stobaeus, *Florilegium* 14.7; Alciphron 3.66.5.

15 Kassel and Austin, *Poetae comici Graeci*, in their commentary ad loc., do not observe that this is a (minor) joke because barley was the cheapest form of bread, cf. Bremmer, 'Marginalia Manichaica', *Zeitschrift für Papyrologie und Epigraphik*, 39 (1980), pp. 29–34, esp. p. 32; T. Braun, 'Barley cakes and emmer bread', in J. Wilkins et al. (eds), *Food in Antiquity* (Exeter, 1995), pp. 25–37.

16 Eupolis, fr. 172, trans. C. B. Gulick, Loeb (slightly adapted).

17 To arrive uninvited was characteristic of the ancient parasites, cf. Asius, fr. 14 West; Cratinus, fr. 46, 47 and 182; Alexis, fr. 213, 259; Timotheus, fr. 1; Apollodorus Carystius, fr. 29 and 31; Lynkeus of Samos in Athenaeus 245a; Lucian, *Demonax* 63; B. Fehr, 'Entertainers at the *Symposion*: the *Akletoi* in the archaic period', in Murray, *Sympotica*, pp. 185–95.

18 Epicharmus, fr. 35 Kaibel, trans. C. B Gulick, Loeb; note for funny parasites also Alexis fr. 188, 229; Philemon fr. 153; H. Nesselrath, *Lukians Parasitendialog* (Berlin and New York, 1985), p. 19.

19 M. Jameson, '*Theoxenia*', in R. Hägg (ed.), *Ancient Greek Cult Practice from the Epigraphical Evidence* (Stockholm, 1994), pp. 35–57, esp. pp. 48f; L. Bruit Zaidman, 'Ritual eating in archaic Greece: parasites and *paredroi*', in Wilkins, *Food in Antiquity*, pp. 196–203.

20 For the relation between these two terms, see Nesselrath, *Lukians Parasitendialog*, pp. 88–121; idem, *Die attische mittlere Komödie* (Berlin and New York, 1990), pp. 309–13; P. G. Brown, 'Menander, fragments 745 and 746K-T, Menander's *Kolax*, and parasites and flatterers in Greek comedy', *Zeitschrift für Papyrologie und Epigraphik*, 92 (1992), pp. 91–107.

21 Pherecrates, fr. 150; Aristophanes, fr. 171; F. Frontisi-Ducroux, 'La bomolochia: autour de l'embuscade à l'autel', *Cahiers du Centre Jean Berard*, 9 (Naples, 1984), pp. 29–49; Nesselrath, *Die attische mittlere Komödie*, pp. 125–8; K. Dover, *Aristophanes: Frogs* (Oxford, 1993), p. 240. Explanation: Harpocration s.v. *bomolocheuesthai*.

22 Eudikos: Aristoxenus, fr. 135 Wehrli (= Athenaeus 19f). Agathocles: Diodorus Siculus 20.63.2.

23 For weddings see R. Hague, 'Ancient Greek wedding songs: the tradition of praise', *Journal of Folklore Research*, 20 (1983), pp. 131–43.

24 E. Romagnoli, *Studi Italiani di filologia classica*, 13 (1905), pp. 226, 251;

E. Fraenkel, *Elementi Plautini in Plauto* (Florence, 1960), pp. 163–4 and Addenda, p. 422; N. Dunbar, *Aristophanes, Birds* (Oxford, 1995), pp. 487f.

25 P. *Heidelberg* 190, cf. R. Kassel, *Kleine Schriften* (Berlin and New York, 1991), pp. 418–21 (= *Rheinisches Museum* 99, 1956, pp. 242–5).

26 Eupolis, fr. 385; Aristophanes, *Frogs* 1451; Anaxandrides fr. 10; A. Brelich, *Gli eroi greci* (Rome, 1958), pp. 167–9.

27 This sanctuary is often, although probably wrongly, identified with that of Heracles in Kynosarges, another Athenian suburb, where Cynics and bastards used to meet, cf. R. Parker, *Athenian History: a history* (Oxford, 1996), p. 306.

28 'Sixty': Athenaeus 260b (from Hegesander), 614d–e (also names, from Telephanes). Cross-eyed Callimedon: Timocles, fr. 29, cf. J. Davies, *Athenian Propertied Families* (Oxford, 1971), p. 279.

29 For similar 'anti-establishment' clubs, see Murray, *Sympotica*, p. 157.

30 Thrace: Xenophon, *Anabasis* 7.3.33 (King Seuthes). Macedonia: Demosthenes 2.19; Theopompus *FGrH* 115 F 162, 236 (Philip II); Plutarch, *Moralia* 60B (Alexander the Great); Athenaeus 130 (the clown Mandrogenes). Successors: Athenaeus 195f (Antiochus Epiphanes danced naked with clowns), 244–5 (Ptolemy), 246 (Lysimachus); Josephus, *Antiquitates* 12.211–14 (Ptolemy).

31 Theopompus *FGrH* 115 F 283b; note also Theophrastus, fr. 548 Fortenbaugh.

32 *Philogelos*, no. 148 (the joke is a 'diluted' version of an *apophthegma* ascribed to the Macedonian king Archelaos [Plutarch, *Moralia* 177A]), cf. Aristophanes, *Birds* 1440ff, *Wealth* 338; Eupolis, fr. 194; Lysias 23.3, 24.20; Demosthenes 25.52; Menander, *Samia* 510–13; Theophrastus, *Characters* 8; Polybius 3.20.5; Philodemus, *De ira* col. 21.23ff; Plutarch, *Nicias* 30, *Moralia* 509A; S. Lewis, 'Barbers' shops and perfume shops: "symposia without wine"', in A. Powell (ed.), *The Greek World* (London, 1995), pp. 432–41.

33 Cf. Diodorus Siculus 20.63.2; Plutarch, *Antonius* 9.5, *Sulla* 2; Dio Chrysostomus 32.86; Athenaeus 261c, 464f; Cassius Dio 80.4; E. Rawson, 'The vulgarity of the Roman mime', in H. D. Jocelyn (ed.), *Tria Lustra* (Liverpool, 1993), pp. 255–60.

34 Plautus, *Stichus* 221: *logos ridiculos vendo . . . cavillationes, adsentatiunculas ac perieratiunculas parasiticas*; 400 *ibo intro ad libros et discam de dictis melioribus*; 454. For the name of Gelasimus, see Fraenkel, *Elementi Plautini*, 33. Plautine parasites: J. C. B. Lowe, 'Plautus' parasites and the Atellena', in G. Vogt-Spira (ed.), *Studien zur vorliterarischen Periode im frühen Rom* (Tübingen, 1989), pp. 161–9.

35 See Herman Roodenburg, Chapter 8 of this volume.

36 For an excellent edition with translation and commentary, see A. Thierfelder, *Philogelos: der Lachfreund* (Munich, 1968). For an English translation, see B. Baldwin, *The Philogelos or Laughter-lover* (Amsterdam, 1983); for the tradition of the text, see also his 'John Tzetzes and the *Philogelos*', *Byzantion*, 56 (1986), pp. 339–41.

37 Cf. G. Ritter, *Studien zur Sprache des Philogelos* (Diss., University of Basel,

1955); L. Robert, *Entretiens Hardt*, 14 (Geneva, 1968), p. 284.

38 W. Gemoll, *Das Apophthegma* (Vienna and Leipzig, 1924), p. 1, observes that the etymology of *apophthegma* is obscure, but the relation with *phthengomai*, 'to speak loudly', defines the word as a more marked speech-act than just a 'normal' answer. For the appearance of the word in the fourth century, see A. Lardinois, *Wisdom in Context: the use of gnomic statements in archaic Greek poetry* (Diss., Princeton University, 1995), pp. 18–19.

39 The jokes have received virtually no attention in recent times, but see J. Rougé, 'Le *Philogélos* et la navigation', *Journal des savants* (1987), pp. 3–12.

40 For the *scholastikos*, see A. Claus, *Ho scholastikos* (Diss., University of Cologne, 1965); add especially C. Roueché, *Aphrodisias in Late Antiquity* (London, 1989), nos. 42–3, 45, 68–9; R. Kotansky, 'Magic in the court of the governor of Arabia', *Zeitschrift für Papyrologie und Epigraphik*, 88 (1991), pp. 41–60, esp. pp. 52–3; T. Hickey, 'A fragment of a letter from a bishop to a *scholastikos*', ibid., 110 (1996), pp. 127–31.

41 See the nuanced discussion by M. I. Finley, *Ancient Slavery and Modern Ideology* (New York, 1980), pp. 93–122.

42 T. Rütten, *Demokrit, lachender Philosoph und sanguinischer Melancholiker* (Leiden, 1992), whose remarks on the sources have to be supplemented with K. Brodersen, 'Hippokrates und Artaxerxes. Zu P. Oxy. 1184ᵛ, P. Beroli. Inv. 7094ᵛ und 21137ᵛ+6934ᵛ', *Zeitschrift für Papyrologie und Epigraphik*, 102 (1994), pp. 100–10; R. Müller, 'Demokrit – der "lachende Philosoph"', in S. Jäkel and A. Timonen (eds), *Laughter down the Centuries*, I (Turku, 1994), pp. 39–51.

43 V. Nutton, 'The medical meeting place', in P. J. van der Eijk et al. (eds), *Ancient Medicine in its Socio-Cultural Context* (2 vols, Amsterdam and Atlanta, 1995), I, pp. 3–22, esp. p. 18. It is typical for the status of jokes that they are not mentioned in these excellent volumes.

44 R. MacMullen, *Enemies of the Roman Order* (New Haven and London, 1966), pp. 128–62; J. Bremmer, 'Prophets, seers, and politics in Greece, Israel and early modern Europe', *Numen*, 40 (1993), pp. 150–83.

45 Pythagoras: Diogenes Laertius 8.20. Anaxagoras: Aelian, *Varia historia* 8.13. Anacharsis: Athenaeus 613d.

46 Phrynichus, fr. 19.

47 Aristophanes, *Peace* 740–50. Aristophanes regularly rejects comic tricks of his competitors, which later he unashamedly uses himself, cf. A. H. Sommerstein, *Aristophanes: Peace* (Warminster, 1985), p. 167; E. Degani and J. M. Bremer, in J. M. Bremer and E. W. Handley (eds), *Aristophane = Entretiens Hardt*, 38 (Geneva, 1993), p. 168.

48 Degani, in ibid., pp. 8f.

49 M. Herzfeld, *The Poetics of Manhood* (Princeton, 1985), pp. 146–9.

50 On Plato, the symposium and laughter, see H. D. Rankin, 'Laughter, humor and related topics in Plato', *Classica et Medievalia*, 27 (1966), pp. 186–213; M. Mader, *Das Problem des Lachens und der Komödie bei Platon* (Stuttgart, 1977); G. J. de Vries, 'Laughter in Plato', *Mnemosyne*, IV, 38 (1985), pp. 378–81; M. Tecusan, '*Logos Sympotikos*: patterns of the

irrational in philosophical drinking: Plato outside the *Symposium*', in Murray, *Sympotica*, pp. 238–60; Z. Stewart, 'Laughter and the Greek philosophers: a sketch', in Jäkel and Timonen, *Laughter down the Centuries*, pp. 29–36. Academy: Aelian, *Varia historia* 3.35. Grouch: Amphis, fr. 12.

51 Davies, *Athenian Propertied Families*, pp. 261f.

52 For a good introduction to the present state of our knowledge, see R. Janko, *Aristotle. Poetics* (Indianapolis and Cambridge, 1987).

53 For Aristotle, his school, and humour see A. D. Leeman et al., *M. Tullius Cicero, de oratore libri III: Kommentar* (3 vols, Heidelberg, 1989), III, pp. 190–200; H. Flashar, 'Aristoteles, das Lachen und die alte Komödie', in Jäkel and Timonen, *Laughter down the Centuries*, pp. 59–70.

54 Alexis, fr. 160 with the commentary of Kassel and Austin; W. J. Slater, 'Sympotic ethics in the *Odyssey*', in Murray, *Sympotica*, pp. 213–20; G. Nagy, *The Best of the Achaeans* (Baltimore and London, 1979), pp. 222–75 (blame poetry); P. O'Leary, 'Jeers and judgments: laughter in early Irish literature', *Cambridge Medieval Celtic Studies*, 22 (1991), pp. 15–29.

55 Cf. P. W. van der Horst, 'Is wittiness unchristian? A note on *eutrapelia* in Eph. V 4', in idem. and G. Mussies, *Studies on the Hellenistic Background of the New Testament* (Utrecht, 1990), pp. 223–37.

56 For this development see J. Bremmer, 'Walking, standing, and sitting in ancient Greek culture', in J. Bremmer and H. Roodenburg (eds), *A Cultural History of Gesture* (Cambridge, 1991), pp. 16–35, esp. pp. 18–20.

57 Aelian, *Varia historia* 8.13 (Aristoxenos), 13.18 (Dionysius); Alexis, fr. 201 (comedy). For Pythagoras, see the brilliant study of W. Burkert, *Lore and Science in Ancient Pythagoreanism* (Cambridge, MA, 1972); J. Bremmer, 'Religious secrets and secrecy in classical Greece', in H. Kippenberg and G. Stroumsa (eds), *Secrecy and Concealment* (Leiden, 1995), pp. 61–78, esp. pp. 63–70 (some additions).

58 E. David, 'Laughter in Spartan society', in A. Powell (ed.), *Classical Sparta: techniques behind her success* (London, 1989), pp. 1–25; N. Fisher, 'Drink, *hybris*, and the promotion of harmony in Sparta', ibid., pp. 26–50.

59 Van der Horst, 'Is wittiness unchristian?', who also discusses the problematic attitude of Christians towards humour; add now H. Rahner, 'Eutrapélie', in *Dictionnaire de spiritualité ascétique et mystique*, vol. 4.2 (Paris, 1961), pp. 1726–9; C. Spicq, *Notes de lexicographie néotestamentaire: supplément* (Fribourg and Göttingen, 1982), pp. 322–5; G. Luck, 'Humor', *Reallexikon für Antike und Christentum*, 16 (Stuttgart, 1996), pp. 753–73 (not quite satisfactory).

60 Wittiness: Ignatius, *Epistle* 4.8; Clement of Alexandria, *Paedagogus* 2.6.50, 2.7.53; Origen, *Fragmenta ex commentariis in epistulam ad Ephesios* 24 (= *Journal of Theological Studies*, 3, 1902, 559); Basil, *Epistles* 2, 22.1; John Chrysostom, *Patrologia Graeca* 49.235; 58.516; 60.72; 62.120 and *passim*. Laughter: N. Adkin, 'The Fathers on laughter', *Orpheus*, 6 (1985), pp. 149–52; add the probably spurious treatise of John Chrysostom, *Ascetam facetiis uti non debere* (*Patrologia Graeca* 48.1053–60).

61 This opposition to buffoons recurs regularly among the Church Fathers. See, for example, Asterius, *Homilies* 1.5.4 (who still combines buffoons

28   Jan Bremmer

and parasites); Gregory of Nyssa, *De beneficentia* 9.105; John Chrysostom, *Patrologia Graeca* 58.665; 60.75; 62.120.

62 Clement of Alexandria, *Paedagogus* 2.5.45–8; Basil, *Patrologia Graeca* 31.961.

63 Cf. J. Bremmer, 'Symbols of marginality from early Pythagoreans to late antique monks', *Greece and Rome*, 39 (1992), pp. 205–14, esp. pp. 205–6; M. van Uytfanghe, 'L'Hagiographie: un "genre" chrétien ou antique tardif?', *Analecta Bollandiana*, 111 (1993), pp. 135–88.

64 B. Steidle, 'Das Lachen im alten Mönchtum', *Benediktinische Monatschrift zur Pflege religiösen und geistigen Lebens*, 20 (1938), pp. 271–80, reprinted in his *Beiträge zum alten Mönchtum und zur Benediktusregel* (Sigmaringen, 1986), pp. 30–9; G. Schmitz, '... quod rident homines, plorandum est. Der "Unwert" des Lachens in monastisch geprägten Vorstellungen der Spätantike und des frühen Mittelalters', in F. Quarthal and W. Setzler (eds), *Stadtverfassung – Verfassungsstaat – Pressepolitik* (Sigmaringen, 1980), pp. 3–15; J. Le Goff, 'Le Rire dans les règles monastiques du haut moyen âge', in C. Lepelley et al. (eds), *Haut moyen-âge: culture, éducation et société. Études offertes à Pierre Riché* (La Garenne-Colombes, 1990), pp. 93–103; Le Goff, Chapter 3 of this volume.

65 H. Rahner, 'Eutrapelie, eine vergessene Tugend', *Geist und Leben*, 27 (1954), pp. 346–53; M.-M. Dufeil, 'Risus in theologia Thome', in T. Bouché and H. Charpentier (eds), *Le Rire au Moyen Âge dans la littérature et les arts* (Bordeaux, 1990), pp. 147–63; J. Morel, 'Pascal et la doctrine du rire grave', in *Méthodes chez Pascal* (Paris, 1979), pp. 213–22; J. Morreall, 'The rejection of humor in Western thought', *Philosophy East and West*, 39 (1989), pp. 243–65; Verberckmoes, Chapter 6 of this volume.

2

Cicero, Plautus and Roman Laughter

FRITZ GRAF

I think that, to a man not devoid of wit, it is easier to talk about anything than about jokes.

Cicero

The Romans were proud of their humour. Other peoples had humour as well – especially the notoriously facetious Athenians – but 'polite ancient Roman wit is wittier than Attic wit', as Cicero has it, quite self-consciously.[1] In order to test the veracity of this assertion even on a superficial level, we must consult Roman literature itself. The two main genres devoted to humour, comedy and satire, were well represented in Rome. In a famous remark, Quintilian, the teacher of rhetoric in the late first century AD, insists that it was the Romans who had invented and cultivated literary satire (though the relationship of humour and satire is not an easy one).[2] The same Quintilian, however, remarks that, 'in comedy, we lag behind': in the wake of Aristotle, he must have taken Attic New Comedy as his standard.[3] A century before, Cicero had asserted that the humour (*urbanitas*) of Plautus, the first full-time Roman comedy writer and stage manager, equalled that of Aristophanes and Athenian Old Comedy, and this was very high praise indeed.[4] On the less superficial level of theory, although the ever inquisitive Aristotle, in the lost second book of his *Poetics*, had been the first to theorize about 'the ridiculous' (*to geloion*) in the context of comedy, it is Cicero's long and excellent chapter on humour – not only in rhetoric – in the second book of his *De Oratore* that remains a major source. The parallel chapter in Quintilian's *Institutio oratoria* (6.3) is heavily indebted to him.

Cicero's chapter is a mine of information, not least about the practice of wit and humour both in public speaking and in the daily life of the Roman upper class. To illustrate and underpin his theoretical framework, he collected a large number of examples. It helped that he himself was thought to be one of the wittiest orators of his day to whom later tradition attributed, in the course of time, a growing number of jokes (his freedman Tiro had already published a collection),[5] and who was, as Quintilian (6.2.2f) reports, open to the censure of having exceeded the good measure of wit – an opinion with which Quintilian disagrees (6.2). But had not Cicero's contemporary, the rigid younger Cato, already called him in (feigned?) anger 'a ridiculous consul'?[6] And did not others, even less benign contemporaries, nickname him *scurra*, the 'clown'?[7]

This disagreement between Cicero's contemporaries and his later admirers already signifies to tensions and evaluations which are not uniform – and it points to the limits of humour. Already Cicero had talked about it more than once.

In his late treatise *De officiis*, Cicero touches upon the problem of wit and its limitations: what marks the limit is 'that which is becoming' (*to prepon*) – a category dear also to Panaetius of Rhodes, upon whom the entire treatise is heavily dependent, and, ultimately, dear also to Aristotle.[8] Wit has to keep itself inside given limits of respectability in order to be socially acceptable. Cicero describes, or rather explores, accepted and unacceptable wit with the help of several terms which are closely related: accepted humour is 'elegant' (*elegans*), 'polished' (*urbanum*, as only a city-dweller could be), 'inventive' (*ingeniosum*) and 'funny' (*facetum*), while unacceptable wit is 'unbecoming to a free-born man' (*inliberale*), 'impudent' (*petulans*), 'disgraceful' (*flagitiosum*) and 'dirty' (*obscenum*). Social categories play a role: city-dwellers versus rustics, free-born versus slaves and disreputable freedmen; bad humour places heavy blame (*flagitium*) on its bearer; elegance and inborn inventiveness (*ingenium*) too are rather upper-class characteristics.

There is more in the chapter on the limits of wit in the earlier rhetorical treatise *De oratore*, and there are also differences from the later ethical work;[9] the categorization follows more Roman practicability than Greek ethical theory. The orator, after all, uses humour as one of his instruments of persuasion, in order to win his audience, not to antagonize it. Cicero proceeds in two steps, from the general to the particular. In the first step, he outlines the general limits of humour: wit has to keep away from great crimes and from great misery – both, obviously, are serious matters, and the orator has to treat them seriously in order to appear credible. Jokes about known criminals and about great misfortune will discredit the one who makes the jokes. The second step concentrates on one specific subject, corporal appearance (2.237–9): 'Deformity and irregularities of the body are a great field for jokes', he says – but again one should beware of going too far, otherwise one would appear as a clown and an actor of mimes, *scurra aut mimus.*[10] Later, the *scurra* is defined as someone who does not know the limits of humour imposed by seriousness (*gravitas*) and intelligence (*prudentia*: 2.247). Likewise, the orator is advised to keep away from overdoing caricature (*imitatio depravata*) lest he seem a *mimus* and *ethopoios*, a parodist of characters, whose bad reputation is well known.[11] In short, not all that is ridiculous is funny:[12] the *sannio*, the rustic jester, is not, though he makes people laugh.

The limits of humour are thus defined by the function it has in rhetoric: wit serves to win over the audience – especially, as Quintilian underlines, the judge whom humour either relaxes or wakes up or diverts.[13] A Roman orator is the embodiment of the perfect member of Rome's senatorial class; to win over his audience, he has to keep as close to this ideal as possible – therefore the importance of *gravitas* and *prudentia*, the chief virtues of this class. The professional entertainers – the clown, the *mimus*, the *ethopoios*, the *sannio* – belong to a different class altogether: they are either Greek foreigners or slaves or freedmen. Both Cicero and Quintilian locate the orator's greatest danger in appearing as an entertainer: the techniques being similar (and actors often being tutors to young orators), the separation is all the more important, and all the more difficult. Again, the difference is one of social standing. Maybe it is clearer now why it was his enemies who called Cicero a clown: he was, after all, a provincial *homo novus*, without all the ingrained refinement of the upper class. To accuse him of overstepping the limits of humour has a class-conscious ring to it, and it was apt to hurt Cicero very efficiently.

The same results arise from Cicero's functional definition of humour: laughter arises 'from the castigation of deformity and disgrace in a not disgraceful way'.[14] Deformity and disgrace arise from social deviance: the function of wit is to correct deviance – in a socially acceptable way. When we look at the examples Cicero gives, a further point becomes clear: it is deviance *within* this same upper class which humour censures. This explains even better the role of humour: direct, unmitigated censure between the members of the same class, haughty and class-conscious as they were, would have been unthinkable, not only for a *homo novus*; but a witty remark takes the sting out of it. And it explains the limits imposed: there is social deviance which is so serious (and transgresses class borderlines) that wit is not a sufficient corrective, and thus a witty remark would seem to take it too lightly. Again, firm knowledge of the social norms imposes the limits on wit and humour.

One now has to beware of a misunderstanding. *Gravitas*, seriousness and respectability, does not exclude humour; the solemn senator is not advised to be humorous in order to please the audience; rather, the rules of the class call for both *gravitas* and for *urbanitas*. In his *De oratore*, Cicero insists that all the rules and classifications he derives from oratorical wit are valid also for day-to-day situations (2.270): it is *urbanitas* which is required, the easy-going presence of mind which offers a witty retort to all situations, and which can function as a polite rebuke. The best example is an anecdote which Cicero reports: 'Once the great Metellus wished to visit old Ennius, the great poet, in his far off house on the Aventine; his maid said that he was not at home – but Metellus, who knew him well, departed with the firm conviction that the maid had not told the truth. Some days later, Ennius came to Metellus' house and asked for the master – but Metellus shouted that he wasn't at home. Understandably, Ennius became angry – but Metellus appeased him: "The other day, I believed your maid (Roman servants were notorious liars), so why don't you now believe me?"' (2.273). Both men, the poet and the senator, stood on an equal footing; to call one openly a liar just would not do.

So far the senatorial, upper-class wit has as its function to preserve the rules of the class – and urbanely to remind those who overstepped them of its limits. Plautus, the writer of comedies, is a different matter – but I hope that the findings up to now will shed some light on him also.

Cicero had compared the wit of Plautus to that of the Athenian Old Comedy – a wit with which Aristotle, as we recall, had his problems: to the coarseness of Aristophanes he preferred the subtleties of Menander and New Comedy.[15] This tells us something about Plautus as well, since this criticism repeats itself in Rome. While, for Cicero, Plautus incorporated Roman *urbanitas*, Horace (who shared the same theory of wit with Cicero) radically differed in his assessment: the first and, to some, the greatest writer of Roman comedies, he insists, is lacking in *urbanitas*.[16] This lack has to do with his *licentia*, 'frivolousness', a characteristic which Horace derives from one of its immediate sources, the indigenous Fescennine jokes of early Roman country people. Not that *licentia* would not have been a catchword for Cicero as well: however, he is not entirely adverse to *licentia* in joking, provided it keeps inside the limits of *honestas*, respectability – as it does, so he thinks, in Plautus. Obviously, Plautus can be measured with different scales: Ciceronian *honestas* is something different from Horatian *urbanitas*. One needs to take a closer look at his humour and to compare it to Cicero's in order to understand the problem.

Humour in rhetoric was regarded by Cicero himself as an instrument of censure inside the same social group. In Athenian Old Comedy, this sort of humour is fundamental: entire plots arise from public situations which call for censure and correction – Cleon's demagogy in the *Knights*, the warmongering of Athenian generals in *Lysistrata* or *Peace*, the lack of tragic talent in the *Frogs*; in a standard scene in all Aristophanic comedies, the *parábasis*, the chorus, usually part of the drama, stepped out of this role to address the public directly, in their author's voice, about those actual problems. When political circumstances changed, Greek New Comedy moved away from political comedy to family problems – young men loving (or seducing or raping) girls below their station, lost daughters found again much later as prostitutes, twins separated as babies and united again as young men. Humour, wit, even indecency are part of this comedy too (to a much greater degree even than scholars tended to believe at the turn of this century, as new papyri have taught us), but there is no social jesting. Archaic Roman comedy continued Greek New Comedy by adapting Greek plays to the Roman stage; and again, direct social censure had no place.[17] It did this not only because the Greek originals had lacked a political dimension; after all, Roman comedy flourished in a period when Roman public life was exciting and controversial enough to offer itself for public comment; rather Roman law forbade ridiculing a citizen (which in practice meant an aristocrat) by name – Naevius, a Roman knight a generation older than Plautus, had to serve a prison sentence for transgression of this law when putting a comedy on stage. Although urbane banter was allowed among the members of the upper class, they never extended the right of making jokes about a nobleman beyond their group, least of all to the popular stage: in-group joking functions as an instrument of group coherence, jokes from outside threaten social status. This does not mean that Plautus refrained entirely from pointing to contemporary events or persons, but such references are much rarer and vaguer[18] – as in the case of Naevius, to whose prison sentence he alludes in the *Miles gloriosus* (vv. 200ff). In addition, this passage is characterized by brilliant metatheatre:[19] while one person, the cunning slave Palaestrio, tries to think up a way to save a difficult situation, a second person, old Periplectomenus, describes his actions:

> Look, please, how he stands, with severe face considering, thinking; he beats his breast with his fingers, I think to call forth his heart; then he turns away, props his left on his left thigh, computes with the fingers of his right, beating upon his thigh. . . . But now he builds: he puts a column under his chin.

Up to this point, humour results mainly from the fact that someone describes what everybody can see on the stage, then also from the wittily naive way this is done. The column under the chin leads to a small commentary: 'Away with it, I hate this sort of building: I heard about a column under the mouth of the foreign poet with whom two guardians always sleep.' The way humour is generated here is complex – and owing to the restrictions imposed by Roman law, the well-known Roman knight Naevius is transformed into a foreigner (*barbarus*),[20] and his sentence due to a speech-act is transformed into a 'columned mouth', *os columnatum*, because he would have been exposed at the pillory on the Forum Romanum. Humour is created here in two ways: first by the clever chain of associations inside the passage (a chin propped upon an arm is compared to a chin under which a column has been built; this metaphorical connection of chin and column leads to mouth and column, that is, to loose talking punished on the pillory), then by the even more clever way of circumventing the prohibition by hiding behind the theatrical effects. The protest against the way the authorities treated a fellow poet is formulated in two ways – first by directly commenting upon a columned mouth ('away with it, I hate this sort of building': in itself, this is not comical), then by the complicated way Plautus bypasses the prohibition on free speech which, exactly by being so complicated, directs the audience to the problem.

Allusions to such specific events which censure Roman authorities or contemporaries are otherwise virtually absent in Plautus. Some related examples come from the prologues, but they do not aim at specific historical events. Rather, they are directed at general and more private shortcomings of behaviour, such as the long list of bad manners in the audience which opens the *Poenulus* and which contains examples of gender humour (directed at the *matronae* who laugh too loud, thus transgressing the *decorum* of their rank), or what one could call humorous group censure (directed at professional or social categories whose individual members do not keep to the rules of their station). Different again are the examples of ethnic humour, jokes at the expense especially of Greeks. Usually, the aim of ethnic humour is not censure, that is, correction, but the affirmation of one's own identity by differentiation. But Plautine ethnic humour has a clever twist: when ascribing to Athens all the immorality he can think of, he implies that Rome is just the contrary; but the audience is well aware that this is not the case.

There is one thing, though, by which Plautine comedy seemed to differ fundamentally from Greek comedy, at least according to a somewhat debated idea of Erich Segal.[21] Greek Comedy, be it Old or New, is set in Greece, mostly in Athens; Roman comedy does not change the setting to Rome but keeps the Greek location. Plautus is well aware of it; in the *Menaechmi*, he explains: 'Poets use to do this in their comedies: they believe that everything takes place in Athens, in order that it looks more Greek to you . . .'[22] – often down to the details of daily life, such as the existence of a *gynaeceum* ('women's quarters') in a house, and the concomitant hesitation of a man to enter it.[23] This implies a fundamental change, from a play staged in a well-known everyday world to a staging in a foreign country associated with luxury, lasciviousness and lack of discipline: 'do not be surprised', he reminds his audience in *Stichus*, 'that slaves drink, make love and invite people to dinner parties: all this is allowed in Athens.'[24] Seen from Rome, this is as scandalous as sons cheating and tricking their fathers (mostly with the help of inventive and unscrupulous slaves), a motif even more common in Roman comedy than feasting slaves – and even more abhorred by Roman morality. Thus, Segal concludes, while Athenian comedy stayed well inside the norms of its society, Roman comedy created a topsy-turvy world of inverted reality where things usually forbidden were allowed. Plautine comedy was a carnivalesque occasion; its specific humour was the humour of carnival, where the rules of ordinary life were suspended.

But the main field of Plautine humour is purely theatrical: witty action, highly entertaining slapstick and word-play of all sorts, such as complex and absurd neologisms, long lists, abrupt changes of style; Plautus insistently directs our attention to how the comical machine works. This categorization (into 'laughter from the incidents' and 'laughter from diction') corresponds to the classes already developed in the Aristotelian tradition for Greek comedy,[25] and most of the Plautine features find their parallels both in Greek New and especially in Old Comedy. There are differences between Plautus and his supposed Greek models, and literary scholarship has tried to analyse these differences for nearly a century; but since Greek New Comedy was virtually unknown until the publication of Menander's *Dyskolos* in 1958, the results were heavily biased by *a priori* assumptions about elevated New Comedy and coarse Plautine humour. The papyrus finds, especially the publication of two scenes from Menander's *Dis Exapaton* in 1968, which were transformed into the Plautine *Bacchides*, gave a new factual basis to such comparisons.[26] The result is somewhat disappointing for those who were looking for a Roman humour categorically different from Greek humour: the Plautine changes enhance the hilarity and the playfulness of the scenes and serve to create livelier, funnier action. It is not Roman humour in any fundamentally different and specific sense: it is the sort of humour needed by a stage professional whose audience tends to be drawn away from a boring performance to more rewarding gladiatorial or circus spectacles – as the other great Roman comedy writer, Terence, knew from hard personal experience. It is a difference in the societal function of the stage in Rome which influences the choice of laughter-inducing techniques.

In a very general way, this is plausible and has been widely accepted in recent scholarship.[27] Still, there are problems. Firstly, Roman – not only Plautine – comedy was enacted during festivals, both irregular occasions (such as funerals, dedications of temples or triumphs) and regular state festivals. Every festival entails a suspension of daily normality, but not every one belongs to carnival:[28] for that, specific features of ritual reversal are necessary. While Greek Dionysian festivals – the ordinary occasions for staging tragedies and comedies – belong to carnival in this narrower sense, among the respective Roman festivals, only the *ludi Megalenses* (celebrated for Anatolian Cybele) show traces of reversal, while the other state celebrations (the *ludi Apollinares* for Apollo and the *ludi Romani* and *ludi plebei* for the Capitoline state gods Jupiter, Juno, Minerva) are not carnivalesque festivals. Secondly, the theory works only for Plautus, not for Terence, whose comedies keep much closer to the spirit of New Comedy, with rather subdued humour and without hilarious joking and emphasis on social reversals. Terentian comedies were staged on occasions similar to the Plautine ones. A carnivalesque character, obviously, was not inherent in the festivals, but, if anywhere, only in the Plautine conception of comedy.[29] Thirdly, a salient feature of carnivalesque humour is its social function: it is a humour which serves to censure the deviant (and sometimes often already deviating) behaviour of group members – as in the 'Schnitzelbank' of the Basel Fastnacht or, to stay closer to Plautus, in the archaic Roman *ioca fescennina*, ritualized jesting which, in the words of Horatius, 'dealt with rustic reproaches'.[30] We saw how direct censure, so common in Old Comedy and satire, was very rare in Plautus, while more general moralizing can be seen as a function of Plautine comedy – but this is a function every comedy has. It is inherent in the literary genre, since comedy is, like satire, basically very conservative, tending everywhere to correct deviant behaviour by ridiculing it (*ridentem dicere verum*, as Horace has it). Direct censure is not at the centre of Plautine comedy: Plautine comedies stress theatrical aspects and excel in creating a sometimes surrealistic musical world and fun for the sake of fun.

There exists a Plautine scene which is emblematical of this complex situation. In *Pseudolus*, young Calidorus has been cheated by the wicked pimp Ballio; the youngster calls his slave Pseudolus, and the two of them attack Ballio with a long verbal insult. In a famous paper, the German classical scholar Hermann Usener long ago argued that this scene reflects an Italian custom of public ritual blaming;[31] even when Plautus found part of the idea already in his Greek model, it certainly gains relief from such an existing ritual background. Such ritual blaming is not humorous *per se*, though it must be quite funny for the bystanders. In Plautus, however, the humour does not stem from the fact that we are viewing a scene of public reproach but from two other sources: from the way the insulting pair acts and speaks – first Calidorus, then Pseudolus, then the two together in a nice climax. And humour results especially from the reactions of Ballio: he cannot be easily impressed:

CA: Violator of laws!
BA: Good!
PS: Seducer of a youngster!
BA: Strong indeed.
CA: Thief!
BA: Aha.
PS: Ex-slave!
BA: By Jove.
CA: Defrauder of the people!
BA: Quite obvious.
PS: Fraudulent man!
CA: Impure person!
PS: Pimp!
CA: Dirt!
BA: Very good singers! (vv. 360–6)

Thus, the theatre is very present, and it is the acting on the stage which is responsible for the humour in this scene, not an intrinsic and traditional humorous quality of what is represented.

So what about Plautus and Roman humour? We saw that Cicero defined humour according to a moralistic function, and limited it along similar lines – 'we laugh about what accuses bad behaviour and demonstrates it in not a bad fashion.'[32] Plautus would have agreed with the second statement: humour cannot be *turpis*, and Plautus refrains from bad language as well as from explicit sexual jokes (the exception is the somewhat salacious *Casina*, but *Casina* is an exception in many ways). But he does not use comedy for the same reason that Cicero or the satirists used humour, for blame and censure, which the label carnivalesque would make us expect. In the long history of his reception, Plautus is admired not for his morals, but for his artistry and his witty entertainment.

NOTES

1 Cicero, *Ad familiares*, 9.15.2: *salsiores quam illi Atticorum Romani veteres atque urbani sales.*
2 Quintilian, *Institutio oratoria* 10.1.93: *satura quidem tota nostra est.*
3 Ibid., 10.1.66: *in comoedia claudicamus.*
4 Cicero, *De officiis* 1.104: *duplex omnino est iocandi genus, unum inliberale petulans flagitiosum obscenum, alterum elegans urbanum ingeniosum facetum, quo genere non modo Plautus noster et Atticorum antiqua comoedia, sed etiam philosophorum Socraticorum libri referti sunt* ('There are two ways of joking, one ignoble, insolent, offensive and sordid, the other one elegant, polished, noble and witty; not only Plautus and the Old

Comedy of Athens, but also the books of the Socratic philosophers are full of this second sort').

5 Macrobius, *Saturnalia* 2.1.12.
6 Plutarch, *Comparatio Demosthenis et Ciceronis* 1.5.
7 Macrobius, *Saturnalia* 2.1.12: *eum scurram ab inimicis appellari solitum*; cf. P. Corbett, *The Scurra* (Edinburgh, 1986).
8 Cicero, *De officiis* 1.103f.
9 Cicero, *De oratore* 2.216–90; cf. the commentary by A. D. Leeman, H. Pinkster and E. Rabbie (eds), *M. Tullius Cicero. De oratore libri III*, vol. 3 (Heidelberg, 1989), ad loc.
10 Ibid., 2.239: *(ne . . .) scurrilis iocus sit aut mimicus.*
11 Ibid., 2.240: *mimus et ethologus.*
12 Ibid., 2.251: *non omnia ridicula faceta.*
13 Quintilian, *Institutio* 6.3.1.
14 Cicero, *De oratore* 2.236: *haec ridentur quae notant et designant turpitudinem aliquam non turpiter.*
15 Aristotle, *Nicomachean Ethics* 1128a 20.
16 Horace, *Ars* 270–4; the catchword is *inurbanum* (273); cf. C. O. Brink, *Horace on Poetry: the 'Ars poetica'* (Cambridge, 1971), p. 308: 'Horace emerges here as the more perceptive literary critic.'
17 M. Fuhrmann, 'Lizenzen und Tabus des Lachens: zur sozialen Grammatik der hellenistisch-römischen Komödie', in W. Preisendanz and Rainer Warnig (eds), *Das Komische* (Munich, 1976), pp. 65–101, here pp. 76f.
18 M. Bettini, *Verso un antropologia dell'intreccio* (Urbino, 1991), pp. 79f.
19 See M. Barchiesi, 'Plauto e il metateatro antico', in *I moderni alla ricerca di Enea* (Rome, 1981), pp. 147ff (orig. *Il Verri*, 31, 1969, 113ff).
20 For this procedure, see E. Fraenkel, *Elementi Plautini in Plauto* (Rome, 1960), pp. 159f.
21 E. Segal, *Roman Laughter: the comedy of Plautus* (Cambridge, MA, 1968; repr., without footnotes (!), New York and Oxford, 1987).
22 *Menaechmi* 7–8: *atque hoc poetae faciunt in comoediis; omnis res gestas esse Athenis autumant, quo illud vobis Graecum videatur magis.*
23 Plautus, *Mostellaria* 755–809; see Nepos, *Praefatio* 7.
24 *Stichus* 446–8: *atque id ne vos miremini, homines servolos potare, amare atque ad cenam condicere: licet haec Athenis nobis.*
25 *Tractatus Coislinianus*: 'laughter from diction and laughter from the incidents'. For a translation of this treatise, see R. Janko, *Aristotle: Poetics* (Indianapolis and Cambridge, 1987), pp. 43–6.
26 E. Handley, *Menander and Plautus: a study in comparison* (London, 1968).
27 See especially Bettini, *Verso un antropologia dell'intreccio*, pp. 79–96.
28 A differentiation not always made in the essays in S. Döpp (ed.), *Karnevaleske Phänomene in antiken und nachantiken Kulturen und Literaturen* (Trier, 1993).
29 Bettini, *Verso un antropologia dell'intreccio*, p. 75, insists on the 'strong historical and cultural difference' ('un forte scarto storico-culturale') between Plautus and Terence.

30 Horace, *Epistle* 2.1.146: *opprobria rustica fudit.*
31 H. Usener, 'Italische Volksjustiz', in his *Kleine Schriften* (4 vols, Leipzig, 1915), vol. 4, pp. 377–80.
32 Cicero, *De oratore* 2.236, above n. 14.

3

Laughter in the Middle Ages

JACQUES LE GOFF

As I begin to present my research into laughter in the Middle Ages, I feel some apprehension. After all, was it not Voltaire who wrote: 'People who seek metaphysical causes for laughter are not cheerful'?[1] However, I am not seeking metaphysical causes for laughter. Rather, I am trying to recover, in particular for the Middle Ages, what society thought about laughter, which theoretical positions it adopted, and how, in its various forms, laughter functioned in medieval society.

I would like to convince the reader that laughter is a subject worth thinking about and, in particular, that it can be studied historically. I hope to validate an initial, very general, observation, but one that we should not neglect because we think it banal: laughter is a cultural phenomenon. Depending on the society and period, attitudes to laughter, the ways in which it is practised, its objects and its forms are not constant but changing. Laughter is a social phenomenon. It requires at least two or three persons, real or imagined: one who causes laughter, one who laughs and one who is being laughed at, quite often also the person or persons one is laughing with. It is a social practice with its own codes, rituals, actors and theatre. I would even say that this is the only interesting point made by Bergson in his otherwise extremely disappointing study of laughter.[2] He emphasized this social dimension, sometimes in a particularly felicitous way, and it was in this area that Freud saw a convergence of his own theories with the ideas of Bergson.[3] As a cultural and social phenomenon, laughter must have a history. That is why I feel compelled to point the reader to the serious side of laughter – something for which I also have my authorities. In 1983, the American John Morreall published his stimulating book *Taking Laughter Seriously*,[4] and five years later the Italian F. Ceccarelli published his study *Sorriso e riso*.[5] After reminding us that every explanation of the ridiculous just kills laughter and that the death of laughter should alarm us, because laughter is a source of pleasure, the author embarks on a long enquiry, at the end of which he concludes: 'It is very difficult to doubt the importance of smiling and laughing, from whatever point of view one considers them.' He adds very shrewdly that the ease with which many people consider a study of laughing and smiling as futile is just part of the problem and function of laughing and smiling. I will end by quoting the Russian author Alexander Herzen, who more than a century ago observed: 'It would be extremely interesting to write the history of laughter.'[6] What I would like to do here is to sketch the problems that arise when constructing the history of laughter in the medieval West.

As I think it may explain my basic assumptions and at the same time account for the weaknesses and lacunae in my approach, I will start by outlining how this subject arose in my research and describing my original motivations and objectives. I will then list the problems I met in the course of my investigation, problems which define its basic assumptions. I must add that my work is still in an exploratory phase. This is not meant as a *captatio benevolentiae*. Some years ago, my friends and I devoted a 'séminaire' to the subject, and many of those who participated have already made very interesting contributions, both at a theoretical and a documentary level. Finally, as an example, I will deal with one particular point that I have by now been able to study in some depth, the laughter of monks, *risus monasticus*, in the early Middle Ages.[7] I will also suggest some guidelines for a history of the evolution in attitudes to laughter and forms of laughter, and to the place of laughter in medieval society, from late antiquity to the Renaissance.

THE BACKGROUND AND OBJECTIVES OF MY RESEARCH

In my view a study of the history of laughter has two aspects. The steps to take, the method, the formulation of the problem, and, most importantly, the documentation are different for each – on the one hand, the attitudes to laughter, on the other, manifestations of laughter by others. One could make a traditional distinction and speak of the 'theory and practice of laughter'. As for the first aspect, it is relatively easy to collect the more or less theoretical, normative texts, which provide us both with attitudes to laughter and with recommendations as to how to laugh. One observes that, as with table manners, there is a whole series of texts on manners of laughing. Perhaps we are best equipped in respect of these texts. The problem of the practice of laughter is far more complex. There again, I think, we meet with two subsets. On the one hand, there are the texts which mention, in a very limited and jejune way, the presence and forms of laughing – for example, in a chronicle where one sees a person start laughing. To try and capture all these instances of laughter is important for an enquiry of this sort, but one immediately sees what a fishing expedition this entails. On the other hand, there is the enormous domain of what is generally described as the comic. Here there is a very different difficulty, because it is necessary to transform an analysis of problems of the comic into an equivalent analysis of laughter, without of course losing track of what is special about the comic or the texts in which it is expressed. In other words, one should distinguish between those texts in which laughter is judged and the texts which seek to make us laugh. They are very different. And here we encounter one of the big problems in our research – the heterogeneity of documents, issues and concepts. We have to find out whether there exists a unifying notion behind it all. I should add that one meets on the one hand a history of values and mentalities and on the other a history of literary and artistic representations: a history of laughing and of making us laugh.

We have then initially a major problem: that of the complex linkages between these four domains – values, mentalities, practices and esthetics of laughter. To make a further preliminary observation: even though there are numerous categories of laughter and even though word-play is not the most important category to cause laughter, we must stress the importance of words and language. Fortunately, here the historian is better equipped. For quite some time now we have known how to use the perspectives of language, vocabulary and semantics, though the number of serious and intelligent studies in this area is still very small. Finally, there is the problem of the linguistic medium, familiar to medievalists: we have to conduct our research both within the domain of Latin and that of the vernacular languages. This second enquiry is all the more important as I think that, for all kinds of interesting reasons, people laughed better in the vernacular than in Latin. If it is its diffusion, heterogeneity and fragmentation which constitute one of the greatest handicaps in studying the subject, this nevertheless enables us to touch upon many fundamental themes of the period under study.

One of the themes which we recognize here is the expressive possibilities of the various languages used in the Middle Ages, in particular of Latin as compared with the vernacular languages. Thorough investigations by expert linguists have stressed that, from the thirteenth century onwards, Latin tends to become if not a dead language at least a language of specialists, used basically in certain religious, liturgical or intellectual exercises, dominated by a new Latin, scholastic Latin. This Latin is hardly appropriate to express what we define as sensibility, the individuality of feelings and ideas, and consequently it fails to observe everything subjective. For that we have to address ourselves to the vernacular languages. Unfortunately, it seems that few medievalists have a good understanding of how to handle both the Latin and the vernacular documents. Finally, we have to realize that, if we want to get hold of the comic and laughter, we have to go beyond the instrument of language, the words, and study the voice, facial expression and gestures, which have their own history.[8]

I turn now to how I became interested in laughter. I think my interest was triggered by reading Curtius's *European Literature and the Latin Middle Ages*, nowadays hardly a fashionable book, though it is a goldmine of texts, themes and ideas. Its brief excursus on the Church and laughter drew my attention to the fact that from early Christianity to the end of the Middle Ages, in particular in ecclesiastical circles, people asked if Jesus had ever laughed in his earthly life.[9] The theme may look anecdotal, but it is extremely interesting, especially when studied in its precise medieval context.[10] I leave aside its emergence, though it is equally interesting. More significant is the fact that this topos, which one encounters in sermons, in homiletic literature, was not restricted to monastic or strictly ecclesiastical society but was also very much alive in university society. In the thirteenth century the University of Paris traditionally organized a yearly *quod libet* (a discussion on a chosen subject, a kind of conference open to the general public) on precisely this subject.

At the same time another topos circulated throughout the Middle Ages, the theme of Aristotle, who advanced the thesis that laughter is a distinctive feature of man. From this arose in the Latin tradition, and in the medieval Christian Latin tradition, an expression which seems to me extremely interesting, though easy to misinterpret – the theme of the *homo risibilis*. This is of course not 'ridiculous man' or 'man to be laughed at', but 'man gifted with laughter', man whose most distinguishing feature is laughter. Around laughter, then, developed what one might call a heated debate and one with far-reaching consequences. For, if Jesus, the great model for humanity who will be more and more held up for imitation, never once laughed in his human life, then laughter becomes alien to man, at least to Christian man. Conversely, if one posits that laughter is a distinctive feature of man, then laughing man will certainly feel himself more able to express his own nature. Both views are found in ecclesiastical authors, and I have not found any heresy of laughter. The various attitudes towards laughter all find their place within a certain orthodoxy. Perhaps this is not altogether true, but this is a frontier of the subject which has not yet been properly explored.

THE LAUGHTER OF KINGS AND MONKS

What was it exactly that brought these two themes together? The situation is the same as that observed in the case of table manners or gestures.[11] During the first stage, the Church, confronted with a phenomenon which it considers dangerous and does not really know how to control, totally rejects it. Later, around the twelfth century, it reaches the stage of bringing the phenomenon under control, distinguishing good laughter from bad, admissible ways of laughing from inadmissible. The Church reaches a sort of codification of the practice of laughter, of which scholasticism assumes ownership. One of the first scholastic texts was written by Alexandre de Halès, the first great Franciscan doctor and *maître* at the University of Paris from 1220 to 1240. Then there are the brilliant texts of Thomas Aquinas and Albertus Magnus, which also had an impact at the level of practices. One of the most striking examples is provided by Saint Louis. Evidently advised by his mendicant – Dominican and Franciscan – entourage, the king solved the question in the following way: he did not laugh on Fridays!

The marvellous Joinville happily shows us a rather unexpected Saint Louis: this was not only a man prone to laughter but also one who clearly fitted another topos, that of the *rex facetus*, the 'jesting king', which became one image of the king.[12] It seems that the *rex facetus* became in particular a topos within a well-defined social and chronological context, that of the court. It is in the context of the court that we find a function of the king that is practically obligatory – making jokes. The *rex facetus* figures in numerous texts, mostly English chronicles from the twelfth century. The first model of the *rex facetus* was Henry II, whose witticisms and the occasions when he laughed about this or that are all recorded. One even senses that laughter was almost becoming an instrument of government or, at any event, an image of power. Some functions of laughter have been studied by anthropologists. The 'joking relationships' in a couple of African societies examined in particular by Radcliffe-Brown are a case in point.[13] There are societies where certain kinship relations, *inter alia* those between son-in-law and mother-in-law, have to be expressed through jokes. Is it possible that similar structures and practices existed in the Christian Middle Ages? Taking a closer look at certain texts, one gets the impression that in the hands of the king laughter was a way of structuring the society around him. He did not make fun of everyone indiscriminately or in the same way. Obscenity is also one of the 'skids' of laughter.

The Name of the Rose played some part in guiding my research, as I noticed that my friend Umberto Eco was no less convinced of the importance of laughter in medieval society and culture. The reader may recall that it was detested by the ultra-rigorous monk Jorge de Burgos. Eco very aptly suggested a connection between his monk's attitude and that of St Bernard, who opposed the representation of monsters in Romance art. One still senses here one of the historical alliances between various forms of mistrust directed to phenomena that are to a greater or lesser extent anarchic, abnormal or provocative. But perhaps what drew me particularly to laughter is that, in the École des Hautes Études and in the Centre de Recherches Historiques many of us are trying to enlarge the domain of history – of orality and gesture – particularly through new documents. I have always been concerned to integrate the body into the study of historical development, not only by looking at the history of attitudes to the body, which is relatively easy and perhaps the most superficial way, but also by a history designed to integrate bodily practices into the great changes of historical societies. I think we are still under the spell of Marcel Mauss's article 'Les techniques du corps', which continues to be useful.[14] Laughter is a phenomenon which is expressed in and through the body. Amazingly, many of those who have written on laughter – historians, literary historians or philosophers (Bergson and even Freud) – are hardly interested in this essential aspect. The codification of laughter and its condemnation in monastic circles result partly at least from its danger-ous relationship with the body.

Broadly, laughter, together with idleness, is the second great enemy of the monk. In the various monastic Rules of the early Middle Ages, the insertion of a passage condemning laughter in a chapter on this or that virtue or on this or that principle of behaviour shows simultane-ously a certain mobility and evolution. In the first monastic Rules, those of the fifth century, laughter generally appears in the chapter on silence, *taciturnitas*. Laughter is the most horrible and most obscene way of breaking the silence. In relation to this monastic silence, which is an existential, fundamental virtue, laughter is an extremely serious viola-tion. Subsequently, one sees, in particular in St Benedict in the sixth century, that laughter evolves from the domain of silence towards the domain of humility: laughter is the opposite of humility; one has clearly entered a different constellation of sensibility and devotion.

The sixth-century *Regula Magistri*, one of those many monastic rules in the medieval West between the fifth and ninth century, especially between the fifth and the seventh, is clearly connected with the Rule of St Benedict, which from the ninth century onwards was the almost universal Rule of the whole of Western monasticism.[15] Careful, con-vincing studies have demonstrated that the *Regula Magistri* antedates the Rule of St Benedict and served as its model, despite considerable differences. One of these is that, whereas the Rule of St Benedict is very succinct (one of the reasons for its success: simplicity and brevity!), the *Regula Magistri* is a very long text, but it is also highly interesting and goes far beyond individual psychology. It exhibits a real Christian physiology, which explains the requirements for comportment, physi-cal and spiritual simultaneously. It is a text firmly anchored in one of the most important phenomena of the Middle Ages, but one which is insufficiently taken into account. Attention has been paid above all to texts which are hostile to the body, those of the ascetic type exemplified by the famous phrase of Gregory the Great, who defined the body as 'the abominable garment of the soul'. I believe that too little attention has been paid to the fact that man is fundamentally conceived as an inseparable union of body and soul. Let us not forget that Christianity offers the resurrection of the body, which singles it out from many other religions, and that one is saved body and soul: good and bad are done through the body.

There has been a tendency to concentrate on the body as an instrument of the devil, despite the fact that it is also an instrument of salvation. It is precisely the *Regula Magistri* which explains clearly how the human body is positioned in relation to good and evil. In fact, good and evil have two sources. On the one hand, there is an exterior source, which is divine grace in the case of good but the devil and his temptation in that of evil. On the other hand, there are two interior sources, both coming from the heart, which are sometimes bad thoughts and other times the opposite, good thoughts. In both directions, from outside to inside or from inside to outside, the human body employs filters: the holes of the face. Eyes, ears and mouth are the filters of good and evil and must be used in order to let the good enter or express itself and to block the road for evil. The *Regula Magistri* speaks of 'the bolt of the mouth', the 'barrier of the teeth', etc. When laughter is starting, it must at all costs be prevented from expressing itself. So we see how, of all the evil forms of expression which come from inside, laughter is the worst: the worst pollution of the mouth. All these ideas are tied to a quite extraordinary Christian physiology, behind which we can detect medical treatises and, as it were, physiological beliefs.

KINDS OF LAUGHTER

Here we encounter a major problem. It is both important and necessary in research to start by venturing hypotheses which cannot yet be based on sufficient studies, analyses and reflections, but without which, I believe, we would not make any progress. Then we must match these hypotheses with our data, adapt them and, if necessary, abandon or replace them. Our first problem, then, is whether we can reduce laughter to a single phenomenon. At this moment I cannot say. It is striking that, when one takes up the study of the various areas of laughter, one is dealing with words, with concepts, and not only with practices, which are comprised by the term 'laughter' or its semantic field. These are often so diverse that one wonders whether one is dealing with the same subject.

This problem has been poorly treated by scholars, even by the greatest among them. In Freud's book on the joke, one of the great works on the subject, I was surprised to find not only that he hardly takes the body into account, but also that he defines three kinds of laughter: wit, the comic and humour, which he qualifies as 'eternal forms of laughter'. It is remarkable that he does not seem to have posed the problem of unity in laughter. He employed the same method to define and analyse these three forms of laughter, but the unity derives from his method of analysis, not from an actual objective unity of the phenomena studied. Among the theories that have been proposed, John Morreall distinguishes three main theories of laughter: the theory of superiority, according to which the person laughing essentially tries to dominate an interlocutor or somebody facing him by his laughter. The second theory is that of incongruity: laughter basically originates from the perception of something outside the normal order of nature or society; this is the theory proposed by Bergson, which he elaborated by his idea of the perception of a mechanical action where there should have been something spontaneous. And finally, there is the relief theory, according to which those who laugh are spared behaviour which would otherwise be much more difficult both in its expression and in its consequences. Having expounded these three theories, Morreall suggests a new one, which is the result of his attempt at a single, briefly formulated explanation: 'laughter results from a pleasant psychological shift'. It is impossible to take this seriously; it is nearly a tautology. And how would we define 'shift'?

Let us return to the cultural legacies which have influenced the concepts of laughter in the medieval West. The biblical legacy is very strong, perhaps even more so in this case than usual. At least until the fourteenth century the Bible remains 'the Book'; all theoretical reflection and practical rules start from the Bible. When the people of the Middle Ages, clerics in particular, tried to understand a phenomenon and form an opinion, they referred first to the Bible, the starting point of their reflections. Clerics and intellectuals always proceeded in this way, and in the first centuries of the Middle Ages compiled dossiers on the majority of the major problems which confronted their society. I have studied this method with regard to work: in the early Middle Ages, Christian intellectuals clearly compiled a dossier beginning with all the biblical quotations referring to work or which could be cited apropos of work.[16] This is a very important 'game' and it is illuminating to see that, depending on the period, certain texts are quoted and others are passed over in silence. It is in this game of quotations, in compiling dossiers, that the evolution of cultural attitudes regarding various phenomena can be perceived. This is also the case with laughter.

We are well armed for our investigation, since there are various good articles, both in dictionaries of the Bible and the New Testament and in monographs, on laughter in the Old and New Testament. It seems to me that the basic distinction in the Old Testament continued to carry weight over a long period, but in new and renewed forms, namely, that between two quite different kinds of laughter, for which Hebrew has two very distinct words. The first is *sâkhaq*, 'happy, unbridled laughter', and the other *lâag*, 'mocking, denigrating laughter'. The first word is also interesting for medievalists because of course it is a legacy which lives on in the Middle Ages. It is this term that gave the name to one of the principal characters of the Old Testament, Isaac, meaning 'laughter'. There is a whole literature on the name Isaac in Jewish thinking, the Talmud and the rabbinic commentaries. Let us therefore take a look at the chapters of Genesis (17 and 18) where the birth of Isaac is announced. It is a comic gem.

One day Yahweh appears to Abraham, as he did quite often, and says to him: 'You know, you are going to be a father.' Abraham: 'A father? But I am a hundred years old and Sarah is ninety.' Abraham keeps silent but he has his thoughts. Some time later Yahweh appears to Sarah and says to her: 'You are going to be a mother.' Sarah openly bursts out laughing. The following year the event happens. A child is born to Sarah and Abraham, who is therefore called 'Laughter', Isaac. The confused Sarah says to Yahweh that she actually had not laughed during the prediction. Yahweh pretends to believe her but finally says: 'You know, you really did laugh.'

This is an astonishing text, and certainly very sensible. It seems to me that there is more than just a conceptual persistence of these two forms of laughter and that the Christian societies of the past had great difficulty thinking of them as being the same kind. But they had to do so because of Latin. Greek has two words from the same root, *gélân* and *katagélân*. *Gélân* is natural laughter and *katagélân* malicious laughter. I think that the efforts of medieval thought to distinguish good and bad laughter merely continue this distinction. Latin had only *risus*; Greek had a word for smiling. Latin had a lot of trouble constructing such a word, *subrisus*, and it succeeded only with difficulty; for a long time *subrisus* did not mean 'smiling' but 'laughing up one's sleeve', 'secret laughter'. It became 'smiling' only after a clear change in values and behaviour – perhaps in the twelfth century? I wonder whether smiling is not one of the creations of the Middle Ages.

If one looks at representations in art of the birth and story of Isaac, one finds no attempt to represent the laughter. This is a problem which I find interesting and fundamental, namely the relation between texts and images, between iconography and theme. Compared with a text, an image may display silences, retardations, displacements and, certainly, discrepancies. The other side of the problem is how to make people laugh through works of art, through the comic and caricature.[17] This is a problem which emerges rather late. One has the impression that for a long time Christianity blocked this whole mocking aspect of laughter, which was defined as particularly bad. On the other hand, one sees smiling blossom forth in paintings and sculpture: the famous smiling angels, the theme of the wise and foolish virgins where the wise virgins smile and the foolish ones snigger.

LAUGHTER AND SOCIETY

Among the problems we encounter there is also that of the relationship between 'laughter and society'. At whom and at what did one laugh? At groups or at classes? Our monks had to respect their particular dos and don'ts. There was a *risus monasticus*, which was an illegitimate, forbidden laughter, but at the same time our good monks certainly had moments of amusement in the monasteries. They even created a type of written joke, the *joca monacorum*, of which there are collections from the eighth century onwards. There are anecdotes about monks, just as there are anecdotes about curates, Jews or Armenians.

Speaking of group laughter: there was a wonderful feudal laughter, the *gab*, a sort of feudal bantering rather reminiscent of 'tall stories'. When the men were not in the women's chambers but with each other, away from battle, they would tell stories of feudal lords, stories about warriors. The aim was to see who could tell the most extraordinary tale of heroic feats. To cut through both a knight and his horse with only one stroke of the sword was the least of such vauntings. It was a riot of imagination, invention and inspiration. This is how, in the oldest *chansons de geste*, the characters pass a good deal of their leisure. In a rather late *chanson de geste*, the *Pèlerinage de Charlemagne*, we are told how, by telling *gabs*, Charlemagne and his twelve peers, as hosts of the emperor of Constantinople, terrorized the spy sent by the emperor to eavesdrop on their plans, who mistook fiction for reality.

As for laughter as communication, Georges Bataille has written that 'laughter is the specific form of human interaction.' When we see how laughter functions, be it at the level of theory or that of practice, laughter can inform us about the structures of a society and its modes of operation. I have just spoken about what I call the 'skids', the erotic, scatological and obscene components, which are very important. They can be found among the oldest comic texts which have come down to us.

I have spoken about anthropological laughter and the connection between laughter and folklore. I have also spoken about 'joking relationships'. There are other astonishing themes, in literature especially – for example, the motif of the child that laughs at the moment it is going to be killed or, in the *Perceval* of Chrétien de Troyes, the young girl who had not laughed for six years. Another type is ritual laughter, of which the laughter at Easter (*risus paschalis*) is the most important example.[18]

CONCLUSION

Let us now formulate a provisional synthesis and a chronological outline. There is a first period, from the fourth to the tenth century, where the monastic model, I believe, prevails, a period of repressed and stifled laughter. I have been struck by a parallelism of attitudes and evolution between laughter and another phenomenon that I have studied to some extent – the dream.[19] There is also a repression and stifling of the dream, just as there is a repression of laughter, since it is diabolical laughter by which people are mesmerized. But let us not forget that, if this is a period in which tears seem to submerge laughter, we meet in the monastic environment itself the counterpoint of the *joca monacorum*. This shows that, even in periods where theories hostile to laughter seem to predominate, a practice which hardly constrains laughter still manages to survive. In any case, in this milieu there is a literary genre which tends in the opposite direction and seems to escape repression.

A second period, in which I would again see a certain parallel with the history of the dream and that of gesture, is the age of liberation and control of laughter, connected *inter alia* with the rise of the laity and with vernacular literature. Society starts to look at itself in the mirror, and the worldly states perceive how ridiculous they look. As a result, satire and parody develop, and within the Church there emerges a control of laughter, like that of dreams and gestures. On the level of practices, it is again the royal courts that function as the centre of the domestication of laughter. I do not think that Norbert Elias is speaking about these aspects of laughter and the comic, but they would fit his categories and theories well.[20]

Next we find scholastic laughter and the establishment of a casuistry of laughter. Who is qualified to laugh? What kind of laughter is permitted? When? How? A time to laugh and a time to cry – that is what Saint Louis is concerned with.

There is a series of fascinating texts (which will beget many others) concerning the term *hilaris*. In general, *hilaris* applies to the face: *vultus hilaris* means a happy, pleasant face; the expression corresponds almost exactly to what we today would call a laughing face, but decidedly not a hilarious face. A fine study by Fernand Vercauteren shows how in charters at the end of the eleventh century the expression 'the smiling donor' (*hilaris dator*) starts to appear.[21] It is not enough for a donor just to make a donation, but he must do it while showing that he is pleased to do so. I suppose this means that donations are becoming less and less important and also are less and less made voluntarily – which is in fact what we know to have happened. That is why the formula of 'the smiling donor' was immediately adopted. Laughter, in *hilaris* form, becomes an attribute of St Francis of Assisi and one of the manifestations of his sainthood. Francis tells his brethren: 'in tribulations, in the presence of those who torment you, always remain *hilari vultu*.' Laughter truly becomes a form of spirituality and comportment. We possess a text which is its counter-proof: the narrative of the arrival of the Franciscans in England in the years 1220 to 1223, written by a thirteenth-century English Franciscan, Thomas of Eccleston.[22] It relates that the Franciscan monastery in Oxford, which had accepted young brethren, tried to apply the recommendations of St Francis in such a scrupulous manner that they abandoned themselves to great crises of mad laughter which ended up disturbing the Franciscan authorities. The Minister General let these young men know that they should not exaggerate: St Francis had not passed his life in mad laughter, neither had he proposed such a 'hilarious' model of sainthood.

Finally, we come to 'unbridled' laughter and to the theories of Mikhail Bakhtin.[23] Bakhtin belonged to a whole school of Soviet scholars who were interested in laughter and the comic and made it one of their main objects of interest. Thanks to *perestroika* we know the essential elements of their work. Around 1980, my friend Bronislaw Geremek, the well-known Polish medievalist, sent me a book by D. S. Lichačev on laughter, which he considered to be fundamental and which has been translated into German; Vladimir Propp was equally interested in the subject, and Gurevich has critically analysed Bakhtin's ideas about laughter. So, here we have a whole school of specialists in laughter, which, I think, reinforces the importance of the theme.[24]

Broadly, according to Bakhtin, the Middle Ages, dominated by the Church, were a time of sadness. Conversely, the Renaissance, the beginnings of which he dated rather early, was the great moment of the liberation of laughter. This is a highly contestable thesis, but one can draw some insights from Bakhtin: first a periodization of laughter, even if it needs to be qualified. Moreover, his theme of a connection with the city and the public area is very interesting. The public area is the place where laughter breaks out. But was there no peasant laughter? Or was it only depreciated and suppressed like the laughter of other despised categories of the Middle Ages – those of children and women? Finally, there is this fine expression, 'the culture of laughter', which is perhaps Bakhtin's most important contribution to the whole question of laughter; it has been translated into German (*Lachkultur*) but, unfortunately, not into French or English. There has been a culture of laughter with all its implications. I believe that we can rediscover the importance of laughter in the operation of cultural and social practices. If we compare another theme which is very close and in a way also the expression of it, it is the battle between carnival and Lent. This is the battle which is the battle between laughter and anti-laughter.

NOTES

This chapter is based on 'Rire au Moyen Age', *Cahiers du Centre de recherches historiques*, 3 (1989), pp. 1–14. It has been translated by Jan Bremmer and Herman Roodenburg, who have kept its oral style but added various notes.

1 *Oeuvres complètes de Voltaire*, ed. L. Moland (54 vols, Paris, 1877–85), vol. 20, pp. 374–5 (from *Questions sur l'encyclopédie*).
2 H. Bergson, *Le rire* (Paris, 1900), Eng. trans. C. Brereton and F. Rothwell as *Laughter* (London, 1935).
3 S. Freud, *Der Witz und seine Bedeutung zum Unbewussten* (Leipzig and Vienna, 1905), Eng. trans. J. Strachey as *Jokes and their Relation to the Unconscious* (London, 1960).
4 J. Morreall, *Taking Laughter Seriously* (Albany, NY, 1983).
5 F. Ceccarelli, *Sorriso e riso: saggio di antropologia biosociale* (Turin, 1988).
6 A. Herzen, in *Kolokol* (*The Bell*: a Russian journal), 1 February 1858, p. 8, also in Herzen, *Ob iskusstve* (Moscow, 1954), p. 223.
7 J. Le Goff, 'Le rire dans les règles monastiques du haut moyen âge', in C. Lepelley et al. (eds), *Haut moyen-âge: culture, éducation et société. Études offertes à Pierre Riché* (La Garenne-Colombes, 1990), pp. 93–103.
8 As we have learned from the fine studies of Paul Zumthor: *Introduction à la poésie orale* (Paris, 1983) and *La lettre et la voix de la littérature médiévale* (Paris, 1987).
9 E. R. Curtius, *European Literature and the Latin Middle Ages*, trans. W. R. Trask (Princeton, 1953), pp. 417–35.
10 J. Le Goff, 'Jésus a-t-il ri?', *L'histoire*, 158 (1992), pp. 72–4.
11 As studied by J.-C. Schmitt, *La raison des gestes dans l'Occident médiéval* (Paris, 1990).
12 Jean de Joinville, *Histoire de Saint Louis*, ed. Natalis de Wailly (Paris, 1874), Eng. trans. M. Shaw as *Chronicles of the Crusades* (Harmondsworth, 1963), pp. 161–353; J. Le Goff, *Saint Louis* (Paris, 1996), pp. 486–8.
13 A. R. Radcliffe-Brown, *Structure and Function in Primitive Society* (London, 1952), pp. 90–116.
14 M. Mauss, 'Les techniques du corps', *Journal de psychologie normale et pathologique*, 39 (1935), pp. 271–93, repr. in his *Sociologie et anthropologie* (Paris, 1950), pp. 365–86; Eng. trans. as *Sociology and Psychology* (London, 1979), pp. 97–123.

15 Cf. A. de Vogüé, *La Règle de saint Benoît* (2 vols, Paris, 1972), Eng. trans. T. Fry (ed.) as *The Rule of St Benedict in Latin and English with Notes* (Collegeville, MN, 1981).

16 J. Le Goff, *Time, Work and Culture in the Middle Ages*, trans. A. Goldhammer (Chicago and London, 1980), pp. 71–86.

17 An important text in this respect is Baudelaire, *Oeuvres complètes*, ed. Pléiade (2 vols, Paris, 1958), vol. 2, pp. 525–43 ('De l'essence du rire et généralement du comique dans les arts plastiques').

18 V. Wendland, *Ostermärchen und Ostergelächter* (Frankfurt and Berne, 1980).

19 J. Le Goff, *The Medieval Imagination* (Chicago and London, 1988), pp. 193–242.

20 Cf. N. Elias, *The Court Society*, trans. E. Jephcott (Oxford, 1983).

21 F. Vercauteren, ' "Avec le sourire . . ." ', in *Mélanges offerts à Rita Lejeune* (2 vols, Gembloux, 1969), vol. 1, pp. 45–56.

22 Thomas of Eccleston, *De adventu fratrum minorum in Angliam*, Eng. trans. L. Sherley-Price as *The Coming of the Franciscans* (Oxford, 1964).

23 M. Bakhtin, *Tvorčestvo Fransua Rable i narodnaja kultura srednevekovja i Renessansa* (Moscow, 1965), Eng. trans. H. Iswolsky as *Rabelais and his World* (Bloomington, 1968).

24 D. S. Lichačev and A. M. Pančenko, *"Smechovoj mir" drevnej Rusi* (Leningrad, 1976; 2nd edn 1984), Ger. trans. as *Die Lachwelt des Alten Rusland*, ed. R. Lachmann (Munich, 1991); V. Propp, *Theory and History of Folklore* (Manchester, 1984), pp. 124–46 [first published 1939]; Gurevich, Chapter 4 of this volume.

4

Bakhtin and his Theory of Carnival

AARON GUREVICH

A history of humour seems to me a rather dubious affair, since scholars who try to elucidate aspects of mentalities (the history of human feelings such as fear, friendship, love, humour and so on) necessarily have to carve out these traditions from a more comprehensive world view, from the complex of human behaviour and sets of values. But, as soon as we try to extract some aspects of reality from their vital contexts, the danger appears that by means of this procedure we destroy the real picture of this reality.

Despite these doubts I would like to make some observations on Bakhtin and his theory of carnival.[1] Mikhail Bakhtin was one of Russia's great thinkers during the first half of this century. His works made a great impression on the general public, not only in my country but also, after the translation of his book, in many other scholarly communities, and his writings remain very popular among historians of culture. Here I should like to concentrate on his main study concerning François Rabelais and medieval and Renaissance carnival culture. Since the content of his book is familiar to everyone interested in the history of humour, I will say only a few words about it and then proceed to discuss his theory.

As is well known, Bakhtin depicted the popular culture of the Middle Ages and Renaissance as a carnival or laughter culture. His idea was that laughter was the main feature of popular culture. The idea of popular culture was not very widespread among historians before the appearance of Bakhtin's book, and it remains rather contradictory. Yet it is difficult to deny that this idea is very fruitful if we use it with caution.

The first edition of Bakhtin's book was published in Russia only in 1965, after his having been ostracized for 25 years. Its appearance was a revelation for all of us. We immediately understood that Bakhtin had touched upon a new world of ideas, beliefs, conduct and behaviour – this so-called submerged Atlantis. Of course, he examined only one aspect of it, the comical, satirical one, but nevertheless he pointed out the main and extremely important problem of popular culture. Bakhtin constructed a picture of medieval culture as divided into two opposite poles. One pole was rather black. It was the official culture, the culture of the Church, the culture of the educated literati. This culture was characterized by Bakhtin as a culture of the *agelastoi*, the people who never laughed and even hated laughter. It was qualified by him as totally serious, frightened and frightening.

On the other pole of medieval culture Bakhtin found popular tradition, which was dominated by laughter. Carnival was, from his point of view, the distillation of this popular culture. It is rather difficult to find in Bakhtin's book a clear-cut definition of popular culture as a culture of laughter, but except for laughter Bakhtin was uninterested in any other aspect of it. Bakhtin treated carnival as a phenomenon whose beginnings were in the extremely distant past. Thus it would be possible from his point of view to connect medieval carnival with the ancient Saturnalia and Bacchanalia. Carnival is a mark on the annual field of time: every year, at the point when winter meets summer, carnival appears.

For many years this idea was known to ethnologists, and the appearance of Bakhtin's book was approved by ethnologists and anthropologists with great joy. One must note, however, that as a rule ethnologists study features which could be connected with carnival celebrations of non-European tribes and peoples. Since Bakhtin studied medieval Christian culture, it seems to me extremely important to stress the difference between European carnival and similar phenomena outside Europe. It appears rather strange that in his book Bakhtin never mentioned Christianity or the Christian God: popular culture of medieval and Renaissance Europe seems to exist without any religion or without any religious connections. It is at this point that my criticism begins.

There is another point which I should like to stress. Bakhtin speaks of popular culture as a culture which was absolutely alien to any kind of phobia or fear. He connects this culture with the idea of the 'immortal collective popular body', as he expressed it – a body which is dying and immediately reborn. This may be true if we speak in a rather abstract philosophical sense, but as soon as our concern is with real medieval and Renaissance history the picture becomes much more complicated. Let us take one example: Bakhtin saw in carnival only a festivity, a point at which popular feelings are free of any obstacles. Some time ago an eminent French historian, Emmanuel Le Roy Ladurie, published a book concerning a carnival in Romans, a town in southern France, which took place at the beginning of the year 1580.[2] The carnival began as usual with dances and songs, with manifestations of the citizens, but very soon it was transformed into a cruel massacre in which the patricians of the town attacked the artisans and killed a lot of them. So the festivity was turned into the kind of civil war which was widespread in the south of France at the end of the sixteenth century, a period well known as the Huguenot wars. Le Roy Ladurie's study is very important in the context of our analysis of Bakhtin's work because Bakhtin stressed the ethnological aspect of carnival as being produced every year, and every new carnival being similar to the previous one. But as soon as a historian tries to study a carnival which has taken place at a specific time and in a specific town, the picture seems to be rather different. Not only joy and humour, not only festivity and popular relaxation, but also cruelty, hate and massacre could be the components of carnival.

As another French historian, Yves Bercé, stressed, there are some features of struggle and revolt which were inscribed in the latent texture of carnival.[3] This seems to me a rather important observation because in real history laughter and joy go hand in hand with hate and fear. It is therefore very difficult to abstract one feeling out of the much more comprehensive and complex set of feelings and emotions of the people.

Other objections come to me when I think about Bakhtin's treatment of carnival as a phenomenon whose beginnings go back to times immemorial. For a historian such a point of view is very difficult to accept, even though in earlier times we can, of course, observe some aspects of the festivities which marked the transition from winter to spring, such as dances, songs and other performances. But I should like to stress that it is possible to speak only of a so-called carnival before real carnival. Carnival as a complete, great festivity with an elaborate scenario we find only at the end of the Middle Ages. All historical indications which could be interpreted as aspects of carnival are dated no earlier than the end of the thirteenth and the beginning of the fourteenth century. The explanation seems to be clear. Carnival is a great festivity in the developed medieval city, with its new kind of population concentrated into one territory and developing into a new kind of medieval culture. Carnival, therefore, is not a feature of popular culture at all different epochs. It appeared only in this specific period of European history at the end of the Middle Ages, at the beginning of the Renaissance.

But my main objection is as follows. Of course, carnival is an expression of the culture of laughter, but is it possible to insist that medieval popular culture was first of all the culture of laughter? When we study medieval sources closely we can see that, first of all, laughter was not alien to the Church. Monks and clerics took an active role in the course of carnival long before the time of Rabelais. Just recently a new study by two historians from Israel demonstrates very clearly that the Church was not opposed to laughter.[4] This is also illustrated by the so-called *exempla*, short didactic stories which since the beginning of the thirteenth century were as a rule included in monastic and clerical sermons. In these *exempla* there is a lot of material which could be interpreted as significant to the history of laughter and humour.

On the other hand, it seems absolutely impossible to characterize popular culture as a culture based first of all and mainly on laughter and joy. If we study historical sources, we see immediately that one of its main aspects was fear. This fear was extremely intense, because it was connected with the idea that after death the majority of simple people would go to hell, and the fear of eternal damnation was fundamental to their world view. So we can state that inside popular culture there was both joy and fear, carnival and terror.

How can we combine these contrasting emotions? This is a problem which is insufficiently elucidated by historians, but I will permit myself to put forward the following hypothesis: precisely because the majority of the people could not rid themselves of this fear of eternal damnation, their fear was, to some extent, psychologically balanced by their attitude towards laughter and happiness. Joy and fear were intrinsically and intimately interconnected. It is only through this combination that we can better understand the popular culture of the Middle Ages.

Bakhtin stressed that at the heart of carnival was the idea of overturning reality, the tradition of turning the established social and religious order upside down. So he supposed that outside the period of carnival the rule of government existed inside popular culture – the idea of order by which all the world was organized. Initially, this idea seemed absolutely true, but after having studied the Church sources which could be connected with popular traditions I have arrived at the conclusion that this strict organization of the universe, which was proclaimed by theologians and philosophers, was not as dominant in popular imagination as it was in the mind of the literati.

In this connection I permit myself to refer to my study entitled 'Evil saints and good demons',[5] in which I try to demonstrate that according to official theory the universe was divided into many different layers, which were subordinated to one another so that God and the angels, together with the saints and other chosen people, were at the top. Beneath them there was a human level, and at the bottom of this pyramid there was hell inhabited by demons and sinners who became the victims of demonic power.

We can observe that in popular imagination this picture could be easily transferred to something substantially different. We find saints who behaved not so much as the representatives of superior values but as creatures who were not absolutely alien from the demonic personages. The saint who was angry with his admirer could beat and even kill him, and the same could be said of the behaviour of Christ himself. He could leave his cross, beat a sinner and even kill him. On the other hand, there are a lot of stories about demons regretting being compelled to leave heaven and follow Lucifer to hell. They try to make peace with God and they even go to confession, but, of course, they cannot be saved because sin of pride prevents their reconciliation with God. In any case, these boundaries between good and evil, between heaven and hell, which seem to be absolutely clear in the official ideology, are not so clear and so polarized in popular imagination. Thus the tendency to turn the universe upside down was not only inherent in carnival but a real feature of everyday popular religiosity. Summing up, I should like to stress that Bakhtin's work was extremely fruitful because it contained a huge intellectual provocation for new studies, but the question remains why Bakhtin constructed such a one-sided picture of medieval laughter and carnival, which is in clear contrast to facts established by historical study.

Of course, Bakhtin worked outside Moscow and St Petersburg, having been exiled to the small provincial town of Saransk, where he was a lecturer at the pedagogical institute and cut off from many historical sources and new foreign literature. But I suppose that his theory of carnival was produced by some different impulses. By constructing an absolute polarity between the official and popular carnival cultures Bakhtin transposed some aspects of contemporary life in Stalinist Russia into the epoch of the Middle Ages and Renaissance. In modern Russia before *perestroika* there were two absolutely different levels of reality. On the one level (the upper, visible level) there was an ideological reality with all its slogans and false ideas. But under this level of expression, behind it, concealed from the official point of view, there was a level of real human life with all its everyday feelings, emotions and ideas which were far distant from the official ideology. It seems that this contrast between the official level of life and life's real content was transposed by Bakhtin into the distant period of the Middle Ages. In reality, though, the distance was not so clear because there were many connections between the Church and the people up to the Reformation.

Some of the distortions of the medieval world view, then, were due to the situation in which Bakhtin lived. Although it was not done consciously or intentionally, such a transposition of the present state onto the past occurs from time to time in historical studies. Bakhtin's theory of carnival in popular culture is one-sided and therefore historically incorrect, but I should like to finish my contribution with the observation that in the study of the history of culture some of the most fruitful intellectually provocative works were produced by historians with rather one-sided ideas. Such is one of the paradoxes of the history of culture. So much for carnival.

Regarding the notion 'popular culture' which was introduced mainly by Bakhtin, it is necessary to stress that this notion is not a very fortunate one. It is too vague, and everybody uses it as they wish. From my point of view the problem is not confined to the opposition of learned culture to popular culture, to the culture of literati on the one hand and the culture of the people, the illiterate, on the other hand.

I suggest that the problem should be defined differently. Everybody who lived in medieval Christian society belonged to different levels of culture. Everybody was Christian and therefore had something in common with the culture and religiosity of the learned people. Of course the monks, the Church prelates, the educated people and theologians had much more information and knowledge about the Christian truth than simple folk, peasants and artisans. But even the most uneducated people possessed some information concerning Christian ideas and Christian beliefs. So I prefer not to speak about popular culture in a pure form, because we do not know what such a phenomenon was. It is necessary to remember that all information we can gather concerning popular culture we have to take from written sources. And these documents were composed by the representatives of the learned strata of society. So the information about popular culture is always transformed and reinterpreted by the learned. I therefore prefer to speak of medieval culture *grosso modo*, remembering that in everyone's mind different levels existed.

One level was concerned with the official culture and religiosity and another level was connected with the beliefs and so-called superstitions which were more characteristic of the mentality of the simple folk. So the opposition of learned culture versus culture of the people is an inner contradiction of the medieval mind. I can give here only one example. In his *History of the Franks*, Gregory of Tours (*c.*539–94) describes in detail theological disputes between orthodox Catholic priests and Arian sectarians, and he finishes with the observation that these disputes ended without any decisive result: neither Catholics nor Arians won.[6]

Gregory returns to a similar episode in his *Libri miraculorum* (1.81). In this hagiographical work he tells that a dispute between the orthodox Catholic and Arian priests was solved by means of an ordeal. A ring was thrown into a cauldron of boiling water from which the disputants had to extract it. As soon as the Arian put his hand into the water in order to take the ring his flesh was burnt. Then a Catholic monk tried to fish out the ring and after searching for a while he managed to find it, his arm intact. So the dispute was solved in the most visible way by the ordeal.

Now the question arises as to what Gregory of Tours had in mind when he wrote this story. Is it possible to suppose that in one case he gave us the true information concerning the dispute and in the other some oversimplified, stylized version? I imagine that the answer must be negative. There were two sides to the same truth, and Gregory expressed them differently because of the different rhetorical and esthetic requirements of both the genres in which he wrote. But the thing which is most interesting to me is that Gregory had the possibility of looking at the same phenomenon concerning religious life from different points of view: there is no inner contradiction in his interpretation of this dispute between Arians and Catholics. This absence of contradictions seems to have been the essential feature of his mentality which combined different approaches to the same question.

So I believe that the problem which is formulated by Bakhtin as a clear opposition between learned culture and popular culture seems to be necessarily transformed into the inner property of the medieval mind, which was able to combine different approaches to the same religious truth.

NOTES

Due to the loss of his eyesight Aaron Gurevich was unable to contribute the written version of his oral presentation at the Amsterdam congress on humour. The text has therefore been edited and annotated from a tape-recording. The editors have aimed at preserving the oral nature of Gurevich's presentation.[7]

1 Cf. M. Bakhtin, *Tvorčestvo Fransua Rable i narodnaja kultura srednevekovja i Renessansa* (Moscow, 1965), Eng. trans. H. Iswolsky as *Rabelais and his World* (London, 1968).

2 E. Le Roy Ladurie, *Le carnaval de Romans* (Paris, 1979).

3 Y.-M. Bercé, *Fête et révolte: des mentalités populaires du XVIe au XVIIe siècle* (Paris, 1976).

4 J. Horowitz and S. Menache, *L'humour en chaire: le rire dans l'église médiévale* (Geneva, 1994).

5 A. Gurevich, 'Santi iracondi e demoni buoni negli "exempla"', in *Santi e demoni nell'alto medioevo occidentale = Settimane di studio del Centro italiano di studi sull'alto medioevo*, 36 (Spoleto, 1989), pp. 1045–63.

6 *Historiae Francorum (Gregorii episcopi Turonensis Historiarum libri decem)*, ed. R. Buchner (2 vols, Darmstadt, 1970–2), cf. 5.43; 6.5, 40; 10.13.

7 For an informative study of Gurevich's work, see C. Castelli, 'Un Diogene alla ricerca dell' uomo: Aaron Gurevic', in A. J. Gurevic, *Lezioni romane* (Turin, 1991), pp. 87–153.

5
Frontiers of the Comic in Early Modern Italy, c.1350–1750

PETER BURKE

When is a joke not a joke? When, where, for whom is a given joke funny or unfunny? What are the limits, the boundaries, the frontiers of the comic? How different do they appear from different viewpoints and how do they shift in the course of time? Apart from Mikhail Bakhtin's well-known discussion of the 'serio-comic', few attempts have been made to answer questions like these.[1] The aim of this chapter is to address such problems by focusing on a single comic genre, the practical joke or *beffa*, replacing it in what might be called the contemporary 'system of the comic', in other words the varieties of humour recorded in Italy in the late medieval and early modern period, their definitions, their functions, their genres and so on.

The approach adopted here will be an anthropological one, in the sense of keeping close to indigenous categories and distinctions (between jest and earnest, cf. private and public, sacred and profane). This is the justification for the many Italian words which will appear below. I shall also be trying to follow the advice given in a well-known piece of historical anthropology, Robert Darnton's essay on the cat massacre, to 'capture otherness', in other words to concentrate on what is most alien to us in the past and to try to make it intelligible.[2] Hence the emphasis here will fall on what is funny no longer, rather than on cultural continuities, important as they are.

THE SYSTEM OF THE COMIC IN ITALY, 1350–1550

Let me first try to sketch this 'system' from Boccaccio to Bandello, or more generally from the Black Death to the Counter-Reformation. Despite the fact that Jacob Burckhardt, in his famous essay on the Renaissance, devoted some perceptive pages to what he called 'modern mockery and humour' (*Der moderne Spott und Witz*), the subject has not attracted many historians.[3] Yet it certainly interested contemporaries, as the language of the period quickly reveals. In the Italian of this time, there was a rich variety of terms available to distinguish varieties of play and humour. Words for the 'joke act' included *baia, beffa, burla, facezia, giuoco, legerezza, pazzia, piacevolezza, scherzo*, while the joker was known as a *beffardo, beffatore, buffone, burlona, giuocatore* or *scherzatore*. Verbs included *burlare, giocare, uccellare*, while a distinction was made between *beffare* and the milder but more continuous *beffeggiare*, which we might translate as 'to tease'. Adjectives were richest of all: *beffabile, beffevole, burlesco, faceto, festevole, giocoso, grottesco, mottevole, scherzoso, sciocco*, and so on. The richness of vocabulary suggests that Italians were indeed connoisseurs in this domain.

The idea of the comic or the playful was not sharply defined in this period but shaded into entertainment, or diversion – *spasso, diporto, trattenimento, trastullo* – at one end of the spectrum, and at the other into tricks and insults – *inganni, truffe, affronti, diffamazioni, offese, scherni*. Two sixteenth-century informants bear witness to the difficulty of marking the boundary. Castiglione defined the *burla* as a 'friendly deceit' (*inganno amichevole*), which 'does not give offence, or at least not very much' (*di cose che non offendono, o almen poco*). Again, Della Casa distinguished *beffe* from insults, *scherni*, only in terms of the intention of the perpetrator, since the effects on the victim were more or less the same.[4]

This ambiguity, or ambivalence, raises the question of the limits of the permissible. How far could one go, in what direction, with whom, about what, without going too far? Although the idea of transgression is central to the comic, the limits or boundaries transgressed are always unstable, varying with the locale, region, moment, period, and the social groups involved. Looking back at Renaissance Italy from today, or even from the seventeenth century, what is most striking, or strange, is the generosity or permeability of the limits. Religious matters might be the object of jokes without causing offence, at least on occasion. Mattello, a court fool at Mantua, dressed as a friar and parodied ecclesiastical rituals.[5] In the introduction to the stories of Antonfrancesco Grazzini, set at carnival, a lady says that even friars and nuns are allowed to enjoy themselves at this time and to dress as members of the opposite sex. Priests might be jesters, like fra Mariano at the court of Leo X.[6] Boundaries existed all the same. In Castiglione's *The Courtier*, for instance, Bernardo Bibbiena criticizes Boccaccio for a joke which 'goes beyond the limits', *passa il termine*.[7]

Ambiguity also leads to the question of function. Was laughter always an end in itself, or might it be a means to another end? We shall soon see examples of laughter as an instrument of vengeance. Another possibility to be taken seriously is Vladimir Propp's idea of laughter on certain occasions as a kind of ritual. Easter laughter in particular may be interpreted as ritual laughter.[8]

The variety of comic genres deserves to be emphasized.[9] Among them was comedy itself, whether 'learned' or popular, including the original 'slapstick' comedy of Harlequin in the *commedia dell'arte*.[10] Stories (*novelle*) were often comic, while jokes often took the form of stories, *facezie*, which were collected and printed. Famous collections include the stories attributed to the Tuscan priest Arlotto Mainardi and those collected by the Humanists Poggio Bracciolini and Angelo Poliziano, the latter published in 1548 under the name of the editor, Ludovico Dolce.[11] Sermons often contained funny stories of this kind, thus combining the serious with the comic. Parody was appreciated in poetry and prose; Pulci's *Morgante*, for instance, mocked romances of chivalry, Aretino's *Ragionamenti* mocked courtesy-books, while now-forgotten works of the seventeenth century parodied epitaphs or the *Aeneid*.[12] So was paradox, as in the mock-eulogies of Berni and Lando.[13] Burchiello's nonsense verse inspired a genre and even a verb, *burchielleggare*.[14]

There were also a number of comic forms in the visual arts. The witty portraits of the Milanese painter Arcimboldo, for instance, who made faces out of fruit, or fish, or books. In the Palazzo del Te in Mantua, however, designed by Giulio Romano, there are visual shocks like the frieze in which some pieces seem to be slipping and the frescoed ceilings which appear to be crashing down on the visitor.[15] They should perhaps be understood as a kind of practical joke.

The imitation of the recently rediscovered classical 'grotesques' included statues for gardens, like Grand Duke Cosimo de' Medici's court fool in the Boboli Gardens in Florence.[16] 'Gardens were the place for play', for liberation from social conventions. In what we might describe as the 'theme park' of Bomarzo, constructed a few miles from Viterbo for one of the Orsini family in the late sixteenth century, there was, for instance, a gigantic stone hell mouth which apparently functioned as a cool site for picnics. That this part of the 'Sacred Wood' was a joke, even if one on the edge of blasphemy, is suggested by the inscription 'lasciate ogni pensiero', parodying Dante, and confirmed by the remarks in a contemporary discussion of grottos that they should be furnished with 'frightful or ridiculous masks'.[17]

No discussion of medieval or early modern humour would be complete without reference to the professional fools who could be found at court and elsewhere. A number of Italians of the time achieved inter-regional if not international fame in this profession, among them Dolcibene, the two Gonellas, Borso d'Este's Scocola at Ferrara (immortalized in the frescoes at Schifanoia), Beatrice d'Este's Diodato at Milan, and Isabella d'Este's Fritella at Mantua.[18]

THE BEFFA

The practical joke, trick or *beffa*, so frequently described in Italian jest-books, stories and other sources, was not of course unique to the peninsula or to the period under discussion. Whether or not practical jokes are a cultural universal, the recurrent figure of the trickster in world folklore (including that of China, West Africa and the Indians of North America) suggests that they are at the very least extremely widespread. Such figures as Panurge and Till Eulenspiegel (not to mention medieval fabliaux) bear witness to the love of *beffe* in Northern and Central Europe, while in parts of the Mediterranean world, from Spain to Crete, anthropologists find them to be flourishing.[19]

All the same, there was apparently an unusual emphasis on this form of humour in Italy, especially in Florence, 'la capitale de la *beffa*'.[20] Boccaccio's *Decameron* makes an obvious starting point for the study of *beffe*, which occur in 27 stories altogether, with 80 references to the terms *beffa*, *beffare* and *beffatore*.[21] Later in the century, *beffe* recur in the stories of Sacchetti. In the fifteenth century, they can be found in the tales of Masuccio Salernitano and Sabadino degli Arienti.[22] There is also the anonymous fifteenth-century story of a joke played on a fat carpenter, an interesting example in the age of 'individualism' (in Burckhardt's formula), because it played with the idea of identity.[23]

As for *beffe* in the sixteenth-century *novella*, one finds them everywhere. In the collection of Antonfrancesco Grazzini (died 1584), the *Cene*, 'the *beffa* is the key', as a French critic puts it, occurring in 18 stories.[24] They are even more important in Matteo Bandello: 70 *beffe* in 214 *novelle*.[25]

The sixteenth-century material also includes plays, such as Machiavelli's *Mandragola* and Pietro Aretino's *Il marescalco*, a carnival entertainment in which the Master of the Horse at the court of the duke of Mantua is informed that the duke wishes him to marry. This was bad news for him, since his tastes were not for the opposite sex, but he goes through the ceremony only to discover that his 'bride' is a page.[26] Books of secrets, a popular kind of how-to-do-it book current in sixteenth-century Italy, included instructions for *beffe*, such as making someone fall asleep at the dining table, alongside recipes for dyeing one's hair or cures for impotence.[27]

To sum up this evidence and place it in comparative perspective, we might compare Stith Thompson's world survey of folk tales with a specialized motif-index of the Italian *novella* by Rotunda. For category X 0–99, 'Humor of Discomfiture', for instance, Thompson gives four examples, Rotunda twenty. In the case of category K 1200–99, 'Deception into a Humiliating Position', Thompson gives 27 examples (including eight from Boccaccio), while Rotunda offers no fewer than 72.[28] The Italians, more exactly the Tuscans, appear to have been obsessed by this theme.

Needless to say there are problems for a social or cultural historian in handling such literary evidence. The stories are stylized, indeed they were subject to a double stylization as they circulated through two media, oral and printed. They are full of topoi. The same stories have different heroes. Can one draw conclusions about society from this evidence? Was the *beffa* a social custom or just a literary game?

Fiction is of course good evidence of fantasy, of the collective imagination. It can be supplemented by evidence of other kinds. At court, for instance, practical jokes were played, for example in Milan under the Sforza or in Ferrara.[29] Other evidence comes from judicial records, regarding everyday joking, or festive joking, which gave offence and so led to legal proceedings. Taverns were a favourite locale for *beffe*, as in the case of the trick played on a certain Furlinfan in the village of Lio Maggiore in 1315, for instance.[30] Carnival was a favourite time, witness the case of the mysterious coil of rope, from Rome in 1551, when seven Jews pretended to arrest a Neapolitan at the time of their carnival (Purim), not the carnival of the Christians. This 'case' could have been made into a *novella*.[31] Again, the painter Michelangelo di Caravaggio, who had a gift for getting himself into trouble, appeared before the Tribunal of the Governor of Rome in 1603 (in company with other painters), charged with insults to their colleague Baglioni (what the victim called 'versi in mio dishonore' calling him *Coglioni, Bagaglia,* etc.).[32]

Turning to the evidence of material culture, let us return for a moment to the Renaissance garden, where there might be hidden fountains activated at a sign from the host, taking the guests by surprise and soaking them to the skin. This mild form of *beffa* was current in aristocratic circles, and can be documented at Caprarola, for instance, designed by Vignola for the Farnese, as well as at Pratolino, designed by Buontalenti for Francesco I de' Medici, where Montaigne was among the victims.[33] It was not very different from the common Italian practice of throwing water at carnival.

It is time to raise the problem of the limits of joking, the frontier between relatively harmless or disinterested deception and more serious trickery or aggression. This is perhaps the moment to observe that, in northern Italy in the sixteenth century, *dare la burla* was a standard phrase employed to describe false promises of marriage.[34] Again, in an age when jokes were often insulting and insults sometimes took playful forms, it was inevitable that someone would overstep the customary limits and that some cases would end up in court. In sixteenth-century

Bologna, one victim of a verbal assault (by means of a sonnet) complained to the tribunal; however, they considered the letter not to be defamatory but only *iocatoria, continens aliqua risu digna*.[35]

Turning to the world of politics, think of Cesare Borgia and the famous trick he played on his enemies at Sinigaglia, a 'torpedo' (as Italo-American gangsters would have called it in the age of Al Capone). The story is told by Machiavelli in his famous *Descrizione del modo tenuto dal duca Valentino nello ammazzare Vitelozzo Vitelli*, etc. Machiavelli wrote in a cool deadpan manner, but elsewhere he expresses his admiration for Cesare. It may not be too far from the mark to suggest a link between his politics and his dramatic interest in *beffe*. His play *Mandragola* is 'Machiavellian' in its interest in stratagems, while his history of Florence is presented in dramatic terms.[36]

Five comments may place the *beffa* more firmly in its cultural context.

1 The *beffa* was often presented as a 'work of art', to adapt Burckhardt's view of the Renaissance in general. It was supposed to give aesthetic pleasure, as well as the more obvious *Schadenfreude*, and it was sometimes described as *bella*. The titles of stories, Bandello's for instance, refer to a 'giocosa astuzia' (2.45), or a 'piacevole e ridicolo inganno' (2.47). It was pleasant, that is, from the point of view of the joker or the bystanders, which is the point of view the reader is generally encouraged to take; unless of course the victim turns the tables on the aggressor, for special pleasure is taken in what is called 'il contracambio', in other words the theme of *beffatore beffato*, the biter bit (Bandello 1.3, for instance).

2 The *beffa* was an appropriate form of joking in a competitive society which was also what might be called a 'culture of trickery', a society ruled by civilians rather than soldiers or, in Machiavellian language, foxes rather than lions. Even today, Italians explicitly approve of people who are cunning (*furbo*), witness the account of a small town in southern Italy in the 1970s by a British anthropologist who described a father repeatedly asking his small son, 'Sei furbo?', expecting the answer 'yes'.[37]

3 The *beffa* was often not 'pure' amusement but a means of humiliating, shaming and indeed of socially annihilating rivals and enemies. This was a culture in which honour and shame were leading values. The titles of some stories reinforce this perception, as in the case of Sabadino degli Arienti, for instance, in which a recurrent phrase is 'se trova vergognato' (no. 1), 'remase vergognato' (no. 16) or 'resta vergognato' (nos. 31, 35). The culture of Renaissance Italy was an agonistic one, most vividly exemplified in Florence.[38] Revenge (*bella vendetta*, as it is sometimes called), is another recurrent motif in the

novelle (Bandello 4.6, Grazzini 2.9, etc.). So is cuckoldry, a source of anxiety and so of joking. Aggression, cruelty, sadism also recur, for instance in two famous stories in which what is supposed to be so funny is the castration of the victim (Bandello 2.20, Grazzini 1.2). These examples underline the point that jokes were not amusing for everyone, that there were victims as well as spectators or listeners.

4 That brings us to what Bakhtin called the 'lower bodily stratum'. In a story told by Sabadino (no. 16), a craftsman goes to the barber to be shaved and sees that the barber's shoes are very large. 'He felt an urge to piss in them' (*li venne voglia de urinarli dentro*), and he does so. In a story by Bandello (1.35), Madonna Cassandra has an affair with a friar, the husband discovers, dresses as the friar, takes laxative pills and shits all over her in the bed. Readers will probably find this story quite revolting. That is precisely why it is quoted here, in order to remind us of the 'otherness' of sixteenth-century Italy.

5 The sense of cultural distance becomes still greater if we call to mind the fact that this particular story is told about a lady, and dedicated to another lady, Paola Gonzaga, by a priest, at the time of the Council of Trent. Today, we tend to think of priests as serious or even as solemn people, at least in public. However, fifteenth-century Tuscans enjoyed the jests they attributed to a rural parish priest of the region, Arlotto Mainardi, and, as we have seen, fra Mariano played the fool at the court of pope Leo X. Again, we tend to think of Renaissance rulers such as Isabella d'Este of Mantua and Cosimo I of Tuscany as serious people, but we should not forget that they are known to have enjoyed the wit and the antics of dwarves and fools.[39] The point to underline, at least for this first period, 1350–1550, is the widespread participation, as both jokers and victims of princes and peasants, men and women, clergy and laity, young and old. Archive evidence confirms the testimony of fiction in this respect. At the court of Milan in 1492, for instance, princess Beatrice d'Este played a trick on the ambassador of Ferrara, causing his garden to be invaded by wild animals who killed his chickens, to the amusement of Beatrice's husband, Lodovico Sforza, the ruler of the state.[40] However, this situation would not last. It is time to turn to change.

CHANGES IN THE SYSTEM

What, then, were the major changes in the system in attitudes to jokes among Italians? Although changes are perceptible by the 1520s, if not before, I shall focus on the period 1550–1650, supporting Welsford's point about 'the decline of the court-fool' in the seventeenth century, and Bakhtin's assertion about the 'disintegration of folk laughter' in the same period.[41] In reflecting on the reasons for these changes, it may be useful to distinguish two religious and secular aspects of what Elias called the 'process of civilization', a European movement which is considered here in the forms which it took in Italy during the Counter-Reformation.

Some traditional forms of joking, which had already been criticized by foreign clergy, from Erasmus on carnival to Oecolampadius on Easter laughter, were now condemned by Italians on religious or moral grounds in an age when Aretino joined Luther and Calvin on the *Index of Prohibited Books* (compiled in Italy though binding on the whole Church). The stories of the jester-priest Arlotto, first published in 1516 or thereabouts, were expurgated in this way from 1565 onwards, with an introductory note explaining the need to remove the jokes 'which seemed to the inquisitor to be too free'.[42] Bandello published his stories just in time, in 1554, while the stories of the Florentine writer Antonfrancesco Grazzini, written around 1580, remained unpublished till the eighteenth century. Oral tales could not easily be censored, but all the same the storyteller Straparola was once summoned before the Venetian Inquisition.

Printed *beffe* were increasingly made to point a moral, underlined by means of metaphors such as 'cures', 'lessons' and 'punishments'. Arlotto had already been described as curing a man of his bad habit of spitting near the altar, and teaching a lesson to the young men who want a quick 'hunter's Mass'.[43] Bandello drew attention to the ethical implications of his stories (in 1.3, 1.35, etc.), although readers may not find this moral packaging altogether convincing. Domenichi made cuts in Poliziano's collection of *facezie* in 1548 and revised them still further for the 1562 edition, changing the title to the more serious *Detti e fatti*, removing blasphemies and anti-clerical remarks, and adding morals to each joke.[44] Guicciardini's collection of jokes was also described on the title-page as 'moralized' (*ridotti a moralità*). A similar collection, published in 1596, claimed to be painting 'the ugliness of vice' (*le bruttezze dei vizii*).[45]

The changing reception of the *Decameron*, especially in the sixteenth century, makes an illuminating case-study in changing attitudes. Boccaccio's stories might have been prohibited altogether by the Council of Trent if the duke of Florence, Cosimo de' Medici, had not sent an ambassador to the council to beg for a reprieve. The stories reappeared in expurgated form in 1582. One story, concerning the hypocrisy of an inquisitor, had disappeared entirely from the collection, while other stories which mocked the clergy suffered drastic revision. Terms like 'friar' and 'archangel' were removed, at the price of making one story completely meaningless – that of friar Alberto, who pretended to be the archangel Gabriel in order to seduce a pious Venetian lady.[46]

The jokes in Book 2 of Castiglione's *The Courtier* were subjected to similar treatment in the expurgated edition of 1584.[47]

The Counter-Reformation clergy had embarked upon a 'cultural offensive', not to ban joking altogether but to reduce its domain. Jokes were increasingly considered indecorous if told by the clergy, whose behaviour should be marked by *gravitas*, or in church, because it was a holy place, or on sacred subjects. The careers of the jester-priests Arlotto and fra Mariano began to seem indecorous – and later, almost unimaginable.

San Carlo Borromeo, for example, in his provincial council of 1565, denounced Easter plays for provoking laughter. He would not have agreed with Vladimir Propp. As Borromeo saw it, the pious custom of representing the lives of Christ and the saints had been corrupted by human perversity, resulting in laughter, contempt and scandal (*ut multis offensioni, multis etiam risui et despectui sit*).[48] Pope Pius V issued a decree against 'immoderate' laughter in church.[49] The Index of Sixtus V (1590), stricter than its predecessors, included the collections of *facezie* edited by Domenichi and Guicciardini, despite their claims to be moralists.[50] Robert Bellarmine, another leading figure of the Counter-Reformation, in a letter of 1608, expressed his opposition to revealing details about the lives of saints which might encourage laughter rather than edification (*quae risum potius quam aedificationem pariant*). Perhaps he was thinking of the traditional image of St Joseph, a figure of fun, cuckolded by the Holy Ghost.

This clerical offensive needs to be seen as part of a wider movement, or at least of a wider shift in attitudes (among the upper classes at any rate), extending from the rise of classicism in the arts to the withdrawal from participation in popular culture, a shift which Norbert Elias described in terms of increasing self-control or 'civilization'.[51] For example, a book of advice for courtiers by Gianbattista Giraldi Cinthio (better known as a playwright) told the reader not to be the first to joke, since this might be construed as disrespect for the prince.[52] The Genoese patrician Ansaldo Cebà emphasized the need for moderation in jokes, which should be adapted to places, times and persons and should not be unworthy of a gentleman (*che non disdicano ad huom libero e costumato*).[53]

CHANGES IN THE BEFFA

To return to the *beffa*: from the 'civilization' point of view, it is surely significant that among its critics, as we have seen, are two authors whose conduct books became famous – the *Cortegiano* of Baldassare Castiglione and the *Galateo* of Giovanni Della Casa. Castiglione's speakers criticize *beffe* on moral grounds in Book 2, preferring verbal jokes to practical ones, while the author censored some of his own jokes in the third manuscript version of his treatise. The criticisms may seem anodyne today, but in the early sixteenth-century context they look almost puritanical, or revolutionary.[54] As for the Counter-Reformation moralist Della Casa, he admitted the need for people to play tricks on one another because life in this vale of tears needed some kind of solace (*sollazzo*), but he also criticized some kinds of *beffa*.[55]

Other evidence also points in the direction of the sharper definition of standards and a shrinking in the area of the publicly permissible. A noble dramatic society of Siena, the *Intronati*, now took care not to offend the modesty of ladies by their *burle*. In the case of the *beffe* recounted by Grazzini, probably in the 1580s, it has been claimed by a recent critic that there was a change of perspective from joker to victim.[56] Another recent writer on Italian literature has remarked on the seventeenth-century 'crisis' and decline of the *beffa*.[57] At the very least, it was purified. Typical of the new regime of humour is Girolamo Parabosco's relatively mild *beffa* in which 'a large jar of water and hot ash' falls on the head of a lover as he arrives at the house of his lady. The tricks played by Bertoldo, the hero of a late sixteenth-century cycle of jests written by Giulio Cesare Croce, include violence but no scatology.[58]

What replaced the traditional *beffa*? There seems to have been a shift among the upper classes in the direction of wit and verbal humour. This shift may be illustrated from the life of the academies, an increasingly important form of upper-class sociability in Italian cities of the sixteenth and seventeenth centuries. These discussion groups, which went back to the early Renaissance, now became at once increasingly formal and increasingly playful, in a respectable way. The change may be illustrated from the humorous names which became virtually *de rigueur* for members and for the academies themselves (the 'Sleepyheads', *Addormentati*; the 'Confused', *Confusi*; the 'Frozen', *Gelati*; the 'Immature', *Immaturi*; the 'Thoughtless', *Spensierati*; the 'Uncivilized', *Incolti*; and so on), as well as from mock-lectures and parodies which figured largely on their programmes.[59]

The seventeenth-century rhetorician Emmanuel Tesauro (who might be described in the language of today as a literary theorist) expressed a new ideal of elegance, dismissing 'popular jokes' (*facetie popolari*). He did not reject the *beffa* altogether, and noted that deception was important in the *novelle*. However, Tesauro was much more concerned with verbal than practical jokes.[60] In this respect he was a typical representative of the cultural movement we now call 'baroque'. It does not seem unreasonable to suggest that the baroque obsession with word-play was a form of psychological compensation, a reaction to the shrinking of the domain of the comic. Another form of compensation was the rise of the caricature, which was invented in the circles of the Carracci and Bernini in the early to mid-seventeenth century. In other words, it was the work of artists famous for their classicism, suggesting that they needed some respite from incessant idealization, while earlier forms of comic relief were now denied them.[61]

Of course the Elias thesis of the rise of self-control or 'civilization' should not be enunciated in too simple a manner. The trend was gradual not sudden, it provoked resistance, and it was successful only to varying extents and at different moments in different places, among different groups, or even in different kinds of situation. For example, Adriano Banchieri, a Benedictine monk, published comic works in the seventeenth century, although he did so under a pseudonym, thus revealing as well as breaking the Counter-Reformation taboo. The Florentine patrician Niccolò Strozzi in the mid-seventeenth century told the story of a *beffa* in which the victim was left on Piazza della Signoria all night.[62] At Pratolino, the fountains were still at work in the seventeenth century or even later, as foreign travellers testify. John Evelyn, for example, visiting in 1645, says that he and his companions were 'well washed for our curiosity'.[63] Richard Lassels recorded visiting 'the Grotto of Cupid with the wetting-stools upon which, sitting down, a great Spout of Water comes full in your face'.[64]

In the eighteenth century we find a return to the Renaissance, but with a difference. Several sixteenth-century comic texts reappeared at this time, but in revised forms. *Bertoldo*, for instance, was republished in 1736, rewritten by 20 men of letters, in verse, with allegories.[65] G. C. Becelli rewrote the exploits of the famous medieval jester as *Il Gonnella* (1739). Grazzini's *beffe*, written about 1580, were published for the first time in 1756. A life of the celebrated jester-priest Arlotto Mainardi was published in Venice in 1763. Thus the eighteenth-century revival of the Renaissance was accompanied by and perhaps depended on a kind of historical distanciation.

As a coda, I should like to turn to a mid-twentieth-century story, told by the novelist Vasco Pratolini in his novel *The Girls of San Frediano*, which evokes traditional working-class culture in the years following the Second World War.[66] The punishment of 'Bob', the local Don Giovanni, by a gang of six girls he has tried to seduce individually, takes the form of a *beffa* in the Florentine tradition, in which he is tied up and paraded through the streets with his genitals exposed. Pratolini is not only placing himself in a high literary tradition, but also in a popular tradition, that of Florentine working-class culture, out of which he came and which he celebrates throughout his work.

What conclusion follows from this coda? We don't seem to have moved very far in the four hundred years separating Pratolini from

Pratolino, or even the six hundred years separating him from Boccaccio. The 'gang', or *brigata*, is central in both instances. However, the social frontiers of the comic have changed. What was represented in the fourteenth century as a general social custom is now associated with young adults of the working class.

At this point it may be useful to go back to Darnton's comments about otherness and suggest a few qualifications to them. Are we less cruel and more civilized, as he suggests? Is a cat massacre impossible today? In the *Cambridge Evening News*, a couple of years ago, an incident was reported in which a young man who had quarrelled with his girlfriend revenged himself on her by putting her cat in the microwave. It might be wise to speak not of a general rise in civilization (still less an irresistible one) but of changes in conventions, in the rules of the game, in the 'frontiers' of the comic (as Elias discussed the frontiers of shame or embarrassment). Like sex, laughter is impossible to repress altogether. Rather than speaking of the 'decline' of traditional forms of humour from the later sixteenth century onwards, we might employ Bakhtin's more precise term 'distintegration', drawing attention to increasing restrictions on the public participation of clergy, women or gentlemen in certain kinds of joke, of a reduction of comic domains, occasions and locales, of a raising of the 'threshold', or of an increase in the policing of the frontiers.

NOTES

This chapter has been given in the form of a lecture in Amsterdam, Budapest and Cambridge, and I should like to thank all three audiences for their questions and comments.

1 M. M. Bakhtin, *Problems of Dostoyevsky's Poetics* (1st edn, 1929; Manchester, 1984), pp. 106–7.
2 R. Darnton, *The Great Cat Massacre* (New York, 1984).
3 J. Burckhardt, *Civilization of the Renaissance in Italy* (1st edn, 1860; Eng. trans. 1878; latest edn, Harmondsworth, 1990), ch. 2, sec. 4.
4 B. Castiglione, *The Courtier* (1528; Eng. trans., New York, 1959), bk 2, sec. 85; G. Della Casa, *Galateo* (1558; Eng. trans., Harmondsworth, 1958), ch. 19.
5 F. Malaguzzi Valeri, *La corte di Lodovico il Moro* (4 vols, Milan, 1913), vol. 1, p. 563.
6 A. Graf, 'Un buffone di Leone X', in his *Attraverso il '500* (Turin, 1916), pp. 365–90.
7 Castiglione (1528), bk 2, sec. 93.
8 V. Propp, *Theory and History of Folklore* (Manchester, 1984), ch. 9; C. Bernardi, *La drammaturgia della settimana santa in Italia* (Milan, 1990), p. 153; Gurevich, Chapter 4 of this volume. On the idea of ritual elements in Bertoldo, P. Camporesi, *La maschera di Bertoldo* (Turin, 1976), p. 92.

9 N. Borsellino, 'Il comico', *Letteratura Italiana*, ed. A. Asor Rosa, 5 (1986), pp. 419–25.

10 K. Lea, *Italian Popular Comedy* (London, 1924); M. T. Herrick, *Italian Comedy in the Renaissance* (Urbana, 1960).

11 D. P. Rotunda, *Motif-Index of the Italian Novella in Prose* (Bloomington, 1942); G. Luck, '*Vir facetus*: a Renaissance ideal', *Studies in Philology*, 55 (1958), pp. 107–21; A. Fontes, 'Pouvoir (du) rire. Théorie et pratique des facéties aux 15e et 16e siècles: des facéties humanistes aux trois recueils de L. Domenichi', *Réécritures,* 3 (Paris, 1987), pp. 9–100.

12 G. B. Lalli, *L'Eneide travestite* (Venice, 1618); G. F. Loredano and P. Michiele, *Il cimiterio* (Venice, 1680); A. M. del Priuli, *Epitafi giocosi* (Venice, 1680); P. Larivaille, *Pietro Aretino* (Rome, 1980); N. Jonard, 'La nature du comique dans le *Morgante* de Pulci', in *Culture et société . . . à A. Rochon* (Paris, 1985), pp. 83–102.

13 P. Grendler, *Critics of the Italian World* (Madison, 1969); N. Borsellino, *Gli anticlassicisti del '500* (Rome and Bari, 1973), pp. 41–65.

14 D. Guerri, *La corrente popolare nel Rinascimento* (Florence, 1931).

15 E. H. Gombrich, 'Architecture and rhetoric in Giulio Romano's Palazzo del Te', in *New Light on Old Masters* (Oxford, 1986), pp. 161–70.

16 E. Battisti, *L'Antirinascimento* (Milan, 1962), pp. 278ff.

17 P. Barolsky, *Infinite Jest: wit and humour in Italian Renaissance art* (New York, 1978); H. Bredecamp, *Vicino Orsini und der heilige Wald von Bomarzo* (Worms, 1985); C. Lazzaro, *The Italian Renaissance Garden* (New Haven, 1990), pp. 137, 142, 306.

18 A. Luzio and R. Renier, 'Buffoni, nani e schiavi dei Gonzaga ai tempi d'Isabella d'Este', *Nuova Antologia*, 118 (1891), pp. 618–50, and 119 (1891), pp. 112–46; Malaguzzi Valeri (1913), vol. 1, pp. 563–4; E. Welsford, *The Fool* (London, 1935), pp. 8–19, 128–37.

19 S. Brandes, *Metaphors of Masculinity: sex and status in Andalusian folklore* (Philadelphia, 1980); M. Herzfeld, *The Poetics of Manhood: contest and identity in a Cretan mountain village* (Princeton, 1985).

20 A. Fontes, 'Le thème de la *beffa* dans le *Décaméron*', in A. Rochon (ed.), *Formes et significations de la beffa* (2 vols, Paris, 1972–82), vol. 1, pp. 12–44, at p. 28.

21 A. Barbina (ed.), *Concordanze al Decamerone* (Florence, 1969); Fontes, 'Le thème de la *beffa*'; G. Mazzotti, *The World at Play in Boccaccio's Decameron* (Princeton, 1986).

22 D. Boillet, 'L'usage circonspect de la *beffa* dans Masuccio Salernitano', in Rochon, *Formes et significations de la beffa*, vol. 2, pp. 65–170.

23 A. Rochon, 'Une date importante dans l'histoire de la *beffa*: la *Nouvelle du Grasso legnaiolo*', in *Formes et significations de la beffa*, vol. 2, pp. 211–376.

24 M. Plaisance, 'La structure de la *beffa* dans les *Cene* d'A. F. Grazzini', in Rochon, ibid., vol. 1, pp. 45–98, cf. R. J. Rodini, *A. F. Grazzini* (Madison, 1970), pp. 153–6.

25 A. Fiorato, 'Le monde de la *beffa* chez Matteo Bandello', in Rochon, ibid., vol. 1, pp. 121–66.

26 The incident is described in the play as a 'burla' (Act 5, scene 11). Cf. M.

74 Peter Burke

Celse, 'La *beffa* chez Machiavel, dramaturge et conteur', in Rochon, ibid., vol. 1, pp. 99–110; M. Marietti, 'Aspects de la *beffa* dans les *Istorie Fiorentine*', ibid., pp. 111–20.

27 W. Eamon, *Science and the Secrets of Nature* (Princeton, 1994), pp. 240, 243, 411.

28 S. Thompson, *Motif-Index of Folk Literature* (6 vols, Copenhagen, 1955–8); D. P. Rotunda, *Motif-Index of the Italian Novella in Prose* (Bloomington, 1942).

29 Malaguzzi Valeri, *La corte di Lodovico il Moro*, vol. 1, pp. 560ff; S. Prandi, *Il cortegiano Ferrarese* (Florence, 1990), p. 78.

30 G. Ortalli, 'Il giudice e la taverna', in *Gioco e giustizia nell'Italia di Comune*, ed. Ortalli (Treviso and Rome, 1993), pp. 49–70, at p. 67.

31 T. V. Cohen, 'The case of the mysterious coil of rope', *Sixteenth-Century Journal*, 19 (1988), pp. 209–21.

32 Documents printed in W. Friedlaender, *Caravaggio Studies* (Princeton, 1955), pp. 271–2.

33 C. Robertson, *'Il Gran Cardinale': Alessandro Farnese, patron of the arts* (New Haven and London, 1992), p. 128.

34 S. Cavallo and S. Cerruti, 'Female honor', trans. in E. Muir and G. Ruggiero (eds), *Sex and Gender* (Baltimore 1990), p. 351.

35 C. Evangelisti, 'Libelli famosi: processi per scritte infamanti nella Bologna di fine '500', *Annali della Fondazione Einaudi*, 26 (1992), pp. 181–237, at p. 221.

36 Cf. Celse, 'La *beffa* chez Machiavel'; Marietti, 'Aspects de la *beffa*'.

37 J. Davis, *Land and Family in Pisticci* (London, 1973), p. 23. For further anthropological analysis of joking in Mediterranean cultures, see Brandes, *Metaphors of Masculinity*, pp. 115ff, and Herzfeld, *The Poetics of Manhood*, p. 148.

38 Burckhardt, *Civilization of the Renaissance in Italy*, pt 2.

39 Luzio and Renier, 'Buffoni, nani e schiavi'.

40 Malaguzzi Valeri, *La corte di Lodovico il Moro*, vol. 1, pp. 560–1.

41 Welsford, *The Fool*, pp. 182–96; M. M. Bakhtin, *Rabelais and his World* (1st edn, 1965; Eng. trans., Cambridge, MA, 1968).

42 Arlotto, *Contes*, ed. P. Ristelhuber (Paris, 1873), pp. xviiff; on the 1516 edition, B. Richardson, *Print Culture in Renaissance Italy* (Cambridge, 1994), pp. 79–80.

43 Arlotto, *Contes*, nos. 5, 6.

44 Richardson, *Print Culture in Renaissance Italy*, p. 135.

45 T. Costo, *Il fuggilozio*, ed. C. Calenda (1st edn, 1596; Rome, 1989), no. 3.

46 A. Sorrentino, *La letteratura italiana e il Sant'Ufficio* (Naples, 1935); P. M. Brown, 'Aims and methods of the second *Rassettatura* of the Decameron', *Studi Secenteschi*, 8 (1967), pp. 3–40.

47 V. Cian, 'Un episodio della storia della censura in Italia nel secolo XVI: l'edizione spurgata del *Cortegiano*', *Archivio storico lombardo*, 14 (1887), pp. 661–727.

48 C. Bernardi, *La drammaturgia della settimana santa in Italia* (Milan, 1990), pp. 256, 259; F. Taviani (ed.), *La commedia dell'arte e la società barocca* (Rome, 1970).

49 Quoted in M. de Azpilcueta, *El silencio ser necessario en el choro* (Rome, 1582), pp. 42–3.

50 F. H. Reusch (ed.), *Die indices librorum prohibitorum des sechszehnten Jahrhunderts* (Tübingen, 1886), p. 481.

51 N. Elias, *The Civilizing Process* (1st edn, 1939; Eng. trans., 2 vols, Oxford, 1981–2); P. Burke, *Popular Culture in Early Modern Europe* (2nd edn, London, 1994), pp. 270–80.

52 G. B. Giraldi Cinthio, *Discorsi intorno a quello che si conviene a giovane nobile nel servire un gran principe* (1st edn, 1565; repr. Pavia, 1569), f. 35 recto.

53 A. Cebà, *Il cittadino di repubblica* (Genoa, 1617), ch. 43.

54 R. Grudin, 'The jests in Castiglione's *Il Cortegiano*', *Neophilologus*, 58 (1974), pp. 199–204; J. Guidi, 'Festive narrazioni, motti et burle (*beffe*): l'art des facéties dans le *Courtisan*', in Rochon, *Formes et significations de la beffa*, vol. 2, pp. 171–210.

55 Della Casa, *Galateo*, chs 11, 19.

56 Plaisance, 'La structure de la *beffa*', p. 46.

57 G. Lebatteux, 'La crise de la *beffa* dans les *Diporti* et les *Ecatommiti*', in Rochon, *Formes et significations de la beffa*, vol. 1, pp. 179–202.

58 O. Guerrini, *G. C. Croce* (Bologna, 1879); P. Camporesi (ed.), *Bertoldo* (Turin, 1978), pp. 18–19, 25, 28, 33, 66, 69.

59 A. Quondam, 'L'accademia', in Alberto Asor Rosa (ed.), *Letteratura Italiana* (Turin, 1982), vol. 1, pp. 823–98, cf. G. F. Loredan, *Bizarrie academiche* (Venice, 1638).

60 E. Tesauro, *Il cannocchiale aristotelico* (1st edn, 1654; repr. Turin, 1670), pp. 38, 223, 583ff, 682.

61 E. Kris, *Psychoanalytic Explorations in Art* (London, 1953), chs 6–7; I. Lavin, 'Bernini and the art of social satire', *History of European Ideas*, 4 (1983), pp. 365–78.

62 J. Woodhouse (ed.), 'Avvertimenti necessari per i cortegiani', *Studi Secenteschi*, 23 (1982), pp. 141–61.

63 J. Evelyn, *Diary*, ed. E. S. de Beer (5 vols, Oxford, 1955), vol. 2, p. 418.

64 R. Lassels, *A Voyage of Italy* (1st edn, 1670; repr. London, 1698), p. 134.

65 Guerrini, *G. C. Croce*, pp. 269ff.

66 V. Pratolini, *Le ragazze di San Frediano* (Milan, 1949).

6

The Comic and the Counter-Reformation in the Spanish Netherlands

JOHAN VERBERCKMOES

The parish priest of St Willibrord's church in Borgerhout near Antwerp was celebrating Twelfth Night among his friends, joyfully drinking. He didn't stay up late, however, because he had a Mass to read the next morning. That morning, before Mass, he sat in the confessional box, still black in the face as a result of the ritualized blacking the night before – at Twelfth Night the fool blacked with soot the faces of those who didn't respond quickly enough to the toast 'the king drinks'. Nobody showed up for a confession. Under the influence of last night's beer, the priest gently dozed off. He dreamt that he was again among his friends and suddenly yelled: 'The king drinks, the king drinks.' This, and the fact that they saw his black face, made the people in the church laugh aloud. Afterwards, the priest was ashamed of himself, and when the bishop heard of this, he got a reprimand.[1]

The Counter-Reformation or Catholic Reformation was a campaign of Christianization as well as a reaction against all kinds of traditional customs, the reform of which had already started before the Council of Trent (1545–63) and outside the Church. Public festivities, with their drinking, dancing and masking were considered a threat to orthodoxy and good morals. In the Southern or Spanish Netherlands the Counter-Reformation got off to a slow start, due to the Revolt against Spain. Only after 1585, when most southern towns were reconquered by the Spanish army, did the Catholic clergy start their swift action to re-establish its power. Initially, up to 1607 (the influential Third Provincial Council of Mechelen) or 1609 (the beginning of the Twelve Years' Truce), it was mainly a repressive movement, to erase the traces the 'heretical' Calvinists had left. From about 1609, and strongly supported by the archduke Albert of Austria (1559–1621) and Isabella Clara Eugenia (1566–1633), the Counter-Reformation made a great leap forward. Participation in sacramental practices, devotions, processions, pilgrimages and vocations were stimulated. Dancing parties, mixed recreation and visits to village taverns were restricted.

However, according to the historians who have analysed the records of episcopal visitations, this Catholic reform presumably had a significant impact on the population in the Southern Netherlands only between roughly 1650 and 1750. On the other hand, the endless repetition of interdictions in the latter half of the seventeenth century might suggest that not much progress was made in reforming public morals. Or was the clergy continually increasing its moral demands? At any rate, the fact that, as late as 1690, for example, the bishop of Ghent, Albert de Hornes, devoted an entire pastoral letter to irreverence in the churches demonstrates the limits of restrictions on bodily expression. 'How impertinent is the miserable worm who laughs in the presence of his God, the humiliated Christ?', was the bishop's rhetorical question. Moreover, secular sources point to a resurgence of popular, non-religious festivities from around 1700. Thus, while some church historians argue that the Counter-Reformation acculturation of the people was successful in some periods, others maintain that the movement actually never took root and instead provoked passive and active resistance, embodied in gluttonous eating and drinking or provocative body language.[2] Challenging the indoctrination concept of the Counter-Reformation as a more or less uniform movement with clear goals to achieve and an identified domestic opponent in the Catholic population, historians have in recent years focused their attention on the ambiguities of such a reform, stressing the interactive communication, also non-verbal, between the different social groups involved.[3]

What I propose to do is to broaden our understanding of the Counter-Reformation in general and its manifestation in the Spanish Netherlands in particular by introducing laughter, which is a non-verbal means of communication metaphorically embracing the key issue of corporality foreign to spirituality in the Christian world view. The Counter-Reformation has a bad reputation regarding humour. The French historian Jean Delumeau quotes several seventeenth-century theologians who thought that man had better refrain from laughter because of his sinful condition. The taste for laughter of many a Counter-Reformation hero had vanished. Robert Muchembled argued in his earlier work that the oppression of popular culture made it more difficult to laugh in the French cities from the late sixteenth century onwards, although he later also qualified that view.[4] In both cases laughter was definitely associated with sensuality, indulgence and licence.

The popular godly chapbook *Duyfkens ende Willemynkens*

pelgrimagie, first published in Brussels in 1627, testifies to this horror of foul laughter. The devout Duyfken – literally 'little dove' – and the playful Willemynken – literally 'my own desire' – are two sisters whose life is represented as a pilgrimage to the heavenly Jerusalem. Their opposite reactions to a puppet show at a village fair (kermis), to mixed dancing and to love songs performed by a group of dancing girls are exemplary for the distinction between profane laughter and pious joy, which the Counter-Reformation emphatically enforced. Willemynken laughs at the puppet show 'until the tears run down her cheeks' ('ick lach dat mijn ooghen tranen'). She watches a dancing party of goats and billy goats, while joking and laughing with a country girl. In the singing contest Willemynken participates with the song 'A Venus creature I have chosen' ('Een Venus dierken heb ick uyt verkoren'), which makes the people laugh and assures the girl of winning the prize. Yet her sister Duyfken each time warns her not to waste time on vain pleasures, a caution reinforced by significant details in the story: Willemynken gets lice at the kermis, excrement is splashed on her at the dancing, and with her song she wins a wreath of rotten medlars. Her life style of indulging in sensuality is literally impure.[5]

This is a simple moral message, the language of which had been developed before the Counter-Reformation moralists reappropriated it.[6] Sixteenth- and seventeenth-century paintings of merry companies, peasant weddings, village festivals or tavern interiors often show crudely laughing participants or a laughing jester, communicating the folly and vanity of unrestrained drinking, eating, dancing and loving. In these paintings similar references to impurity are made as in the godly chapbook. The Antwerp artist Jacob Jordaens, for instance, painted several versions of Twelfth Night parties in the 1630s and 1640s. While the temporary king lifts his glass and the room resounds with the cry 'The king drinks', a drunken man vomits, a child pisses and another child's bottom is being cleaned.[7] The type of laughter expressed in these genre paintings and enjoyed by Willemynken is that associated with the lower functions of the body, the popular culture of laughter as Bakhtin analysed it in Rabelais.[8]

It is beyond doubt that this kind of laughter was condemned in the Counter-Reformation, but that it actually disappeared or only functioned within the limits imposed by the official culture, as Bakhtin alleged, is much less certain. In *Duyfkens ende Willemynkens pelgrimagie* Willemynken defends her conduct, arguing that laughter is typical of man. It is impossible to be serious all the time, she claims: 'I have to laugh every now and then, so that my heart feels it.' Moreover, 'people are seduced by laughter and therefore prefer listening to comic songs.' And, Willemynken continues, 'what would the people say? They would mock us if we would look for no other recreation than picking flowers.'

On the other hand, the pious Duyfken acknowledges that there is nothing against cheerfulness, as long as there is a good and pure reason. For her there is no doubt that she will find the perfect joy in the heavenly Jerusalem, where her groom waits for her.[9]

But postponing one's laughter until a next life was certainly not something everybody was eager to do. The argument that people first of all look for something comic encapsulated a familiar complaint among religious writers in the Counter-Reformation. The regular canon of Windesheim, Pieter Croon from Mechelen, observed that books containing a virtuous message were left aside until people were older, whereas jokes and foolishness were read immediately and ten times over.[10]

The obvious way of suppressing the secular laughter which was considered a real obstacle to a true Christian life was simply to forbid laughter. 'Do not laugh and do not say anything which arouses laughter', Ignatius of Loyola admonished in the additions to the first week of his *Spiritual Exercises*.[11] At Provincial councils and synods following the Council of Trent the regular and the secular clergy were instructed to avoid provoking laughter during the services. Moderation of the clergy's own laughter was imperative, even during recreation, as the gravity of their function had to be displayed to the outside world at all times. At the beginning of the seventeenth century the dean of Hulst in Zeeuws-Vlaanderen – at that time still a part of the diocese of Ghent – heard rumours about the parish priest Petrus Stevens of Onssenisse, who read Mass in such a bizarre way that he was looked upon more as a clown than a priest ('tam mirabili modo celebrat ut potius histrionem quam sacerdotem referat'). In his visitation report the dean wrote that he would pay him a surprise visit, but we hear nothing more about it.[12] Two visitators of the Benedictine abbey of Affligem in 1634 found to their displeasure that jokes were made in the infirmary and that the silence in the dormitory was disturbed by immoderate laughter.[13] In 1645 Antoon Triest, bishop of Ghent, confirmed the rules of the Beguines in Ghent, in which it was stated that these women were forbidden to sing indecent or worldly songs, to tell frivolous stories, to roar with laughter or to sleep with two in the same bed.[14] Yet a strict application of the rule of suppressing laughter does not seem to have been a major concern of the Counter-Reformation hierarchy in control of the clergy.

The double admonition not to provoke laughter and not to indulge in laughter dated back to the Church Fathers, such as John Chrysostom, and to the monastic rules of Benedict of Nursia and many others. For Benedict, not to be moved too quickly to laughter and to talk without laughing were signs of humility.[15] Excessive laughter was condemned especially because it was often linked to sinful carnal pleasures. Some even considered laughter as such as an insult to God, as the learned monks could read in the *Apophthegmata christianorum* of the Antwerp canon Laurentius Beyerlinck: 'An old man saw somebody laughing and said: "we have to account for our whole life to the Lord of heaven and earth and you laugh." '[16] The crucial theological argument against laughter, however, was that according to the gospels Christ had never laughed, whereas his weeping had been recorded. Developed by the Greek Church Fathers John Chrysostom and Basil, this argument was introduced to Latin Christianity by Rufinus of Aquileia around 400. After that time it became a topos in theological writing, which undoubtedly contributed to the negative judgement on laughter in the Christian tradition.[17] Yet the argument could be interpreted in different ways. The twelfth-century scholastic Petrus Cantor declared that Christ, although he had never laughed, had actually been capable of doing so, because laughter was a property of man. For the Christ incarnate, the denial of laughter can only have been a virtue if he really had the capacity to laugh, like any human being, Cantor argued.[18]

This last argument was amplified by the humanist and professor at the University of Louvain Erycius Puteanus, who in 1611 publicly defended laughter and the Greek philosopher Democritus during the *quaestiones quodlibeticae*, disputes about every possible subject, which were organized yearly around St Lucia's day on 13 December. This intellectual contest was integrated in the period of carnivalesque winter festivals, which in this Latin milieu was associated with the Roman Saturnalia. Although the occasion legitimized a speech on such a trivial topic as laughter, Puteanus explicitly put forward the thesis that laughter is an expression of wisdom, thus giving it a privileged position in his philosophy of life. One of Puteanus' arguments concerned Christ's refusal to laugh. According to Puteanus, Christ had chosen not to laugh to set an example. By deliberately refusing to do something which was an essential part of human nature, he had found the best way of convincing people that true laughter could only be found in God. In short, laughter was of divine origin, as could also be established, Puteanus continued, when considering that Isaac, whose Chaldean name means 'laughter', had been a victim, just like Christ himself.[19]

God was the secret of true and good laughter. Stressing that message was another way of solving the difficulty of reconciling laughter and Christian virtue. Counter-Reformation moralists referred to this matter introducing a sequence of weeping and laughing. There is a time for weeping and a time for laughter, the Bible said, and moralist writers like the regular canon Pieter Croon of Mechelen or the Antwerp Premonstratensian Jacob Moons repeated the verdict of the Church Father Origines: 'now is the time for weeping and in heaven will be the time for laughter.' The Christian only had to wait until the redemption of the sins in the heavenly Jerusalem, where he would find the only natural laughter. This Augustinian pessimism made Bossuet or de Rancé condemn laughter and led to rigorous moral principles. In an epigrammatic manner, but also expressed in the seventeenth century, for instance by the Jesuit Adriaen Poirters, this meant nothing less than: 'he laughs best who laughs last.'[20]

The most horrible consequence of the Augustinian theology of eternal damnation was the threat that God would laugh at the unrepentent sinners in hell. The Italian historian of literature Piero Camporesi has shown that this perverse idea was phrased at the end of the seventeenth century in the sermons of the Lombardic discalced Augustinian eremite Angelo Maria de San Filippo and others. As a second Nero, God would ridicule the damned in the crackling flames, thus denying them the final chance of salvation. Already in 1682, and before these Italian preachers, Jacob Moons had given his Flemish audience an idea of what they could expect from such a *Deus ridens* or 'laughing god': those who during their lifetime mocked the clergy and other people who had turned their back on the world would be ridiculed by God himself in the hour of their death.[21]

I summarize briefly. Both from a theological and a moral point of view, secular, immoderate laughter was considered harmful for a good Christian, although it was also a natural thing to do. The strictest discipline meant renouncing laughter, but while this was a nearly utopian demand, spiritual writers promised that earthly tears would be followed by heavenly laughter, eventually threatening persistent sinners that God would laugh last. However, the identification of profane laughter also allowed the acceptance of other types of laughter, which could contribute in a positive way to the perfection of a Christian life style. For some saints and mystics, among whom Filippo Neri is the best known, laughter could have a deeper religious meaning. Teresa of Ávila wrote that laughter helped her to understand her own suffering ('me rió y conozco mi miseria'). The mystic Maria Petyt from the Flemish village of Hazebroek, now in the north of France, knew the same kind of laughter. When children paid reverence to her in the beguinage of Ghent because she had acquired a reputation of holiness – 'look the saint is there, make space' – Maria Petyt sometimes laughed, thinking that they mocked her. These were the fools for Christ and the heirs of an old Christian tradition.[22]

Laughter could therefore be the expression of true Christian sentiments. 'It must come from the inside and tickle the heart, that which makes us laugh well', the Jesuit Adriaen Poirters maintained.[23] According to her spiritual biography, the Louvain nun Catharina Daneels was 'much inclined to laughter, not out of vanity or imprudence, but out of a natural cheerfulness, to avoid quarrel and discord and to evade dismay and wrath. When somebody in the house had broken something or had done something else wrong and expected to be scolded, Catharina started laughing and thus showed her gentleness.'[24] Laughter for the sake of peace and quiet seemed the perfect marriage of stoicism and Catholic self-sacrifice. After all, laughter was natural, and those who laughed only once a month barely had a soul, alleged the Brussels popular writer Joan de Grieck.[25] Even in the monasteries, monks of a melancholic complexion, such as the Benedictine Jacques Rahier in Stavelot, were openly urged to laugh.[26]

The most convincing argument for Christian laughter was called *eutrapelia*. According to Aristotle in his *Nicomachean Ethics*, *eutrapelia* is the property of being funny in a civilized way, to strike a balance between too much and too little. Thomas Aquinas interpreted this *eutrapelia* theologically as a moderate laughter which does not interfere with charity.[27] In the seventeenth century this Christian *eutrapelia* was defended by, among others, François de Sales, in his *Introduction à la vie dévote*, which was also very influential in the Spanish Netherlands. *Eutrapelia*, he said, 'means good conversation, word-play in an atmosphere of modest gaiety and joy. It is an honest recreation on the frivolous occasions which the human imperfections offer. It must, however, not become mockery, which is aimed at contempt of one's neighbour.'[28] Blaise Pascal called truthfulness, discretion and piety, which can be summed up as charity, the secrets of true Christian laughter, principles which, according to him, contribute to the success of a joke.[29]

Theoretically, blending funniness with morals and Christian charity was the ideal solution. Even popular festivals became acceptable when the rule of honest recreation was applied. Twelfth Night parties, the regular canon Pieter Croon argued, are tolerable when the participants behave moderately, when the jester makes honourable jokes, when everybody laughs virtuously, when there is love and affability. Remodelling the ritual, Croon legitimized the drinking ceremony at Twelfth Night, referring to the explanation given in the 'gospel of the distaff' ('Evangelie vanden spin-rock'), which actually meant that it was a manifest lie: during one of their visits to the little Jesus in Bethlehem, the three Wise Men saw the baby suckling the blessed breasts of his mother. They said among each other, 'the king drinks', which became the popular cry at Twelfth Night.[30]

Notwithstanding the many public declarations of moderating one's laughter, the Counter-Reformation also produced its own brand of unrestricted humour. Under the pretext of rebuking the imperfections of others, all kinds of jokes were unleashed. Calling these 'honest recreation' and labelling the jokes of their opponents 'mockery' was simply a matter of self-justification. Consider for example the jest told by Franciscus Costerus, a Jesuit born in Mechelen in 1532 and one of the most important figures of the Counter-Reformation in the Spanish Netherlands between 1585 and 1619, the year of his death. In 1604 Costerus wrote that about twenty years before he had lived in the German Fulda, where the Jesuits had a cook, Michiel, who had learned Latin and even some Greek sayings from the students who came to his kitchen.

> When Michiel went to the village to buy oxen, the local Reformed minister wanted to convert the Jesuit cook. He asked him some things in Latin, but the cook was able to answer him in the same language. The minister even turned to Greek, but to his amazement the cook answered with a Greek saying, which he had heard from the students and which said: 'this is somebody who will answer you'. After that, the minister gave up and prided himself that he had talked to the most learned of all Jesuits. When he came home, the cook told the rector and the other Jesuits what had happened in a jocular manner, so that all laughed. When a couple of days later, a lay student from Würzburg who had heard about this came to Fulda, he warned the minister: if their cook is already such a learned man, what to expect then from their doctors?[31]

The imperfections of others as a proper object of ridicule meant for the Counter-Reformation clergy first of all laughing at the Reformed ministers. Up to 1621 – the end of the Twelve Years' Truce – and even beyond that year, some Jesuits, such as Costerus, Johannes Gouda or Maximiliaan van Habbeke, used the pulpit to mock their adversaries. Although they were admonished by their superiors to moderate their language and although they formally rejected the *opportuna jocatio* – the use of jokes in sermons – there is some evidence that these Jesuits showed caricatures in the pulpit, spoke facetiously and used grotesque body language, in short did everything to appeal to the oral and visual culture of their audience. In pamphlets and pasquinades Costerus, Johannes David and other Jesuits used a Rabelaisian language.[32]

Jokes about Reformed ministers were definitely integrated in the Counter-Reformation culture, stressing in a carnivalesque way its theological and educational foundations. The Catholic English refugee Richard Verstegen, for instance, filled anecdotes, dialogues, epigrams, comic epitaphs, proverbs, news reports and character sketches with anti-Reformed stereotypes. Verstegen was from a family which had emigrated from Guelderland to England in the early sixteenth century, while he himself had settled in Antwerp in 1587. He published many pamphlets, books and news reports in Antwerp between 1617 and

1633, and his works were plundered by Counter-Reformation writers throughout the seventeenth century.[33]

But jests about Reformed ministers were also popular in oral traditions. Basically, these jests on the Protestants were all quite alike, focusing on the deemed defective Bible knowledge of the Reformed ministers or Bible sisters, highlighting their theological opinions and dissensions and displaying their eagerness for disputes. In every punch line they are forced to keep silent.

> A Protestant or Dutch minister was a passenger on the barge between Ghent and Bruges. He immediately started to dispute with the Catholics present, as they were not as well instructed in the Bible as he was. Two Observants were also present on the barge. One of these monks had a pack on his back. When the Protestant saw this, he turned to the Observant and challenged him to talk about the Scriptures. The father refused to answer, knowing that he would not gain credit by such a dispute. The minister then asked him what he was bearing in the large pack on his back. 'It's an organ', the Observant answered. 'Play us a tune', the Protestant said. The father immediately replied: 'put your mouth at the back and blow in the hollow pipe, it will sound like an organ.' Hearing that answer, everybody laughed at the minister.[34]

I mention this last sentence of the anecdote in particular, because it is an example of 'textual laughter', which is often found in jest-books and which helps prove that these anecdotes were indeed considered comic in the seventeenth century. It can also be interpreted as the collector's advice to the reader that the anecdote has a comic intention.

Crucial in the strategy of the Counter-Reformation (and the Reformation) was the insistence of the reformers on the separation between the realms of the sacred and the profane. This also involved a remodelling of the emotions. Tears were promoted as characteristic for a truly devout life style. Laughter, on the other hand, was acceptable only in the context of theological defence or moral reaction against worldly vanity and folly. The latter resulted in a reassessment of the theme of folly in didactic-moralistic writing in the wake of the Jesuit Adriaen Poirters. It did not result in funny books, however, although these writers reused comic anecdotes to illustrate their mockery of worldly vanity. Laughter was in their case more a state of the soul than a straightforward bodily expression.[35]

More importantly, the enforced separation between the realms of the sacred and the profane created a whole new field of humour. Those who publicly showed irreverence were brought before ecclesiastical or secular courts and convicted, among them the puppet players Jacob

Cobbeniers and his wife Elisabeth Lauwers, who around 1600 in a puppet play let St Peter and St Paul kiss and feel a woman, Margrite, and even let the two saints embrace each other, or Elisabeth Blondeel, who on Christmas night 1622, in the parish church of Impe near Brussels in the presence of forty people, sat down in the confessional box, placed the priest's biretta on her head and heard the confession of a young man.[36]

But there were more subtle ways to go beyond the limits – for instance jests, which could always be interpreted in different ways. In spite of continued censorship jest-books were being published in the Spanish Netherlands up to 1627. After that date no more collections were printed, although there is some evidence to suggest that copies of the old editions were still being sold. In the latter half of the seventeenth century moralistic collections of anecdotes seem to have replaced the jest-books. Yet around 1700 at least three new jest-books in the vernacular were printed, one of which was a supplement to a popular almanac for the year 1701 containing only three (sixteenth-century) anecdotes.

In these last collections and in the earlier named manuscript about one-sixth of the anecdotes are concerned with priests, monks, nuns, the holy sacraments and the Church. The sixteenth-century allegations of gluttony, stupidity and greed were repeated, referring especially to the behaviour of the regular clergy. But more important, and relatively new with respect to the sixteenth century, were jokes in which the point was about Christian practices and the dominant position of the priest in his parish. According to these jests, priests in the pulpit made their audiences roar with laughter. They made funny comparisons – for instance, comparing an attendant colleague, who was an ugly hunchback, to the biblical tax-collector Zacchaeus in the tree.[37] Joking manifestations of resistance in the confessional were also recorded, like the anecdote about the peasant who was admonished by the priest to learn his prayers and who for his part advised the priest to learn how to make a straw hat.[38] This last pattern was frequently adopted in jests concerning the catechism. Often it is from the child's mouth that the reply comes. 'In 1682', one anecdote goes, 'near Bruges, a parish priest scolded the children for not learning anything. One boy replied: "Do you know how to drown a frog?" "No", the priest said, "how?" "Well", the boy answered, "take the frog, put a little stick between his jaws and throw him into the water. He will drown immediately." '[39] Even the bishop of Ghent, Antonius Triest, one of the most zealous Counter-Reformation bishops, did not escape ridicule. In an anecdote a servant takes a chamber-pot from under the table where Triest is sitting, and this causes loud laughter among his table companions.[40]

Jests, even of a scatological nature, were integrated in the culture of the Counter-Reformation in the Spanish Netherlands. Of course, based on an old Christian distrust of laughter, limits were imposed and legitimized by appeals to decency as well as by theological arguments – according to the Bible, Christ had never laughed himself. Yet laughter as such might also be considered a pale reflection of the divine happiness. Refining one's humour and attuning it to the principles of Christian charity, one practised an *eutrapelia* which was beneficial to the soul. Even unrestricted humour found its advocates among the Roman Catholic clergy, as long as the goal and the opponent were appropriate. Moreover, entirely new fields of humour emerged out of the Counter-Reformation. This way, laughter can be understood as the means of communication which invested the spiritual learning and the cultural hegemony of the Counter-Reformation with codes of visual and oral expression drawn from daily life and common, corporal experiences.

NOTES

1 Ghent, University Library, Manuscripts, 1816, *'t Verdrijf des droefheyts ende melancolie*, f. 107. The research for this paper is based on J. Verberckmoes, *Schertsen, schimpen, schaterlachen: het komische in de cultuur van de Spaanse Nederlanden (16de–17de eeuw)* (Diss., Louvain, 1993). See also *Schertsen, schimpen, schateren: geschiedenis van het lachen in de Spaanse Nederlanden* (Nijmegen, 1996) and *Laughter, Jestbooks and Society in the Spanish Netherlands* (London, 1997).

2 The Christianization thesis is defended by M. Cloet, *Het kerkelijk leven in een landelijke dekenij van Vlaanderen tijdens de XVIIde eeuw: tielt van 1609 tot 1700* (Louvain, 1968), and other church historians, whose research is mentioned in M. Cloet, 'Een kwarteeuw historische produktie in België betreffende de religieuze geschiedenis van de Nieuwe Tijd', *Trajecta*, 4 (1995), pp. 198–223. The resistance thesis is defended by R. Muchembled, *Culture populaire et culture des élites dans la France moderne, XVe–XVIIIe siècles* (Paris, 1978); H. Soly, 'Openbare feesten in Brabantse en Vlaamse steden, 16de–18de eeuw', in *Het openbaar initiatief van de gemeenten in België: historische grondslagen (Ancien Régime)* (Brussels, 1984), pp. 605–31; and A. K. L. Thijs, *Van geuzenstad tot katholiek bolwerk. Antwerpen en de contrareformatie* (Turnhout, 1990). Cf. J. Tracy, 'With and without the Counter-Reformation: the Catholic church in the Spanish Netherlands and the Dutch Republic, 1580–1650. A review of the literature since 1945', *Catholic Historical Review*, 71 (1985), pp. 547–75 and C. Harline, 'Official religion and popular religion in recent historiography of the Catholic reformation', *Archiv für Reformationsgeschichte*, 81 (1990), pp. 239–62. For the quote from de Hornes' letter, see P. F. X. De Ram and J. F. Van de Velde (eds), *Synodicon Belgicum*, vol. 4 (Mechelen and Louvain, 1858), pp. 349–52.

3 See, for instance, A. Lottin, *Lille, citadelle de la contre-réforme? (1598–*

1668) (Dunkirk, 1984); P. Burke, *Historical Anthropology in Early Modern Italy: essays on perception and communication* (Cambridge, 1987); G. Levi, *Inheriting Power: the story of an exorcist*, trans. L. G. Cochrane (Chicago and London, 1988).

4 J. Delumeau, *Le péché et la peur: la culpabilisation en Occident (XIIIe–XVIIIe siècles)* (Paris, 1983), pp. 510–11; R. Muchembled, *Culture populaire et culture des élites dans la France moderne, XVe–XVIIIe siècles* (Paris, 1978), p. 201, and his *L'invention de l'homme moderne: sensibilités, moeurs et comportements collectifs sous l'Ancien Régime* (Paris, 1988).

5 Boetius a Bolswert, *Duyfkens ende Willemynkens pelgrimagie tot haren beminden binnen Ierusalem*, ed. H. J. A. Ruys (Utrecht, 1910), pp. 174–8, 187–90 and 295–9.

6 For the Christian and medieval interpretations of laughter, see J. Le Goff, 'Le rire dans les règles monastiques du haut moyen âge', in C. Lepelley et al. (eds), *Haut moyen-âge: culture, éducation et société. Études offertes à Pierre Riché* (La Garenne-Colombes, 1990), pp. 93–103; G. H. M. Posthumus Meyjes, *Geloven en lachen in de historie* (Leiden, 1992); J. Horowitz and S. Menache, *L'humour en chaire: le rire dans l'église médiévale* (Geneva, 1994); J. Le Goff, Chapter 3 in this volume.

7 A. A. Van Wagenberg-Ter Hoeven, 'The celebration of Twelfth Night in Netherlandish art', *Simiolus. Netherlands Quarterly for the History of Art*, 22 (1993–4), pp. 65–96. For the debate on the interpretation of genre scenes, see P. Vandenbroeck, 'Verbeeck's peasant weddings: a study of iconography and social function', *Simiolus*, 14 (1984), pp. 79–124, and W. S. Gibson, 'Verbeeck's grotesque wedding feasts: some reconsiderations', *Simiolus*, 21 (1992), pp. 29–39.

8 M. Bakhtin, *Rabelais and his World*, trans. H. Iswolsky (London, 1968).

9 Boetius a Bolswert, *Duyfkens*, ibid.

10 P. Croon, *Almanach voor heden en morghen ende daer op vermaeckelijcke uyt-legginghen met gheestelijcke bemerckingen: voor een nieuw-iaer* (Antwerp, 1665), p. 339. Cf. also D. Idinav [=J. David, sj], *Lot van wiisheyd ende goed geluck: op drije hondert ghemeyne sprek-woorden: in rijme gestelt* (Antwerp, 1606), pp. 4–5.

11 I. De Loyola, *Écrits*, ed. M. Giuliani (Paris, 1991), pp. 98–9.

12 T. B. W. Kok, *Dekenaat in de steigers: kerkelijk opbouwwerk in het Gentse dekenaat Hulst, 1596–1648* (Tilburg, 1971), p. 389.

13 H. Verleyen, *Dom Benedictus van Haeften, proost van Affligem, 1588–1648: bijdrage tot de studie van het kloosterleven in de Zuidelijke Nederlanden* (Brussels, 1983), p. 99.

14 Ghent, Archives Klein Begijnhof, K1S9/8, chap. III, point IV (I am indebted for this reference to H. Cailliau and M. Cloet).

15 Cf. G. Perduyn, *LXXII instrumenten der goede wercken van den H. Benedictus: alles getrocken op sermoonen voor alle de zondagen des jaers* (Brussels, 1697), instruments 54 and 55 (with thanks to H. Storme).

16 L. Beyerlinck, *Apophthegmata christianorum* (Antwerp, 1608), p. 514.

17 Cf. Le Goff, 'Le rire', pp. 93–5; Delumeau, *Le péché*, p. 511.

18 Cf. E. R. Curtius, *Europäische Literatur und lateinisches Mittelalter* (6th edn, Berne and Munich, 1966), pp. 422–3.

19 Puteanus' speech was published under the title *Democritus, sive de risu dissertatio saturnalis: publice Lovanii habita* (Louvain, 1612) and reprinted several times. Democritus and laughter: Bremmer, Chapter 1 of this volume.

20 P. Croon, *Cocus bonus oft geestelycke bemerckingen op de tafel ende spysen van een volkommen maeltyt* (Bruges, n.d.), pt II, pp. 16 and 257; J. Moons, *Sedelyck vermaeck tonneel* (Antwerp, 1675), pp. 384–5; Posthumus Meyjes, *Geloven en lachen*, p. 14; Delumeau, *Le péché*, pp. 330–1; A. Poirters, *Het Masker van de wereldt afgetrocken*, ed. J. Salsmans and E. Rombauts (Oisterwijk, 1935), p. 50: 'T is soo, Philothea, al soo veel hebbense jae meer, de ghene die naer lacchen, als die voor lacchen.'

21 P. Camporesi, *L'enfer et le fantasme: une théologie baroque*, trans. M. Aymard (Paris, 1989), pp. 117–21; J. Moons, *Sedelycken vreughden bergh* (Antwerp, 1682), p. 344 (referring to Wisdom 4:18).

22 A. Deblaere, *De mystieke schrijfster Maria Petyt (1623–1677)* (Ghent, 1962), p. 33; cf. J. Saward, *Perfect Fools: folly for Christ's sake in Catholic and orthodox spirituality* (Oxford, 1980); M. De Certeau, *La fable mystique: XVIe–XVIIe siècle* (Paris, 1982), pp. 58–70; J. Poitrey, *Vocabulario de Santa Teresa* (Madrid, 1983), p. 598, lemma 'reír'.

23 Poirters, *Het Masker*, p. 370.

24 F. De Smidt, *Doorluchtich ende stichtich leven van Iouffr: Catharina Daneels* (Antwerp, 1647), pp. 163–4 (I owe this reference to H. Storme).

25 J. De Grieck, *De Sotte Wereldt, ofte den waeren af-druck der wereldtsche sottigheden* (Brussels, 1682), p. 292.

26 J. Hoyoux, 'Les moines de l'abbaye de Stavelot en 1633', *Bulletin de l'institut historique belge de Rome*, 37 (1966), pp. 361–9 (p. 366: 'Jacobus Rahier . . . humoris melancolici, et pusillanimis . . . ipsum semper potius ad hilaritatem oportet excitare quam ad tristitiam inducere').

27 Cf. J. Suchomski, *'Delectatio' und 'Utilitas': ein Beitrag zur Verständnis mittelaltlicher komischer Literatur* (Bern, 1975), pp. 55–61; Le Goff, 'Le rire', pp. 95–6; H. Rahner, 'Eutrapelie, eine vergessene Tugend', *Geist und Leben*, 27 (1954), pp. 346–53; Bremmer, Chapter 1 of this volume.

28 François de Sales, *Oeuvres* (Paris, 1969), p. 207 (*Introduction*, pt III, chap. 27); cf. A. L. J. Daniels, *Les rapports entre St François de Sales et les Pays-Bas, 1550–1700* (Nijmegen, 1932).

29 B. Pascal, *Les Provinciales*, ed. L. Cognet (Paris, 1965), pp. 193–214; cf. J. Morel, 'Pascal et la doctrine du rire grave', in *Méthodes chez Pascal* (Paris, 1979), pp. 213–22.

30 P. Croon, *Almanach*, pp. 131–8, cf. Van Wagenberg-Ter Hoeven, 'The celebration', pp. 77–8.

31 Cf. R. Hardeman, *Franciscus Costerus (1532–1619)* (Alken, 1933), pp. 19–20 (quoted from the *Weder-legginghe Francisci Costeri . . .* (Antwerp, 1604), p. 131). I have paraphrased the quote rather than translating it literally.

32 J. Andriessen, *De jezuïeten en het samenhorigheidsbesef der Nederlanden, 1585–1648* (Antwerp, 1957), pp. 184–90; R. Mortier, *Un pamphlet jésuite 'rabelaisant', le 'hochepot ou Salmigondi des folz' (1596): étude historique et linguistique suivie d'une édition du texte* (Brussels, 1959); K. Porteman,

'Na 350 jaar: de "Sermoonen" van Franciscus Costerus', *Ons Geestelijk Erf*, 43 (1969), pp. 209–69; H. Storme, *Preekboeken en prediking in de Mechelse kerkprovincie in de 17e en de 18e eeuw* (Brussels, 1991), pp. 203–6, considers, on the evidence of printed collections of sermons, comic sermons to have been exceptional; compare, however, with the remarks by H. Roodenburg, *Onder censuur: de kerkelijke tucht in de gereformeerde gemeente van Amsterdam, 1585–1700* (Hilversum, 1990), p. 41. See in this context also V. Wendland, *Ostermärchen und Ostergelächter: brauchtümliche Kanzelrhetorik und ihre kulturkritische Würdigung seit dem ausgehenden Mittelalter* (Frankfurt am Main, 1980), M. J. Jacobelli, *Il 'risus paschalis' e il fondamento teologico del piacere sessuale* (Brescia, 1990).

33 Cf. E. Rombauts, *Richard Verstegen: een polemist der Contra-Reformatie* (Brussels, 1933); W. J. C. Buitendijk, *Het calvinisme in de spiegel van de Zuidnederlandse literatuur der contra-reformatie* (Groningen and Batavia, 1942), pp. 155–228; idem, 'Richard Verstegen als verteller en journalist', *De Nieuwe Taalgids*, 46 (1953), pp. 21–30, and 'Richard Verstegen's playsante conterfeytsels en concepten', *De Nieuwe Taalgids*, 46 (1953), pp. 71–9.

34 Ghent, University Library, Manuscripts, 1816, ff. 22–3 (see note 1). In this manuscript collection, dated around 1700, the as yet unidentified author refers back to written as well as to oral traditions ('I heard from my father', etc.).

35 Poirters, *Het Masker*; the main reference for this literature is still E. Rombauts, 'De letterkunde der XVIIe eeuw in Zuid-Nederland', in *Geschiedenis van de letterkunde der Nederlanden*, vol. 5 (Antwerp, Brussels and 's Hertogenbosch, 1952), pp. 379–482.

36 E. Peeters, 'Van poppenspel naar brandstapel: een proces voor de vierschaar van Eppegem in 1601–1602', *De Brabantse Folklore*, 199 (1973), pp. 325–34; J. De Brouwer, *De kerkelijke rechtspraak en haar evolutie in de bisdommen Antwerpen, Gent en Mechelen tussen 1570 en 1795*, vol. II (Tielt, 1972), p. 81.

37 Ghent, University Library, Manuscripts, 1816, f. 2; compare also ff. 2–3, 14–15, 30–2, 43–4, 65–7 and 139.

38 A. J. W. L., *Den seer vermaeckelycken kluchtverteller* (Ypres and Antwerp, n.d.), p. 47, and compare pp. 78–9. See also the anecdote at the beginning of this chapter.

39 Ghent, University Library, Manuscripts, 1816, f. 48, and compare ff. 1 and 69; see also A. J. W. L., *op. cit.*, pp. 29–33, 119–20 and 139.

40 Ghent, University Library, Manuscripts, 1816, ff. 21–2.

7

Prose Jest-Books Mainly in the Sixteenth to Eighteenth Centuries in England

Derek Brewer

A jest is a verbal mini-art form designed to produce laughter. It is in origin oral, spoken to an in-group, hence in prose, concerned with the accidents and stresses of ordinary life. It is a brief narrative of some piquant reversal or incongruity or smart reply embodying such, appealing to a group of people of similar tastes. It is a part therefore of the more general culture of humour in a society, and is to some extent an index of what is there thought to be funny. The history of such jests, especially as they exist in collections of items all of a similar kind, i.e. jest-books, is of some considerable though neglected interest in the history of literature and culture.

A Necessary Social Setting

The nature of a jest is to promote the humour and harmony of the group who share it and its implicit assumptions. All groups by their very existence imply and may deliberately exclude outsiders, and virtually all traditional jests are at the expense, however small, of a victim who either is, or becomes, an outsider. It is for this reason paradoxically that the nineteenth-century notion that jokes are subversive in part arises.[1] The outsider may well be, but does not have to be, a superior, or the embodiment of conventional rather than actual morality. Traditionally jests tend to endorse popular prejudice, as with the universally practised ethnic joke,[2] or almost equally universal anti-feminism in many forms, or mockery of physical handicaps. Political jokes especially in the former communist countries were subversive because they expressed the solidarity of ordinary people against the 'outsiders' who oppressed them. Traditional jests, which include new ones of the traditional kind, are thus very frequently 'politically incorrect', corresponding to the feelings of ordinary people in the ordinary groupings hostile to dominant minorities, whether political or intellectual, who are outsiders.

The political joke in modern times is perhaps the quintessential traditional jest in its oral nature, being sometimes even dangerous to write or print. Hence a paradox arises from historical discussion, since we can only discuss written or printed jests. The recorded form decontextualizes the jest, deprives it of much of its emotional power, of the privilege and protection of the in-group. Only in so far as we imagine ourselves back into something like the original circumstances, and remember our common humanity, can we appreciate most of these ancient jests. (But I have had the experience of attempting to demonstrate the feebleness of one of these well-worn chestnuts by telling it to a group, and finding both myself and my audience laughing.) The solitary reader can imagine himself or herself into the group, but may also be cast as the outsider, in which case the jest may offend where no personal offence was originally intended.

The absence of the social group and communal jollity, the 'coldness' of print, allows cultural analysis and history. But there is no reason to find analysis and history amusing, though there are irony and paradox in plenty. With these preliminary considerations in mind we can turn to the history of the genre itself, emphasizing first of all the cultural circumstances – the classes and situations of the men and women involved.

There were of course jests in classical antiquity and in the Middle Ages, some of which survived for many centuries, but the first jest-book proper – rather, improper – is normally reckoned to be the *Facetiae*, the collection of jests made by Poggio Bracciolini, the great Humanist scholar (1380–1459).[3] It is a series of scabrous, sometimes ancient anecdotes said to have risen from the gossip during the fifteenth-century equivalent of coffee-breaks among the papal secretaries in Rome. Written in Latin about 1450, the learned language being indicative of the educated and socially cohesive group among whom they originated, they circulated widely in Europe and were printed in 1477. Poggio claims they were told by named persons about others – witty, malicious gossip – but they have received literary polish. As they were immensely popular, others adopted individual items, and similar books began to be published in Europe.

An important and neglected insight into the cultural place of jests in the sixteenth century is given by the large place assigned to them by that highly influential book on courtly behaviour *Il libro del cortegiano* (1528) by Baldassare Castiglione (1478–1529). It is based on conversations said to have taken place at the court of Urbino under Duke Guidobaldo (1504–8). The book was much reprinted, and translated into several languages, including an English version, *The Courtyer*, by Sir Thomas Hoby (1530–66), first published in 1561. In *The Courtyer* the first of four substantial books making up the whole instructs what should be the qualities of a courtier, and the second, to quote Hoby, is about 'the vse of them [i.e. the qualities] and of merie Iestes and Pranckes', which include such jests as those against hunchbacks (a favourite for several centuries). It is the courtier's duty to lace his conversation with jests. But Castiglione refers to professional jesters with contempt, and he deplores rough or dirty jokes. The courtier should not taunt or scoff at the weak. Yet Book II of *Il Cortegiano* is a veritable jest-book in itself, with jests often decidedly unkind, though some of them are so long and circumstantial as to verge on that closely related genre the comic tale.[4]

No medieval courtesy-book has much to say about the art of conversation, and less still about jests. By contrast, from the sixteenth century onwards there is a sequence of courtesy-books which normally refer to the art of conversation and have some reference to jests, with a slightly increased emphasis on the need to avoid indecency. An example may be found in *The Refin'd Courtier, or A Correction of Several Indecencies Crept into Civil Conversation*.[5] There were more versions based on a Spanish translation. The work is a paraphrase of another famous Italian sixteenth-century courtesy-book written by Giovanni Della Casa, archbishop of Benevento, *Galateo,* first translated into English by Robert Peterson in 1576, which emphasizes decorum and self-control in personal manners and is rather less friendly to jests, as being 'biting', but admits them into polite conversation.[6]

These foreign works and their English translations, adaptations and imitations undoubtedly had their influence in England at an upper-class level from the sixteenth century onwards. Related to them, the product of the same Humanist interest in behaviour both educated and polite, are the various works on rhetoric. The most important book in English on rhetoric in the sixteenth century was Thomas Wilson's *The Art of Rhetorique, for the Use of all Suche as are Studious of Eloquence,* first published in 1553, revised and improved in 1567.[7] Though based on classical sources it has its own individuality and lively style. Most of the second of the three parts of the work is devoted to analysing and exemplifying all sorts of jests. The humour is always derisive. The remarkable Humanist scholar Gabriel Harvey owned a copy of the second edition and wrote in it, 'One of my best for the art of jesting: next Tullie [Cicero], Quintilian, the Courtier in Italian ... Of all, the shortest, & most familiar, owr Wilson.'[8] The general ambiance and the Humanist connections are clear.

For a more specific account in England we have two invaluable sources for the seventeenth century, Burton and Pepys. Burton is the more general. Pepys gives us the very flavour of jests in both courtly and middle-class life.

Robert Burton (1577–1640) was a Student (i.e. Fellow, faculty member) of the college called Christ Church in Oxford. He wrote an immense treatise with the self-explanatory title *The Anatomy of Melancholy*, first published in 1621 and enlarged in successive editions until the posthumous edition of 1651, from which final version my quotations are taken. His range is encyclopaedic. He analyses the various causes of melancholy, including love and religion, noting various cures through a huge series of literary references that makes him a great comparatist in several fields. He leads us into our subject when he considers the recreations of the English people among possible cures for melancholy. He makes clear the social background against which humour, and specifically the jest-books, should be considered.

The ordinary recreations which we have in Winter, and in most solitary times busie our minds with, are Cardes, Tables and Dice, Shovelboard, Chesse play, the Philosopher's game, small trunks, shuttle-cock, balliards, musick, masks, singing, dancing, ulegames, frolicks, jests, riddles, catches, purposes, questions and commands, merry tales of errant Knights, Queens, Lovers, Lords, Ladies, Giants, Dwarves, Theeves, Cheaters, Witches, Fayries, Goblins, Friers, etc, such as the old woman told *Psyche* in *Apuleius* [i.e., as a marginal note suggests, Milesian tales, which are the oldest recorded jokes], Boccace Novels, and the rest . . . which some delight to hear, some to tell; all are well pleased with.[9]

Burton adds, further down the page,

Some mens whole delight is, to take Tobacco, and drink all day long in a Tavern or Alehouse, to discourse, sing, jest, roare, talk of a Cock and Bull over a pot, etc. Or when three or four good companions meet, tell old stories by the fireside, or in the Sun, as old folkes usually do.[10]

Old stories they may well have been. These jests survived sometimes for centuries, maybe even millennia, through various cultures, normally in prose, only superficial circumstances of the narrative being changed.

The larger social group-setting of the jests and jest-books is all-important for their true understanding, though the evidence is scanty and scattered. The books imply social groups and an oral influence. Burton sketches the possible tavern setting; other settings are suggested by the action and the social level of Shakespeare's *The Taming of the Shrew*, *Twelfth Night*, *The Merry Wives of Windsor* – domestic settings of nobility, prosperous bourgeoisie and artisans, to which we may add bishops' households, and even churches occasionally in the sixteenth century. To this add the teeming life of the streets illustrated in so many ways in the jest-books themselves, peopled with artisans, tradespeople and ordinary townsfolk, as well as with passing clergy, courtiers, gentry, nobility and country simpletons. In *Howleglas* of the early sixteenth century, and *The Hundred Mery Talys* of 1526, there are villages with churches and graveyards, even warrens and isolated country houses; in *Ratseis Ghost* (1605) there is a glimpse of a highwayman and strolling players on the road in the country. But Ratsey's advice to the players is 'Get you to London', and this reflects the bias towards town life, especially London, of the jest-books themselves. Probably for this reason countrymen are the butt of a number of jokes, though sometimes the countryman mocks with his apparent simplicity the townsman or scholar.

The best glimpses of merry social life in seventeenth-century London are those given by Pepys in his *Diary*.[11] He notes many social occasions, either with men alone or in mixed company, when 'we were very merry'. He records a variety of kinds of humour. For example, on 7 May 1662 he quotes a fairly gross parliamentary joke – the group implied here being the all-male membership of the House of Commons, and by extension those interested in their business. On 21 May 1662 he went with his wife and Sarah, Lord Sandwich's housekeeper, to see a 'droll' – a short comic play. On 21 September he made 'mirth' in the evening at his aunt's house by praising the Roman Catholic Mass, teasing his Protestant aunt because she was mourning her sister's death (a good example of malicious humour). On 30 October 1662 he heard at dinner a couple of gross jokes from Sir John Mennis, a well-known wit and part-author of a scurrilous partly comic book.[12] On 31 December 1662 he saw in the evening the king and noble ladies dancing to the jest-song *Cuckolds All A-Row*. On 29 April 1663 he called on Lord Sandwich at his mistress's house in Chelsea and, walking in the garden, was 'finely wetted' by what must have been a joke-fountain. On 24 October Pepys was mighty merry with pleasant stories by Coventry and Sir John Mennis, and again at another dinner with the whole Navy Board on 5 December 1663 he was much pleased 'for the many excellent stories told by Mr Coventry; which I have put down in my book of tales, and so shall not mention them here.' He had also written them down in October, but alas the book of tales is lost. There is another reference to it for 28 March 1664. (Pepys does record the story of an ingenious insurance fraud on 30 November 1663, but it is not clear that he found it funny.)

These entries illustrate the garnering of stories from and for conversation, but also for and in books. Pepys records hearing on 12 May 1660 'an exceeding pretty story and worth my getting without book [i.e. memorizing] when I can get the book.' This well illustrates how such stories float in and out of the oral, written and printed traditions, and explains why their style usually retains some oral characteristics. The social informality accounts for the variations in different versions (a characteristic of traditional literature) and explains the dominance of prose. No one speaks in verse at a party of friends (except briefly in a riddle – there were books of merry riddles in verse, some owned by Pepys – or perhaps in a quoted proverb). Educated men, often in the company of women as shown above, throughout our period, with few exceptions, are interested in hearing, telling, and recording what are often very old jokes. On 9 October 1660 Pepys and his friends 'were very merry at table, telling of tales'. On 14 November 1660 in the evening they drank a great quantity of sack 'And did tell many merry stories, and in good humours were we all.' (The nuance of 'merry' is well conveyed by the entry for 1 June 1663, when Pepys had a 'very pretty dinner' at his brother Tom's with clerical friends, when 'we were very pleasant but not very merry, the Deane being but a weak man, though very good.') Different again, but still social, was the merry evening of 4 March 1669, when Pepys watched the duke and duchess of York and some great ladies 'sitting upon a carpet on the ground, there being no chairs', playing at 'I love my love with an A because he is so and so . . . and some of them, but perticularly the Duchess herself and my Lady Castlemayne, were very witty.' This illustrates not only the company of women but their participation in general merriment.

Pepys notes some practical jokes. On one occasion Sir William Batten and other colleagues of Pepys for a time stole a silver tankard from Sir William Penn. Pepys wrote letters pretending to be the thief who stole it on 28 August 1661, and when they met they all teased him about it, 'which makes very good sport' (1 September 1661). On 2 September Pepys wrote another letter demanding a thirty-shilling ransom, and when he paid up they all got so drunk on the money on 9 September that Sir William was unable to understand what they had done when they confessed the jest, 'which caused us more sport'. On 12 September Pepys heard from Sir William Batten 'that Sir W. Penn doth take our jest of the tankard very ill – which I am sorry for'; but the reader is not surprised. Here the group makes one of its own members, Penn, a temporary outsider.

A bizarre account is given (from the trial proceedings) on 1 July 1663 of Sir Charles Sedley stripping himself naked on the balcony of a cook's shop in Covent Garden, before 1000 people, then engaging in various obscene acts, 'abusing scripture', and preaching an obscene 'Mountebank sermon'. The story is apparently true and Sedley was fined £500. The aggressiveness and subversiveness of jests are notable here.

On 23 October 1668 Sedley and Buckhurst are noted as having run up and down the streets 'with their arses bare', fighting with and being locked up by the watch. The king took their part so that the watch was accused, 'which', says Pepys, 'is a horrid shame'. He concludes that it is a mad world, 'God bless us out of it.' One would not be surprised to have read such stories as exploits of Tyl Eulenspiegel or other jest-book heroes, including the king's favour to the perpetrators and the unjust treatment of the watch, formed of respectable and responsible citizens. The subversiveness here is very ambiguous.

Pepys's *Diary* for 1668 notes many merry gatherings and has other references to comic tales (e.g. 'the old woman of Woolwich' told to his boatman, 2 June 1668). A good many other examples of occasions for laughter, illustrating various types of humour – physical, gross, bawdy, brutal, witty, etc. – can be garnered from the *Diary*, but these examples must suffice. Judging from these and the continued production of jest-books throughout the century and beyond even to the present day there does not seem, from this point of view, to have been less laughter at the end of the century than at the beginning. The Puritan interregnum, 1640–60, may have limited some humour with the licensing act of 1643, but even during that period a few jest-books were published, and from 1660 onwards there is not surprisingly something of an outburst of humorous writing of various kinds.

Burton does justice, as already noted, to the warm group feeling generated by jests. He recognizes the deeper element of hostility as well. His chief discussion of jests is not as a relief for melancholy, as one would expect, but as a cause of melancholy.

There is an important psychological truth here too, which is often rather neglected by the purveyors of jests in all ages, and by students of humour. One group's jest is often another person's pain. Burton's target is 'biting jests' with which he groups sarcasm, calumny, desire to hurt, and so forth, giving several instances from classical history of jesters who paid dearly for mocking, even with justice, their superiors.[13] He wants kindness to be practised, and sees that there is no geniality in jests. This is the traditional view. Pepys notes 'the absurd nature of Englishmen, that cannot forbear laughing and jeering at everything that looks strange' (*Diary*, 27 November 1662).

Nowhere does Burton recommend jests as a cure for melancholy. But after a tolerant account of adultery, he does passingly refer to one jest-book jest. He quotes an old one about a boaster who fails comically to carry out his threat against the stronger man who has cuckolded him.[14] Burton seems to misunderstand the joke, and praises the cuckold's restraint.[15] He regards 'playbooks and jests' as not worth reading.[16] He does in fact quote Ben Jonson (1572–1637) a few times, but he never quotes Shakespeare or other playwrights. Ben Jonson presumably squeezes in because of his neoclassicism. Burton in this respect antici-pates later scholarly disdain but also the collector's interest, for he did own, as will be noted, two jest-books. He also refers very briefly *en passant* to Marcolphus as a figure of repellent ugliness.[17] Marcolphus is a strange figure. In Old English there was a *Dialogue between Salome and Saturn*, a piece of 'wisdom' literature. It is quite serious. Somehow Saturn became Marcolf, and in the medieval period Marcolf is a coarse jester against Solomon's wisdom – an indulgence of subversion, at the least. Burton presumably knew a Latin version (the English was published with the name Marcolf in 1492 from Amsterdam and no later text survives). This intelligent but coarse parody and mockery of conventional wisdom seems not to have been much to Burton's or the general English taste. (However, the equally coarse Howleglas, not mentioned by Burton, took his place.)

Burton's consciousness of the bitterness of jests is at one with the writers of courtesy-books, but may also be due to his great emphasis on reading. Though cheerful in company he was no tavern-haunter, no good fellow, and must have spent most of his time alone to acquire his prodigious reading and write hardly less prodigiously about it.

POPULAR CULTURE INCLUDES GENTLEMEN

Jest-books are always regarded with some ambivalence by the educated, but, as Pepys illustrates, if they were not valued they were certainly read, even to pieces. Pepys was a graduate of Magdalene College, Cambridge, and he made his way among the higher social classes with no sense of class inferiority.

The later examples from the eighteenth century only reflect more clearly the interrelatedness of many kinds of verbal recreation and expression implicit in the jest-books of earlier centuries. Attitudes to the jest-books on the part of educated writers become slowly more explicit and probably more differentiated. While *A Hundred Mery Talys* was the product of a highly educated Humanist circle, being printed and probably compiled by John Rastell, and in 1526 appearing in folio, it was soon issued in the cheaper octavo form, presumably designed for a wider audience. Since such books were cheap and little prized in themselves they easily fell to pieces. Their printing history is impossible to reconstruct in full (but see note 14). The dismissive references to *A Hundred Mery Talys* by Shakespeare's courtiers Benedick and Beatrice (*Much Ado About Nothing*, II, i, 137) may well suggest that that particular jest-book had become old-fashioned. Nevertheless the jokes and witticisms exchanged by Beatrice and Benedick and their friends are redolent of very similar jest-book humour, in that as in other of Shakespeare's plays. Dogberry and Verges, the Watch, are pure (in every sense of the word) jest-book heroes. The jest-books continued to be used. Jests themselves and jest-books were collected by scholars and gentlemen throughout the seventeenth century. Burton's own books, now in the Bodleian Library, include two jest-books. One of them is the 1630 edition of the sixteenth-century jest-book with strong medieval roots which is attributed to the versatile Rabelaisian monk-turned-physician Andrew Boorde, whose very surname means 'jest'. The book is *The Merry Tales of the Mad-Men of Gottam*.[18] Burton's other book is *The Banquet of Jests* (1630), which in later editions became attached to the name of Archie Armstrong. Pepys collected a considerable number of small merry books, classified under *Vulgaria* in his catalogue.[19] Another collector was Bishop Moore (*d.* 1714) of Ely (where there is a splendid monument to him in the cathedral), to whom we owe one of the fragments of an octavo edition of *A Hundred Mery Talys*. Moore had also a substantial collection of chapbooks, and left his library to the Library of the University of Cambridge. The situation is summed up by Thomas Hearne in 1735, who remarks of jest-books that they 'are much bound up by those that to their collections of books of the first class aim at adding little pieces that tend to promote mirth.'[20]

Gentlemen also made their own personal manuscript collections. Pepys's own book of tales, now lost, has already been mentioned. Sir Nicholas Le Strange (1603–56) in the 1630s and 1640s made a collection he called *Merry Passages and Jests*, containing over 600 items, and records the name of the person who told him each story. Many of these are old jokes.[21] One of my predecessors as Master of Emmanuel, the austere bachelor William Sancroft (1617–93), left the college a remarkable learned library of some 6000 volumes, but also compiled a manuscript now in the Bodleian Library containing 105 jests of the traditional kind, though much abbreviated. Some are in Latin. None is gross. One is about hunchbacks.

These gentlemen had not lost their sense of proportion, nor were they yet cultural historians *avant la lettre*, except perhaps for Burton. They seem to have read but not highly valued the jest-books that they themselves sometimes compiled for their own private amusement. Anthony à Wood, historian of Oxford University, refers in his *Athenae Oxoniensis* (1692), I, col. 60, to *The Merry Tales of the Mad-Men of Gottam* (one of Burton's collection). It was printed, he says, in the reign of Henry VIII (*d.* 1547), 'in whose reign and after it was accounted a book full of wit and mirth by scholars and gentlemen. Afterwards, being often printed, it is now sold only on the stalls of ballad-mongers'.[22] It was from such stalls that collectors like Pepys and Moore made their collections. But as Pepys and the others show, the change of taste from that of straightforward enjoyment to that of a collector is not clear-cut. The collector may still enjoy, for its own sake, if perhaps a little dismissively, what he collects out of antiquarian or social interest.

The jests lived between the oral, written and printed word, as is clear from the examples already cited. They were, and are, protean, fluid, variable, like almost all traditional secular literature. Their existence is peculiarly a part of social life – for what community, however solemn, exists without jokes? *A Hundred Mery Talys* includes tales with a probable oral base but derives from a specifically literate circle, the Humanists associated with Sir Thomas More (himself a notable joker). Brother-in-law to More, Rastell had a variety of intellectual and literary interests, wrote an interlude, *The Four Elements* (*c.*1520), and a couple of comedies. His son-in-law was John Heywood (?1497–?1580), to whom one of the supposed Rastell comedies has also been attributed. Heywood wrote an interlude, *The Four Ps* (first printed ?1545), and several comedies which are close to the jest-book vein, as well as collections of proverbs and epigrams which are again within this same area of popular literature, like riddles. Heywood was great-grandfather of John Donne but apparently no relation of Thomas Heywood (?1575–1641), several of whose works, for example, *The Wise Woman of Hogsdon* (*c.*1604, printed 1638), are close to jest-book tradition. In these cases, while it would be perhaps extravagant to talk of the 'influence' of jest-books on better literature, it is clear that jest-books are part of a whole tradition of humour shared with major works.

In the sixteenth century the various literary and social classes mingled together in a quite medieval way, and so did some of their recreational literature. As always, the most interesting example is Shakespeare. He was a grammar-school boy, like Burton, from the English Midlands (in Burton's case Sutton Coldfield). But Burton the scholar differs somewhat from the creative writers, who remain in the popular tradition, both drawing from it and contributing to it, joining in oral, written and printed transmission. 'Popular' does not mean 'low-class'. In Burton we already see the beginning of the withdrawal of the scholar from the general mainstream, and the beginning of a sharper class-division in English literature. A comparison between Burton and Shakespeare in a particular instance is illuminating.

JEST-BOOKS AND ENGLISH LITERATURE

Burton reports one of what he calls 'the harmless jests of great men'.[23] He drew this from a Latin history of Burgundy by Heuterus published in 1584, where the story is told as having actually happened. It is a practical joke on a drunken peasant almost identical with the jest presented by Shakespeare as played on the drunken tinker Christopher Sly in *The Taming of the Shrew*, written about 1592. The same general pattern of the drunken marvellous dream is remembered by Shakespeare when he presents Bottom's dream in *A Midsummer Night's Dream*. The episode has been called by editors 'The Waking Man's Dream', but it is Folktale Type 1531, called by Aarne-Thompson 'The Man thinks he has been in Heaven'.[24] It is also found as an Italian novella.[25] In Heuterus a lord finds a drunken peasant asleep, dresses him finely, wakes him and pretends he is a great lord, treating him to fine entertainments. He then puts him to sleep again, and restores him to his old clothes and former poverty. It is very unlikely that Shakespeare read Heuterus as his source. He may have found the story in some early collection of printed anecdotes such as that in which it appeared in 1630.[26] If he did, the book, like so many others of the kind, has disappeared. But it does not matter. The main point is that the anecdote is not of a historical episode but is an old widespread popular comic folk tale, a traditional tale, perhaps originating like so many others in Asia. It appears in *The Arabian Nights*, not known in Europe until the eighteenth century. These stories wander between oral, written and printed forms. Shakespeare shows himself effortlessly in the general popular tradition, comprising high and low, learned and illiterate.

Seventeenth-century neoclassical learned writers, such as Milton and Jonson, tended to patronize Shakespeare's 'native woodnotes wild'. Burton, by his neglect or ignorance of Shakespeare (in contrast with his knowledge of Ben Jonson), shows himself within the same neoclassical tradition.[27] Shakespeare by contrast is old-fashioned, still medieval, or 'Gothic', in the language of art-historians. His princes, even the melancholic Hamlet, but especially Prince Hal in the two *Henry IV* plays, and his courtiers are, however, strongly in the Humanist tradition of gentleman-like jesting, even though his clowns and many actions are of the general tradition – though indeed there is little difference, as I have argued, between gentry and people in this genuinely popular humour. Shakespeare combines traditional jests with witty repartee, yet he shows a gentleness, humanity and sympathy superior to the heartlessness of much traditional jesting. His sexual jokes are not coarse by modern standards, there is almost no scatology and, while some of his practical jokes may seem a little rough to tender modern hearts, none is savage. He protects the victims of the practical jokes he presents by showing them armoured with an impenetrable self-confidence, a kind of essentialist egoism. 'Simply the thing I am shall make me live', as Parolles says indomitably in *All's Well that Ends Well* (IV, iv, 373–4), which is another of Shakespeare's plays whose basic structure in the popular folkloric tradition is too little understood today. Shakespeare in another such play, *The Merchant of Venice*, started out to present Shylock the Jew as comically villainous, at whom we jeer, though there is no anti-Jewish streak in the English jest-books until the nineteenth century. We all know how Shakespeare's, and the audience's, sympathies shift for a while to the Jew. Such is Shakespeare's humanity. Yet the verbal trick played on Shylock to lead to his well-deserved defeat at the end is of a jest-book kind. Even more so is the elaborate practical joke played on Malvolio in *Twelfth Night*. Malvolio's name, unusually explicit and self-descriptive for Shakespeare, makes clear that he is rightly duped. Yet his admirably undefeated puritanical spirit, paradoxically similar to that of Milton's Satan, and to Shylock's refusal to be abashed, attracts our sympathy and renders the joke at once more comical and less offensive.

While Shakespeare's literary learning, especially in comedy, has been done ample justice in recent years, his place, like that of many other scholars and gentlemen, particularly in the sixteenth century, within a truly popular but socially inclusive tradition of humour, especially as found in the jest-books, has not been sufficiently appreciated.[28] Editors and critics either disregard jest-books or treat them with the disdain of the neoclassical high literary, exclusive culture. In *The Taming of the Shrew* not only the framework of 'The Waking Man's Dream', but the whole story of Petrucchio's taming of his wife, who begins as the very stereotype of the shrewish wife, is of the same kind as jest-book marital humour. *The Merry Wives of Windsor*, as I have shown in detail elsewhere, is pure jest-book stuff. Shakespeare, in a hurry for material for a commissioned comic play, turns to traditional jest-book humour as the readiest material to hand.[29] Nor does he need to find specific sources. In this field alone, it would appear, Shakespeare can and does invent a plot, though of an entirely traditional kind.

The seventeenth century sees some development in specialization in literature. Class distinction begins to make itself felt. This is the first century in which aspects of both literature and social class could be called 'low', and were, often wrongly, identified with each other. We have the growth of neoclassical literary criticism in Britain, but led by continental influences. This is not the place to characterize it, and I have touched on various aspects of it elsewhere.[30] The genre of jest-books flourished and, as already noted, was not highly rated. Yet it was essentially a Humanist genre, for all the traditional base of many of the jests, and Humanism becomes neoclassicism. Moreover, as F. P. Wilson remarks, the appearance of the realism of ordinary life in jest-book anecdotes feeds into the realism that is one of the many streams that join in what becomes the mighty river of the novel, which is essentially a neoclassical genre.[31] An early example of this development, more extended than jest-book anecdotes but with much of their flavour and occasionally similar incidents, is provided by the stories, which are not yet quite novels, of Thomas Deloney (1560–1600).

Two great sixteenth-century continental writers who much influenced the novel in Britain, and who are very often close to jest-book humour, are Rabelais and Cervantes. In Rabelais the trickster element, the uproarious farce, the scatological elements, the comic reversals, which it is fashionable nowadays to call 'carnivalesque', have very obvious connections with jest-books. Rabelais is an infinitely greater version of our own Dr Andrew Boorde. In Spain the anonymous early 'novel', or picaresque romance, *Lazarillo de Tormes*, printed in 1553, is a string of jest-book episodes, one of them independently shared with a sixteenth-century English jest-book *Tales and Quicke Answeres*. *Lazarillo* links the episodes together to make a greater book than any equivalent volume of its kind in English, but there are jest-book 'biographies' in plenty in the second half of the sixteenth and the seventeenth century in England which are of the same kind as *Lazarillo*.[32] From *Lazarillo*, we come to Cervantes' *Don Quixote*, like the works of Rabelais so much more than only a jest-book, but of which it is not too much to claim that the basic inspiration is identical with jest-book humour. In all of them the humour is harsh, unsympathetic, derisive, even brutal. Many of the incidents are close to, if not actually paralleled in, the jest-books. Both Rabelais and Cervantes were translated into English during the seventeenth century. Swift and Sterne were directly influenced by Rabelais while Cervantes's influence is widespread. Then later, fragments of Swift, in particular, were incorporated in the jest-books of the later eighteenth century, an interesting reversal of the flow of borrowing and influence.

Pope and Swift were close in some of their works to the vein of jest-book humour. Matthew Prior retails the indecent and very typical jest-book story of Hans Carvel's ring without using an immodest word.[33] Pope, Prior and Gay also, to go no further, wrote comic verse in 'Chaucerian' style retailing anecdotes of jest-book character.

The eighteenth century saw a blossoming of humorous writing in general. It may be a little different in tone from that before the Civil War, but moderate change is not surprising. It reflects a wider reading public and greater interest in 'decorum' of a kind. It was the eighteenth century in England which set the stamp on Chaucer as primarily a comic and somewhat indecent poet, though this development had been preceded by such as Sir John Mennis (above). Up to then he was regarded as the noble philosophical poet of love.[34] The notion of Chaucer as primarily a bawdily comic writer is fostered even in the present day, and now, as in the eighteenth century, promoted by distorted versions of the *fabliaux*-type tales, for example the *Miller's*, *Reeve's*, *Summoner's* and *Shipman's*, which are basically very similar to jest-book anecdotes. They differ in their elaboration and great poetic skill. There were a number of modernizations of these tales of Chaucer's in the eighteenth century, and it is curious that in several cases a substantial scatological element was added, while the sexual element was a trifle minimized.[35] The eighteenth century did not devote amazing ingenuity to extracting bizarrely obscene meanings from Chaucer's text as do some modern Chaucer critics; it simply wrote the scatology into modernizing visions. The history of 'reception' tells us as much or more about the later readers as it does about the original author.

The recorded practical joke virtually dies out in jest-books by around 1700 (but do practical jokes in actual life ever really die out? Can we not all remember them, more or less cruel to their victim?). Stories of jesters or rogues like Ratsey die out with Archie Armstrong, though names of actors, for example, Joe Miller, continue to be used, and Mrs Pilkington flourishes mid-eighteenth century, though not as a jester herself. Part of the change of manners, fairly superficial at that, may be summed up on the one side by the response of Elizabeth I to 'How Tarlton plaid the drunkard before the Queene', 'Whereat Her Majestie laughed heartily', and similarly, as late as *c.*1631–2 (the presumed date of composition of *L'Allegro*), how the young Puritan Milton portrays 'Laughter holding both his sides'.[36] On the other side we note Goldsmith's line in *The Deserted Village* (1770), 'The loud laugh that spoke the vacant mind' (l. 122). This latter inevitably calls to mind Lord Chesterfield's famous strictures on laughter. His Letter 144 of 9 March O.S. 1748 has a substantial passage condemning laughter (the mob 'call it being merry'). According to Chesterfield, laughter is very illiberal and ill-bred, a disagreeable noise, beside 'the shocking distortion of the face it occasions'. Letter 146 of 19 October O.S. 1748 told Chesterfield's son (to whom the letters were originally written) that 'Loud laughter is the mirth of the mob, who are only pleased with silly things; for true wit or good sense never excited a laugh . . .'[37] There is in fact only a little new in this. Peterson's *Galateo* (1576) noted above praises 'grace' in manners, and condemns 'unseemly laughinges', laughing at one's own jokes, and improper jests.[38]

It is a nice paradox that no sooner had Chesterfield died than a quite traditional jest-book should have appeared in his name. It is paradoxical too that Goldsmith championed laughter and opposed Chesterfield's comments on it.[39] In fact, as the history of jest-books shows, we should not attach too much general importance to Chesterfield's remarks. Chesterfield, though a wit, whose wit according to Dr Johnson consisted mostly in puns (Boswell, 3 April 1773), was also a snob. By contrast Johnson, who once remarked of Chesterfield's letters that 'they teach the morals of a whore and the manners of a dancing master', but who yet prided himself on his refinement, had a heartier zest for laughter.[40] On one occasion at least he outdid the Thames watermen in scurrilous comic insult (Boswell, October 1780), though Boswell remarks that this custom, so close to derisive jest-book humour, was now of the past. Johnson could also laugh heartily. Of 17 May 1775 Boswell comments that they had 'much laughing' and that Johnson's laugh was remarkable, 'a kind of good-humoured growl'. Tom Davies said 'He laughs like a rhinoceros'. For all its hyperbole, Paulson's characterization of Boswell's *Life* as the culmination of the jest-book has its point – not least in seizing on the oral element in jests by giving the social setting of various kinds of repartee.

THE JESTER: CONTINUITY AND CHANGE

A side glance here at the history of the fool and court jester reveals another aspect of this complex topic. The subject is discussed by Enid Welsford, who devotes a valuable chapter to 'The Court Fool in England'. She discusses in particular Archie Armstrong. He represents a long line going back to antiquity of natural or calculated fools, buffoons, jesters and clowns, whose varied functions are surveyed in Welsford's classic study.[41] Such persons enjoyed a varied degree of licence. Some could get away with criticism, appropriately formulated, of their superiors. They could indulge in mockery, rough horseplay and practical jokes, or penetrating witticisms, or appropriate satire. Some rather primitive societies maintained them, along with dwarves and other unfortunates, to be jeered at, to mock and be mocked, long into the eighteenth century. Elizabeth I enjoyed, though she sharply controlled, her jesters. For England, and perhaps for Europe, Shakespeare makes the most remarkable use of the fool/clown/jester, once again establishing himself in the general popular tradition, though with more humanity.

Archie Armstrong was unusually prominent, and also unusually fortunate. In the time of Henry I of England, the minstrel Luke de Barra, who satirized the king in his songs, had by the king's orders his eyes torn out as a punishment and so died.[42] Archie's happier fate illustrates some progress in civilization. His conceit was abounding, he was a malicious trouble-maker, and almost his only resource was foul-mouthed insult. Nevertheless James I and Charles I cherished and rewarded him until he went too far with Archbishop Laud, and was dismissed in 1637. He was a Scotsman who had made a comfortable fortune from a monopoly granted by James I in the manufacture of clay pipes, to the disadvantage of many poor men, it was said. He retired to a country estate in northern England and died as a landed proprietor in 1672.

The collection of jests first published anonymously in 1630, *A Banquet of Jests and Merry Tales*, eventually and wrongly attached to his name, was reprinted and added to nine times throughout the Commonwealth period and later. The jests are old, and one episode told of his life by the anonymous nineteenth-century editor of *A Banquet of Jests* is a variant of the story of Mak the sheep-stealer in the medieval miracle play, the Townley Second Shepherds' Play.[43]

The fall of Archie Armstrong may have indicated a change of manners, for his successor, Muckle John, made no great impression, being no money-grubber. Welsford charts their decline in the latter part of the seventeenth century in both France and England. But Charles II's early companion in debauchery in France, Tom Killigrew (1612–83), became known as court jester. Pepys met him on 24 May 1660 on the ship bringing the king to England, 'with persons of Honour among others, Thom Killigrew (a merry droll, but a gentleman of great esteem with the King): among many merry stories he told one how he writ a letter three or four days ago to the Princess Royall about a Queen Dowager of Judæa and Palestine . . . etc.' This was a gentler and less dangerous practical joke than many.

Pepys records on 13 February 1668 that Killigrew 'hath a fee out of the wardrobe for cap and bells, under the title of the King's foole or Jester, and may with privilege revile or jeere anybody, the greatest person, without offence, by the privilege of his place.' On 8 December 1666 he was reported to have given very forthright and honest advice to the king about his idleness except in lechery. Killigrew's official position was as Groom of the Bedchamber to the king, having been also Master of the Revels, and manager of the Theatre Royal, where he kept a whore for 20 shillings a week for the use, in order to retain their services, of some eight or ten of his actors, as Pepys notes on 24 January 1669. There is a strong connection between fools, folly, jesters, jests and the stage. On 16 February 1669 Pepys heard the story of how Lord Rochester boxed Killigrew's ear for his impudence, but Pepys blames the king for being friends with Rochester, so that for once Killigrew was on the side of the angels.

Thomas Killigrew was also a playwright whose most popular play was a bawdy comedy, *The Parsons' Wedding*, though this was first performed in 1640/1, and printed in 1664 with other plays. In status and activity he was superficially somewhat different from earlier court jesters, being more of a boon companion, a Falstaff, but there is little fundamental difference. Again we note continuity after the Puritan interregnum.

The Killigrew family had some prominence. Thomas Killigrew had one son, Henry, 'young Killigrew' (1637–1705). 'One of the most disreputable of the court sparks', 'A most notorious lyer', according to the king, 'twice banished from the court' (*Diary*, Vol. X, 'Companion', s.n.) for his violent and licentious behaviour, but he was apparently appointed jester to the king (William III of Orange, the Dutchman) in 1694. I find no references to court jesters in England after that. The usual view has been that Archie Armstrong, or Thomas Killigrew, was the last, and it seems clear that this indicates a general truth. The end of the seventeenth century marks the end of an era, the fading though not total disappearance of the medieval world view, but not the end of jest-books, nor of humour, nor of laughter. The objects of humour changed a little, and jests at the unfortunate (except for the Irish) became a little less popular. Hunchbacks were not so frequently and openly mocked.

The fool is part of a world view that characterizes agrarian societies that are hierarchical and aggressive, but also collective, with clear moral bounds that are often infringed, but with hope of repentance, as well as fear of damnation. They lived in a harsh physical world that was also often felt to be the expression of a more real spiritual one. Within that world serious-minded men had usually condemned folly, but it was also possible to ask, with Shakespeare's Fool, 'Who is the wise man, who is the fool?' St Paul could say 'I speak as a fool' (II Corinthians 12: 23), though he could speak sharply to the fool also (I Corinthians 15: 36). A true fool needs a true king, as a true king needs a true fool. The king, like the fool, has the mystery of absoluteness, whatever the shortcomings of the individual. 'The King, the Priest and the Fool all belong to the same régime, all belong essentially to a society shaped by belief in Divine order, human inadequacy, efficacious ritual.'[44] And, Welsford might have added, a society which recognized the inevitability of pain, with a myriad ways of adjusting to it rather than abolishing it. That collective psychological landscape, its 'sense of glory' was dissolving, though like Charles II it was 'an unconscionable long time a-dying', and many parts of English society shared – still share – its fundamental feelings, its mockery of 'everything that looks strange', its hostility to the handicapped and effeminate.

Underlying the change there was the continuing, intrinsic absurdity of being human, and the jest-books continue because in their realistic unambitious way they play on ever-present human absurdities, self-contradictions, fears, satisfactions, and frustrations. We are still subject to those factors, even if our circumstances are different.

The preface to the 1657 print of *A Banquet of Jests* tells the reader that it would have contained more jests had not the licence curbed them. This seems to refer to the Parliamentary Ordinance of 1643, which provoked the writing and (unlicensed) publication of Milton's noble and patriotic protest, a plea for (limited) freedom of expression, *Areopagiticus* (1644). (His protest did not prevent him from acting as Licenser himself in 1651–2.) He rehearses, and the list is easily lengthened, and he condemns, the names of those in the past who had attempted to control free expression. Such control is not the prerogative of any single religious faith or sect or political party. Revolutionaries have always by definition reacted against and condemned repression until they are in power, when they have themselves often enforced repression more rigidly. The Puritans may have condemned May games, not altogether without reason, but they seem not to have objected to jests, except perhaps political ones.[45]

There seems to have been no significant falling-off of publication of jest-books after 1640 except for a diminution in the years 1640–60, during the Commonwealth, though in the 1650s especially there seem to have been a number of satirical or comical accounts of the exploits of rogues. In the 1660s there were satirical attacks on 'the Presbyters', and Pepys records a good and comical sermon against them and Hugh Peters (*Diary*, 3 April 1663). Jest-books are not especially anti-religious, either early or late. In the early period they satirize false or ignorant religion in priests or laity. In the later period there are fewer jokes about ignorant or vain priests, but less humorous blasphemy than earlier. In so far as they are less satirical they may be said merely to accept what is immoral, confused, or ridiculous in life as it is. The jest-books continue unabated until today, though with some change of emphasis.

The Puritans, having begun as a party advocating a special form of church government, rapidly acquired in the popular mind of the late sixteenth and early seventeenth centuries, as represented by the dramatists, a reputation, not entirely ill-deserved, for being killjoys, often hypocritical; Shakespeare's Malvolio in *Twelfth Night*, Ben Jonson's Zeal-of-the-land-busy, in *Bartholomew Fair*, represent the type. There is a brilliant later evocation of it in the person of Mr Thomas Trumbull, the apparently pious smuggler in Scott's *Redgauntlet* (1824), Chapter XIII, who reads, bound in sable, as it might be a psalter, what but 'Merry thoughts for Merry Men; or Mother Midnight's Miscellany for the small hours'. The young hero of the novel is disgusted by the book's profligacy; the educated but debauched sailor Nanty Ewart calls it 'sculduddry which after all, does nobody any harm'; they summarize a debate for and against obscenity in literature which continues to the present day. At the same time Scott marks a cultural change in the latter part of the eighteenth century and the first quarter of the nineteenth. He reflects the beginning of the rejection of public indecency in the nineteenth century, which later in the century created a dark underside apparently not at all funny and far more radical than the rather schoolboyish indecencies of the 'merry books'.

The subject-matter of the old jests fades with social circumstance, but the basic nature of jests shifts only slightly. At no period does there seem to be less laughter. And as a last irony medical science, no less, now authorizes us to agree with the Bible, and with Andrew Boorde, that laughter really is good for us.[46]

108   *Derek Brewer*

NOTES

I wish to record my gratitude to Peter Burke, FBA, of Emmanuel College, and Julian Roberts of the Bodleian Library for their helpful suggestions, and the editors for their valuable editorial advice.

1 *Medieval Comic Tales*, 2nd edn rev. and enlarged, ed. with introduction by Derek Brewer (Cambridge, 1996).
2 C. Davies, *Ethnic Humor Around the World: a comparative analysis* (Bloomington, 1990).
3 Poggio Bracciolini, *Liber facetiarum*, in *Opera omnia*, con una premessa di R. Fubini = *Monumenta politica et philosophica rariora*, Series II, 4–7 (4 vols, Turin, 1964–9), Vol. I: *Facetiae*, trans. B. J. Hurword (New York and London, 1968).
4 T. Hoby, *The Courtyer*, trans. from *Il Cortegiano* by B. Castiglione, 1528 (London, 1561).
5 N. W., *The Refin'd Courtier, or A Correction of Several Indecencies Crept into Civil Conversation* (London, 1663; further edns appeared in 1679 and 1686, and other versions in 1673, 1698, 1701, 1703, 1774).
6 *John della Casa Galateo . . . A treatise of the Manners and Behaviours . . . done into English by Robert Peterson* (London, 1576; facsimile in *The English Experience Series*, No. 120, Amsterdam, 1969).
7 Thomas Wilson, *The Art of Rhetorique*, ed. G. H. Mair (Oxford, 1909).
8 V. F. Stern, *Gabriel Harvey: his life, marginalia and library* (Oxford, 1979), pp. 199, 238–9.
9 The Philosopher's game was a peculiarly complicated form of chess; 'small trunks' was bagatelle, 'questions and commands' was a parlour game using often apparently sexual questions and commands, as appears from *Joe Miller's Jests, or The Wits Vade-Mecum*, ed. Elijah Jenkins [pseudonym for John Mottley] (London, 1739), no. 168, pp. 46–7. This book was hugely popular: three editions in the first year, five more in the next six years; editions in 1742, 1745, 1832, 1845, and 1848. See, with useful introduction, John Wardroper, *Jest upon Jest: a selection from the jestbooks and collections of merry tales published from the reign of Richard III to George III* (London, 1970).
10 Robert Burton, *The Anatomie of Melancholy* (London, 1651), Pt 2, Sec. 2, Member 4.
11 R. Latham and W. Matthews, *The Diary of Samuel Pepys* (11 vols, London, 1970–83).
12 Sir John Mennis, *Musarum deliciae or The Muses Recreation* (London, 1655).
13 Burton, *The Anatomie*, Pt 1, Sec. 2, Member 4, Subsec. 4.
14 It appears, for example, in *A C Mery Talys. Revised Short Title Catalogue*, 1976, Vol. 2, lists 23663, J. Rastell, 1526?, 4 fragments fol. (British Library); 23664, Anr ed. – Göttingen; 23664.5, Anr ed. 8', R. Copland?, 1548. 4 leaves in binding of another book, Univ. Lib. Camb. Peterborough E.4.28. See also *Shakespeare's Jest Book, A Hundred Mery Talys*, ed. with introduction and notes by H. Oesterley (London, 1866); *Shakespeare Jest-*

Books, ed. with introduction and notes by W. Carew Hazlitt (3 vols, London, 1864).

15 Burton, *The Anatomie*, Pt 3, Sec. 3, Member 4, Subsec. 1.

16 Ibid., Pt 2, Sec. 2, Member 4.

17 Ibid., Pt 3, Sec. 2, Member 5, Subsec. 3, cf. *The Dialogue or Communing between the Wise King Solomon and Marcolphus* (Antwerp, 1492; facsimile ed. E. G. Duff with introduction, London, 1892); M. Jones, 'Marcolf the Trickster in late medieval art and literature: or the mystery of the bum in the oven', in G. Bennett (ed.), *Spoken in Jest* (Sheffield, 1991), pp. 139–74.

18 S. J. Kahrl, 'The medieval origins of the sixteenth-century English jest-books', *Studies of the Renaissance*, 13 (1966), pp. 166–83; Wardroper, *Jest upon Jest*, p. 152.

19 See *Catalogue of the Pepys Library at Magdalene College Cambridge*, ed. R. Latham and others (7 vols, Cambridge, 1975–93), q.v.; K. H. Göller, 'Die Bedeutung der Vulgaria-Sammlung von Samuel Pepys', *Archiv*, 216 (1979), pp. 109–16; M. Spufford, *Small Books and Pleasant Histories: popular fiction and its readership in seventeenth century England* (London and Cambridge, 1981).

20 Wardroper, *Jest upon Jest*, p. 199.

21 Sir Nicholas Le Strange, *Merry Passages and Jests: a manuscript jestbook of Sir Nicholas Le Strange* (1603–55), ed. and with an introduction by H. F. Lippincott = *Salzburg Studies in English Literature, Elizabethan and Renaissance Studies*, 29 (Salzburg, 1974); Wardroper, *Jest upon Jest*, p. 11.

22 Wardroper, *Jest upon Jest*, p. 199.

23 Burton, *The Anatomie*, Pt 2, Sec. 2, Member 4.

24 A. Aarne, rev. S. Thompson, *The Types of the Folktale* (2nd edn, Helsinki, 1973).

25 D. P. Rotunda, *Motif Index of the Italian Novella* (Bloomington, 1942), Type J2322.

26 Shakespeare, *The Taming of the Shrew*, ed. H. J. Oliver (Oxford, 1982), p. 35.

27 D. Brewer, 'Some observations on the development of literalism and verbal criticism', *Poetica*, 2 (1974), pp. 71–95.

28 L. G. Salingar, *Shakespeare and the Traditions of Comedy* (Cambridge, 1974); W. Riehle, *Shakespeare, Plautus and the Humanist Tradition* (Cambridge, 1990).

29 D. Brewer, 'Elizabethan merry tales and The Merry Wives of Windsor: Shakespeare and popular literature', in T. Takamiya and R. Beadle (eds), *Chaucer to Shakespeare: essays in honour of Shinsuke Ando* (Cambridge, 1992), pp. 145–61.

30 Brewer, 'Some observations'.

31 F. P. Wilson, 'The English jestbooks of the sixteenth and early seventeenth centuries', in H. Gardner (ed.), *Shakespearian and Other Studies* (Oxford, 1969), pp. 285–324.

32 Brewer, 'Elizabethan merry tales', pp. 150–1.

33 M. Prior, *Poems on Several Occasions* (London, 1721), p. 97.

34 D. Brewer (ed.), *Chaucer: the critical heritage* (2 vols, London, 1978).

35 As can be seen in the texts reprinted in B. Bowden (ed.), *Eighteenth Century Modernizations from the Canterbury Tales* (Cambridge, 1991).

36 Brewer, 'Elizabethan merry tales', p. 153.

37 C. Strachey (ed.), *The Letters of the Earl of Chesterfield to his Son* (London, 1901).

38 Peterson, *Galateo*, p. 120.

39 Oliver Goldsmith, 'A comparison between laughing and sentimental comedy', *The Westminster Magazine or The Pantheon of Taste*, no. 1 (1773), pp. 4–6, repr. in A. Friedman (ed.), *Collected Works of Oliver Goldsmith* (Oxford, 1966), vol. 3, pp. 209–13.

40 Quoted by M. Drabble (ed.), *The Oxford Companion to English Literature* (5th edn, Oxford 1985), s.v. Chesterfield.

41 E. Welsford, *The Fool: his social and literary history* (London, 1935). See also P. V. A. Williams (ed.), *The Fool and the Trickster: studies in honour of Enid Welsford* (Cambridge, 1979); a penetrating theoretical analysis, A. C. Zijderveld, *Reality in a Looking Glass: rationality through an analysis of traditional folly* (London, 1982).

42 J. Strutt, *The Sports and Pastimes of the People of England*, ed. William Hone (London, 1838), p. 197.

43 *A Banquet of Jests and Merry Tales by Archie Armstrong*, ed. with introduction anonymously (London, 1889).

44 Welsford, *The Fool*, p. 195.

45 Welsford, *The Fool*, p. 154.

46 L. Hodgkinson, *Smile Therapy* (London, 1991).

ADDITIONAL BIBLIOGRAPHY

The basic works are those by Schulz, Wilson (note 31), Wardroper (note 9) and Zall. A good list of jest-books up to 1660 is found in G. Watson (ed.), *The New Cambridge Bibliography of English Literature* (2 vols, Cambridge, 1974, 1971), Vol. I; there is no such section in Vol. II.

Aernout van Overbeke, *Anecdota sive historiae jocosae*, ed. R. Dekker and H. Roodenburg (Amsterdam, 1991).

Petrus Alphonsi, *The 'Disciplina Clericalis' of Petrus Alphonsi*, trans. and ed. Eberhard Hermes, Eng. trans. P. R. Quarrie (Berkeley, 1977).

John Ashton, *Chap-Books of the Eighteenth Century* (London, 1882).

James Boswell, *The Life of Dr Johnson*, 1791, ed. E. Malone, 6th edn (London: Everyman Library, 1933).

J. A. Burison (ed.), *Storytellers: folktales and legends from the south* (Athens and London, 1989), pp. 99–100, 234, 239.

Peter Burke, *Popular Culture in Early Modern Europe* (London, 1978).

W. Caxton, *The Fables of Alfonce and Poge* (London, 1484).

The Cobbler of Canterbury: Frederic Ouvry's edition of 1862, ed. with introduction by H. Neville Davies (Cambridge and Totowa, NJ, 1976).

Robert Hays Cunningham, *Amusing Prose Chap-Books Chiefly of Last Century* (London, 1889).

The Douce Collection in the Bodleian Library, Oxford.

M. Douglas, *Purity and Danger* (London, 1966).

——, *Implicit Meanings* (London, 1975), pp. 90–114 ('Jokes').

D. F. Foxon, *Libertine Literature in England, 1669–1745* (London, repr. with revisions from *The Book Collector* [1963], 1964).

The Harding Collection, Bodleian Library. Section E 10 has a number of jest-books.

Howleglas (?1528), ed. P. M. Zall, *A Hundred Mery Tales etc.*, pp. 151–237: see Zall, 1963.

Sir John Mennis, *Musarum Deliciae or the Muses Recreation* by Sir J. M. and Ja. S. [James Smith] (London, 1655).

——, *Recreation for ingenious head-pieces . . . of epigrams, 700. Epitaphs, 200. Fancies a number. Fantastickes, abundance . . .* (London, 1654).

R. Paulson, *Popular and Polite Art in the Age of Hogarth and Fielding* (Notre Dame, 1979).

A. Pope, *Imitations of English Poets I, Chaucer*, in *The Poems*, Vol. VI, Minor Poems, ed. N. Ault and John Butt, Twickenham Edition (London, 1954).

Paul Radin, *The Trickster: a study in American Indian mythology* [with commentaries by Karl Kerényi and C. G. Jung] (London, 1956).

The Pastyme of People and *A New Boke of Purgatory by J. Rastell with a facsimile of The Pastyme*, ed. Albert J. Geritz, *The Renaissance Imagination*, Vol. 14 (New York and London, 1985).

Ratseis Ghost, or The Second Part of his Madde Pranks and Robberies, 1605. Reproduced in facsimile from the copy preserved in the John Rylands Library, Manchester, with an introduction by H. B. Charlton MA (Manchester, 1932).

W. Redfern, *Puns* (Oxford, 1984).

E. Schulz, 'Die englischen Schwankbücher bis herab zu *Dobson's drie bobs* (1607)' = *Palaestra*, 117 (Berlin, 1912).

Solomon and Saturn: the poetical dialogues of Solomon and Saturn, ed. R. J. Menner = *Modern Lang. Assoc. of America*, Monograph Ser. 13 (New York, 1941, Old English texts).

R. P. Stearns, *The Strenuous Puritan: Hugh Peter, 1598–1660* (Urbana, 1954).

J. R. Tanner, *Constitutional Documents of the Reign of James I, 1603–1625* (Cambridge, 1930).

A. Taylor, *The Literary Riddle before 1600* (Berkeley and Los Angeles, 1948).

K. Thomas, 'The place of laughter in Tudor and Stuart England', *Times Literary Supplement*, 21 January 1977, 77–81.

J. H. Würster, *The Cobler of Canterburie* (Diss., Regensburg, 1983).

P. M. Zall (ed.), *A Hundred Merry Tales and Other English Jestbooks of the Fifteenth and Sixteenth Centuries* (Lincoln, 1963).

——, *A Nest of Ninnies and Other English Jestbooks of the Seventeenth Century*, selected and ed. P. M. Zall (Lincoln, 1970).

8

To Converse Agreeably: Civility and the Telling of Jokes in Seventeenth-Century Holland

Herman Roodenburg

Once meeting a distant acquaintance, the lawyer Aernout van Overbeke (1632–74) was branded by this man as a *halve geck*. Van Overbeke, so we read, took the compliment 'but passably well'. Still, we know that he was fond of jokes and, moreover, himself a gifted joker. The facts are clear. First, this respectable Hague citizen left behind an extensive manuscript containing some 2500 jokes and anecdotes. Second, in another such manuscript he emerges as a good-humoured fellow, ever ready to crack a joke or give a smart retort. Third, in several anecdotes that circulated after his death he emerges as an indefatigable joker – and a glutton at that. In short, there is ample reason for devoting an entire chapter to this 'half-wit' alone.

JOKES AND THE HISTORIAN

What we have, then, is a large collection of humorous material. We also know the identity of its author, we know that he loved telling jokes and we have a good idea to whom, where and when he told them. Such complete data are far from common for the seventeenth century. Indeed, they distinguish his collection, the *Anecdota sive historiae jocosae*, from all the jest-books published in that century.[1]

For a long time jokes and folk narratives, such as fairy tales, legends and proverbs, were studied from a 'historical-geographical' perspective: the classical approach employed by scholars, mostly within a single genre, to position the content of their material within a long chain of variants of the same 'type' or 'motif'. In this way they finally hoped to arrive at an overall picture of the tales' origins, their dissemination routes, and the changes they underwent in the process. But such a synthesis remained elusive. As has been noted, most of the studies undertaken from this perspective resulted in narrow paths followed over long stretches of time. To put it somewhat critically, what they amount to are long lists of isolated instances with the people, the actual storytellers and their culture, largely left out.[2]

Another approach was developed in the 1960s. Instead of making cross-sections over time, the method adopted was that proposed by some early critics of the historical-geographical school, in particular Johannes Bolte and Albert Wesselski, to work breadthwise. While the search for types and motifs was certainly maintained, students now tended to focus on a single period and study the available source-material in breadth. This proved to be a fruitful approach, especially with regard to the early modern period. Many of these more recent studies not only contain valuable contextual information, they also elucidate the complex relationship between texts and their re-creation in oral tradition, and have contributed substantially to our understanding of the cultural and social structures of the period.[3]

Even so, questions of the sort posed by students of contemporary storytelling – removing the focus of interest from the texts to the competence of the performers and their particular performances – proved hard to answer. Confining ourselves to forms of humour, we still face the most simple questions. For example, who were the jokers and their audience, what were the occasions for telling and listening to jokes, and what level of communicative competence was needed by the performers? In other words: who told what jokes to whom and how?[4] Sadly, although most students of early modern humour would be receptive to such questions, their sources are not. The many jest-books published in seventeenth-century Holland are a case in point. They provide virtually no data on authorship or audience, making it almost impossible to point out the social circles in which this humour must have thrived, let alone that we might recover how these narratives found their way into orality, into daily conversation. Let us cast a brief glance at this literature.

JOKES IN PRINT

In 1653 it was observed that 'nowadays the best books remain on hand . . . ; the printers, so they say, earn the most on Till Eulenspiegels.'[5] While the author just cited exaggerated in an effort to promote his own jest-book, he nonetheless had a point. Jest-books were in great demand, both in the Northern and the Southern Netherlands. For the seventeenth century alone, a rather conservative survey lists 25 jest-books that went through more than seventy printings and editions. Before 1600 the production of all this wit was confined to the Southern Netherlands or, more precisely, to the city of Antwerp. After 1600 jest-books were also published in cities such as Amsterdam and Leiden, though it was only in the second half of the seventeenth century that the genre attained its greatest popularity. Most of the books were published after 1650.[6]

Who were the authors or compilers of such books? We have some information on the (mostly French) originals on which several of the books were based,[7] but data about Dutch authorship are scarce. Two of the jest-books published in the republic, the *Klugtige tyd-verdryver* (1653) and the *Schimpigen Bolwormspiegel* (1671), were probably compiled by the Utrecht printer and bookseller Simon de Vries (1628–1708).[8] Another one, *Het leven en bedrijf van Clément Marot* (1653), may have been compiled by the actor, printer and bookseller Jan Zoet (1615–74), though the evidence for this is slight.[9] And the same is true of *De geest van Jan Tamboer* (1656); the question of its authorship remains unsolved.[10] Most of the compilers, then, are unknown to us, which would probably have suited them! As the jest-book was the lowest of literary genres, there was little honour to be gained from such work. The notion that the compilers desired anonymity to circumvent allegations of piracy is less likely, for plagiarism did not plague this sort of literature.[11]

Clearly such practices constitute a serious setback to any search for types and motifs. While claiming novelty and originality, the authors of Dutch jest-books borrowed right and left. Many of the jokes were even taken from jest-books and other collections of humour published in France, England and Germany, just as Dutch collections offered material for jest-books printed elsewhere in Europe, especially in Germany, as was established by the late ethnologist Elfriede Moser-Rath.[12] In other words, many of the narratives included in the jest-books were not bound to local or national culture, and circulated all over Europe in a lively international exchange.[13] Moreover, the majority of the Dutch compilers made use of material ranging from novellas, exempla, facetiae and mock prognostications to riddles, epigrams and apophthegms. That such variety was appreciated by the readers may be gathered from the subtitles of jest-books, where it was recommended time and again. Although paradoxical, it was precisely this variety, this variety of genres, which ultimately defined the genre of the jest-book.[14]

What about the readers, the audience for the jest-books? Sadly, data on ownership are rare as well. In the sixteenth century, intellectuals were probably the primary 'consumers' of jest-books – for example, both the nobleman Philips of Marnix, lord of St Aldegonde and secretary to William of Orange, and the Leiden burgomaster Jan Dircksz van Brouckhoven owned a German edition of Johannes Pauli's *Schimpff und Ernst*.[15] In the first years of the seventeenth century, the genre was still popular among intellectuals, including a minister from the city of Flushing, Daniel de Dieu (*d*. 1607), who owned a copy of Georg Wickram's *Rollwagenbüchlein*, originally published in 1555. Similarly the great philologist Joseph Scaliger, known for his lively table-talks, the *Scaligeriana*, owned a copy of the *Nederlantsche wechcorter*, a jest-book published just before his death in 1609.[16]

A fascinating source in this respect is a diary kept by the Frisian gentleman-farmer Dirck Jansz. Around 1605 he compiled a list of the more than forty books he owned, including such well-known chapbooks as *Tijl Uilenspiegel*, *Reinaert de Vos*, the *Fabelen van Aesopus* and *Floris ende Blancefloer*. But the farmer also mentioned an anonymous jest-book, from which he may have copied the jests entered elsewhere into his diary 'to instruct and edify his children'.[17] By then the genre may have started to trickle down the social ladder, though we have no information to confirm or even qualify the process. In later years, when drawing up inventories, notaries simply omitted the smallest and cheapest books, or listed them under such irritating headings as 'several books'.[18]

The jest-books may have sold well, but to the historian or ethnologist trying to establish who cracked what jokes to whom and how, they remain annoyingly reticent. One of the very few clues they provide – often found in the frontispiece – is that they were meant for the *kluchtlievende jonckheyt*, for 'jest-loving youth'. Of course, a jest-book intended for 'jest-loving old people' would not have been in great demand. Still, it is an indication to keep in mind.

JOKES IN MANUSCRIPT

Fortunately, texts other than jest-books and similar products of the printing press have also come down to us. For example, there are some seventeenth-century manuscripts which may have been meant for publication, though it is far more likely that they were merely intended for private use, similar to Dirck Jansz's practice of copying jests for the edification of his children. What makes these manuscripts so fascinating is that they do inform us, if poorly, on questions relating to the joker, his performance, his audience and the social occasions for his joking.

For seventeenth-century England, for example, there is a manuscript by the nobleman Nicholas Le Strange (1603–55), in which he recorded a great number of jokes and anecdotes taken from his daily environment, including some pretty bawdy ones from his own mother, Dame Alice.[19] For seventeenth-century Holland we know of three such manuscripts, though one of these, written by Constantijn Huygens the Younger (1628–97), private secretary to prince William III, was lost in the nineteenth century.[20] A second document, written by Samuel van

Huls the Elder (1596–1688), a city father from The Hague, still exists,[21] as does van Overbeke's *Anecdota sive historiae jocosae.*

Remarkably, both authors lived in The Hague, and both recorded a host of dialogues in which they cheerfully put their family, friends and acquaintances on stage. Whether these men and women actually did or said the things imputed to them is another matter. Literary historians and ethnologists have often warned against such pitfalls, and their sensible advice, especially on considering the presence of first-person narrators as autobiographical evidence, should be taken very seriously indeed.[22] As was the case with the jest-books, no matter how lively and genuine the events may seem to us, much of the humour may have been borrowed from other sources.

However, one of the most interesting aspects of the two manuscripts is their surprising degree of correspondence. We encounter Van Overbeke cracking a joke or making a smart retort in some 37 anecdotes recorded by Van Huls. Some of them even figure in both manuscripts, including a dialogue between the two men and recorded in both versions with a first-person narrator. In other words, just as this anecdote was derived from an actual conversation, so other anecdotes in which Van Huls or Van Overbeke put themselves on stage may have been more truthful, more autobiographical, than we have been trained to think. Without the information provided by Van Huls, the most we might have said of the jokes in Van Overbeke's *Anecdota* is that they have been the kind that circulated among the upper circles in The Hague. Having his testimony at hand, showing that Van Overbeke was both a chronicler and a performer of jokes, we have every reason to focus on the narrator and his performance and, of course, on matters of context: on his audience and the occasions for telling jokes.

WOLFING WARFLES

Interestingly, the life and times of Van Overbeke, who recorded so many jokes and anecdotes related to others, are partially obscured by anecdotes on the man himself. As Mariët Westermann describes in Chapter 9, something similar happened to Van Overbeke's contemporary Jan Steen. Contending that Steen's life was as farcical as his art, his earliest biographer, Arnold Houbraken, noted many a juicy anecdote on the painter's life. As has been argued, this was a well-known rhetorical convention, which the unknown editor of Van Overbeke's *Geestige werken* may have been following when he included a couple of such anecdotes in his preface to the book. Published four years after Van Overbeke's death, the book contains a selection of his comic verse (including some 'parlour games' performed at the weddings of friends and acquaintances) and even a few instances of his serious verse. However, to whet the reader's appetite the editor added a couple of anecdotes presenting the poet both as a joker and an incredible glutton. Visiting the Rotterdam fair (so one of the stories goes), Van Overbeke gave three *schellingen* to a waffle-baker for the privilege of eating as many waffles as he could. To the baker's bewilderment Van Overbeke wolfed down 84 waffles, one after the other, before finally losing his appetite.[23]

Of course, such voracity would fit any 'half-wit'. Much later, at the end of the nineteenth century, the poet was even dismissed as a *vrolijke lichtmis*, a 'lighthearted libertine', whose work by and large could not pass muster.[24] Clearly his critic, the literary historian J. A. Worp, did not appreciate Van Overbeke's sense of humour (he was also familiar with the *Anecdota*) and therefore sought to trivialize his poetry as the product of an irresponsible, though good-natured, layabout. In this way the nineteenth century's lofty image of the Golden Age, exalted as an era of frank and honest men, was deftly left intact. But was our lawyer really such a 'libertine', was he really a 'half-wit'? Is it not significant, as Van Huls noted, that Van Overbeke took the compliment 'but passably well'? Let us briefly review the few facts we do know about the man.[25]

BEATING THE ENGLISH

Born in Leiden in 1632, Aernout van Overbeke was the fourth of five children. His parents, Matthijs van Overbeke and Agatha Scholiers, both members of the Lutheran Church, were born in Flanders and moved to Holland after a long stay in Germany whither their families had fled. Both their religious affiliation and their Flemish origin constituted serious obstacles for obtaining high positions in the Dutch Republic and consequently for entering the urban regent class. However, Aernout's father was a wealthy man, in a position to acquire one of the finest houses in the city of Leiden as well as a country estate. Moreover, he was respected by intellectuals and artists alike. For some years, a group of scholars, including Gerardus Vossius and Caspar Barlaeus, assembled at the Van Overbekes to discuss theological and other issues; Barlaeus was even a friend of the family. Matthijs was also known for his patronage of the arts and his impressive collection of paintings, books and coins. He owned works by Rubens, Bailly, Van Coninxloo, Porcellis, Van de Velde, Savery and Vrancx, all of them highly valued painters at the time. The poet Constantijn Huygens Sr., who in his capacity as secretary to the House of Orange took an active and well-informed interest in the art of painting, wrote approvingly of

'Overbeke who makes such good use of his wealth'. He probably saw the collection in 1630. A few years later, Van Overbeke even purchased 14 precious volumes from the library of a Humanist, most of them incunabula of important Greek texts printed in Venice around 1500 and illuminated by Albrecht Dürer. In the same period, however, he encountered increasing financial difficulties. The ensuing lawsuits, partly with his own brothers, may have precipitated his death in 1638 of *morbo melancholico*, as a family chronicle informs us, leaving his widow and children with serious debts. Even the paintings had to be sold.

Financial woes were also part of Aernout's life: probably even more so as he could hardly handle money, another point in common with Jan Steen. After studying law at Leiden University, he received his doctoral degree in 1655 at the age of 22 and began practising law some years later in The Hague. There he made the many friends and acquaintances that figure so markedly in the *Anecdota*, meeting them at all sorts of occasions: at dinners, at the fives court, at a musical evening (Van Overbeke played the violin) or taking a walk in the surroundings of The Hague. It was in these circles, just below the top layer of regents and nobility and consisting mostly of lawyers, notaries, doctors, merchants and high-ranking officials, that Van Overbeke told his jokes and anecdotes.

Judging from the long trail of bonds in the city's notarial archives, the young lawyer lived in style, as was probably normal for the sons of well-off families. From one of the first-person narratives, related both in the *Anecdota* and the Van Huls manuscript, we learn how Van Overbeke once complained about the bills of his tailor to Christiaan Huygens, the famous mathematician and son of Constantijn Huygens Sr. 'Just pay the goat', Huygens replied, 'for they make it so that their children will be noblemen and we arrange it so that ours will be tailors. They may then avenge us.' Still, Huygens could afford such a way of life. Van Overbeke, who was less well-off and an easy spender at that, could not.[26]

In 1663 things got worse. Van Overbeke composed a new Lutheran version of the psalms, in itself a notable achievement for a 'lighthearted libertine', and had it published at an Amsterdam printing house. Unfortunately, the version was not approved by the Lutheran ministry, and the unlucky poet was forced to buy back the entire edition. Many years later he cheerfully ridiculed himself as looking 'as amiable, as if I had been peddling Lutheran psalms all day', but at the time it must have been a bitter pill to swallow.[27] In 1668 he even had to leave for Batavia, the present city of Jakarta. This was a well-known way out for individuals whose creditors were clamouring at the door, but Van Overbeke obtained a good position. At the intercession of Cornelis

Backer, a director of the East India Company, he was appointed to the *Raad van Justitie*, the highest court of justice in the Dutch East Indies. His stay was brief: he sailed back to Holland in 1672 and, as the highest-ranking official on board, he even served as admiral of the fleet. What is more, our 'half-wit' returned home a national hero. Just off the Frisian coast, the richly laden fleet – consisting of 15 ships – was attacked by the English. Van Overbeke triumphed and was brought to safety by the republic's most famous admiral, Michiel de Ruyter. The directors of the company awarded the hero a chain of gold, or 500 guilders net, despite their dismay at the fact that, while waiting for De Ruyter's convoy in the harbour of Delfzijl, Van Overbeke had already spent the outrageous sum of 2000 guilders entertaining the Princess of East-Frisia. He died two years later, in 1674, at the relatively young age of 41.[28]

THE 'ANECDOTA'

At first sight, the *Anecdota*, containing exactly 2440 jokes and anecdotes, appears to be little different to contemporary jest-books. Though there is little overlap, most of the jokes in the jest-books as well as the *Anecdota* refer to famous persons (from Socrates to Henry IV), to sex and marriage, and to the comedy of rank and manners. These key themes were followed by jokes on fools and lunatics and the jokes performed by 'fools', such as the Frenchmen Clément Marot and Simon Goulart, or the German Claus Narr.[29] Within these themes, both the jest-books and the *Anecdota* teem with such age-worn characters as the hen-pecked husband, the nagging and insatiable woman, and the simple-minded peasant. That the roles were often reversed, for example the slovenly peasant or the lusty woman getting the better of their 'betters', was even funnier. Yet the humour was double-edged and did little to alter the well-established social and sexual hierarchies.

Other aspects of the *Anecdota* were quite different. First, Van Overbeke recorded the shortest version possible of his material, an aspect to which I will return. Secondly, the jokes on sex are certainly more numerous and less purified. And thirdly, many jokes, including a number of the sexually straightforward ones, feature people from Van Overbeke's own environment. This bawdy humour included jokes that were no longer appreciated openly in the second half of the seventeenth century and others that, to my knowledge, never appeared in print. For example, Van Overbeke's joke on 'Spanish and Turkish manners' had already been recounted by Poggio, Marot and also Béroalde de Verville, in his *Le moyen de parvenir* of 1610. It is about a man who put a child's shoe on his 'nose' because his wife had her private parts shaved and, as he explains to her, he does not like to go barefoot through the stubble. Jokes such as these were no longer printed in Van Overbeke's time. In the 1660s some new compilations, among them the *Eerlycke uren* (1661) and *De droeve, ende blyde wereldt* (1671), condemned older and well-known jest-books, such as the *St Niklaesgift* (1644), *De gaven van de milde St Marten* (1654), *Het leven en bedrijf van Clément Marot* (1656) and *De geest van Jan Tamboer* (1656). Yet even in these controversial collections, criticized for their crudity and bawdiness, the sexual jokes were already less explicit, and none had to do with sodomy.

This was different in Van Overbeke's *Anecdota*, where he records a joke about a man and his son-in-law who were forced to share a bed in a tavern, a situation that was not uncommon even among the seventeenth-century elite. What followed was less common. In the middle of the night, so we read, 'the son mounts the father in great fury and starts to caress him vigorously'. The man wakes up and then cries out: 'Damn! What are you up to? To be rid of that I gave you my daughter' (207). Although a rather innocent joke, it must have been considered too risqué, since it was partly crossed out.[30]

Of course, this joke was not about specific individuals; however, other bawdy jokes were. For example, one is about the Amsterdam sheriff Aernout Hooft, who when he was a student joined a boating party near Leiden. Seeing a young woman looking out at the river from a garden house, he got ready to urinate at the stern of the ship. Then, like a real macho, he displayed his penis and shouted: 'You don't have this.' But the woman, simultaneously questioning Hooft's manliness and confirming the lustiness and insatiability of all women, retorted: 'I've seen better' (537).[31] There are dozens of such jokes. It was very much a man's world.

However, this robust humour is just one side of the *Anecdota*. Another feature is the hundreds of jokes in English, French, German, Latin and even in Spanish and Italian. To master all these languages was exceptional, even among the elite. Moreover, many of the Latin jokes contain tacit references to the Vulgate or to classical authors, including Horace, Virgil and Lucan. Without identifying these references one would easily miss the clue. And, if the *Anecdota* derive much of their inspiration from the popular tradition of the jest-books, they equally rely on the more learned tradition of the apophthegms.[32]

Among the material Van Overbeke consulted – directly or indirectly – are the apophthegms of Alphonso, king of Aragon and first king of Naples and Sicily. This important collection titled *De dictis et factis Alphonsi regis Arragonum*, written by Antonio degli Beccadello, surnamed Panormita, and published in 1455, was followed by an enlarged edition produced by Aeneas Sylvius. The Amsterdam edition of this work, which came out in 1646, was probably the source for a number of the apophthegms included in the *Anecdota*.[33] More important is Erasmus' collection of apophthegms and those of Francis Bacon and Julius Wilhelm Zincgref.[34] The latter's book, enlarged by Johann Leonhard Weidner, was also published in Amsterdam in 1653;[35] in his book of epigrams, the *Korenbloemen*, which was first published in 1658, Huygens Sr. borrowed extensively from Zincgref.[36] One of the books which Van Overbeke may have pillaged directly is a collection of apophthegms published in 1609 by the Leiden professor of law Gerardus Tuning (1566–1610).[37]

Van Overbeke thus recorded a remarkable range of humour. Although dominated by typical jest-book humour with its classical themes and characters, the collection also included a kind of sexual humour not found in the jest-books of his time, and a subtle and sophisticated sort of humour appealing to an educated and even erudite audience. Obviously he could appreciate both.

PERFORMING THE 'ANECDOTA'

Having all of this rich material at hand, how did Van Overbeke proceed? How did he formulate his jokes? Surprisingly, in most cases he noted them in the shortest version possible, almost in telegraphic style and without any embellishment whatsoever. We could see this as another indication that our twentieth-century jokes, with their sharp phrasing, are far older than students of the genre have assumed.[38] However, it is more likely that Van Overbeke simply preferred brevity in order to have the essentials, the crucial dialogues, readily at hand. The material, we might say, is still in dead-colour, waiting for the narrator to come alive.

Without the embellishments, even without such basic elements as dialect features, it is hard to say anything about the techniques used by Van Overbeke. Still, in some cases he seems to have keyed the narratives to their actual performance, to the telling of the joke. For example, one of his strategies was to enliven the material by allotting the actual author or compiler of the joke a role in his own plot. Witness the following 'anecdote' about the publisher and poet Adriaen van Steyn. 'Lately, when Steyn left home very early', we read, 'Jochum the baker blew hard on his horn. "What's going on?", he asked, "is somebody in distress, is there cause for alarm?" "No [replied somebody], it's the baker, it's a sign that his bread is hot." "Oh, if the bread is hot, no wonder he is blowing."' This story, in Van Overbeke's typical telegraphic style, sounds quite genuine (bakers actually blew a horn when the bread was ready), but van Steyn was also the author of a collection of epigrams called *De puntige poëet in de wapenen*, in which we find exactly the same pun, staging just a first-person narrator.[39]

Another victim of Van Overbeke's techniques was Huygens Sr. The poet figures in 16 of Van Overbeke's anecdotes, suggesting that the two were well acquainted. However, all of them go back to Huygens' epigrammatic poetry, to his *Korenbloemen*, which we know Van Overbeke took with him on his voyage to Batavia. In one of the stories Huygens, feeling neglected by his 'mistress', complains that she has stolen his heart and that she ought to give it back to him. Should she refuse, he will tell everybody that she is a 'double-hearted' madam (112). But reading the epigram we encounter only 'Moy Anne' (lovely Anne) and a first-person narrator. Interestingly, Huygens had culled the pun from an English jest-book called *A Banquet of Jests and Merry Tales*, published in 1630.[40] Of course, by introducing the authors or compilers of his material into the material itself Van Overbeke could substantially enhance the dramatic and semantic impact of his performances. More than just memorizing the narratives to reproduce them word by word, he subjected his written sources to a process of appropriation, of 'productive re-creation'.

Among his other techniques was to locate an epigram in his own circles, to stage individuals from his own environment as the leading characters in his material. Witness the following, rather unfunny pun (no. 633 in the collection) on the Dutch word for parsley, *pieterselie*.[41] The point is that Pieter is a man's first name and Celij a woman's first name (popular in the seventeenth century). Three of Van Overbeke's acquaintances have gathered in a country inn. When one of the friends (called *Pieter*) is ravishing the maid (called *Celij*) on the staircase, the innkeeper's wife, being busy in the kitchen, calls for *pieterselie*. The punch line is delivered by one of the other friends, who cheerfully calls back: 'You will find them on the staircase.' Again, initially the story rings true, but the very same pun had already been exploited by Huygens in 1658. In fact, it is often the flatness of the jokes (most of them work better as epigrams) that betrays their provenance.

These examples suggest that much of the published humorous material – jest-books, collections of epigrams, apophthegms – received a 'second life' when it was selected and appropriated by a capable joker, a proficient storyteller. That Van Overbeke was such a performer may be gathered from the pet name *Nout*, sounding almost like a stage name, bestowed upon him by both Van Huls and the unknown editor of his *Geestige werken*. What, however, were the social and cultural contexts for his performances? What meaning did they derive from these contexts and what did they contribute to them? In other words, what prompted Van Overbeke, Van Huls and Huygens Jr. to start their manuscripts in the first place?

To Converse Agreeably

In the last ten years or so, the manifold relations between writing and speaking, between texts and performance, have not only engaged students of language but have started to intrigue cultural historians as well.[42] Roger Chartier, for example, has argued that many early modern European texts 'had the precise function of disappearing as discourse'. As instances of such texts he refers to the well-known *artes moriendi* and the numerous conduct and civility books.[43] Another, less-known, example consists of the writings on the 'art of conversation'. As Peter Burke has observed, they constituted an important subgroup of the manuals on civility.[44]

Of course, jest-books, collections of apophthegms and similar compilations of humour are a very different sort of text. To put them in the same category of 'discourse' as used by Chartier would be valid only for the older jest-books with their miscellany of *ernst en luim* ('solemnity and mirth'). The art of joking, however, was an integral part of the art of conversation, of the communicative competence demanded from the upper classes.[45] Well-bred people were supposed to know not only how to engage in conversation but also how to be witty and amusing, a virtue of which champions of urbanity were well aware. To quote the most famous of them all: 'A collection of anecdotes and maxims is for a man of the world the greatest treasure, when he knows how to scatter the first at the appropriate places into conversation and to remember the last at felicitous moments.'[46]

Although Goethe wrote this at the beginning of the nineteenth century, he merely endorsed what had been emphasized in all the manuals on civility from before his time: mastery of witty and amusing conversation was a hallmark of civility. This ideal was most aptly expressed in Castiglione's *The Courtier* published in 1528. Relying on ancient rhetoric, in particular on the writings of Cicero and Quintilian, the author presented his readers with an amusing colloquy on such conversation along with an appealing selection of jokes and anecdotes, thereby combining the art of joking with the humorous material itself.[47]

Later treatises on civility, certainly those written in the seventeenth century, largely omitted humour, though they continued to emphasize that knowing how to be witty was a desirable social grace, integral to what was often called 'the science of conversing agreeably'. For example, in a Dutch manual entitled the *Hoofsche Welleventheid*, published in 1677, it was observed that the art of joking will make one 'be esteemed with all gentle people, and agreeable in every company'. And it once more repeated Cicero's distinctions between sociable and aggressive joking and his condemnation of indecent language and too much mimicry.[48]

In the jest-books such objectives were generally only intimated, but in the more aspiring compilations, such as Zincgref's *Apophthegmata* or Jan de Brune the Younger's *Iok en ernst* published in 1644, the message corresponded exactly to the codes expressed in the civility books.[49] In his introduction, De Brune extolls the proper use of witty sayings (*aardige hofredenen*). As he explains, they help 'to make oneself agreeable in company and they kindle friendship.' He also cautions his readers that the sayings should be inserted cleverly (*met abelheit*) into the conversation.[50] That jest-books were nevertheless exploited in conversation emerges from an important eighteenth-century manual on civility, the *Groot ceremonie-boeck der beschaafde zeeden*, which even explains how *not* to be funny. The reader is introduced to a less cultured gentleman, 'who always carries a dictionary of witty sayings in his pocket, which he studies day after day, and he never turns up in any company without having learnt twenty-five sayings by heart and then he is on the watch for a chance to conjure one of them up.'[51] The gentleman's error was not so much that he had recourse to the book, but that he used it far too conspicuously, having memorized the quips word by word – a perfect example of communicative *in*competence. Again, as the manual indicated, the joking should appear spontaneous and effortless, as if one's *bons mots* originated at the spur of the moment and flowed naturally from the conversation.[52] Even Quintilian's discussion of laughter was enlisted for such sociability. A Dutch translation of his ideas, taken from the *Institutio oratoria*, recommended itself as 'serving to skilfully invent witticisms, and to be able to jest, quip and joke properly.'[53]

In fact, diaries and other such documents may have served equally as 'toolboxes' for the art of conversing. For example, the diaries of Huygens Jr. are riddled with anecdotes, gossip and related bits of information to be used at the proper moment in the proper company. Possession of such social ammunition could not but impress one's company. A comparable phenomenon was the 'table-talks', among them the famous *Scaligeriana*,[54] or the collections of curiosities culled from all over the world and published by polyhistors at home and abroad.[55] How such literature functioned, how knowledge of it was wielded in conversation, is well illustrated by Huygens' diaries. In 1694 he recorded a Dutch diplomat's attempt to impress his company by revealing all sorts of intrigues at the court of Versailles. But Huygens knew better. Much of what the man related was taken from *Les galanteries des rois de France*, a book Huygens had recently lent him.[56]

Returning to our argument, it may well be that the three manuscripts, or at least parts of them – omitting, for example, the coarsest sexual jokes – had been destined for publication. Yet it is significant that none ever reached that stage and that the anecdotes, both in the Van

Overbeke and the Van Huls manuscripts, were recorded without any embellishments, in an almost telegraphic style. Moreover, publishing one's own collection had its hazards, as Gerardus Tuning was to discover. Once his apophthegms had been printed, so De Brune tells us in his *Wetsteen der vernuften*, the professor was no longer considered quite the agreeable company he had been previously: his witticisms had become public property and he failed to devise new ones.[57]

Perhaps the manuscripts were not meant entirely for personal use. They may have circulated among family or friends, just as Van Overbeke's *Geestige en vermaeckelijcke reys-beschryving*, a comic letter on his voyage to Batavia, was read by a few friends before being sent by them to a publisher in 1671.[58] Such readership might also explain why in his manuscript Van Huls addresses himself 'to the readers' and to those who 'hear or read' his 'pranks'. Indeed, Van Huls may have seen Van Overbeke's collection, perhaps after the latter's death in 1674, as some of the overlapping anecdotes are remarkably similar in their composition and choice of words. Still, the primary purpose of the Van Overbeke, the Van Huls and the Huygens manuscripts must have been to serve the art of their authors' conversation.

MELANCHOLIA, INTELLECTUALS AND COMIC CULTURE

Of course, the jest-books were also read in silence. One easily imagines a solitary reader, spending the hours before bedtime ('these long evenings', as one jest-book put it) with such literature. The contents, so other jest-books tell us, could help 'to shorten time', 'to shorten the way' or to 'dispel melancholia', but boredom could be fought in more sociable ways as well. The books probably served both functions. For example, the *Vermeerderde Nederlandtschen wech-corter* of 1609 advertised itself as 'very pleasant to read, and convenient to tell when travelling to shorten the way, instead of gossip on waggons and in barges.'[59] Even melancholia could be dispelled by conversation and good company. In 1637 Huygens Sr. wrote a letter to his friend Barlaeus urging him to fight his melancholia: 'The main thing is that matter be found for laughing and joking', and for that he should seek out the company of friends. To cheer the patient, Huygens enclosed some witty verse, though Barlaeus answered that he was not in the mood now 'to joke about anything' and that he had 'almost scrubbed urbanity from the ranks of the virtues'.[60]

Obviously, the sociability suggested by the jest-books and the manuscripts was not exactly the art of conversation propounded in the French treatises which were written at the end of the seventeenth century and soon reached the Dutch Republic.[61] Van Overbeke belonged to an earlier period, in which Jan Steen, among others, could still exploit his earthy jokes, a period in which popular farces had not yet been cleaned up in the wake of French classicism. These changes may be viewed as part of a more general rise of self-control and discipline, a major theme in the work of Norbert Elias, but still leaves us in the dark about the generation of Steen and Van Overbeke. Were they so much less refined or is our view of them too much influenced by the disparaging comments of the generation after them?

In 1682 the Dutch printer of Rabelais excused the author's language by pointing out 'that he, being from another century, is all too straightforward and the opposite of a dissembler' (*dat hy van een ander eeuw, al te openhartig en een averechts huigchelaar is*).[62] Even more enlightening is what La Bruyère wrote in 1690. He simply found Rabelais 'incomprehensible' and 'inexcusable for the muck he spread in his writing'. But he also called the *Gargantua and Pantagruel* an 'enigma' and a 'chimera': 'It's a monstrous assembly of fine and ingenious observation and foul corruption. Where it is bad, it goes well beyond the worst, it's the kind of thing that charms the rabble; where it is good, it is even exquisite and excellent, it can be a dish fit for the most delicate.'[63]

As has been argued, in imitating the chapbooks of his time and also adopting the 'low corporeality' associated with the popular classes, Rabelais strove to undermine the hierarchy of literary genres. It is this playfulness – the mixing of all genres and styles, the celebration of deception and ambiguity – which would continue well into the seventeenth century: Jan Steen was a master of the art. However, in the last decades of the century, when social and aesthetic standards started to converge, such latitude was no longer allowed. Under the impact of the latest codes of civility the elite was no longer to enjoy low comedy and all its corporeality. Henceforth the farces performed in the Amsterdam theatre, which had appealed to the elite through their focus on deceit and ambiguity, could survive only in the cleansed versions produced by the protagonists of French classicism. Nor were genres to be mixed up or lofty subjects to be treated in any other than in the lofty style. Rembrandt's biblical women portrayed with the welts of their stockings on their knees were now condemned, just as painters in general were no longer supposed to take a plump housemaid and paint her like a damsel or to take an awkward schoolboy and dress him as a gentleman. As Gerard de Lairesse explained, a history painter (which was the highest to which one could aspire) should take his models solely from the well-behaved and elegant upper class.[64] What seems to have happened, then, is that the elite started to withdraw, not so much from popular culture as from its own playful exploitation of this culture or from what it saw as such.

It is also this mixing of genre and styles which helps us to understand, as Westermann explains, why Steen portrayed himself in his own paintings, more or less in the same way as the jest-book narrators in *De geest van Jan Tamboer*. Interestingly, Van Overbeke did a similar thing. In an unpublished letter about his journey to the East Indies, he put himself on stage in the following words:

> Mostly in the morning I delight in talking to the sailors about their former villainies and how they got to the East Indies or, as the highflown discourses are a bit too profound, I turn to my jokes and pleasantries, about which they split their sides with laughter. When I tire of jesting, I get my violin and sit down before the mainmast and play and sing like mad. There is no shortage of tobacco and arrack, which fits the music pretty well. Indeed, it is a poor village that does not hold kermis (village-fair) once or twice a week.[65]

The smoking and drinking, the singing and the music, the joking and the allusion to kermis: this scene could have been painted by Jan Steen, including the portrayal of himself.[66]

NOTES

1 Aernout van Overbeke, *Anecdota sive historiae jocosae: een zeventiende-eeuwse verzameling moppen en anekdotes*, ed. Rudolf Dekker, Herman Roodenburg and Harm Jan van Rees (Amsterdam, 1991) [= Publikaties van het P. J. Meertens-Instituut, vol. 16]. Parts of the present chapter are based on the introduction to this edition; the original manuscript is in the Royal Library in The Hague. It was only in the nineteenth century that the collection received its present title. For these and other technical aspects, see the Introduction.

2 For an interesting critique, in which the author uses examples taken from her own research on humour, see Elfriede Moser-Rath, 'Gedanken zur historischen Erzählforschung: Kurt Ranke zum 65. Geburtstag', *Zeitschrift für Volkskunde*, 69 (1973), pp. 61–81, esp. 64–6. For an English translation, see idem, 'Some thoughts on historical narrative research (On the occasion of Kurt Ranke's sixty-fifth birthday)', in *German Volkskunde: a decade of theoretical confrontation, debate and reorientation (1967–1977)*, ed. and trans. James R. Dow and Hannjost Lixfeld (Bloomington, 1986), pp. 212–28, esp. 214–15.

3 For a few pioneering studies, see Elfriede Moser-Rath, *Predigtmärlein der Barockzeit: Exempel, Sage, Schwank und Fabel in geistlichen Quellen des oberdeutschen Raumes* (Berlin, 1964); Rudolf Schenda, *Volk ohne Buch: Studien zur Sozialgeschichte der populären Lesestoffe, 1770–1910* (Frankfurt am Main, 1970); Wolfgang Brückner, *Volkserzählung und Reforma-*

tion: ein Handbuch zur Tradierung und Funktion volkstümlicher Erzählstoffe im Protestantismus (Berlin, 1972). On German jestbooks, see especially Elfriede Moser-Rath, *'Lustige Gesellschaft': Schwank und Witz des 17. und 18. Jahrhunderts in kultur- und sozialgeschichtlichem Kontext* (Stuttgart, 1984).

4 For the theoretical background to such questions, see the classical texts by Dell Hymes, 'Introduction: toward ethnographies of communication', in D. Hymes and J. J. Gumperz (eds), *The Ethnography of Communication* = special issue of *American Anthropologist*, 66 (1964), pt 2, pp. 1–34; and Joshua Fishman, 'Who speaks what language to whom and when', *La linguistique*, 2 (1965), pp. 67–88. The study of performance has been strongly influenced by Hymes's formulations. See also his *Foundations in Sociolinguistics: an ethnographic approach* (Philadelphia, 1974). For a helpful introduction to the ideas of Hymes and other scholars who contributed to the development of the field, see Muriel Saville-Troike, *The Ethnography of Communication: an introduction* (2nd edn, Oxford, 1982); for a useful introduction to the study of folklore and performance, see Richard Bauman (ed.), *Folklore, Cultural Performances and Popular Entertainments: a communications-centered handbook* (New York and Oxford, 1992).

5 'De beste boecken blyven leggen/Nu onverkoft, soo is 't gestelt/De druckers winnen, soo zy segge/Aen Uylespiegels 't meeste gelt.' Quoted from *De verloore uren van Mons. D. Ouville, Anders het 1e Deel van Milde St. Marten* (Rotterdam, 1653), introduction.

6 P. P. Schmidt, *Zeventiende-eeuwse kluchtboeken uit de Nederlanden: een descriptieve bibliografie* (Utrecht, 1986). It should be pointed out that the author employs rather strict criteria. He does not include the small jestbooks printed as addenda to the popular almanacs, nor the so-called *Schwank*-biographies: pseudo-biographies based on jests. For some criticisms, see A. P. J. Plak and P. J. Verkruijsse, 'Een bibliografie van zeventiende-eeuwse kluchtboeken', *Dokumentaal*, 16 (1987), pp. 37–40; and J. Koopmans and P. Verhuyck, *Een kijk op anecdotencollecties in de zeventiende eeuw* (Amsterdam and Atlanta, 1991), pp. 47ff.

7 See Schmidt, *Kluchtboeken, passim.*

8 Arianne Baggerman, *Een drukkend gewicht. Leven en werk van de zeventiende-eeuwse veelschrijver Simon de Vries* (Amsterdam and Atlanta, 1993), pp. 270, 276–7.

9 Koopmans and Verhuyck, *Een kijk op anecdotencollecties*, pp. 143ff.

10 Schmidt's attribution to the printer and bookseller Jan van Duisberg is not convincing, as his argument is based partly on Van Duisberg's authorship of the *Schimpigen Bolwormspiegel*, which has also been ascribed to Simon de Vries. See Schmidt, *Kluchtboeken*, p. 42.

11 Cf. Elfriede Moser-Rath, '"Burger-Lust": unterhaltende Gebrauchsliteratur im 17. Jahrhundert', in *Literatur und Volk im 17. Jahrhundert: Probleme populärer Kultur in Deutschland*, ed. W. Brückner, P. Blickle and D. Breuer (2 vols, Wiesbaden, 1985), vol. 2, pp. 881–98, esp. 882–3.

12 Elfriede Moser-Rath, 'Clément Marot als Schwankfigur', *Fabula*, 20 (1979), pp. 137–50; idem, *'Lustige Gesellschaft'*, pp. 23–6.

13 For such an argument relating to Dutch jest-books, see Koopmans and Verhuyck, *Een kijk op anecdotencollecties*, pp. 33–45.

14 Moser-Rath, *'Lustige Gesellschaft'*, pp. 8ff; cf. Koopmans and Verhuyck, *Een kijk op anecdotencollecties*, pp. 47–61.

15 Among the other books owned by Marnix were editions of Erasmus' *Apophthegmata*, Bebel's *Facetiae*, Boccaccio's *Decamerone*, and *La vida de Lazarillo de Tormes*.

16 *Een nyeuwe cluchtboeck*, ed. H. Pleij, J. van Grinsven, D. Schouten and F. van Thijn (Muiderberg, 1983), p. 43; B. van Selm, *Een menighte treffelijcke boecken: Nederlandse boekhandelscatalogi in het begin van de zeventiende eeuw* (Utrecht, 1987), pp. 121–2.

17 *Het aantekeningenboek van Dirck Jansz*, ed. P. Gerbenzon (Hilversum, 1993), pp. 126–8, 157ff.

18 Cf. Margaret Spufford, *Small Books and Pleasant Histories: popular fiction and its readership in XVIIth century England* (Athens, GA, 1981), p. 48.

19 *'Merry Passages and Jeasts': a manuscript jest book of Sir Nicholas Le Strange (1603–1655)*, ed. H. P. Lippincott (Salzburg, 1974); see also D. Brewer, Chapter 7 of this volume.

20 The manuscript was still extant in 1869. See D. Veegens, 'Aanteekeningen van Constantijn Huygens jr.', *De Nederlandsche Spectator*, 10 April 1869.

21 The manuscript, called *Eenighe Duijtsche, Latijnsche, Engelsche ende Fransche Annotatien, bestaende in verscheijde leeringen, vragen ende antwoorden, raedsels, gedenckweerdige spreucken, oock kluchten, spreeckwoorden, bedriegerijen, botticheit, en fijne en grove storien*, is in the Hague Municipal Archive.

22 Interestingly, Koopmans and Verhuyck, *Een kijk op anecdotencollecties*, pp. 93–4, suggest that Nicholas Le Strange, in staging people from his own surroundings, may have adhered to the literary tradition of frame tales and fictive narrators. In her informative review of our edition of Van Overbeke, Tineke ter Meer, 'Overbeke en Huygens', *Nieuwe Taalgids*, 86 (1993), pp. 315–60, also adopts a rather 'orthodox' point of view.

23 'Vermaeckelijcke voor-reden', in Aernout van Overbeke, *De geestige werken van Aernout van Overbeke, in syn leven advocaet voor den E. Hove van Hollant* (Amsterdam, 1678). The book was a great success. An enlarged second and third edition under the name of *De rijm-wercken van wijlen den heer en meester Aernout van Overbeke* appeared in the same year. A tenth and last edition was published in 1719.

24 J. A. Worp, 'Mr. Aernout van Overbeke', *Oud-Holland*, 1 (1883), p. 266.

25 For a more extensive biography (and for some technical aspects of the manuscript), see the introduction to Van Overbeke, *Anecdota*, xi–xvii.

26 Van Overbeke, *Anecdota*, no. 509: 'Ick klaegde eens aen Christiaen Huijgens, dat mijn Fransche kraemer François de la Smagge mijn rekening uyttermaeten goddeloos hadde overgegeven. "t Is geen noodt", seyde hij, "betaelt den bock, sij schryven doch en maecken het daernae dat haer kinders jonckers, ende wij klaeren het soo, dat de onse noodtsakelijck Fransche kraemers sullen moeten worden. Die mogen dan voor ons revenge nemen en bruyen haer kinders sooals sij oude duyvels ons gedaen hebben."'

27 Van Overbeke, *De rijm-wercken*, 16.

28 For further details, see the introduction to Van Overbeke, *Anecdota*, xii–xvii.

29 Claus Narr and Marot received their own collections, but other jest-books related their stories as well. See *Het leven en bedrijf van Klaas Nar* (Amsterdam, 1652); *Het leven en bedrijf van Clément Marot* (Amsterdam, 1655). For the original Goulard collection, see Étienne Tabourot des Accords, *Les apophthègmes ou contes facétieux du sieur Goulard* (Paris, 1614); some 88 jests from this book reappeared in *De gaven van de milde St Marten* (Amsterdam, 1654); on the Marot collection and its problems, see Moser-Rath, 'Clément Marot'; Koopmans and Verhuyck, *Een kijk op anecdotencollecties*.

30 'Seker edelman reysde met zijn schoonvader nae den bisschop van Spier. Onderwegen wierden sij, door gebreck van beddens, gedwongen om saemen te slaepen. (Crossed out, but still legible:) Des nachts springt de soon de vader op 't lijf in groote furie en begint hem braef te caresseren. R. "Wat donders begint gij? Om daervan vrij te zijn heb ik u mijn dochter gegeven."'

31 'Aernout Hooft, noch student sijnde, was tot Leyerdorp met eenige mackers tot Haesje's vrolijck geweest. In 't wederkeeren sagh hij een juffer uyt een speelhuysjen op den Rhijn uytkijcken. Hij stapte buyten het tentje van de schuyt en ontrent het roer staende, trock hij van leer om sijn water te maecken en hem een slinger gevende riep hij tot de juffer: "Dat en hebt gij niet." Sij, sonder haer om te keeren, antwoorde: "Ick hebb'er wel beter gesien."'

32 An apophthegm may be defined as a memorable saying (*sententia*) occasioned by a concrete and often very ordinary situation (*occasio*). Such statements could be serious and instructive, but they could also include a witty observation, a *bon mot* or a quick repartee. On the genre, see T. Verweyen, *Apophthegma und Scherzrede: die Geschichte einer einfachen Gattungsform und ihrer Entfaltung im 17. Jahrhundert* (Bad Homburg, 1970); see also Bremmer, this volume, Chapter 1, note 39.

33 Antonio degli Beccadelli, *Speculum boni principis, sive vita Alphonsi regis Aragoniae* (Amsterdam, 1646).

34 Erasmus compiled a large collection of apophthegms from antiquity (his *Apophthegmatum opus*, first published in 1531) but was interested only in the sayings of famous persons. In the early seventeenth century the genre acquired a different, more 'democratic' outlook. For example, in his *Apophthegms, Old and New* of 1625, Francis Bacon included the sayings of ordinary people, as did Julius Wilhelm Zincgref in his influential collection of German apophthegms, the *Teutsche Apophthegmata*, first published under a different title (*Der Teutschen scharfsinnige kluge Spruch*) in 1626. The 'democratic' character of the two collections was enhanced by the fact that both authors preferred their native language.

35 Julius Wilhelm Zincgref, *Teutsche Apophthegmata* (Amsterdam, 1653); in 1669 a Dutch edition was published: Julius Wilhelm Zincgreven and Johannes Leonard Weidner, *Duytsche Apophthegmata of kloeck-uyt gesprokene wysheydt bestaende in sin-pit-pant- en spot-redenen* (Amsterdam, 1669).

36 Tineke ter Meer, *Snel en dicht: een studie over de epigrammen van Constantijn Huygens* (Amsterdam 1991), pp. 60–71.

37 *Apophthegmata Graeca, Latina, Italica, Hispanica collecta à Geraerdo Tuningio Leidensi* (Leiden, 1609).

38 German ethnologists have assumed that the modern *Witz* arose only at the end of the eighteenth century. See Hermann Bausinger, *Formen der 'Volkspoesie'* (2nd and enlarged edn, Berlin, 1980), p. 148; Lutz Röhrich, *Der Witz. Figuren, Formen, Funktionen* (Stuttgart, 1977), p. 8. But see Moser-Rath, '"Bürger-Lust"', pp. 881–2.

39 Van Overbeke, *Anecdota*, no. 7; Adriaen van Steyn, *De puntige poëet in de wapenen of de nieuwe stapel punt-dichten* (Rotterdam, 1669), pp. 41–2; for other examples, see the *Anecdota*, no. 482, and Steyn, p. 99; for a slightly different procedure: *Anecdota*, no. 239, and Steyn, p. 91.

40 These and other borrowings were pointed out by Ter Meer, 'Overbeke en Huygens', pp. 315–60; see also her *Snel en dicht*, pp. 57–60. Among the other foreign sources used in the *Korenbloemen* we find the Spanish *Floresta Española* and also the collections of Lycosthenes, Erasmus and Bacon.

41 Nowadays it is spelled *peterselie*.

42 See Peter Burke, 'The social history of language', in idem, *The Art of Conversation* (Cambridge, 1993), pp. 1–34, esp. 7ff.

43 Roger Chartier, *The Cultural Uses of Print in Early Modern France* (Princeton, 1987), p. 6.

44 Peter Burke, 'The art of conversation in early modern Europe', in idem, *The Art of Conversation*, pp. 89–122, here p. 90.

45 As summarized by Muriel Saville-Troike, *The Ethnography of Communication*, p. 21: 'Communicative competence involves knowing not only the language code, but also what to say to whom, and how to say it appropriately in any given situation.' The notion was originally developed by Hymes as a corrective to Chomsky's definition of linguistic competence.

46 'Eine Sammlung von Anekdoten und Maximen ist für den Weltmann der größte Schatz, wenn er die ersten an schicklichen Orten in's Gespräch einzustreuen, der letzten im treffenden Falle sich zu erinnern weiß.' Quoted by Verweyen, *Apophthegma und Scherzrede*, p. 14.

47 For the Dutch edition, see Baldassare Castiglione, *De volmaeckte hovelinck* (Amsterdam, 1662), pp. 209ff. On the reception of Castiglione, see Peter Burke, *The Fortunes of the Courtier: the European reception of Castiglione's 'Courtier'* (Cambridge, 1995). For Cicero and Quintilian see also the Introduction by Bremmer and Roodenburg, and Graf, Chapter 2 of this volume.

48 *Nieuwe verhandeling van de hoofsche wellevendheit, en loffelyke welgemanierdheit, in Den Haag aan het Hof, en voorts door geheel Nederland, by treffelijke lieden gebruikelijk* (Amsterdam, 1677). The text of this little treatise is based largely on Antoine de Courtin's *Nouveau traité de la civilité qui se pratique en France* (Amsterdam, 1671). It is noteworthy that the pages on jokes and joking were not taken from De Courtin. For a helpful overview of decorum and the telling of jokes, mainly in the eighteenth century, see Jacqueline de Man, 'De etiquette van het schertsen:

opvattingen over de lach in Nederlandse etiquetteboeken en spectators uit de achttiende eeuw', *De Achttiende Eeuw*, 25 (1993), pp. 93–136.

49 For example, in the preface to the Zincgref edition of 1669 we read: 'Hier zijn sin-spreucken, aerdige hofredenen, gedenckwaerdige spotteryen, deftige gelijckenissen, en geestige antwoorden, die alle dagen, in maeltyden, byeenkomsten, en geselschappen voorvallen, en nodigh zijn.' See Zincgreven and Weidner, *Duytsche apophthegmata*, preface.

50 See the author's introduction: 'Nu, het is een zaak van onverwrikkelike vastigheit, dat, onder andere dingen, die, in den ommegang, aangenaam maken, en vrientschap verwekken, het bescheiden gebruik van aardige hofredenen, geen van de geringste plaatsen toekomt. Zy dienen om, tussen allerlei voorvallende praat, met abelheit ingeschoten te worden: oock kan menze zomtijts op hun zelven verhalen.' The title of the book is worth quoting in full: Jan de Brune de Jonge, *Iok en ernst: Dat is, Allerlei deftige hofredenen, quinkslagen, boerteryen, raadsels, spreuken, vragen, antwoorden, gelikenissen; En al wat dien gelijkvormigh met de naam van Apophthegmata verstaan wort. Gevonden en gesproken van prinssen, mevrouwen, geletterden, en andere staatspersoonen, die alt'samen dicht by onze tijden geleeft hebben, of oock tegenwoordig leven* (Amsterdam, 1644).

51 It is no coincidence that the story refers to a pocket book. Jest-books and other humorous collections were very often editions in octavo, as people preferred to have them ready at hand. On such aspects, see the introduction by Herman Pleij to *Een nyeuwe clucht boeck*, pp. 44–5; and Moser-Rath, *'Lustige Gesellschaft'*, pp. 50–2.

52 C. v[an] L[aar], *Het groot ceremonie-boeck der beschaafde zeeden, welleevendheid, ceremonieel, en welvoegende hoffelykheden onderwyzende hoe ieder een ... zich behoorden te gedraagen, om zich zelven in deeze wereld, bemind en gelukkig te maaken* (Amsterdam, [1735]), p. 191: 'die altoos een woordenboekje van geestige zeggingen in zyn zak draagt, daar hy dagelyks in studeert, en hy verschynt nooit in het gezelschap, dan nadat hy'er vyf-en-twintig van buiten heeft geleerd, en dan staat hy op wacht om gelegenheid te hebben van'er een uit de mouw te schudden.' See also p. 192: 'Men moet ook niet ... eenige van buiten geleerde en bestudeerde zeggingen gebruiken als men vermakelyk boerten wil, maar zy moeten op het zelve oogenblik geformeerd en ter wereld gebragt worden, zy moeten uit het onderhoud natuurlyker wyze voortspruiten, want zonder het zelve zyn ze laf, droog, en zonder leeven.' On this important manual, see Herman Roodenburg, ' "The Hand of Friendship": shaking hands and other gestures in the Dutch Republic', in J. Bremmer and H. Roodenburg (eds), *A Cultural History of Gesture from Antiquity to the Present Day* (Cambridge, 1991), pp. 156ff.

53 *Van het lachen uyt M. Fabius Quintilianus van den Spreekkunstelijke Onderwijsing. Dienende om bequaemlijk quinkslagen uyt te vinden, en wel te passe te konnen schertsen, jokken, en boerten* (Leiden, 1677).

54 See, for example, *Scaligeriana, sive excerpta ex ore Jos. Scaliger* (2nd edn, Leiden, 1668); *Scaligeriana, Thuana, Perroniana, Pithoeana, et Colomesiana: ou remarques historiques, critiques, morales, et litteraires de*

Jos. Scaliger, J. Aug. de Thou, Le Cardinal du Perron, Fr. Pithou, et P. Colomies (Amsterdam, 1740). As its compiler put it, 'Disciples des ces grands hommes, qui leur entendoient dire tous les jours des particularitez d'Histoire, de Critique, et de Literature curieuses et interessantes, les escrivoient pour leur propre usage.' Scaliger also figures in the *Anecdota* (no. 1855).

55 A famous Dutch polyhistor was the Utrecht publisher Simon de Vries. See Baggerman, *Een drukkend gewicht*, esp. pp. 209–10, where she mentions the significance of such books for conversation and sociability. Cf. Wilhelm Kühlmann, 'Lektüre für den Bürger: Eigenart und Vermittlungsfunktion der polyhistorischen Reihenwerke Martin Zeillers (1589–1661)', in Brückner et al., *Literatur und Volk*, vol. 2, pp. 917–34, esp. 926–7.

56 *Journaal van Constantijn Huygens jr.* (2 vols, Utrecht, 1877), vol. 2, p. 379 (7 July 1694).

57 Jan de Brune de Jonge, *Wetsteen der vernuften*, 'Aen den lezer'.

58 One of these friends may have been the Delft regent Pieter Teding van Berkhout, who noted in his diary: 'Je . . . passoys le reste de la soyrée a la lecture d'un grand Journal que Naut Overbeeck avoit envoyé des Indes.' The diary is in the Royal Library in The Hague. I owe this information to Jan van der Waals.

59 *Vermeerderde Nederlandtschen wech-corter inhoudende verscheyden nieuwe vertellingen, van warachtighe geschiedenissen, seer genoechelijck om lesen, ende dienstelijck om in plaetse van achterclap op waghens ende in schuyten, oockck op weghen te vertellen tot vercortinghe des weghs* (Amsterdam, 1629).

60 Both letters cited in Blok, pp. 58–61, where the Latin originals are also quoted.

61 Most popular was Morvan de Bellegarde's *Modèles de conversations pour les personnes polies* (Paris, 1697), which knew five editions between 1699 and 1709 alone.

62 *Alle de geestige werken van Mr. François Rabelais* (Amsterdam, 1682), 'Den Hollandze drukker tot de leesers'.

63 Quoted in Mikhail Bakhtin, *L'oeuvre de François Rabelais et la culture populaire au Moyen Age et sous la Renaissance* (Paris, 1970), p. 114. I have followed the translation of this passage in Jerry Palmer, *Taking Humour Seriously* (London and New York, 1994), pp. 122–3; La Bruyère also refers to the humour of Clément Marot.

64 Gerard de Lairesse, *Het groot schilderboek* (2 vols, Amsterdam, 1707), vol. 1, pp. 56, 64, 173–4.

65 'Reisbeschrijving van Aernout van Overbeke', 1669. The manuscript is at the Royal Library in The Hague.

66 For a further exploration of these correspondences, see the forthcoming article by Rudolf Dekker in the *Annales ESC*.

9

How Was Jan Steen Funny?
Strategies and Functions of Comic
Painting in the Seventeenth Century

MARIËT WESTERMANN

Like his contemporary Rembrandt, the Dutch painter Jan Steen frequently portrayed himself, and in a variety of guises. But while
Rembrandt most often struck serious attitudes, Steen preferred to
present himself as a rotund, belly-laughing fellow or as a sly, smiling
rake (see figs. 9.1 and 9.3). How funny was Steen to seventeenth-
century viewers of his self-portraits and his dissolute households, the
messy interiors that are still proverbial for domestic mismanagement?
Or rather, how was Steen funny? Through these questions I will attempt
to recover some of the thematic and formal means that rendered
seventeenth-century paintings comic, some of the pictorial strategies
that bear on the functions of comic painting.

Although some of my observations about Steen's comic practices
apply equally to painters such as Adriaen van de Venne, Adriaen
Brouwer and Judith Leyster, Steen offers especially promising pros-
pects for a study of painted comedy. In 1721 his earliest biographer,
Arnold Houbraken, made elaborate claims for the comic character of
his life and art.[1] Houbraken jumps right into what he calls Steen's
'farcical life': 'He was a pupil of Jan van Goyen, who loved him
especially for his wit and sometimes, after painting, took him along for
a beer and a little banter. Jan likewise loved his master, but even more
his daughter, whom he treated so farcically that she began to swell ever
more.' Over another drink Steen apprises his teacher of this circumstance, and in a more sober encounter with his father, a brewer, he
obtains approval to marry the woman, after reassuring the anxious old
man about the dowry. ' "That'll be all right", said Jan, "my master is
already a fat fellow." ' Houbraken clarifies that Steen was referring to
his teacher's body rather than his purse, and that Steen's father had to
support the newly-weds by putting them in charge of a brewery in Delft.
Steen's life in and around the brewery then unrolls into a continuous
yarn of quips and practical jokes that have disastrous financial

Figure 9.1 Jan Steen, *Self-Portrait with Lute*, c.1665–8. All rights reserved. © Fundación Colección Thyssen-Bornemisza, Madrid

consequences but reduce even his wife to laughter. The brewery soon bankrupt, Jan resorts to painting a picture of his disintegrated household, which in Houbraken's description looks most like Steen's *The Dissolute Household*, now in the Wellington Museum (see fig. 9.2). He sets up a tavern, closing the establishment whenever the barrels are empty to 'paint an occasional picture for the wine merchant, who then sent another cask in return.' The inn reopens, 'but this did not last long, for he was his own best customer.' Houbraken finishes his account with a few descriptions of paintings, all 'witty of thoughts', and a few more anecdotes, noting that he has received them hot from the press.

Until recently, art historians reviled Houbraken's tales as untruthful attempts to badmouth a painter who was not to his classicist taste.[2] But the archival evidence does not invalidate all of Houbraken's scenarios: Steen married Van Goyen's daughter; his father put him in a brewery that went broke; he did get a licence to serve alcohol at his house; he ran into debts; and the owners of his works included a brewer, an innkeeper and a beer delivery man.[3] To Houbraken, Steen's curriculum vitae and painterly thematics corresponded so well that he had to conclude 'that [Steen's] paintings are as his way of life, and his life as his paintings.'[4] This identification of a painter with the themes of his work was no peculiarity of Houbraken's, indebted as it was to the Renaissance topos that 'every painter paints himself'. Although this

Figure 9.2 Jan Steen, *The Dissolute Household*, *c*.1661–4, by courtesy of the Board of Trustees of the Victoria and Albert Museum, London

Figure 9.3 Jan Steen, *Self-Portrait*, *c.*1668–70, Rijksmuseum, Amsterdam

proverb originally meant that artists involuntarily impose their own physical features on the human figures they draw, Renaissance biographies soon applied the notion to the overall character of an artist's production.[5] In emulation of Italian biographies such as Vasari's of Piero di Cosimo or Michelangelo, Netherlandish writers thus used anecdotes to enliven their biographies of artists and to evoke the character of their art. Karel van Mander, for example, in 1604 immortalized Pieter Bruegel as 'Pier the Droll', an artist born among peasants whose witty paintings and conversation made everyone laugh.[6] In the same vein, Cornelis de Bie dwelt on Brouwer's rough, pranksterish conduct and on Adriaen van Ostade's love of the peasant fair.[7]

Steen provided Houbraken with overwhelming evidence for an equation of his life and work, with his self-portraits in comic roles or compromising situations. Although the number of Steen's self-portraits within his paintings is debatable, their presence is beyond doubt. A mezzotint by Jacob Gole (*c.*1660–1737) after Steen's *Self-Portrait with Lute* (see fig. 9.1) already identified the sitter as the painter himself, and Houbraken wrote that Steen included himself in his very first painting, 'for a joke . . . with a tankard in his hand'.[8] Numerous characters in his paintings have features akin to those in his self-portrait in the Rijksmuseum (see fig. 9.3) and in his engraved portrait in Houbraken's biography. The frequent appearance of these traits even raises the possibility that Steen jestingly exploited the topos that every painter portrays himself in his figures.[9] In his laughing self-portrait, the lute and the tankard appear to be his sources of inspiration (see fig. 9.1).[10] The round face and body, expanded by his bulging breeches, mark the drunken jester in the Western tradition, although, in the estimation of Johan de Brune Jr., the round head also signified 'a great presence of mind and an uncommonly good wit'.[11] Steen often cast himself in this rotund form, derived from the comic Silenus type of drunk with a fat belly (see figs. 9.5, 9.11, 9.13). In a different incarnation, Steen is the rake whose red-stockinged leg and swaggering arm leave no doubts about his intentions (see fig. 9.2).[12]

In language echoing Van Mander's life of Bruegel, Houbraken asserted that Steen's practical jokes and farcical paintings alike forced viewers to laugh. To evoke and emulate Steen's comic effect, Houbraken wrote a biography that is itself indebted to the structure, idiom and motifs of comic literature. At the end of it, he expressed his faith that his readers would have 'howled about the farce' on his own literary stage.[13] Steen's biography resembles the type of jest-book in which anecdotes revolve around or are told by a central comic narrator.[14] Houbraken's string of practical jokes, descriptions of paintings, moralizing commentary, art theoretical digressions and claims for his veracity also resembles the structure of anecdotal volumes compiled by scholars such as De Brune. His consistent use of rollicking sentences and colloquial expressions contrasts with the more graceful prose in his biographies of courtlier artists such as Govert Flinck. The life of Steen is larded with proverbs, just as seventeenth-century comic texts and images are. Houbraken's banter about Steen's premarital impregnation of his wife has close parallels in contemporary jokes, as does the motif of the debauched painter making pictures for innkeepers.

To test Houbraken's claims for the comic character of Steen's work I have examined theoretical statements on comic representation as well as comic texts, whether meant for performance, recital or reading alone. These writings include farces, classically structured comedies, witty epigrams, occasional songs, jest-books, and parodies of serious literature such as mock encomia and travesties of domestic conduct books.

Netherlandish comic theorists drew on classical and Renaissance poetics to define themes suitable for comedy and to indicate the representational modes proper to those topics.[15] In 1638, Cornelis vanden Plasse, editor of the collected works of the comic poet Gerbrand Adriaensz Bredero, enumerated ancient comic themes:

> The comedies jumped merrily onto the stage with the lightest sort and the scum of the people, shepherds, peasants, workers, innkeepers male and female, matchmakers, whores, midwives, sailors, spendthrifts, tramps, and spongers: in fields, in woods, in hovels, in shops, taverns, pubs, in the street, in back alleys and slums, in the meat hall, and at the fish market.[16]

All of these types and situations indeed form the stock-in-trade of comedy, along with well-to-do burgers, doctors, lawyers and misers. If amended to include these figures, the list also reads like a catalogue of contemporary genre paintings.

Theorists were less explicit about the representational manner proper to these themes and characters. They repeated the Aristotelian view that the comic poet represents people as they are, or as worse than they are, as opposed to the tragic writer, who creates people better than life. Vanden Plasse reiterated the statement attributed to Cicero that comedy should be 'an imitation of life, a mirror of good mores, an image of truth', and he therefore suggested that 'the banter should be that of the common man: the scenes farcical and jolly', full of 'almost excessive exuberance, and roaring laughter'.[17] In practice, such lifelike depiction of human behaviour required honesty about bodily needs, about eating and drinking, elimination processes and concupiscence. Comic theorists and practitioners were a little squeamish about these motifs, though, and came to be more so as Dutch urban culture continued to civilize itself in the course of the seventeenth century.[18] The effort to cleanse cultural products and events was spearheaded jointly but for different reasons by principled moralists, concerned city magistrates and classicizing poets. By 1680, the members of Nil Volentibus Arduum, the Amsterdam society for the reform of theatre, had begun to rewrite comedies in purified verse and imagery. Their spokesman Andries Pels heatedly rejected the most obscene farces, although even to Nil Volentibus Arduum a modest uncouthness remained central to comedy.[19]

Figure 9.4 Jan Steen, *The Lean Kitchen*, c.1650, National Gallery of Canada, Ottawa

Vanden Plasse, Pels and others actually defended the bodily realism of comedy against Calvinist charges of immorality, arguing that the lifelike representation of comic scenes was essential to their function, which was to edify an audience by holding up a mirror of improper behaviour. In other words, they advocated comic realism by recourse to the familiar poetic requirements of combining the sweet and the useful, of telling the truth while laughing. They also appealed to the mechanisms of a shame culture, claiming that the viewer-reader of comic transgressions would not want to be caught dead engaging in them.[20] These are the purposes comedy should accomplish, according to Pels and his predecessors; they are the same functions recent iconographers have claimed for genre painting.[21] A closer look at Steen's production and at comic texts may clarify how humorous works acquitted themselves of these tasks, and if they could not fulfil others.

So how was Jan Steen funny? Most fundamentally, by his choice of themes. Remarkably often, Steen painted historic episodes that thematize mockery, wit and laughter, from the mocking of Samson to the ridicule of Ceres.[22] But it is in so-called scenes of everyday life that Steen worked most deliberately as comic painter. If we believe Houbraken, Steen's very first painting was born of his comic circumstances. Although Steen did not paint the type of farcical household described by Houbraken until well into his career, his earliest pictures do suggest a conscious effort to enter a market for comic and anecdotal scenes. His first documented paintings, finished by 1651, included a toothpuller, a peasant wedding and two pendants of a fat and a lean kitchen.[23] With the kitchens and the peasant wedding Steen placed himself in the Bruegelian peasant tradition, and those works would have been seen as comic by that referentiality alone. In *The Lean Kitchen*, which may be identical with the painting mentioned in 1651, Steen gave impetus to the notion that he painted his own life, as he included an easel and a scrawny fellow with Steenish features who grins towards the viewer (see fig. 9.4). The quack toothpuller and his screaming yokel of a patient were sixteenth-century comic fixtures as well, and, judging from their frequent appearance in jokes and images, remained so in Steen's time.

In the three decades following these modestly comic beginnings, Steen developed a production largely to do with the pleasures and woes of love and marriage that formed the favoured territory of comic texts. Exemplary for the close thematic links between comic literature and Steen's paintings are two parodies of domestic conduct books by Hieronymus Sweerts, best translated as *The Ten Amusements of Marriage* and *The Confession of Married People*.[24] These texts describe the milestones of marriage from the contract, wedding and first childbirth to budget management, child rearing and the extramarital

Figure 9.5 Jan Steen, *The Doctor's Visit*, *c.*1667–70, John G. Johnson Collection, Philadelphia Museum of Art

pleasures of the spouses. Steen painted all of these themes in a corpus that adds up to a comic exposition of the amusements of love and marriage. My examples address these central comic narratives, from seduction and lovesickness to marriage and childbirth celebration.[25]

Steen's themes can resemble those of comic literature so closely that a painting may seem to enact a text or a text to describe a painting. This is the case with Steen's representations of doctors visiting lovesick maidens (see fig. 9.5).[26] Art historians have historicized this theme by reference to medical and legal lore, all of it illuminating.[27] But the comic treatment of doctors and patients suggests that these painted jokes would have been obvious to viewers without such information. In a jest-book of 1665, one anecdote reads:

> It happened recently in Zwolle that a certain young daughter, from sorrow over a lover she could not get, became sick, and laid down in bed, so that a doctor was brought along, to see what might ail her. Coming to her he grabbed her hand to learn what hurt her. The manservant, knowing her illness, said: 'my lord, you have touched in the wrong place, because you have felt her arm which is not where she suffers, and you have left her abdomen, where she aches, unconsoled'. 'Oh!' said she, 'my sweet Klaes, that's just what I thought: I would rather entrust my healing to you than to this doctor.'[28]

This anecdote, which appears in at least two other Dutch jest-books, is characteristic of seventeenth-century jokes in its leisurely description of an event in which both doctor and girl are made laughable. In Steen's painting, the young woman perks up at the sight of the lover entering. Her accelerating pulse confounds the doctor, who signals his incompetence with his costume, outmoded for the 1660s, and with his bewildered expression. The smiling girl at the virginals and the grinning character at far right, who sports Steen's features, enhance the comic flavour. Letting us in on the joke, Steen suspends a herring and two onions in a farcical simile for the cure, a transparent image in early modern Europe well before Freud.[29] The prankster's costume proclaims his role as well: the cap with slits, familiar from Steen's self-portrait (see fig. 9.1), is even more antiquated than the doctor's attire, and was customary for fools in plays and in illustrated comic texts.[30]

Even in this case, joke and image don't quite match, however, as the lover in the painting is distinct from the witty commentator, and the joke does not use the culinary metaphor of the painting. A gustatory remedy does provide the clue to a humorous riddle, in which a doctor writes out a dinner prescription for an ill maiden: 'take the first of a Melon, center of a hAm, last of a heN'.[31] The clever reader easily spells the answer. A recipe-writing doctor appears in Steen's painting in Rotterdam (see fig. 9.6), but the somewhat different cure is advertised by a laughing boy at left, who is surely too young to apply it. His metaphor for sexual healing is the punch line to a steamy song about a girl expiring from desire, who sends a matchmaker to fetch her a doctor. His prescription: 'You are in great need of clystering', seventeenth-century slang for 'What you need is a good bang.'[32] A matchmaker type is present in some lovesickness paintings, but then again, the

Figure 9.6 Jan Steen, *The Doctor's Visit*, *c*.1663–7, Museum Boymans-van Beuningen, Rotterdam

painted doctor is usually a slightly daft physician rather than the energetic administrator of enemas in the song.

Texts thus slip and slide alongside images, and it would be pedantic to call one a source of the other. Just as the literary doctor's visits shift emphases and details, never repeating precisely, so Steen was at pains to reinvent the narrative. In several paintings of faint maidens revived by wafts from ribbons smouldering in braziers, the joke may be the doctor's inability to diagnose pregnancy.[33] In one such work Steen even makes the presumably male beholder a protagonist, perhaps standing in for the anecdotal lover, wittily diagnosing where she should be touched (see fig. 9.7). The only clues for the knowing viewer are the folksy aromatherapy, the doctor's old-fashioned costume and the girl's rather too frivolously coloured dress. Her costume as well as her direct look and smile signify a somewhat improper interest in the object of her attention, the viewer. In comic and libertine texts, brightly coloured silks, and especially satin, frequently mark female seductiveness.[34] Jokes and songs also attest a fascination with the erotic effect of female

Figure 9.7 Jan Steen, *The Sick Woman*, *c.*1663–7, Rijksmuseum, Amsterdam

Figure 9.8 Jan Steen, *The Marriage Contract of Sarah and Tobias*, c.1667–70, Herzog Anton Ulrich-Museum, Braunschweig

eyes on men and with the need for women to control their own looking. In the oft-repeated joke 'On looking', a woman in the street gawks 'with a lustful eye' at a 'dignified man'. Taking offence, he asks why she does not keep her eyes to the ground. She quips that she is only following the proper inclinations of her sex: man, who was made from earth, should look down, but woman, who was born of the male chest, will look there.[35] Addressing the viewer directly, Steen's finely attired maiden jests with these conventions as she makes the beholder a participant in the joke. While this pictorial strategy was not available in like manner to the written tale, the theatre employed it. In the farce *Bremer Hans*, Katrijn confesses to a young man and the audience that she 'suffered a certain illness . . . that cannot be cured otherwise, than by you and other young *Monsieurtjes*.'[36]

If lovesickness were properly treated, the next comic stage of courtship involved marriage contract negotiations, depicted in Steen's large painting in Braunschweig (see fig. 9.8). This practice was as widespread in the Dutch Republic as it was viewed negatively by moralists such as Jacob Cats and Petrus Wittewrongel. Marriage contracts which stipulated the different possessions brought into the marriage by the two spouses contravened the Calvinist ideal of wedlock based on mutual affection; this ideology bolstered the socially stabilizing practice of marriage between partners of about equal means and social standing. The marriage negotiation is a motif of comedies staged in the Amsterdam theatre, and Sweerts described it as the first of *The Ten Amusements of Marriage*.[37] Sweerts illustrated his facetious account of haggling and false promises with an explicit engraving of numerous men loading large scales (see fig. 9.9). Earlier engravings by Van de Venne had established a simpler formula for properly restrained marriage arrangements (see fig. 9.10).[38] The tone of Steen's version lies between this seriousness and Sweerts's extravagance. Steen modified Van de Venne's composition to indicate the slight ridiculousness of the situation. He turned the attitudes of the parents at left into more meddlesome hunches, and gave the sober demeanor of the lawyer a sharper-nosed intensity, casting doubts on the man's legal credentials by giving him old-fashioned costume. He transformed the demure stance of the couple into double-jointed, eye-rolling anxiety, and redressed them in fanciful costumes. He also elaborated the scene by referring to preparations for the sort of exaggerated festivity described in *The Ten Amusements of Marriage*.

But the joke is on collectors and art historians as well. As was rediscovered in 1926, the bride and groom have good reasons for their anxious antics: they are Sarah and Tobias, the biblical couple defying the unfortunate history of Sarah's previous seven marriages.[39] Steen appears to have cast a minor biblical episode in the guise of a genre

Figure 9.9 Anonymous engraving, *The Marriage Contract*, from H. Sweerts, *De tien vermakelikheden des houweliks* (Amsterdam, 1678), by courtesy of Universiteitsbibliotheek, Amsterdam

BRVYT,

MET DE

MANLICKE-TEGEN-

PLICHTEN,

A dien ick, teere Maeght, u plichten
heb befchreven ;
Vind' ick als by gevolg , mijn finnen
aengedreven ,
Om door een nieuw' ghedicht te
brengen aen den dach ,
Hoe dat een echte-vrou haer ampt
bereycken mach ,

M iiij   On -

Figure 9.10 Anonymous engraving after Adriaen van de Venne, *The Marriage Contract*, from J. Cats, *Houwelyck* (Dordrecht, 1634), reproduced by permission of The British Library, London

painting, to make comic comment on contemporary wedding contracts. When the moralist Cats condemned marital conditions, he cited the contract of Sarah and Tobias, in the apocryphal book of Tobit, as the only scriptural instance of such haggling.[40] Steen or his customer may well have owed the idea for the painting to this passage in Cats's popular book, but by putting the story on a large, comic stage, he also seems to mock Cats's futile attempt to underscore the triviality of marriage negotiations. The apocryphal text mentions only the writing of a contract, without any details.

The Marriage Contract of Sarah and Tobias also appears to make a painter's joke for the connoisseur about the categories of history and genre painting, whose borders it blurs. Steen's biographer Houbraken, who once owned the painting, described it as the highest accomplishment of Steen's witty realism:

> I cannot pass up mentioning the contents of a large piece (which was for a long time in my house, and later was sold to the Prince of Wolfenbüttel) in which stood represented a bridegroom and bride, two old folks and a notary. All of these figures were depicted so naturally in their actions, as if one saw the very thing happening. The old folks appeared to indicate with the greatest seriousness their intentions to the law fox, who listened with attention, with pen perched to paper. The groom stood (as if extremely displeased about this) in a posture, as if he was stamping his feet from distress, having thrown his hat and marriage tokens to the floor, with shoulders and hands raised. He gives the bride a sideways look, as if he wants to blame the old ones for all this, and as if to apologize to her; who stands there looking sad with tears on her cheeks. All this was as clearly and obviously visible from the features, and postures of the figures, and other circumstances, as if it had been written down. Equally witty and naturally painted by him is . . . a St Nicholas Eve.[41]

While Houbraken in the early eighteenth century already misidentified the history painting as a witty genre scene, early connoisseurs seem to have understood the joke. Several early sale catalogues refer to a painting of 'the marriage of Tobias', surely identical with one of the several versions of the Braunschweig painting.[42] To appreciate fully Steen's comic craft, such viewers would have had to be familiar with the arguments and comic texts about wedding conditions, with other representations of marital contracts, with the apocryphal book of Tobit, with Cats's use of its example, and with the conventions of history and festive group paintings. An especially sophisticated beholder might have delighted in all of these references. But without recognizing every allusion, less prepared viewers would have found pleasure and social truths in Steen's comic marriage contract, as Houbraken implies. Steen's *Village Wedding Contract* in St Petersburg, an explicitly farcical scene set in a disorderly household, may have aimed more directly at such viewers.[43]

Once the marriage contract had been signed, the comic calendar called for a wedding celebration. The extent and semi-public character of such revelry were of grave concern to seventeenth-century authorities. The endless sermons against excessive celebrations and the occasional sumptuary legislation indicate that those who could afford it continued to put on elaborate feasts and dances.[44] It is unlikely, however, that the festivities were quite as disorderly or lewd as suggested by proscriptive rhetoric or comic representations. Steen's paintings and comic texts could depict such rowdy revelry by situating it in less privileged environments than, say, the homes of the lovesick maidens or the marriage partners. Characteristically, they displaced exuberant festivity onto peasants and fops (see fig. 9.11). Bredero acknowledged that he described the transgressions of his urban peers 'in peasant mode, even though they are the responsibility of numerous city folks ... knowing that [the poems] would otherwise bite too sharply ... and that many wouldn't mind, as long as they were disguised in peasant forms with changed names and clothes.'[45]

Steen's *Peasant Revel* at the Wellington Museum (see fig. 9.11), which suggests marital celebration with its prominent dance around the egg and its floral and vegetal decorations, positions viewers slightly above the scene to afford a survey of the activities. Steen's distanced but detailed reportage of conversations, music making, fish peddling, love play, dancing and eating evokes comic accounts of festive crowds. A rambling poem on a peasant wedding gives a similar surveyor's view, although more richly ornamented with scatological flourish. Like Steen, the reporter at first remains invisible, as he or she observes from above fops such as 'Lord of Apes' and 'Madam du Shit to Onion' and boors such as 'Lubbert Emptybarrel' and 'Grossman Gruelbag', dancing, fondling, shedding dress and worse. Only in the last of four stanzas, the narrator appears in the midst of it all: 'from laughter I had to piss lots.'[46] Slow perusal of Steen's swirling crowd eventually reveals the painter, too, as reveller among revellers, toasting us with a generous laugh from the far end of the table. Where the poet uses tell-tale names to characterize boorish and pretentious folks, Steen distinguishes them by customary body types: peasants are well-rounded, hunched, bulging, with prominent orifices; the elongated fops at right sway modishly. No participant sits or stands straight, as decent citizens would.[47] The only guests who do not lean, hunch or reel are an innocent girl and a woman in an old-fashioned portrait on the wall, ignored by all. Steen's

Figure 9.11 Jan Steen, *Peasant Revel with an Egg Dance*, c.1670–3, by courtesy of the Board of Trustees of the Victoria and Albert Museum, London

Figure 9.12 Anonymous engraving, *The Hazardous Gathering of Toilet Inscriptions*, from H. Sweerts, *Koddige en ernstige opschriften*, 3rd edn (Amsterdam, 1698–1700), by courtesy of Universiteitsbibliotheek, Amsterdam

careful differentiation of social types and ages accords with theoretical prescriptions for comic playwrights and actors. Houbraken recommended Steen's truthful representation of attitudes and gestures as a model for young painters, and considered it an index of his comic inclinations.[48]

As in the case of the doctor's visits, it is unnecessary to see the literature about marital contracts and celebrations as a comic storehouse pillaged by painters. Even when texts predate images there are good reasons not to expect perfect matches of visual and literary comedy. Theorists of poetry accepted that the comic poet invents, that is finds his or her own themes, while the tragic writer chooses them from historical texts. Paradoxically, the inventiveness of the comic poet followed from the assumptions that comedy mirrors life, and that the comic poet finds material in ever-changing experience. Bredero, for example, repeatedly claimed to write in the folksy dialects he found in Amsterdam. Farce books for ever announce the newsworthiness of their anecdotes, the never-heard-before quality, even as they shamelessly borrow and vary each other's jokes.[49] Hieronymus Sweerts published a large collection of amusing inscriptions on windows, walls and toilets, and assured readers that he gathered them personally. An engraving in his book graphically thematizes the process, as the collector raises his spectacles to read the graffiti high up on a male loo (whose occupant is squatting in full view) while he is about to be hit by bird droppings (see fig. 9.12).[50] The topos of comic imitation from life gave Houbraken added support for his assumption that Steen's life must have been like a string of his painted episodes. In this view comic painters, too, invent life as they find it.[51]

Apart from the comic imperative to render life, there is another reason not to expect exact correspondences between texts and paintings. Seventeenth-century observers were keenly aware of the limits of what could be represented visually. Calvinist theologians and classicist theatre critics agreed that seeing naughty comedy was riskier than reading it. The preacher Wittewrongel argued that it was

> one thing to write or read a play, but from writing to go to acting does not properly follow. The Holy Spirit also wrote songs, especially the Song of Songs of the wise King Solomon: but should one therefore have to play it in a theatre? It is one thing to write or read an edifying comedy or tragedy, but quite another to show them for money, in a pagan manner, with so much commotion to the purpose of fleshly pleasure.[52]

Analogously, moralist as well as libertine writers claimed that paintings of lovers or lascivious themes caused dangerous arousal.[53] And indeed, where texts occasionally detail sexual exploits and bodily elimination, such references are more limited and less direct in painting. I have already noted the scatological ornamentation of the peasant wedding poem that is otherwise comparable to Steen's peasant revels. The bare bottoms and breasts that spice comic description are also rare in genre painting, as they must have been in performance, and exposed genitalia and full-length nudity are virtually absent outside history painting.[54]

Besides scouring comic literature for thematic correspondences to paintings, then, it seems equally or more instructive to compare the ways in which texts and images make their subjects laughable. To create a frame for comic interpretation, literature has titles at its disposal, or genre indications on title-pages; to trigger laughter it employs more complex signs. Like comic texts, comic paintings orient their public

Figure 9.13 Jan Steen, *Merry Company under a Pergola*, c.1673–5, Metropolitan Museum of Art, Fletcher Fund, 1950, New York

Figure 9.14 Anonymous title engraving to *Den nieuwen clucht-vertelder* (Amsterdam, 1665), reproduced by permission of The British Library, London

with markers of their genre. These indices are particularly effective if they upend familiar signifiers of 'serious' truth. Thus Steen ensured the comic interpretation of doctor's visits and marriage contracts with costumes, gestures and attributes that would have been improper in contemporaneous portraiture or history painting. He marked his wedding celebrations as comic by situating them among peasants and fops, and by letting no revellers stand or sit as proper citizens would. I will try to tease out a few more comic markers favoured by Steen.

Steen's *Merry Company under a Pergola* (see fig. 9.13) demonstrates abundantly a device I consider the laughing prompt: the laughing face of a figure in the painting, often aimed directly at the beholder and reinforced by fingers pointing out objects of ridicule. The laughing prompt is as ubiquitous in Steen's work as it is in comic texts. Comic actors frequently announce they are about to burst out laughing at some indecency or predicament. In jest-books, witnesses of jokes erupt in peals of laughter, while authors of quips are said to speak with a laughing face or mouth.[55] We have seen Houbraken use several versions of this strategy, describing Steen and his wives and his own readership as laughing.[56]

Horace's dictum that 'a face which laughs, makes us laugh too' provided theoretical confirmation for the infectiousness of the laughing face.[57] Encouraging such reader response must have been the purpose of the laughing narrators on the title-pages of jest-books, including a Father Christmas type in a collection of 1665 (*Den nieuwen cluchtvertelder*: see fig. 9.14). A portrait by Barend Graat of Jan Pietersz Meerhuysen (1618–c.1667), a comic actor, apparently had just such a laughter-inducing effect (see fig. 9.15). Contemporary poems called attention to its laughing face, and encouraged readers to beg some pranks from it, since 'like Democritus, it invites everyone to laughter'.[58] Like other comic markers, the laughing prompt works so well because it would be highly unusual in serious portraiture or history painting.

For painters, the use of a figure within the painting to model the beholder's emotional response had been traditional in theory as well as practice.[59] Unusual, however, is the frequency with which Steen used his own laughing face, and the functions to which he put it. In his *Merry Company under a Pergola* he appeals to the viewer from lower left (see fig. 9.13). There, he participates in the revelry, states his authorship of it by appearing in a signature's corner, and suggests the proper response. Steen thereby assumes overlapping roles similar to those of the jest-book narrator, a burly joker in antiquated get-up who flashes a wrinkly grin (see fig. 9.14).

Figure 9.15 Anonymous engraving after Barend Graat, *Jan Pietersz Meerhuysen*, also known as *Jan Tamboer*, 1650s, Rijksmuseum, Amsterdam

Figure 9.16 Adriaen Brouwer, *The Smokers, c.*1633–5, Metropolitan Museum of Art, The Friedsam Collection, 1931, New York

Although there are few parallels for the extent of Steen's comic posturing, several of his contemporaries engaged in similar role-play, drawing attention to their comic voices in their texts and eliding the border between their actual and represented lives. The actor Meerhuysen, whose portrait I have just discussed, became a comic media personality in mid-century Amsterdam, nicknamed Jan Tamboer, or 'John Drummer', for his role in a militia company. He not only acted comic parts, but also had jest-books attributed to him.[60] David Questiers, the author of the poem I quoted about Meerhuysen, wrote almost exclusively comic poetry, and according to someone else's joke he enjoyed his drink. He worked with other comic personalities, such as Sweerts and the 'serious' painter but funny poet Willem Schellinks.[61] The distinguished lawyer Aernout van Overbeke assembled a vast manuscript of jokes and, in anecdotes that evoke Steen's self-portrait as musician (see fig. 9.1), described himself in jolly gatherings, making music, smoking and jesting with his social equals and subordinates.[62] The painter Adriaen Brouwer emerges from his biographies by De Bie and Houbraken as a practical joker and drinker, an image perhaps created partly by Brouwer's self-portrait with friends, smoking and drinking in a tavern (see fig. 9.16).[63]

Laughter directed at the viewer in one sense ruptures the fiction of a comic reality spied upon and caught on canvas. This breach of illusion was a common strategy of comic texts and plays as well.[64] Paradoxically, the self-conscious address to the viewer can also function as a realist ploy. Mindful of its charge to mirror life, the comic representation is at pains to guarantee the authenticity of the situation represented. One of its reassuring strategies is the indication that the author witnessed an event and turned it into a representation. In a play, an actor can express his expectation or fear that the events represented are likely to end up on the stage, thus turning the audience into observers of the comic play in the making.[65] The joke often uses a reporter who details the event with the specificity of an eye-witness, providing seemingly unnecessary information such as designations of time or location. Steen's presence in his paintings identifies him as a similarly reliable witness.

Like the laughing prompt, several other comic strategies guarantee the comic truth of Steen's fictions. Another episode from his collected works on love and marriage, *The Childbirth Celebration*, demonstrates some of these realist devices (see fig. 9.17). A print from *The Ten Amusements of Marriage* represents the same event as a rather staid affair (see fig. 9.18). Surprisingly, this engraving illustrates the feasting and bawdy bantering of women who have come to celebrate a birth – quite literally the climax to the book. Only the outsized caudle glass with a cinnamon stick inserted, held by the woman at right, hints at the tallness of their tales, which detail the insatiability of female sexual appetite, the varying abilities of men to satisfy it, and the spectacular deliveries that result. These titillating stories provide vicarious compensation for women and readers who find themselves less well-served in life, and the illustrator must have felt the text needed no amplification.[66] Steen did not have the luxury of written description to establish the comic and ribald character of his monumental childbirth celebration. But with pictorial means he surely created an equally compelling image of comic reality, a rendering of the event that transforms the polite visits to the

Figure 9.17 Jan Steen, *The Childbirth Celebration*, 1664, reproduced by permission of the Trustees of the Wallace Collection, London

Figure 9.18 Anonymous engraving, *The Childbirth Celebration*, from
H. Sweerts, *De tien vermakelikheden des houweliks* (Amsterdam,
1678), by courtesy of Universiteitsbibliotheek, Amsterdam

lying-in chamber painted earlier by Gabriel Metsu and Gonzales Coques.[67]

A pointed use of gesture and a carefully structured disorder are organizing principles of this as of Steen's other crowd scenes. The impressive servant in red, blue, yellow and white moves into the pictorial space ahead of me, oblivious to my presence and therefore serving as realist guarantee. She and the others are there before me, spatially but also temporally: they have been there a while.[68] She also sets the direction for my look and models it for me: I must not miss the baby swaddled in the same red and white, held by its presumed father in tell-tale antiquated costume. Two women beleaguer him, after his money for tips and more delicacies.[69] Above all, I must not miss the horning gesture of the smiling man with Steen's features at the back, who implies that the financial father is not the natural one. Jokes about horn-carriers were the stock-in-trade of European comic literature, and Steen makes it difficult to miss the punch line, not least because he reinforces it by laughing prompts.[70]

But the amusement of comic painting, and especially of such a large, expensive painting, cannot end there. Comic representation needs to be fleshed out to fulfil its realist brief and, as significantly, to sustain repeat viewings. Thus my looking is distracted almost as soon as it has begun: to the prominent woman at right, whose ample décolletage alerts me to the tenor of the conversation; to the woman behind her, who looks at me and reinforces the message by pulling on a sausage. I am disoriented by the revellers, who are disarranged spatially as well as compositionally. They overlap and cut each other off; they are on and around furniture that has been placed at oblique or sharp angles, both within the pictorial space and as surface pattern. Figures and furnishings hardly seem to fit the ground plan of the room – but that plan would be impossible to draw despite the promising indications of the marble tiles in the foreground. The necessary information for a mathematically constructed space is lacking: the joinings of walls and floor have been carefully obscured. The servants and visitors mirror and model my dispersed attention: seven of them occupy themselves with the cuckolded father and the baby, but for differing reasons; two busy themselves with the new mother in bed; the remaining women are absorbed in the preparation and consumption of food and drink. The swollen womb of the woman drinking at left hints at another topic of conversation as we know it from the equivalent scene in the *Ten Amusements*. And finally the painter himself distracts, with his signature above the door that frames the joker, and with his conspicuous skills, with his gleaming bed warmer, delicate egg shells, glazed ceramics, silvery pewter, crusty roll. The casual presence of these bits, ignored by the revellers and observed only by me, asserts once more the veracity of the scene, just as the apparently superfluous details of jokes do.

Such carefully structured disarray cannot be accidental. That disorder appeared more truthful than order was obvious to at least one contemporary creator of it, the playwright Jan Vos. In defence of his spectacular productions for the Amsterdam theatre he wrote:

> The lives of the great and the small, which one shows on the stage, exist mostly in licentious extravagances; whoever wishes to keep order in this disorder of life, will himself become disorderly; for he would depart from the truth; but whoever wants to represent disorder properly, must use disorder, and thus disorder becomes order.[71]

Steen, too, seems to have ordered disorder or disordered order for the invention of comic truth.

But to what purposes all this comic disarray, written, performed or painted? I can give only preliminary indications. There were the traditional Humanist arguments already cited: that pleasure and laughter facilitate the learning of important truths, that they bring necessary, entertaining relief to the studious mind, and that they fill empty time and drive away sleep.[72] Like music and wine, laughter at comic entertainment was often cited as an effective remedy against melancholy.[73] In his self-portrait in Madrid, Steen uses all three preventive medicines (see fig. 9.1). There is no reason to doubt that comic authors and consumers believed in the efficacy of these functions. The moralizing justification for the representation of comic behaviour – that it would deter such actual conduct – appears more sophistical, as it did to Calvinist theologians.[74]

However sincerely meant, these consciously expressed rationales do not explain why certain themes and figures were favoured for comic treatments. The examples I have given suggest that comic fictions also offered alternative modes of addressing urgent social concerns – alternative to the more official treatments of the theological tracts, medical texts, domestic conduct books, legislative ordinances and serious images that circulated in the Dutch Republic. Anxiety about female sexuality and women's talk, the qualifications of professionals, the need for financially and socially balanced marriages, and the censorship of adultery were all as central to 'serious' discourse as they were to comic representation. This is not to say that comic musings on these issues constitute explicit resistance to dominant ideologies of gender, marriage, property, festivity and professionalism, but rather that comic practice tests and plays with these concepts even as it accepts their validity. New comic authors were aware that their works reinforced in jest what other texts argued seriously. Dirck Pers, for example, published a serious condemnation of alcohol and a mock eulogy to it within one volume, noting he intended 'all of it . . . as exhortation to virtue and sobriety'.[75] As literary and cultural historians such as Natalie Davis, Umberto Eco and Herman Pleij have shown for the early modern carnivalesque, a comic inversion of prevalent norms confirms and enhances their truth value, because the challenge is branded as temporary and ridiculous. In this sense, comic painting dispenses morals even when it does not appear to preach actively.[76] Steen's laughing self-portraits, at once within and outside his topsy-turvy revels, must have sharpened the message, as they make viewers complicit in pleasure as well as censorship. Houbraken acknowledged this ambivalence of Steen's comic resources in an epitaph that credits his 'witty painting' for its demonstration that people run wild if not disciplined, without identifying Steen's attitude towards the behaviour represented.

But in the process of buttressing ideological givens and thus reinforcing viewers in their proper identities, the boisterous and bawdy means of comic painting could offer relief from unarticulated stresses of politesse. Seventeenth-century comic painting showed people laughing uproariously; it lingered on illicit pleasure; it made dirty puns; it celebrated material stuffs; and it put all this together in disorder. Courting such unruliness in life would have been bad form for the rather well-off urban buyers of Steen's paintings, but those types of owners, as they present themselves in portraits, are obviously different from comic characters with their hunched or rotund bodies, wide-open mouths, coarse gestures, and outlandish or indecent costumes. Laughter at the indulgences of such buffoons, at pleasures one could never grant oneself, allows the leisurely scrutiny of them, free of moral charge.[77] In this reading, Steen's mildly grotesque bodies do not hold out the communal, regenerative, unofficial power Bakhtin celebrated in the Rabelaisian comic. Steen's works sublimate transgressions into the private, perhaps nostalgic pleasures of an urban elite; they are very much art, as indeed are Rabelais' learned Gargantuan debauches. In their compelling political critique of Bakhtin's carnivalesque, Peter Stallybrass and Allon White have suggested that the development of Western middle-class identity was predicated on the reform of a medieval festive culture – a set of forms and motifs that was already on the wane as Rabelais drew on it.[78] Gargantua and Pantagruel, Bredero's comedies and Steen's undisciplined households manifest and participate in different stages of this civilizing process.

This view of comic efficacy may be apt for the more obvious themes of comic painting, such as doctor's visits and peasant revels. My variety of examples suggests, however, that comic images knew as many nuances as comic texts, some blurting out one-liners, others jesting more ambiguously by hinting at unfinished narratives, and the most

Figure 9.19 Jan Steen, *The Oyster Girl*, *c*.1659–60, Mauritshuis, The Hague

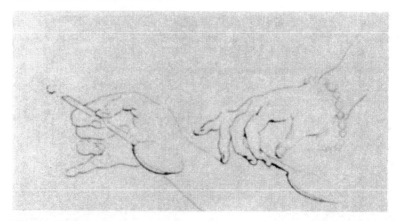

Figure 9.20 Anonymous engraving, *Two Proper Ways to Hold a Spoon*, from G. de Lairesse, *Groot schilderboek* (Haarlem, 1740; 1st edn Amsterdam, 1707), by courtesy of Mariët Westermann

ambitious pictures engaging a viewer's awareness of the conventions of painting itself. Steen's most delicate comic works, concise and presupposing an informed viewer, are more comparable to witty epigrams than to bantering jests and farces. Their functions, too, would seem to differ from those of more plainly humorous works.

Steen's display of wit in his famous *The Oyster Girl* is so economical that the painting has rarely been seen as comic at all (see fig. 9.19). The rediscovery that oysters were considered aphrodisiacs has recently turned her from an icon of Dutch realism into a dangerous woman, and the painting into a 'viewer, beware' statement.[79] But the small cabinet piece does, or did, much more. A young woman smiles at the beholder, establishing the subtlety of the joke in Steen's most refined version of the laughing prompt. Her direct look engages the viewer in a way contemporaries would have understood as improperly forward, as we have seen. She enhances the piquancy of the oyster and the joke with pepper, on the pewter dish and the oyster, and especially with the salt she is just now sprinkling on. In a popular misconception, salt was considered an effective means of catching a bird, the category of animals then as now used metaphorically for male genitals and their owners.[80] But the girl's handling of salt holds out more delicate pleasures. 'Not forgetting the salt', in seventeenth-century lore, marks her a virgin.[81] And yet her looks and actions suggest differently, as do the painting's composition and meticulous execution.

Steen borrowed the illusion of an arched window from a successful genre of painting developed in his home town Leiden, in which young women handle obvious vegetal and animal metaphors for sexual favours.[82] This girl, too, may have something more on offer. She tries hard to mask her dubious status, bending her salting fingers into a gesture which Gerard de Lairesse was to illustrate as proper for an upstanding young woman (see fig. 9.20).[83] Steen's girl has often fooled viewers. A story of 1873 claims her as the apotheosis of Steen's self-rehabilitation. 'No Madonna could be more beautiful and chaste . . .', a woman whispers.[84] The arch frame may indeed wink at the Virgin's pictorial tradition, a convention of which the Catholic Steen must have been aware.

The Oyster Girl plays with appearance: she may not be what she seems to be, and she is as seductively deceptive as painting, and especially this painting, itself. The deceptiveness of painting, ape and rival of nature, was of course an old saw. In seventeenth-century Dutch the words for deception and seduction could be interchanged, and they often were in reference to painting. As Eric Jan Sluijter has argued, painters from Leiden embodied this pun in meticulously crafted young women, seductresses who metaphorize the deceptive technique that engendered them.[85] In his finest exercise in eye-fooling painting, Steen flaunted his awareness of these pictorial musings on the seduction of appearance.

Not everyone would have understood Steen's joke in all its complexities, but those initiated into the culture of salt would have savoured it. Salt in literary, and especially epigrammatic, theory served as metaphor for the sharp, the unexpected, the witty. Constantijn Huygens, master of the *puntdicht* or sharp epigram, and one of the highest officials in the land, devoted one such poem to this quality:

> *A quick, and salted poem, to amuse the clever folks,*
> *Is not a food to please the tongues of common blokes:*
> *Salt your speech; less than a salt dish yokels comprehend;*
> *Not one in hundred readers, the true salt understands.*[86]

The point of the wittiest representations must be quick and sharp, and thereby obscure. In *The Oyster Girl* Steen's salty wit meets the epigrammatic challenge. This is comic art for the discerning 'clever folks', and as such it works as social discriminant, separating the sophisticates from the thigh-slappers.

NOTES

I presented parts of this article at the Courtauld Institute of Art in February 1992, and at the Conference of Historians of Netherlandish Art in October 1993. For their perceptive responses to those papers and to this one, I am grateful to Perry Chapman, Egbert Haverkamp-Begemann, Elizabeth

Honig, Herman Roodenburg, Eric Jan Sluijter, Marina Warner and Joanna Woodall. The David E. Finley fellowship of the Center for Advanced Study in the Visual Arts in Washington, DC, enabled me to write this essay. My book *The Amusements of Jan Steen: comic painting in the seventeenth century* (Zwolle, 1996) gives more comprehensive documentation of the theoretical positions and comic strategies discussed in this essay.

1 A. Houbraken, *De groote schouburgh der Nederlantsche konstschilders en schilderessen* (3 vols, Amsterdam, 1718–21), vol. 3, pp. 12–30. Fuller consideration of Houbraken's life of Steen in H. P. Chapman, 'Persona and myth in Houbraken's life of Jan Steen', *Art Bulletin*, 75 (1993), pp. 135–50; Westermann, *The Amusements*.

2 L. de Vries, 'Achttiende- en negentiende-eeuwse auteurs over Jan Steen', *Oud Holland*, 87 (1973), pp. 227–39, examined Houbraken's theoretical stakes in his biography of Steen, but still considered his account libellous. For recent revisions of this view, see H.-J. Raupp, 'Ansätze zu einer Theorie der Genremalerei in den Niederlanden im 17. Jahrhundert', *Zeitschrift für Kunstgeschichte*, 46 (1983), pp. 401–18, and accounts cited in note 1.

3 Most archival information in M. J. Bok, 'The artist's life', in the exhibition catalogue *Jan Steen: painter and storyteller* (Washington, DC, 1996), pp. 25–37; for the early owners of paintings by Steen, Westermann, *The Amusements*, Chapter 2.

4 Houbraken, *Groote schouburgh*, vol. 3, pp. 12–13.

5 R. Klein, *La forme et l'intelligible: écrits sur la Renaissance et l'art moderne*, ed. A. Chastel (Paris, 1970), pp. 341–52, esp. 341–2 ('Giudizio et gusto dans la théorie de l'art au Cinquecento'); M. Kemp, '"Ogni dipintore dipinge sé": a neoplatonic echo in Leonardo's art theory?', in *Cultural Aspects of the Italian Renaissance: essays in honour of Paul Oskar Kristeller*, ed. C. H. Clough (Manchester and New York, 1976), pp. 311–23; F. Zöllner, '"Ogni pittore dipinge sé": Leonardo da Vinci and "automimesis"', in *Der Künstler über sich in seinem Werk: Internationales Symposium der Bibliotheca Hertziana Rom 1989*, ed. M. Winner (Weinheim, 1992), pp. 137–60.

6 K. van Mander, *Het schilder-boeck, waer in voor eerst de leerlustighe ieught den grondt der edel vry schilderconst in verscheyde deelen wort voorghedraghen, daer nae in dry deelen t'leven der vermaerde doorluchtighe schilders des ouden, en nieuwen tyds, eyntlyck d'wtlegghinghe op den Metamorphosen pub. Ovidij Nasonis* (Haarlem, 1604), fol. 233r; for the early historiography of Bruegel, J. Muylle, '"Pier den Drol" – Karel van Mander en Pieter Bruegel: bijdrage tot de literaire receptie van Pieter Bruegels werk ca. 1600', in H. Vekeman and J. Müller Hofstede (eds), *Wort und Bild in der niederländischen Kunst und Literatur des 16. und 17. Jahrhunderts* (Erftstadt, 1984), pp. 137–44.

7 C. de Bie, *Het gulden cabinet vande edele vry schilder-const* (Antwerp, 1661), pp. 91–4. For Ostade's early reputation, ibid., p. 258, and Houbraken, *Groote schouburgh*, vol. 1, pp. 347–9. On Brouwer's reception, K. Renger, *Adriaen Brouwer und das niederländische Bauerngenre 1600–1660* (Munich, Alte Pinakothek, 1986), pp. 12–20 [exhibition catalogue].

8 Houbraken, *Groote schouburgh*, vol. 3, p. 15. For Gole's print, F. W. H.

Hollstein, *Dutch and Flemish Engravings and Woodcuts ca. 1450–1700*, vol. 7 (Amsterdam, 1952), p. 216, ill.

9 The topos of involuntary self-representation was not beyond comic reach; see S. van Hoogstraeten, *Inleyding tot de hooge schoole der schilderkonst: anders de zichtbaere werelt* (Rotterdam, 1678), p. 168.

10 For facetious treatment of wine as a source of poetic inspiration, see D. P. Pers, *Bacchus wonder-wercken . . . Hier is by-gevoeght de Suyp-stad, of dronckaerts leven . . .* (Amsterdam, 1628), pp. 105–6.

11 J. de Brune de Jonge, *Alle volgeestige werken, bestaande in I. Wetsteen der vernuften, of bequaam middel om van alle voorvallende zaken aardiglijk te leeren spreken* (Amsterdam, 1681), bk 2, ch. 1.

12 The slung leg and arm akimbo with hand bent back mark sexual prowess in an etching by Romeyn de Hooghe in G. Boccaccio, *Contes et nouvelles de Bocace Florentin . . . enrichie de figures en taille-douce gravées par Mr. Romain de Hooge* (2 vols, Amsterdam, 1697), vol. 1, p. 177. See further L. Steinberg, 'Michelangelo's Florentine *Pietà*: the missing leg', *Art Bulletin*, 50 (1968), pp. 343–53. For the frivolity of red finery, including stockings, see *Klucht van de koeck-vreyer* (Amsterdam, 1659), pp. 11–12, and H. Sweerts, *Koddige en ernstige opschriften, op luyffens, wagens, glazen, uithangborden, en andere tafereelen* (4 vols, 3rd edn, Amsterdam, 1698–1700), vol. 1, p. 49.

13 Houbraken, *Groote schouburgh*, vol. 1, p. 372, and vol. 3, p. 30.

14 The biographic character of some farce books is discussed by J. Koopmans and P. Verhuyck, *Een kijk op anekdotencollecties in de zeventiende eeuw: Jan Zoet, het leven en bedrijf van Clément Marot* (Amsterdam and Atlanta, 1991), pp. 72–5, 111–42.

15 A. G. van Hamel, *Zeventiende-eeuwsche opvattingen en theorieën over litteratuur in Nederland* (The Hague, 1918), Chapter 4: 'De theorie van het drama'; J. H. Meter, *De literaire theorieën van Daniël Heinsius: een onderzoek naar de klassieke en humanistische bronnen van De tragoediae constitutione en andere geschriften* (Amsterdam, 1975), pp. 228–49; A. J. E. Harmsen, *Onderwys in de tooneel-poëzy: de opvattingen over toneel van het kunstgenootschap Nil Volentibus Arduum* (Rotterdam, 1989), text and commentary of days 8, 10, 20, 24, 27, 35, 36 and 37, and *passim*; more briefly B. F. W. Beenen and A. J. E. Harmsen (eds), *De Tweeling van Plautus: twee zeventiende-eeuwse Plautus-bewerkingen* (Utrecht, 1985), pp. 87–106, and M.-T. Leuker, *'De last van 't huys, de wil des mans . . .': Frauenbilder und Ehekonzepte im niederländischen Lustspiel des 17. Jahrhunderts* (Münster, 1992), pp. 64–9.

16 C. L. vanden Plasse (ed.), *Alle de wercken so spelen gedichten brieven en kluchten van den gheest-rijcken poëet Gerbrand Adriaensz Bredero Amsterdammer* (Amsterdam, 1638), p. [A3v]. His statement is indebted to the first Netherlandish description of comic themes, published in 1555 by C. van Ghistele, ed. and trans., *Terentius comedien nu eerst wt den latine in onser duytscher talen . . . over ghesedt* (Antwerp, 1555), dedication.

17 Vanden Plasse, ibid., pp. [A3v], [B1v]; compare C. Schrevelius, ed., *Publii Terentii comoediae sex post optimas editiones emendatae, accedunt, Aelii Donati, commentarius integer* (Leiden, 1662) and the theoretical

statements of Nil Volentibus Arduum in Harmsen, *Onderwys*, text and commentary of days 20, 27, 35, 36 and 37.

18 Van Ghistele, *Terentius*, dedication; Meter, *Literaire theorieën*, pp. 230–8, 245; T. Rodenburgh, *Eglentiers poëtens borst-weringh* (Amsterdam, 1619), cited by Van Hamel, *Zeventiende-eeuwsche opvattingen*, pp. 88–9. For the purification of verse and idiom in later seventeenth-century comedies and farces, and their shift of setting from peasant and lower middle class to more 'civilized' urban milieus, Van Hamel, ibid., pp. 90–3; P. H. van Moerkerken, *Het Nederlandsch kluchtspel in de 17de eeuw* (2 vols, Sneek, 1898), vol. 1, pp. 7–8; and Leuker, *'De last'*, pp. 65, 68–9, 72, 90–1, and 103–7. For the active promotion of a cleaner theatre by Nil Volentibus Arduum, Harmsen, *Onderwys*, and A. Pels, *Gebruik én misbruik des tooneels*, ed. M. A. Schenkeveld-van der Dussen (Culemborg, 1978 [Amsterdam, 1681]), pp. 11–16, 18–25. Calvinist polemicists condemned the lasciviousness and 'uncleanliness' of comedies; see the translation of the English Puritan tract by W. Prynne, *Histrio-mastix ofte schouw-spels treur-spel, dienende tot een klaer bewijs van de onwetlijckheden der hedendaechsche comedien* (Leiden, 1639), and P. Wittewrongel, *Oeconomia Christiana ofte Christelicke huys-houdinghe* (2nd revised edn, 2 vols, Amsterdam, 1661), vol. 2, pp. 1168–86.

The seminal study of the early modern civilizing process is N. Elias, *Über den Prozeß der Zivilisation: Soziogenetische und psychogenetische Untersuchungen* (Bern, [1939], 2nd edn, 1969).

19 A. Pels, *Gebruik én misbruik des tooneels* (2nd edn, Amsterdam, 1706; for 1st and modern edns, note 10), pp. 21–4, 25–8, 33, 37, 42; idem, *Q. Horatius Flaccus dichtkunst, op onze tyden, én zéden gepast*, ed. M. A. Schenkeveld-van der Dussen (Assen, 1973 [Amsterdam, 1677]), pp. 85–6; this is an expanded edition of Horace's *Ars poetica*. Pels admired Bredero's unsurpassed imitation of 'the flourish of the old coarse customs, / And the uncouthness of the street language of Amsterdam' (*Gebruik én misbruik*, 1706, p. 15). For his own jocular poems, A. Pels, *Minneliederen én méngelzangen* (Amsterdam, 1684), and an early poem in the comic songbook *Het eerste deel van de Amsterdamse mengelmoez* (Amsterdam, 1658), p. 68. Pels and Nil Volentibus Arduum produced several comedies, including cleansed versions of earlier plays, that retained motifs abhorrent to Reformed moralists, such as stupidity, drunkenness and adultery; see Pels's comments on his comedy *Julfus* (*Gebruik én misbruik*, 1706, p. 64), and the Nil version of Plautus's *Menaechmi*, edited by Beenen and Harmsen, *De Tweeling*.

20 The ancient claim that explicit comedy offers a way of *ridentem dicere verum* circulated through all genres of Dutch comic theory and literature, documented by Westermann, *The Amusements*, Chapter 3. Nil Volentibus Arduum formulated the shame avoidance argument: 'One obtains this [moral improvement] not only from Tragedies, but even and often much more from comedies and farces: for as in these the foibles and vices are represented in mockery to the entire world, and as the unvirtuous person usually tolerates chastising much better than being laughed at and mocked, it is no wonder that this will make him watch out', Harmsen, *Onderwys*,

Day 7. For shame as behavioural regulator in the Dutch Republic, Leuker, *'De last'*, pp. 279–92; H. Roodenburg, *Onder censuur: de kerkelijke tucht in de gereformeerde gemeente van Amsterdam, 1578–1700* (Hilversum, 1990), *passim*; S. Schama, *The Embarrassment of Riches: an interpretation of Dutch culture in the Golden Age* (New York, 1987).

21 Most fundamentally E. de Jongh, *Zinne- en minnebeelden in de schilderkunst van de zeventiende eeuw* (Amsterdam, 1967) and E. de Jongh et al., *Tot lering en vermaak: betekenissen van Hollandse genrevoorstellingen uit de zeventiende eeuw* (Amsterdam, Rijksmuseum, 1976), pp. 27–8 [exhibition catalogue].

22 Steen's historical themes of mockery include *Wine is a Mocker* (Proverbs 20: 1; Pasadena, Norton Simon Museum of Art), *The Mocking of Samson* (Cologne, Wallraf-Richartz Museum), *The Mocking of Ceres* (private collection), and *The Satyr and the Peasant* (The Hague, Museum Bredius and Santa Monica, J. Paul Getty Museum). Steen also represented a scene from Bredero's comedy *Ascagnes and Lucelle* (Washington, DC, Corcoran Gallery of Art, and private collection), and added mockers where the story did not require any, as in his *Amnon and Tamar* (Cologne, Wallraf-Richartz-Museum) and in the *Banquet of Ahasuerus* (Cleveland Museum of Art). For these paintings, see K. Braun, *Alle tot nu toe bekende schilderijen van Jan Steen* (Rotterdam, 1980), nos. 125, 146, 191, 279, 297, 300, 310, 312, all ill., and A–30.

23 A *Peasant Wedding* that cannot be identified was shipped from Utrecht to Denmark in 1650; A. Bredius, *Jan Steen* (Amsterdam, 1927), pp. 90–1. The *Fat and Lean Kitchens* were bought for the Swedish field marshal Wrangel in 1651; O. Granberg, 'Schilderijen in 1651 voor Karl Gustav Graf von Wrangel te 's-Gravenhage aangekocht', *Oud Holland*, 25 (1907), p. 132. *The Lean Kitchen* may well be the painting now in the National Gallery of Canada in Ottawa (see fig. 9.4); its pendant *The Fat Kitchen* is on the art market. *The Toothpuller*, dated 1651, is in the Mauritshuis in The Hague; Braun, *Jan Steen*, nos. 27, 28 and 32, all ill.

24 H. de Vrye [pseudonym for Hieronymus Sweerts], *De tien vermakelikheden des houwelyks, spotsgewijze beschreven door Hippolytus de Vrye* (2nd edn, Amsterdam, 1678); idem, *De biecht der getroude, zijnde het tweede deel van De tien vermakelikheden des houwelyks* (Amsterdam, 1679).

25 For the centrality of love and marriage as themes of written and painted comedy, see P. Barolsky, *Infinite Jest: wit and humour in Italian Renaissance art* (Columbia, MO, 1978), and L. Salingar, *Shakespeare and the Traditions of Comedy* (Cambridge, 1974).

26 Around 1657 Frans van Mieris introduced this theme in painting; Steen almost immediately adopted it. See L. de Vries, *Jan Steen 'de kluchtschilder'* (Diss., Groningen, 1977), pp. 98–101, 128 n. 68; and O. Naumann, *Frans van Mieris the Elder (1635–1681)* (2 vols, Doornspijk, 1981), vol. 1, pp. 48–50, 99.

27 J. B. F. van Gils, 'Een detail op de doktersschilderijen van Jan Steen', *Oud Holland*, 38 (1920), pp. 200–1; J. B. Bedaux, 'Minnekoorts-, zwangerschaps- en doodsverschijnselen op zeventiende-eeuwse schilderijen', *Antiek*, 10 (1975–6), pp. 17–42; E. Petterson, 'Amans Amanti Medicus: Die Ikonologie

des Motivs "der ärztliche Besuch" ', in *Holländische Genremalerei im 17. Jahrhundert: Symposium Berlin 1984*, ed. H. Bock and T. W. Gaehtgens (Berlin, 1987), pp. 193–224.

28 *Den nieuwen clucht-vertelder* (Amsterdam, 1665), p. 187.

29 On the fish as phallic metaphor, see D. Bax, *Ontcijfering van Jeroen Bosch* (The Hague, 1949), pp. 34–5, 166–8 and *passim*; P. Vandenbroeck, 'Jheronimus Bosch' zogenaamde *Tuin der lusten*, I', *Jaarboek van het Koninklijk Museum voor Schone Kunsten Antwerpen* (1989), pp. 9–210, esp. 102, 170–3, 185; and the examples cited by J. H. Böse, '*Had de mensch met één vrou niet connen leven': prostitutie in de literatuur van de zeventiende eeuw* (Zutphen, 1985), *passim*; the references in this fascinating study are often imprecise.

30 On Steen's anachronistic doctor's costumes, see S. J. Gudlaugsson, *De komedianten bij Jan Steen en zijn tijdgenooten* (The Hague, 1945), trans. J. Brockway as *The Comedians in the Work of Jan Steen and his Contemporaries* (Soest, 1975), pp. 8–23; for valid criticism of Gudlaugsson's use of theatrical prints, see A. McNeil Kettering, *The Dutch Arcadia: pastoral art and its audience in the Golden Age* (Montclair, NJ, 1983), pp. 113–14.

31 Sweerts, *Koddige en ernstige opschriften*, vol. 4, p. 107.

32 [D.] Questiers, 'Oubollige lijf-artz', in *Amsterdamse mengelmoez*, 1658, pp. 64–7. On clystering and its ideological charges in early modern Europe, see L. S. Dixon, 'Some penetrating insights: the imagery of enemas in art', *Art Journal*, 52 (1993), no. 3, pp. 28–35; M. Warner, *From the Beast to the Blonde: on fairy tales and their tellers* (London, 1994), pp. 59–62.
   The song ridicules the girl's sexual needs, the matchmaker, and the doctor's remedy by the epithet 'oubollig', or droll, and by the 'low' Amsterdam dialect of the protagonists. Dialects and descriptive names in comic literature function much like facial and body types and costumes in comic painting. Doctors frequently speak Dutch with bastardized German or French accents, or have pig Latin names indicating their preoccupations with bodily functions; in pictures they are hunched and haggard, have long noses or fanciful costumes, look bewildered or crave drink.

33 For the malodorous remedy, see Van Gils, 'Een detail'; L. S. Dixon, *Perilous Chastity: women and illness in pre-enlightenment art and medicine* (Ithaca, NY, 1995), pp. 143–7, rightly notes that the ribbon in the brazier is not a pregnancy test, as often claimed. But a viewer might well have attributed the patient's fainting to morning sickness. Doctors unable to recognize pregnancy are stock characters in comic texts; in Sweerts, *De tien vermakelikheden*, p. 126, one is aptly named Dr Stultoris.

34 *Klucht van de koeck-vreyer*, p. 11; [C. W. Barth,] *Incogniti scriptoris nova poemata...Nieuwe Nederduytsche gedichten ende raedtselen* (3rd edn, Leiden, 1624), p. 109; *'t Amsterdamsch hoerdom, behelzende de listen en streeken, daar sich de hoeren en hoere-waardinnen van dienen* (Amsterdam, 1681), p. 46; [J. Kabeljau,] *De verreezene Hippolytus, ontdekkende de natuur, eigenschappen, toomelooze hartstochten, onkuische liefde, en ydelheid der vrouwen* (2nd edn, Amsterdam, 1710 [Amsterdam, 1679], after the anonymous Latin text *Hippolytus redivivus, id est remedium*

contemnendi sexum muliebrem [n.p., 1644]), pp. 82, 87. For various views of painted satin, see A. McNeil Kettering, 'Ter Borch's ladies in satin', *Art History*, 16 (1993), pp. 95–124, esp. 99–101, 111–15.

35 *Den kluchtigen bancketkramer, of 't leven en bedrijf van Frans de Geck* (Dordrecht, 1657), p. 78.
36 Excerpted in J. van Vloten, *Het Nederlandsche kluchtspel van de 14e tot de 18e eeuw* (3 vols, Haarlem, 1878–81), vol. 3, p. 126.
37 Sweerts, *De tien vermakelikheden*, pp. 19–31. For marital contract negotiations in the Dutch Republic, see D. Haks, *Huwelijk en gezin in Holland in de 17de en 18de eeuw: processtukken en moralisten over het laat 17de- en 18de-eeuwse gezinsleven* (Assen, 1982), pp. 137–8; J. de Jong, *Een deftig bestaan: het dagelijks leven van regenten in de 17de en de 18de eeuw* (Utrecht and Antwerp, 1987), pp. 90–1; and Leuker, '*De last*', pp. 175–94. Calvinist critiques in J. Cats, *Houwelyck: dat is de gantsche ghelegentheyt des echten staets* (Dordrecht, 1625), ed. *Alle de wercken* (2 vols, Amsterdam and Utrecht, 1700), vol. 1, pp. 288–9; idem, *'s Werelts begin, midden, eynde, besloten in den trou-ringh, met den proef-steen van den selven* (Dordrecht, 1637), ed. *Alle de wercken*, 1700, vol. 2, p. 13; Wittewrongel, *Oeconomia*, vol. 1, p. 46.
38 The engraving designed by Van de Venne opens the section entitled 'Bruyt' (bride), in Cats's *Houwelyck*, (Dordrecht, 1634) p. 271. For similar compositions, see the engraving after Van de Venne in the octavo edition of *Houwelyck* (The Hague, 1628), p. 335, and an engraving of 1633 by Abraham Bosse, first in his series of six prints on *Le mariage à la ville*; N. Villa, *Le XVIIe siècle vu par Abraham Bosse, graveur du Roy* (Paris, 1967), pl. 58; for the series, J. Habert et al., *Abraham Bosse: les gravures du Musée des Beaux-Arts de Tours* (Tours, Musée des Beaux-Arts, 1982), no. 3a [exhibition catalogue].
39 August Fink, 'Jan Steen's Hochzeit des Tobias', *Zeitschrift für bildende Kunst*, 60 (1926–7), pp. 230–3.
40 Cats, *Trou-ringh*, p. 13; Tobit 7: 11–15. Cats notes that Adam and Eve did not need a marriage contract and that Netherlandish custom never required one; Cats's comments clarify the presence in Steen's painting of the picture at back left, which represents the creation of Eve from Adam's rib.
41 Houbraken, *Groote schouburgh*, vol. 3, pp. 16–17. In Steen's other versions of this composition the archangel Raphael behind Tobias has wings and thus facilitates identification of the history theme; Braun, *Jan Steen*, nos. 309, 355, ill. For Steen's frequent elision of the borders between pictorial genres, see Westermann, 'Jan Steen, Frans Hals, and the edges of portraiture', *Nederlands Kunsthistorisch Jaarboek*, 46 (1995), pp. 298–331.
42 Bredius, *Jan Steen*, p. 100, debt settlement of 1676; G. Hoet and P. Terwesten, *Catalogus of naamlyst van schilderyen* (3 vols, The Hague, 1752–70), vol. 1, p. 110: Sale, Anonymous, Amsterdam, 6 March 1708, no. 4 (f 205); and Rijksbureau voor Kunsthistorische Documentatie, The Hague, fiches HdG: Sale, Anonymous, Amsterdam, 13 July 1740, no. 32.
43 Braun, *Jan Steen*, no. 236, ill.
44 Schama, *The Embarrassment*, pp. 129–220; for weddings and sumptuary laws, pp. 182–7, 336.

45 G. A. Bredero, *Groot lied-boeck,* ed. A. A. van Rijnbach (Rotterdam, 1966 [Amsterdam, 1622]), p. 9.

46 *Den nieuwen clucht-vertelder,* pp. 122–4.

47 For elite concerns with straight posture, see H. Roodenburg, 'Over scheefhalzen en zwellende heupen: enige argumenten voor een historische antropologie van de zeventiende-eeuwse schilderkunst', *De zeventiende eeuw,* 9 (1993), pp. 152–68; Westermann, *The Amusements,* Chapter 3.

48 Houbraken, *Groote schouburgh,* vol. 1, p. 377; vol. 3, pp. 16–17, 18–19.

49 Van Hamel, *Zeventiende-eeuwsche opvattingen,* pp. 87, 139–40; Meter, *Literaire theorieën,* pp. 239–40; Pels, *Gebruik én misbruik,* pp. 7, 47–51. Pels argued that comic material is so 'easily found in common talk' that it makes no difference whether the playwright takes it from life, popular literature or his own brain (pp. 50–1), but he censored the tragic poets' own inventions of stories (pp. 47–8). Pels also noted Bredero's perfect imitation of Amsterdam street life (p. 15); for Bredero's own statements, see the prefaces to his *Groot lied-boeck,* pp. 7–9, and to *Den Spaanschen Brabander,* in *De werken van G. A. Bredero,* ed. J. ten Brink et al. (3 vols, Amsterdam, 1890), vol. 2, pp. 143–6; as well as his *Voor-reden vande sotheyt,* discussed by K. Porteman, ' "Lacht wel": Bredero's *Voor-reden vande sotheyt',* *Spektator,* 4 (1984–5), pp. 280–7.

   Although jest-books always took material from each other and from other genres of literature, the details and phrasing of the anecdotes vary as much as one would expect in oral retellings. The wandering of anecdotes throughout Europe is documented by Worp's edition of Huygens's epigrams (*De gedichter van Constantijn Huygens,* ed. J. A. Worp [9 vols, Groningen, 1092–9]) and by the jest-book studies of Koopmans and Verhuyck, *Een kijk,* and E. Moser-Rath, *Lustige Gesellschaft: Schwank und Witz des 17. und 18. Jahrhunderts in kultur- und sozialgeschichtlichem Kontext* (Stuttgart, 1984). Despite this borrowing practice, jest-book compilers claim to 'pick up many things from the street'; *Den vaeck-verdryver van de swaermoedighe gheesten* (Amsterdam, 1620), p. Aii. Titles such as *Den schimpigen bolwormspiegel, vol aartige Amsterdamsche en uytheemsche geschiedenissen en nieuwigheeden* (Amsterdam, 1671) stress the local specificity and novelty of anecdotes.

50 Sweerts, *Koddige en ernstige opschriften,* vol. 1, engraving between pp. 8 and 9; the titles and introductions of the different volumes assert Sweerts's compiling activity.

51 Houbraken, *Groote schouburgh,* vol. 3, p. 12, prefaced Steen's biography by pointing out that painters 'of a jocular mind' are especially adept at the most natural imitation; throughout the life of Steen he emphasizes Steen's lifelike representation. On the requirement for comic painters, see Westermann, *The Amusements,* Chapter 3.

52 Wittewrongel, *Oeconomia,* vol. 2, p. 1190; compare Prynne, *Histrio-mastix,* p. a3; Pels, *Gebruik én misbruik* (1706), pp. 26–8; and J. van Beverwyck, *Schat der ghesontheyt* in *Alle de wercken, soo in de medecyne als chirurgye* (Amsterdam, 1652), pp. 46–7.

53 Cats, *Houwelyck,* pp. 296, 387–8; Van Beverwyck, *Schat,* pp. 46–7; comic

texts: [S. de Vries?] *De klugtige tyd-verdryver waar in de alder-aardigste vermaaklijkheden van verscheide schrijvers t'zaam gezet zijn* (Utrecht, 1653), p. 22; [Barth], *Incogniti scriptoris*, p. 111. See the fundamental study of E. J. Sluijter, 'Belering en verhulling? Enkele 17de-eeuwse teksten over de schilderkunst en de iconologische benadering van Noordnederlandse schilderijen uit deze periode', *De zeventiende eeuw*, 4 (1988), no. 2, pp. 3–28, esp. 13–15, trans. as 'Didactic and disguised meanings? Several seventeenth-century texts on painting and the iconological approach to northern Dutch paintings of this period', in *Art in History/History in Art*, ed. D. Freedberg and J. de Vries (Santa Monica, 1991), pp. 175–207; also his 'Venus, visus en pictura', *Nederlands Kunsthistorisch Jaarboek*, 42–3 (1991–2), pp. 337–96, esp. 352–81.

54 For characteristic sexual references and nudity, see *'t Amsterdamsch hoerdom*; *Den vaeck-verdryver*, p. 16 no. 36; *Den nieuwen clucht-vertelder*, pp. 12, 23–4, 72–3, 115, 214–15; J. Westerbaen, *Gedichten van Jacob Westerbaen, Ridder van Brandwijck en Gybland &c.* (3 vols, The Hague, 1672), vol. 2, pp. 506, 507–8, 522, 527–8; for scatological motifs, *Klucht van de koeck-vreyer*, pp. 16, 20, 22; an epigram of Constantijn Huygens of 21 February 1655 in Huygens, *Gedichten*, vol. 5, p. 182; *Den nieuwen clucht-vertelder*, pp. 21, 23–4, 47, 50–1, 56–7, 59, 69, 97, 115, 119, 130–1, 139–40, 140–2, 143, 194–5, 210; Westerbaen, ibid., vol. 2, pp. 511, 520, 525. These texts for private reading are more explicit about nakedness, sex and scatology than plays. Like paintings and prints, performances relied on metaphors for sex and genitalia.

55 For laughing prompts issued in plays and jest-books, see Westermann, *The Amusements*, Chapter 3.

56 Houbraken, *Groote schouburgh*, vol. 3, pp. 15, 18, 20, 21, 22, 25, 26, 30.

57 Pels, *Dichtkunst*, p. 68: '[A poem] should lead one's mind where the author wants to lead it. / Just as a face, which laughs, makes us laugh too, / so a crying one can press sympathy from us.'

58 The comic poet David Questiers contributed the poem cited to the *Amsterdamse mengelmoez*, p. 32. Ibid., p. 157, for a similar poem by his sister, the painter Catharina Questiers; for four others, see J. Zoet, *D'uitsteekenste digt-kunstige werken ... bestaande in verschaiden ernsthaftige en boertige stoffen* (Amsterdam, 1675), p. 195. Democritus: Bremmer, Chapter 1 of this volume.

59 L. B. Alberti, *On Painting*, trans. J. R. Spencer (New Haven, 1956), p. 78; Van Mander, *Het schilder-boeck*, fol. 18r–[18v].

60 J. Tamboer, *Het toneel der snaaken* (Amsterdam, 1700); P. P. Schmidt, *Zeventiende-eeuwse kluchtboeken uit de Nederlanden: een descriptieve bibliografie* (Utrecht, 1986), pp. 118–23, doubts the title-page's attribution of the collection to Meerhuysen, and suggests it was a marketing ploy because Tamboer was legendary for his comic persona. Meerhuysen indeed died some 33 years before the first known edition of this volume. During his life, one jest-book already claimed to be written in 'the spirit of Jan Tamboer'; *De geest van Jan Tamboer* (Amsterdam, 1656); Schmidt, ibid., p. 42, tentatively identifies the printer Jan van Duisberg as author. Further on Meerhuysen, E. F. Kossmann, 'De polemiek over de vertooningen van

Jan Vos in 1660 en *De t'zamenspraeck van Jan Tamboer en Jan Vos'*, *Oud Holland*, 30 (1912), pp. 37–49.

61 This coterie contributed poems to comic compilations such as *Klioos kraam, vol verscheiden gedichten*, ed. H. Rintjus (2 vols, Leeuwarden, 1656–7), and the *Amsterdamse mengelmoez*. Questiers responded to the joke about him in the latter volume, p. 121.

62 Herman Roodenburg, Chapter 8 of this volume; see also R. M. Dekker and H. Roodenburg, 'Humor in de zeventiende eeuw: opvoeding, huwelijk en seksualiteit in de moppen van Aernout van Overbeke (1632–1674)', *Tijdschrift voor sociale geschiedenis*, 10 (1984), pp. 244–6, and their edition of Van Overbeke's manuscript: A. van Overbeke, *Anecdota sive historiae jocosae: een zeventiende-eeuwse verzameling moppen en anekdotes* (Amsterdam, 1991), pp. xii–xviii.

63 W. A. Liedtke, *Flemish Paintings in the Metropolitan Museum of Art* (2 vols, New York, 1984), pp. 5–10. I discuss other self-consciously comic personae in Dutch literature and painting in Westermann, 'Jan Steen, Frans Hals'.

64 Typographic conventions of printed plays show when asides to the audience were used to comic effect. The theorizing poets of Nil Volentibus Arduum attempted to curtail the use of 'alleenspraaken' (monologues) and 'terzydespraaken' (asides) to preserve the unified illusion of reality presented in tragedy and comedy; characteristically, they made an exception for drunken characters, stock figures of comedy; Harmsen, *Onderwys*, text and commentary of Day 19; and Beenen and Harmsen, *De tweeling*, pp. 95–100.

65 The characters Hansje in M. Fockens, *Klucht van dronken Hansje* (Amsterdam, 1657); Pieter in the *Klucht van de koeck-vreyer*, p. 30; Koen in J. Lemmers, *De jalourse Lammert ... vertoont op de Amsterdamsche schouburg* (Amsterdam, 1680), p. 15; and six others cited by Van Moerkerken, *Nederlandsch kluchtspel*, vol. 1, p. 5.

66 Sweerts, *De tien vermakelikheden*, pp. 117–26 and engr. IX opp. p. 112. An engraved *Visite à l'accouchée* by Bosse, from his *Mariage à la ville* series, is almost as straightforward as the illustration to Sweerts's text. A poem recording the women's conversation suggests the event's piquancy, however, as does the presence of a male eavesdropper, peeking from behind the bed curtain; Villa, *Le XVIIe siècle*, pl. 60, and Habert, *Abraham Bosse*, no. 3d.

67 F. W. Robinson, *Gabriel Metsu (1629–1667): a study of his place in Dutch genre painting of the Golden Age* (New York, 1974), pp. 52–6, fig. 130; for Coques, T. H. Lunsingh Scheurleer, 'Enkele oude Nederlandse kraamgebruiken', *Antiek*, 6 (1971–2), pp. 297–332, esp. 302 fig. 4b. Compare the paintings by Matthijs Naiveu and Cornelis Troost; E. J. Sluijter et al., *Leidse fijnschilders: Van Gerrit Dou tot Frans van Mieris de Jonge, 1630–1760* (Leiden, Stedelijk Museum De Lakenhal; Zwolle, 1988), no. 58, ill. [exhibition catalogue]; J. W. Niemeijer, *Cornelis Troost, 1696–1750* (Assen, 1973), nos. 593S, 594T, 595T, and 597T, all ill.

68 For the functions of the figure seen from behind, see M. Koch, *Die Rückenfigur im Bild von der Antike bis Giotto* (Recklinghausen, 1965),

and J. L. Koerner, *Caspar David Friedrich and the Subject of Landscape* (London, 1990), pp. 149–244.

69 Sweerts, *De tien vermakelikheden*, pp. 126–8, 139–41, ridicules the midwife's preoccupation with tips and the stinginess of the father and guests in dispensing them.

70 A nineteenth-century restorer obscured the primary joke by painting out the cornuto gesture; it re-emerged when the painting was cleaned in 1983. J. Ingamells, *The Wallace Collection Catalogue of Pictures*, Vol. IV: *Dutch and Flemish* (London, 1992), no. P111. J. B. Descamps identified the man making the gesture as Steen himself; *La vie des peintres flamands, allemands et hollandois* (4 vols, Paris, 1753–64), vol. 3, pp. 30–1.

71 J. Vos, *Medea* (Amsterdam, 1667), introduction. Comic writers attained disorder by the discursive structure of their plays or tales. To mimic the unruly cadences of actual speech, they used ametrical verse, broken rhyme and prose, which was still exceptional in fictional writing.

72 For the didactic power of comedy, see note 20. Prefaces to comic texts emphasize their recreational function; see Bredero, *Spaanschen Brabander*, pp. 141–2. The jest-book title *Den vaeck-verdryver* means 'sleep-chaser'.

73 Many cultures view the comic as salutary, and seventeenth-century Dutch society was no exception; see, for example, Van Beverwyck, *Schat*, p. 63.

74 For claims that comic representations deter licence, see note 20. Among the vocal skeptics were Wittewrongel and even Pels.

75 Pers, *Bacchus wonder-wercken*, title-page.

76 On the functions of 'world-upside-down' processes, see B. A. Babcock (ed.), introduction to *The Reversible World: symbolic inversion in art and society* (Ithaca and London, 1978), pp. 13–36; D. Kunzle, 'World upside down: iconography of a European broadsheet type', ibid., pp. 39–94; N. Z. Davis, 'The reasons of misrule' and 'Women on top' in her *Society and Culture in Early Modern France* (Stanford, 1975), pp. 97–151; H. Pleij, *Het gilde van de blauwe schuit: literatuur, volksfeest en burgermoraal in de late middeleeuwen* (2nd edn, Amsterdam, 1983); U. Eco, 'Frames of comic freedom', in U. Eco et al., *Carnival!* (Berlin, 1984), pp. 1–9.

77 This psychological function was worked out for modern joke culture by Sigmund Freud in *Der Witz und seine Beziehung zum Unbewußten* (Leipzig and Vienna, 1905); trans. J. Strachey as *Jokes and their Relation to the Unconscious*, vol. 8 of the Standard Edition of the Complete Psychological Works of Sigmund Freud (London, 1960).

78 P. Stallybrass and A. White, *The Politics and Poetics of Transgression* (London, 1986), esp. pp. 149–202. This book historicizes both Freud's joke analysis and the celebratory interpretation of the Rabelaisian comic by M. M. Bakhtin, *Rabelais and his World*, trans. H. Iswolsky (Cambridge, MA, 1968).

79 See H. R. Hoetink et al., *Mauritshuis: Dutch painting of the Golden Age* (Washington, National Gallery of Art, and three other venues; The Hague, 1982), no. 33 [exhibition catalogue]; on the aphrodisiac character of oysters, see Cats, *Houwelyck*, p. 394, and De Jongh, *Tot lering*, no. 62. For a joking reference, *Klucht van de koeck-vreyer*, p. 24.

80 On catching birds with salt, see J. R. ter Molen, *Zout op tafel: de*

geschiedenis van het zoutvat (Rotterdam, Museum Boymans-van Beuningen, 1976), p. 23 [exhibition catalogue]. For the bird as phallic metaphor, E. de Jongh, 'Erotica in vogelperspectief: De dubbelzinnigheid van een reeks 17de eeuwse genrevoorstellingen', *Simiolus*, 3 (1968–9), pp. 22–74, esp. 27–31 and 49–52, and Vandenbroeck, 'Jheronimus Bosch', pp. 183–5.

81 Sweerts, *Koddige en ernstige opschriften*, vol. 1, p. 121; Van Beverwyck, *Schat*, p. 151.

82 Sluijter, *Leidse fijnschilders*, *passim*, and idem, 'Over fijnschilders en "betekenis": naar aanleiding van Peter Hecht, *De Hollandse fijnschilders*', *Oud Holland*, 105 (1991), pp. 50–63.

83 G. de Lairesse, *Groot schilderboek, waar in de schilderkonst in al haar deelen grondig werd onderweezen, ook door redeneeringen en prent-verbeeldingen verklaard* (2nd edn, 2 vols, Haarlem, 1740; 1st edn, Amsterdam, 1707), p. 54. Contemporary theorists described misapplied gesture as laughter-inducing.

84 W. P. Wolters, 'Het oesteretende vrouwtje van Jan Steen', *De Gids*, 37 (1873), no. 1, pp. 317–61, esp. 357.

85 Sluijter, *Leidse fijnschilders*, pp. 13–15; Sluijter, 'Over fijnschilders'. For additional statements of seduction as metaphor for the deceptiveness of painting, see F. Junius, *De schilder-konst der oude* (Middelburgh, 1641), pp. 42–3; Sweerts, *Koddige en ernstige opschriften*, vol. 4, p. 64; J. van Hoven, *Schildery van de Haagsche kermis, nevens de rarekiek van de Amsterdamsche kermis* (The Hague, 1715), p. 7; and the contributions of Sweerts and the painter-poet Willem Schellinks to *Klioos kraam*, pp. 224, 351–2.

86 Epigram of 5 February 1656, in Huygens, *Gedichten*, vol. 6, p. 4. On salt as metaphor for epigrammatic sharpness, see T. ter Meer, *Snel en dicht: een studie over de epigrammen van Constantijn Huygens* (Amsterdam and Atlanta, 1991), pp. 22–3, 29.

10

Parliamentary Hilarity inside the French Constitutional Assembly (1789–91)

Antoine de Baecque

On Monday 3 August 1789, in the midst of parliamentary discussion about the Declaration of Human Rights and Citizenship Rights, following the contradictory and 'metaphysical' orations of Malouet, Mounier and the count of Antraigues, a priest mounted the rostrum to stammer out the following request: 'I am asking indulgence from this assembly for a shy novice who is speaking before you for the first and, quite possibly, the last time. One must not set one's sights too high, and I would like to speak to you about a matter related to my line of work ...' It was at that point in his speech that the journalist from the *Moniteur universel*, in common with most of the other 'logographers' transcribing the 'national discourse' for publication in their periodicals, noted: 'Loud laughter broke out in the assembly.' These journalists were watching from the same gallery the mood and pace of the work being carried out by the 945 assemblymen at the new amphitheatre of the Salle des Menus-Plaisirs at Versailles. The priest hesitated, rather bewildered in front of his audience just as he had admitted when introducing himself, then went on to propose dedicating the National Assembly to religion with an altar inside and a chaplain in an adjacent office, 'to whom each member of the assembly, before and after undertaking legislative action, could confess his sins.' Once again, the journalists noted that at that very moment 'laughter erupted'. Not having completed his speech, the priest, 'without becoming flustered, continued in spite of the amused mood of the assembly with his spiritual suggestions.' After a few minutes, against a backdrop of general laughter, the president of the assembly interrupted the speaker and officially closed what had become a long session, leaving the bemused priest alone at the rostrum. His propositions had barely been listened to, let alone accepted, yet they do reveal to the historian a characteristic specific to the National Assembly: on occasion, the political body laughed.

With further consideration, this statement should not come as a surprise. The work of the assembly, extremely hectic, at times highly stressed, often difficult and austere, nonetheless provided the occasion for outbursts of loud laughter. These outbursts could be construed as a simple release of tension and were ostensibly perceived as being out of place, given the dignity of the institution; or, they could be construed as a particularly well-constructed piece of political discourse authored by one of the masters of the art. The anecdote I have just presented has led me to a more systematic analysis of the behaviour of this very first French National Assembly, a body nearly a thousand members strong, which met during the period May 1789 to September 1791. This analysis is based on the observation of laughter, which in transcriptions of debates (beginning with the 'Chambre de la Restauration') was regularly classified under the heading of 'hilarity'.

At the beginning of the revolution, when the organization of the parliamentary sessions had not yet been established, these moments of humour were considered a collective action. We read: 'Laughter broke out', or sometimes, with a little more detail, 'loud bursts of laughter were heard'. On other occasions there might be a digression on the overall state of mind of the people's representatives: 'That statement incited widespread laughter, and the members of the assembly, exhausted by an overly long day of work, seized this moment of gaiety to ask for the suspension of the session' (28 July 1789). In any event, laughter had become a recurrent practice within the assembly, albeit ambiguous. When I re-read the parliamentary archives of the Constitutional Assembly,[1] over the 28 months of parliamentary sessions I counted 408 distinct incidents of laughter in the assembly recorded by the three major parliamentary journals of the time, *Le moniteur*, Bertrand Barère's *Le point du jour* and Le Hodey's *Le logographe*.

The 408 incidents could be interpreted in a variety of ways. The members of the assembly, considered collectively, laughed on average every other day, or over 14 times a month. This statement in itself, of course, may not amount to much, even if the assembly could be taken as representative of the enlightened elite at the end of the Old Regime. I do not maintain that a lawyer, a member of nobility open to new ideas, a philosopher-priest, would have laughed publicly 14 times per month in the past, as these outbursts of laughter did not occur on a regular basis. For several days, indeed several weeks on occasions, the assembly would not laugh a single time. For example, in 1789 no laughter is recorded between 5 May, the date of the meeting of the 'États Généraux' (States General), and 8 June, when the first collective laugh of the assembly was recorded by a journalist; there was no laughter, either, between 8 June and 4 July, or between 8 July and 28 July. The summer of 1789, unsurprisingly, was much less favourable to laughter than to political initiatives, to drafts of declaration and to what contemporaries were quick to label the 'moods' of the assembly – fear, enthusiasm, strictness and lyricism. On the other hand, some debates, especially those during the autumn of 1789 on religious statutes and the property of the clergy, incited both violent confrontations and remarkably burlesque scenes in the National Assembly.

My project, based on these 408 instances of recorded laughter, is not a chronology of humorous moments inside the Constitutional Assembly, since this would not be very significant. Rather, I will look mostly at the question of why there was laughter, which presumes a typology of laughter at this point in history: what were the circumstances and the context of laughter during parliamentary sessions? This approach also involves a typology of 'jokes' and comical situations specific to this group of almost 1000 men of culture. Other lines of enquiry will also be pursued: how, at the beginning of the revolution, was a collective political humour established as a tool of persuasion and combat? This humour inside the assembly filled out the texts, images and gestures of the culture of laughter, the 'French gaiety',[2] that observers often note, whether to criticize it or to praise it, and which was also prevalent when the National Assembly was convened. If this body of recorded information is studied seriously, the historian can witness the construction of a political arena perceived as being in danger of becoming a 'public comedy stage'. The danger was one of divisiveness and corruption, quite contrary to hopes and expectations of a renewed public stage for political modernism.

Certainly, the chroniclers of the day judged very harshly the presence of laughter within inner parliamentary circles. Laughter was provoked by 'out-of-place comments'; laughter was provoked by allowing the better part of the French spirit to yield to that traditional gaiety which the new, reborn generation sought to suppress; finally, laughter was provoked by a partisan spirit, which the revolutionaries, even amidst the most fundamental divisions, had always deplored. In assessing these 408 incidents the historian contributes somewhat to the notion of 'revolution by default', a reality opposite to the proclaimed ideal because of the imperfectibility of the world. Methodologically, this statement is no less interesting: laughter is best measured when it clashes with the sources of official culture (in this case, the records of the parliamentary proceedings); when it is inappropriate to laugh; also, when the historian has difficulty understanding it. Robert Darnton wrote that it was precisely when the historian feels utterly lost, having come across something abnormal and unexpected, that he becomes a discoverer, that he is able to forward his most stimulating interpretations.[3] This is the situation with laughter in the very assembly that was supposed to regenerate France.

Laughter, Out-of-Place Comments

A stern ideal for political assemblies was proclaimed on 6 June 1789 in the first internal code of conduct of the 600 members of the *tiers état*. This advocated a state of impassiveness, of solemnity, which would silence the outbursts of the group as a whole and restrain its collective affections: 'The members of the assembly will remain silent and will not change seats. Absolutely no sign of applause or approval will be allowed. Insults and displays of individual character are forbidden along with any outbursts of laughter.'[4] The quietness of the deliberations suggests an ideal of reason, and the manner of assembling reasonably, 'philosophically', at the end of the enlightened eighteenth century suggests those 'long-established assemblies where no tension or strong affection upsets the physical and natural presence of the community.' The same precepts were applied to public celebrations at the end of the Old Regime and during the revolution. There was a general mistrust, of cheerful gatherings, of carnivals, of overly joyous receptions and even of the spirited mood of crowds, as they were considered harmful and dangerous and able to excite the group literally into a state beside itself. Within the framework of a more limited assembly, such as the *tiers état* in 1789, and subsequently the National Assembly, the mistrust of public speech during riotous orations and the praise for public impassiveness, initially perceived as mutually incompatible, end up finding common ground: four 'censors', 'selected to enforce the internal code of conduct, are to be placed in each corner of the hall.'

Furthermore, the passage from the state of gaiety, at the outbreak of laughter, to that of philosophy and legislative wisdom was often described as a leap from one era to another. In renouncing laughter inside their political assembly, the French people would be able to change themselves: 'I know that, at first, the assembly will be in a joking mood, and that is to be expected', wrote the author of the *Première lettre à un ami sur l'Assemblée des États Généraux*, in January 1789:

The French always have to begin and end by singing and buffoonery; however, political affairs are simply too serious and too important. Even further still: despite the often maligned superficiality of this nation, I am quite far from believing that its core is as frivolous as it appears. Involve it in the more serious issues, and you will see what kind of lift it will get, what kind of boost it can enjoy from its patriotism. Believe me, my dear friend, this nation, which is so joyous, so spiritual, so friendly, so ready to laugh, is capable of serious efforts, profound reflection, noble enthusiasm, once it gets itself fixed on important goals. Up until now, this nation has seemingly been in a joking spirit only because it was prohibited from reasoning, because joking was all it was allowed, because it was forbidden instruction and denied the chance to take care of public affairs. Yet, a nation that has produced a Montesquieu, one in the midst of which a Jean-Jacques Rousseau developed the greatest moral and political truths, one where the wise Mably traced with such a sure hand the principles of law and government and the eternal alliance of politics with morals, such a nation, I continue, is in no way an essentially frivolous and laughing nation. It is, quite the contrary, capable of raising itself to the heights of seriousness just as it is of delving into the most sublime discussions.

And yet, this alliance of politics with morals, sealed by philosophical underpinnings and then extended as an ideal by the new assembly, was circumvented at times by previously prevailing attitudes. As in the case of public celebrations, where, from the early years of the revolution, the municipality of Paris was obliged to give in to French gaiety at special celebrations 'of eating and drinking to excess', of watching hot-air balloons and fireworks, of laughing at shows and of participating in jousts, reviving 'the games of slaves', 'children of the past'.[5] Likewise, even the political assembly turned to laughter at times, but not only laughter: more often, it would murmur, applaud, and even heckle. No code of conduct or censor could prevent it. Symptomatically, just two days after the adoption and public announcement of the assembly's first regulation, the *tiers état* assembly was jolted by its first collective outburst of laughter, a doubly improper outburst because it challenged a regulation and was not mere amusement but a political affront, a loud demonstration of a divisive, riotous mood.

On 8 June 1789, Malouet, a member much in evidence, as at previous sessions, returned to present a motion that this time was not on the legislative agenda. An anonymous member from Languedoc made a snide comment to put his loquacious colleague in his place, and this witty remark unleashed a guffaw from the hall: 'We are beholden to Mr Malouet for the ideas he has transmitted to us. Up until now, he has been willing to do so at almost all of our sessions; let us hope that for the sake of his patriotism, he will be intent on addressing us motions better suited to the day's agenda and on more propitious occasions (laughter).' Offended, Malouet tried to justify himself, but a reproving murmur forced him to remain silent. Ultimately, he even admitted to feeling a kind of public remorse, intending thereby to soften the angry mood of this large political body, 'a recognition that the motion presented was in fact premature'. This initial moment of laughter, after a month of daily sessions, was significant: first of all, from a political perspective, it acted to restore order. Though explicitly forbidden by the internal code of conduct, this resort to humour was in accordance with a tacit rule which the collective moods of the members were called upon to enforce: no single member, not even the most brilliant, not even Malouet or Mirabeau, should wield an excessive influence on his colleagues. This instinctive rule, expressed through moods and affections, was in its way the natural complement, the watchdog, of the internal code of conduct and one that was adopted by reason. Laughter was, exceptionally, authorized because it restored order and injected a dose of humility, and it served as a natural antidote to the 'hybris' of men in power.

Yet, most of the laughter by the assembly was not intended for this virtuous purpose. Humour mostly opposed out-of-place discourse, behaviour and actions: a whimsical aside lost amidst an arduous discussion, unintentional absurdities discovered in a decree, illogical expressions out of the mouth of a rather strait-laced member – for instance the bishop of Chartres, who proposed, on 7 August 1789, 'that the decree have appended to it the stipulation that game animals could only be hunted with innocuous weapons'. These were the most common 'comical moments' in the assembly, 200 by my count.

Sometimes, a few moments of delirium so shook the assembly that – often after a long day of work and debate – it found itself 'in another world', a world beyond its internal code of conduct, beyond its impassiveness, beyond its legislative concerns. This was a world in which behaviour followed a regressive kind of rationale denounced by the most critical observers and journalists of the time. Such was the context when the abbé Grégoire wanted to read aloud a series of anonymous letters he had received: 'A categorical "no" was heard throughout the assembly hall. The abbot insisted; and the same "no" was repeated with the same fervour. He then made the observation that the author of these anonymous letters had threatened to denounce him at the Palais-Royal if the letters were not read. For each response, and in unison, one resounding laugh was screamed from all sides: "Burn 'em, burn 'em, burn the letters" . . .'[6]

This type of conduct or incongruous expression could sometimes reach a state of parodic art. At this point, we are delving not just into another genre of laughter – after all it still falls into the realm of taking words, expressions and gestures out of context – but also into another type of rationale: purposely twisting a word, an expression or a gesture to provoke laughter. An unintentional, comic antic was followed by a kind of provocation: the idea was not so much to convince colleagues by resorting to laughter, but to amuse them in order eventually to be heard. For a few seconds, even minutes, the assembly would actually leave the confines of its designated role and listen, in spite of itself, to a virtuoso or an aficionado performing a pun, a pastiche or a parody. These were generally short-lived escapes, since a member would normally invoke censorship and quickly restore order to the institution, thereby preventing this digression from becoming, in the absence of any restraint, a loss of control. For example, when the Viscount Mirabeau, younger brother of the patriotic orator, attempted to capitalize on an initial pun that had generated widespread laughter, he was immediately interrupted sternly and insensitively by a colleague: 'Mr Lavie promptly retorted from his seat, "I ask whether we have been convened here for a course in epigrams and whether the rostrum is a stage."'[7] If the assembly, reacting by laughter, actually did at times find itself in another world – though only temporarily – beyond its habitual role and rationality, it nevertheless did not stray far from the sophistication of the times. This type of laughter could be analysed as repositioning a traditional high-society culture towards the new political culture, a brief reorientation, basically unauthorized, often poorly esteemed, and fragmented. It was as if, occasionally – about ten times a month – a jumble of various approaches (parody, pastiche, misquotation) could suddenly grab hold of the political agenda, provoking a short and contained outburst of laughter, one spurred by a collective bad conscience. The high-society 'way' to shine would then intervene and short-circuit the political 'way' to impress. Each time it happened, these encounters were significant: a kind of misplaced laughter exploited the art of pastiche, parody and travesty that generally surrounds the world of politics – one of the techniques dominating political writings and pamphlets at the time: misquotations from the Bible, parodies of mythological fables or pastiches of taxonomical work. This culture of travesty, from 1789 on, utilized the political arena to a great extent as a preferred source of material – pastiches of the Declaration of Human Rights, parodies of decrees, mock 'national assemblies' (consisting of cuckolded husbands, prostitutes, rascals, etc.) – and sometimes succeeded in penetrating the very heart of the 'real' assembly's most respectable political debates. From one perspective, a kind of cultural contamination was taking place: laughter, a common practice of high society and of journalism, reached the National Assembly through a few individual characters.

An art of diversion and a few individual characters – these were the two key ingredients for the 'misplaced' laughter within the National Assembly. This diversion was rooted in the major, common cultural bases of the period: Latin culture, religious culture and scientific culture were the most often cited sources. It is worth noting that outbursts of laughter would systematically accompany puns related to these three cultural bases, as in the case of the priest quoting Horace, only to be repeated by the president of the assembly, who, against a backdrop of widespread laughter, silenced the priest and further rattled him by adding a parodical Latin saying.[8] Along the same lines, on 3 August 1789, the assembly decided not to limit the time allotted to orators' speeches, and a priest, 'in the midst of the most fervent bouts of laughter', pronounced as a biblical parody of the end of the world, 'The Lebanese cedars are upside down!' Each period had its preferred parodic themes, and in so doing sought to corrupt, through the use of laughter, a common cultural base. These out-of-place, reinvented Latin and biblical citations that upset the serenity of the assembly were, perhaps, the period's version of false advertising, or at least something very close.

The assembly quickly identified its most jovial merrymakers – and came to mistrust them just as quickly. Yet, there was only a single one among them who systematically utilized his comic weapon as a political practice and, often out of provocation, regularly employed the out-of-place word, gesture or behaviour in front of his colleagues, namely the Viscount Mirabeau, traditionalist and notorious counter-revolutionary. His 'course in epigrams' began in September 1789; and, over a period of some ten months, he led the charge in this 'war of laughs'. Interjecting frequently to contradict his brother, whether from his seat or from the rostrum, he would introduce himself as the 'ordinary hornet of legislative power', endowed with 'the most epigrammatic buzzing' and the 'most joyous gullet of the aristocracy'. His parliamentary tactic of portraying himself as a counter-revolutionary 'guerrilla' drove him to parody and, though he did not lack verve, he nonetheless deeply irritated his colleagues during the decrees and legislation of the assembly. In January 1790 he proposed, against the backdrop of both laughter and jeers, a 'declaration of horses' rights' during the discussion devoted to the national stud farms. Along the same lines, during his tenure as secretary of the assembly, in September 1789, he took the minutes with a certain liberty of expression not necessarily appreciated by the other members. On 26 September 1789, after the public reading of his minutes from the previous day's session, the younger Mirabeau – already nicknamed 'Mirabeau the barrel' because of his stoutness and the gluttony he details in his satirical writings – was brusquely singled out:

> There were long discussions over the editing of the minutes, punctuated by murmurs and snickers. The transcriptions of the minutes were not deemed dignified. One member cried out: 'When will the minutes of the proceedings be composed in epigrams, for how long will the dignity of our sessions be ridiculed?' The Viscount Mirabeau then apologized, saying that for the preceding session he had been accused of verbosity, and

that for this session he had simply deleted all the details (murmurs). A member continued: 'Only to be replaced by your witticisms . . .' To which he replied: 'I simply don't know what to do in order to obey this assembly; a door must be either open or closed' (laughter). And it was the viscount once again who, at the end of the very long and tumultuous session of 16 January 1790, addressed President Target of the assembly in terms so disrespectful and unexpected that they incited a widespread riotous reaction: 'Mr President, send us to dinner, and we'll send you packing, and everyone will be happy' (general laughter).

So we can see that laughter played a central role in the assembly, even if initially it was out of context and became funny precisely by being exceptional and fanciful. It made its impact felt by contaminating the internal workings of the National Assembly – a space preserved by its code of internal conduct, its set of attitudes and an ideal of impassive and deferential behaviour – with the external environment, a political space open to the most contradictory of moods.

The National Assembly at the Heart of French Gaiety

Shortly afterwards, though, the assembly, this ideally preserved space, was placed at the centre of French gaiety. Actually, political writers working in a public forum from the end of 1788, thanks to the freedom of the press, had two good reasons to summon laughter. First, they sought to acknowledge the traditionally 'gay' character of the French, presumed difficult to reform even if each individual was striving to create a new man, a regenerated man. The second reason had to do with developing a powerful technique for conviction, also traditional in its own right, and most essential at a time when, faced with a multiplication of political events and competing journalists, each author was seeking to attract potential readership. Laughter, in terms of 'French spiritedness', had therefore been connected with laughter as a 'persuasive ingredient' in order to mould a political framework in which the two factions, royalist and patriotic, rivalled one another by presenting to their eager, attentive readers fictional characters, puns and comical situations. Everyone, from then on, would invoke, albeit in contrasting terms, that useful virtue of *eutrapélie*,[9] which had first been extolled by François de Sales, then by de Sales' followers or the Jesuit schools that tried to provide a theoretical, ethical and practical framework for using 'decent joyousness' to lure and convince its followers. This application of gaiety was at the very heart of the discussions held by the revolutionary journalists, in spite of its strong condemnation by the National

Assembly. This condemnation stemmed from a basic mistrust of any humour that would shift legislative discourse away from the ideal of reason, or, as we shall see later, anything that could divide the political body into rival factions.

To illuminate this debate on the correct use of laughter that gripped the National Assembly, I will look for support from the period's key author who, undoubtedly thanks to his Jesuit training (he was a brilliant instructor at the institution), paid most attention to 'French gaiety'. Joseph-Antoine Cérutti, at the end of 1788, reworked one of his previous manuscripts for republication as the political situation developed: *Les avantages et les origines de la gaieté française* ('The advantages and the origins of French gaiety').[10] Cérutti defined the French personality there by its 'vivaciousness' and its 'cordiality': 'You possess', he wrote to the 'French man',

> a core of joyfulness all your own that inspires those around you and that allows you to reconcile with your most obstinate of enemies. I would be able to distinguish one of your compatriots solely by the manner in which he would listen to me speak. A friendly smile, maybe even a sly one, would be his first response; a joke would immediately thereafter enliven the conversation; and had we started with the most serious matter, I do not doubt that we would finish by the most enjoyable banter.

The author went on to assign himself the mission of convincing through participation in the 'bantering': 'Nothing strikes me as being friendlier than your gaiety, nothing strikes me as being more useful either: it's ornamental, it's resourceful.' An ornament of spirit, a resource for persuasive discourse – this is how Cérutti viewed the rhetoric of this 'decent joyousness' appropriate to preachings. And yet he introduced this rhetoric into a political context. Cérutti undertook to define the use of laughter politically.

In so doing, he provided an in-depth portrayal of political customs related to the penchant for gaiety. Laughter and 'despotism' are incompatible:

> Gaiety cannot exist under despotic rule. It cannot be within the despot who is too highly revered to be despised, too encased in his opulence to be encumbered, too pleasure-driven to have any. Neither can it be transmitted to those misfortunate subjects of despotism. The reason is quite clear: just like herds of cattle that frolic in the prairie when left to graze freely, upon entering the barn, they become saddened, and they bellow with horror before being slaughtered.

Yet, laughter and 'republic' are scarcely more compatible: 'War could only break out in a republican state where some kind of joviality could be heard. In a republic, happiness is attained, but without playfulness. The idea of amusement and banter does not tend to coincide with the seriousness of the republic; a song would rejoice only a few people preoccupied by a political system, and the foolishness of one individual does not mean a thing for those who contemplate incessantly the needs of the greater public.' Between the 'horror' of despotism and the rather stern 'happiness' of the republic, only the 'tempered monarchy' could favourably accommodate the French sense of humour:

> Your climate primes you for gaiety, your government ties you to it. There is only one monarchic state, and monarchic like yours, where gaiety can be expressed positively and reign unobstructed. You possess enough freedom, but not enough independence, and powerful and affable leaders who govern out of passion; subjects who are obedient out of honour. Such a system provides the flexibility for a dynamic and playful spirit. To be completely convinced of the difference that exists on this particular point between a republic, a despotic state and a tempered monarchy, consider a family where the father governs, the slaves languish, and the children play. The father represents the republicans; the slaves, those misfortunate victims of despotic rule; and the children, those cheerful subjects of a monarch such as the King of France.

Gaiety, then, is ascribed to the tempered monarchic regime: the French are the 'children' of the king and of laughter. The revolution did not exactly take place on new ground, and had to welcome these children. Some revolutionaries would seek to reform these children through the application of republican principles, to show them the way to 'happiness'. In this case, condemnations of 'frivolity', of 'lack of substance' and of 'bantering' were pronounced one after the other in order to contrast this version of a 'Frenchman of the past' with the 'renewed man', whose body and soul had been shaped by the revolution. However, from Cérutti's perspective, the power of conviction is transmitted through childish antics themselves: politics, respecting the regime specific to the jovial French spirit (the 'constitutional monarchy', a revised version of the previous 'tempered monarchy'), was drawn through bantering and laughter into 'vivaciousness' and 'cordiality'.

A certain number of patriotic authors supported Cérutti in this domain of 'seduction by the decency in laughter'. For example his friend Ginguené, the closest collaborator on the *Feuille villageoise* (*The*

Village News), provided a civilized and useful interpretation of Rabelais,[11] in whom Ginguené recognized the same aim as in the ex-Jesuit. Initially, these selections consisted essentially of the language of the body. Rabelais 'wrote at a time when it was necessary to protect oneself with an allegoric veil, no matter how transparent it may have been.' He invoked the 'narrative form' of allegory in order to thwart censors and 'feudal superstitions' alike, thereby veiling every truth. 'At this time, however', as Ginguené continued, 'truth marches on with its head held high', but the playful imagination that, in the past, had veiled the truth, can and must, thanks to the revolution, raise this veil and give the persuasive laugh free rein. It was with this demonstration of the utility of Rabelais' allegorical comedy that Ginguené invited his audience to read 'Maître François'.

However, the reading was somewhat selective because the reputation of Rabelais continued to slide, even if his rediscovery dated back to the 1770s. His grotesque, his farce and his 'obscene images' could have threatened the decorum of French gaiety. It had been necessary to keep his work within the realm of the comic imagination by rejecting all elements of grotesque exaggeration:

> I am cautious about all that is approved and about re-reading everything: what is exaggerated, extravagant, obscure in mean-ing, obscene without gaiety, grotesque without beauty, trivial, insignificant and vulgar has only had the chance to bore me but once. Yet, the pleasant tales, the many features of an ingenious and delicate style, the images that brush the philosophical ideas by their cheerful appearances, all those bold expressions that were suitable for the past were still so for our times up until a few years ago, and they shine today with a frankness, a superior reason, a wisdom that I find charming. Each time I would take my Rabelais, it was only after having re-read all the passages marked in my copy that I could put it down. I thought that what accurate, pleasant and imaginative material they contained on 'les Grands', on warrior fantasies, on parliamentary pillaging, on monks and even on the Pope; that all this, let me repeat, would have something spicy to it, maybe even useful, and could make an impression on attitudes by its comedic authority.

Ginguené developed a code from his reading of the 'marked passages', namely the proper usage of laughter. He proceeded to take advantage of a few of Rabelais' characters to laugh a restrained laugh at the king with the 'big gullet', at the queen with the 'big billy-can', at the 'seventeen thousand nine hundred and thirteen cows' necessary for maintaining the census, at the 'noble stuffed cats', at 'Grippeminaud' the Farmer General and at the prelates of the 'island of Papimanie', the rascals and drunks venerating the 'papacy' that endows them with a 'sovereign disguise'.

In addition, statements of intentions extracted from brochures demonstrated the strong grasp which persuasion by decorous laughter had on the playful imaginations of the 'new generation' of the revolution. 'Beneath a very jovial, and even rather smudged, wrapping, this work has sealed within it a set of pure morals, some philosophical ideas and several comments borne out by the ongoing revolution. Young man, read and laugh; then re-read and ponder. Perhaps, you won't be wasting your time' – so ran an 'avertissement' by the same author who republished the naughty and light-hearted brochure *La vie et l'oeuvre de feu l'abbé Bazin, evêque de Mizoura en Mizourie* (*The Life and Work of the Late abbé Bazin, Bishop of Mizoura in Mizourie*). This theme found support in an anti-clerical brochure printed in January 1790, *Le régiment de la calotte*, which, after an explicit inscription, 'Readers . . . read and laugh at the aristocracy', tried to lead the French revolutionary, who had become 'a bit too serious, dreaming only of punishment and vengeance', to a more 'serene gaiety', and one no less patriotic:

> Public expressions of amusement must especially be encouraged provided they remain honourable, and those works that, in the guise of laughter, provide salutary advice should particularly be emphasized. And I feel that this joyfulness, far from hindering the operations necessary for assuring our liberty, would instead serve to maintain each and every individual in his proper duties, thwart any potential intrigue, warn of self-aggrandizing intentions and, most importantly, punish bad citizens by denouncing with excessive irony their turpitude and their baseness.

In a similar fashion, several patriotic brochures of May 1789 were aimed at promoting the *tiers état* through gaiety, contrasting it with the 'contemptuous faces' of the nobility and the 'blank faces' of the clergy. These brochures celebrated, in this '*tiers état*, the soul to laugh to the point of crying', the 'best of orders', the one that succeeds in mocking the 'ridiculous ceremony' imposed by the hierarchy of seating and dress during the procession and then the opening session of the *États Généraux*.

In appropriating the notion of 'decent joyousness', counter-revolutionary satire very quickly found its place. There was even a kind of renaissance taking shape: the literary movement born at the beginning of the 1780s and counting among its followers masters of irony and virtuosos at their craft, such as Rivarol, Champcenetz, Palissot, Sabathier and Dorat, carried on into the revolution. It rose up against the likes of

Cérutti, Ginguené and Grouvelle, all rivals in the *République des lettres* of the Old Regime before becoming rivals at the forefront of revolutionary literature. The 'patriotic humorists' attacked their adversaries as 'overly subtle souls' and portrayed them in these terms: 'Rivarol convinced the bookseller Le Jay that satire is the first genre of literature. Two entire centuries were spent educating the world; the time has now come to entertain this world in order to make it forget all it has learned and to force it to become mean.'[12] The weapon used by these 'traditionalist humorists' was the satirical dismembering of the bodies of their victims. The art of caricature practised by groups of satirists (whose sharp-edged, biting humour was best illustrated by Rivarol in his *Petit almanach de nos grands hommes* in 1788 followed by the *Petit dictionnaire des grands hommes de la Révolution* in 1790) actually did take aim very precisely at dismembering bodies. On the basis of a single detail, a subtle imagination could draw a distasteful feature that served to 'slice up the bodies of innocent victims with the satirical pen', and from one feature draw a defamatory portrait. Subtle minds could find in these galleries of characters an opportunity to exercise the virtuosity of their writing, the 'corruption and decadence of laughter' in the words of Cérutti. As an aside, Cérutti was not spared the daggers either, as he assumed the nickname of 'Des Superficies' in the *Bibliothèque de la cour et de la ville* and solicited this comment from Rivarol: 'Nothing indifferent has ever been produced by the hand of such a great author since even boredom can be so nicely followed up.'[13] It was to combat this 'boredom' that the group of satirists was formed; they then concentrated on deriding the pretentiousness of the revolutionaries-turned-politicians.

From the beginning of November 1789, the *Actes des apôtres* (*Acts of the Apostles*), the journal created by the group of satirists, caused a stir by its caustic writing. The group, supported by a powerful publisher of the Palais Royal, Gattey, having located a talented engraver, Weber, presented one caricature an issue, soon to be joined by, and I quote, 'the most joyous souls of the entire country, heirs to the marquis de Bièvre, the inventor of the French version of the pun'. It set its sights on the very heart of the new political system, the National Assembly itself. Between autumn 1789 and spring 1790, the image of the assembly had been decisively degraded by these humorous attacks. There also appeared in the same vein as the *Actes des apôtres* a biblical parody, 'relating with amusement the actions and the gestures of the new apostles of liberty' (in other words, the members of the assembly), together with several other publications followed by series of 'comic pamphlets'. The assembly was thereby transformed into a comic stage, which represented a complete about-face from the ideal of impassiveness and solemnity. The Salle du Manège, where the Tuileries sessions were held, was transformed in these works into a theatre of laughter, into (from the title of one of these comic pamphlets) a 'National Spectacle'. The pamphlet inspiring this title went on to state: 'The great comedians of the Salle du Manège will perform today *Le roi dépouillé*, a very highly acclaimed old comic show.'[14] This comic stage was associated with parody-inspired specialized journals, chronicles, revealing and anecdotal details in the counter-revolutionary satirical press, such as the *Almanach des métamorphoses nationales*, *La chronique du manège*, *La grande ménagerie*, *Il est possible d'en rire*, *Le livre nouveau des charlatans modernes*, *Les chevaux au manège* and *Mes étrennes aux douze cents*. Here, amidst this body of literature of political satire, we find the Viscount Mirabeau, who, in June 1790, when abolishing the titles of nobility was high on the agenda, was nicknamed 'Riquetti-la-tonne'. He was the author of a journal devoted entirely to a humorous narration of the debates within the National Assembly: *Les dîners, or the truth comes out while laughing*. In this work, the younger Mirabeau had entered into a sort of contract with his reader: the author has to 'entertain, while instructing, his reader'. He discussed the nature of this contract in one of the very first issues of *Les dîners*, in January 1790:

> It is a kind of contractual commitment, one that I will do my best to fulfil, and one that consists of reporting each day the most salient features of the deliberations of our august body of senators. An entirely accurate journal should not be expected; those already exist in sufficient quantities and, like Egyptian grasshoppers, tend to devour one another. Besides which, my intention herein is not at all to establish myself as a journalist, as I rather despise that line of work. No, our National Assembly's sessions are far too captivating for that: they actually serve the purpose of amusing us.

In the space of 15 issues, Mirabeau developed, through the use of anecdotes, parodies of decrees and jokes, the most derisive portrait of members acting grotesquely on the stage of the 'Comédie Nationale'.

At the beginning of January 1790, this satire of the National Assembly was still mounting. Taking advantage of the forthcoming carnival, a celebration of laughter and travesty that the newly created municipality of Paris had formally banned from the street out of a fear of masked enemies and to break away from previous attitudes, the royalists once again eagerly seized upon the theme of subversive attacks perpetrated through laughter. They picked up on this notion of carnival and foisted it, in writing, upon the National Assembly as a 'test of laughter'. It was the *Actes des apôtres*, as expected, that ignited the laughter, by proposing, in the chapter dated from the 'day of the kings', a description of the opening of the 'Club de la Révolution' fit for a carnival-like costume party.

> Those with malicious intentions spread the word that the current revolution would not be a lasting one because it had altered the joyous French spirit, and that the cheerfulness so essential to their spirit seemed banished forever from the capital. We can only respond in a victorious manner to the objections of these dissidents. Dare we say that today the severe and sad revolution has been consummated, and that France, after having set the example, for all Europe, of courage and rigor, after having given Europe models for the constitutions already written and those to be written, yes France, let us say it, will continue to be the centre for the art of dramatic mime, for the appreciation of travesty and for joyous entertainment.

Thus wrote the satirist, delicately suggesting the language of a defender of the revolution.[15] The description did not spare either Condorcet, who was called 'Masque Sérénissime' (a reference to the Venetian carnival), or the Constitutional Assembly, which had become the 'National Circus of Travesty'. This carnival-inspired story spread very quickly, since two major *Carnavals politiques* were published at the time of Mardi-Gras, on 9 February 1790. Satire would now be used for pastiches of denunciatory language, not removing masks as the patriotic journalists struggled to do, but describing the masks meticulously in order better to reveal the 'real nature' of revolutionary politicians. *The Great Patriotic Costume Ball* latched onto these denunciatory signs, commenting, 'Advertising is the safeguard of the people', and then introduced the masquerade and the 'masked members' of this patriotic carnival led by the Jacobins: Le Chapelier as a 'butler', Guillotin as a 'locksmith carrying his new machine', Théroigne de Méricourt as 'Flore', Talleyrand as a 'grippe-sol', the duke of Orléans 'disguised as a blood-related prince', Aiguillon as a 'hermaphrodite', Mirabeau as an 'honest man' and the abbot Grégoire as a 'rabbi'.

This art of the 'revealing disguise', as it was called in the brochure, was carried even further by the *Carnaval politique* of 1790 or the *Mardi-Gras Exile at the National Assembly*. Since Mardi-Gras, incarnated in one single grotesque character with a 'ruddy and bloated body', was chased from the street, it decided to seek refuge in the Assembly:

> Carnival is prohibited to the people; yet, since the time of the revolution, you have established one among yourselves, and you get much enjoyment from it without modesty or reserve. You

forbid, under penalty of fines, merchants from presenting masks and costumes in their stores, and yet you are not ashamed to wear them yourselves for the most serious and most important events . . . Since you strive to unmask others, I will go one step further, I would like to disguise you as close as I can to your real physical appearance.

The gaze of Mardi-Gras across the hall of the assembly saw each and every one, especially the patriotic heralds, 'with his own individual mask' that he hastened to transcribe 'in its fullest and most amusing detail'. The 'war of epigrams' led by the royalist satirist was of a very great literary virtuosity: it succeeded in returning to the carnival its subversive function, turning it against the new revolutionary powers – the municipality of Paris and the National Assembly as revealed by several individuals behind their 'hideous masks'.

The carnival of 1791 seemed to head in the same direction: Bailly, the mayor of Paris, did not rescind his ban from the previous year, and royalist satire did not yield, attempting as always to 'assign each individual his appropriate disguise'. Supported by the 'joyous nature' of the French, a nature that the municipality 'scorned' and one that the Jacobins 'ignored', royalist satire counted on renewing its success of 1790. 'As long as France will remain France, the French will remain French, or, in other words, we'll always have our carnival days, and we'll adapt them to our morals. The folly of the people may change name and may change face, but it will always assume the personality that suits it best', explained *Le carnaval jacobite* or *The Patriotic Ball, Banquet and Masquerade*. The royalist sense of humour naturally seized upon this 'joyous French spirit', defined as being eternal, forged over the centuries by the 'fair monarchy', in order to turn it against innovation, ridiculing the 'happiness decreed by our new sovereigns, I mean to say the Directory of the Jacobins . . .' Laughter became specific to the royalist writer, corresponding with the 'most accurate veracities about French gaiety'. Therefore, once again the grotesque processions of paper took over the revolutionary assemblies to make up and cast their members. *The Carnival of 1791*, a pamphlet reusing the previous year's title without any real changes, described the 'list of masks that would be on display at the 'Club des Jacobins', during the 'trois jours gras'. A few new faces were introduced in it, such as a Robespierre 'ghost' 'in a long, white costume, with a veil over his head' whose presence 'was forewarned so as not to frighten'. Along the same lines, *La Jacobinière*, a show like no other, invented the encounter and battle of 'three masquerades', adding complexity to the royalist version of Mardi-Gras. Equally disguised and ridiculous were the shows of Santerre, the 'Jacobinière du Faubourg Saint-Antoine', or those of La

Fayette (the 'municipal acrobat') and of Mirabeau (the 'Comédie Nationale'), where the encounter and battle finished, after clashes and concoctions of disguises, with 'a beautiful revolutionary torrent'.

A 'war of laughs', virulent, virtuoso and funny, foisted itself upon the National Assembly: opposing the patriotic journalists (Cérutti, Ginguené, the caustic Camille Desmoulins and his *Revolutions de France et de Brabant*, the subtle Gorsas and his *Courrier des départements*, the ingenious Mercier and his *Literary and Patriotic Annals*) with Mirabeau's satirical groups of the *Actes des apôtres* and *Les dîners*. From that point on, this war of laughs, having besieged the National Assembly, or so it seemed, became politicized and, despite the serene and impassive idealism, forcefully entered into the national representative body. In so doing, it was able to split the members of the assembly along 'party' lines, inside a meeting hall that had been conceived as fostering unanimity.

THE PARTISAN USE OF LAUGHTER

Now we are in a position to reassess the outbursts of laughter within the National Assembly from a more political angle. The 408 instances of laughter that spread over the members' benches had initially been considered as out of place, a concession to the French spirit. Yet, this gaiety very quickly met head on with the world of politics through the battles waged in performances: laughter had been used as a political weapon. In addition, when party battle lines were first being drawn at the National Assembly, with sharp splits apparent as of September 1789, laughter at that point was no longer simply an out-of-place intermission between two debates, no longer simply incited by a stray, confused priest standing at the rostrum. It had in fact become, from the inside of the nation's walls, from the inside of the 'Sainte Masure', a weapon as powerful as it was from the outside. Its power derived from its ability to distinguish between the opposing partisan camps. Laughter, from that point forward, like applause, murmurs and boos, though prohibited under the internal code of conduct, nonetheless contributed to sketching a partisan map of the members. This power of laughter was so sensitive that when a novice member stepped up to the rostrum, on 10 October 1789, hesitating, stammering, and delivered jokes that up until then had provoked an incongruous laughter, now spoke politics: the laughter that his comments generated became political laughter within a few months. To take one's seat in the assembly had become tantamount to choosing one's political camp, and this member, who has remained anonymous, did not know where to sit: 'I took a seat', said this new arrival at the rostrum, 'right in the middle of the hall to show that I was neither from the right side nor from the left (laughter). I understand it is said that there are no sides to an assembly shaped in a circle (laughter once again), but I contend that it is impossible to perceive the truth amidst the clash of opinions.' The members, beginning in the autumn of 1789, knew perfectly well that laughter had become one of the attitudes most suited to this 'clash of opinions'. It was something that Mirabeau had grasped faster than the rest, for he had provided in January 1790 in his *Les dîners, or the truth comes out while laughing* this small, amusing and significant anecdote: 'A member on the right side of the room cried out like Titus [in other words, by cheerfully parodying Titus in a genre that mimicked the strictest Romans of the National Assembly]: "This day for us won't be lost, we will have destroyed something."' The members from the right side of the room laughed riotously at this skilful imitation, yet it has been presumed that the 'sane side' of the hall, in other words the side that sits to the president's left, booed the imitation.

In reconsidering the tactic employed by Mirabeau, which often relied on provocation, the humorists sought to place themselves on the president's right. By doing so, they also followed the group of satirists who were waging a very active campaign of using laughter to counter the new ideas. This political tactic founded on the war of laughs was soon uncovered by someone close to Mirabeau, his brother, the patriotic orator himself, who, on 19 September 1789, reprimanded the viscount sternly following a dubious pun inserted into the minutes of the sessions:

I always considered as proof of a good attitude that work is performed joyously. As such, it does not behove me to reprove the persistence of this individual [his brother] with his tone of joyfulness, since it has remained decent. It is neither in my heart nor in my intention to criticize his amusements, but it is in my obligation to refute his opinion and his sources when they seem to me to be dangerous. This obstinate member engages in merry amusement in order to divide us, and if indeed gaiety is a blessed tradition of the French spirit, divisiveness is a disastrous one.

The elder Mirabeau comprehended with great acuity the political strategy of royalist humour, that of his brother; he understood it, yet from then on he could not extirpate it from the assembly: French tradition had decided otherwise. For him it became essential to be able to perceive clearly the harmful consequences of this strategy.

Patriotic members of the assembly could not help engaging in humour, and they could, as Mirabeau had requested, neutralize laughter by making a simple concession to joke-making in accordance with

French gaiety, but they could also utilize it to their own advantage. Parallel to the royalist satirists, a group of patriotic humorists could be seen taking shape within the assembly itself. This group was less individualistic than the royalist group, relying on the younger Mirabeau, Duval d'Espréménil, Maury and Cazalès, but it was no more effective. On 28 August 1789, for example, when the crucial debate on the royal veto, a debate that would profoundly divide the assembly, was commencing, laughter had been transformed into politics in the minds of the patriots: a royalist was actually at the rostrum and uttered this traditionalist statement: 'Under the monarchy, power depended essentially upon the monarch.' The chronicler noted the immediate reactions of the members: 'Loud screams brought the obstinate member back to order; a voice was heard above the background murmurs of the crowd: "We are talking about a monarchy here, and our obstinate colleague, for his part, is discussing a despotic regime."' Another voice promptly sent the traditionalist speaker back to his seat amidst an eruption of laughter: 'I suggest sending the opinionated one to Constantinople.' An ecclesiastic then mounted the rostrum: 'We are finally going to take care of this constitution. It is now high time that we devote ourselves, as never before, to the religion that we profess.' Once again, laughter broke out: 'With this motion also leaning towards establishing despotic rule, protests came from all sides. One comment was heard above all the ensuing tumult: "May our obstinate colleague be joined by the preceding speaker in Constantinople." This sarcastic rejoinder immediately forced the speaker to sit down against a backdrop of widespread laughter.' From then on, laughter was fairly equally split between the president's left side and his right side. Laughter had entered into politics at that very instant, when the conflict of humour of the Palais-Royal, rue Saint-Jacques, had infiltrated the rows and benches of the assembly.

The 408 instances of laughter in the French National Assembly between 1789 and 1791 sketch out a fascinating itinerary of the use of humour. It could be construed as out-of-place humour when related to the ideal kind of solemnity demanded by the new representatives of a free and regenerated people; laughter was initially considered as a concession to French gaiety, a tradition that could not simply be set aside and which it would have been disastrous to ignore. Little by little, however, the war of paper at the beginning of the revolution allowed laughter to be something more than a temporary or out-of-place concession: it had become a political weapon among others in the arsenal, an effective weapon that individual parties utilized to distinguish themselves, to attack one another within the assembly. The left and the right achieved this distinction in large part by playing on these political moods. The use of applause, murmurs and outbursts of laughter all constituted a sort of ritual, a ceremony of mutual and parallel recognition, a vital ritual in French parliamentary practices. To a certain extent, laughter operated within the National Assembly much like a *principe rituel de réalité* ('a principle of the ritual of reality'). Through laughter, the members renounced the philosophical ideal of impassiveness in order to rally around a very effective practice that was both real and ritual: group laughter. Similarly, these instances of laughter stretched from being directed at simple, out-of-place remarks all the way to the reconstruction of a real political ceremony. Or even further, these instances were directed against the constitution of a democratic parliamentary setting, or an assembly divided by its moods, and one that sometimes could even be, out of laughter, cruel to its minority constituents, yet one where groups could also lead guerrilla attacks of irony against the powers that be.

NOTES

1 *Archives parlementaires de 1787 à 1860 recueil complet des débats législatifs et politiques des chambres françaises, sous la direction de MM Mavidal et Laurent* (Paris, 1867–).
2 A. de Baecque, 'La gaieté-française: essai sur un "état sensible de la nation française" au XVIIIe siècle', *Annales ESC* (forthcoming) [special issue on the history of laughter].
3 Robert Darnton, *The Great Cat Massacre* (New York, 1984).
4 A. Castaldo, *Les méthodes de travail de la Constituante* (Paris, 1989).
5 A. de Baecque, 'Les corps du carnaval politique', in *Le corps de l'histoire: métaphores et politique (1770–1800)* (Paris, 1993), pp. 303–41.
6 Session of 3 August 1789, in *Archives parlementaires*.
7 Session of 26 September 1789, in *Archives parlementaires*.
8 Session of 3 August 1789, in *Archives parlementaires*.
9 See also Bremmer, Chapter 1 of this volume.
10 Joseph-Antoine Cérutti, *Lettre sur les avantages et les origines de la gaieté française* (Paris, n.d.).
11 Pierre-Louis Ginguené, *De l'autorité de Rabelais dans la révolution présente* (en Utopie et à Paris, 1791).
12 *La satyre universelle: prospectus dédié à toutes les puissances de la terre* (Paris, 1788).
13 Antoine Rivarol, *Petit dictionnaire des grands hommes de la Révolution* (Paris, 1790).
14 *Spectacle de la Nation* (Paris, n.d.), no. 1.
15 *Les actes des apôtres*, ch. XXIII (1790), pp. 19–20.

11

Humour and the Public Sphere in Nineteenth-Century Germany

Mary Lee Townsend

In 1848, much as in 1989, revolution swept across the continent of Europe, defining in blood and iron the issues that would shape European history for the next 150 years. During the decades beforehand, in Germany as elsewhere, the voice of the people had been stifled and forced to express itself through the ambiguities of humour and satire. Popular humour thrived in these pre-revolutionary years, allowing Germans to participate in a lively underground culture of dissent, much like their counterparts in Cold War Eastern Europe, where humour became a major political weapon against repressive regimes.

However, humour was more than just 'politics by other means'. At a time of enormous social change, as a traditional society based on estates gave way to a confusing new world marked by industrialization, urbanization and social mobility, popular humour filled a variety of needs. It provided simple entertainment, it encouraged Germans to vent their spleen, and it allowed them to explore and negotiate the shifting boundaries of the brave new world around them.

The power of humour became increasingly apparent in nineteenth-century Germany as it exploded from a traditional pastime into a commercial, mass-market product. During the first half of the century, popular humour moved out of the streets and into the drawing rooms. This was a German, indeed a European phenomenon, but it happened most strikingly in the state of Prussia, particularly in the city of Berlin. Here popular humour, which was called *Berliner Witz*, burst onto the literary and artistic scene, routinely zigzagging across conventional boundaries: between dialect and *Hochdeutsch*, caricature and art, low culture and high culture.[1]

This humour was not simply a shallow commercial product, sprung up overnight to satiate a craving for innovation and amusement. The inhabitants of Prussia's capital city had long prided themselves on their wit, and during the pre-revolutionary publishing boom they translated this oral tradition into texts and pictures. Guidebooks hailed Berlin as the 'mother city of wit', citing the natives' reputation for mockery, ridicule, bluntness and cheek. Enthusiasts claimed that this peculiar dry wit was almost a natural phenomenon, an inborn characteristic of Berlin's lower classes.[2]

Given the importance of wit, observers had many different ideas about its function in society. Some, including radicals and conservatives, believed that humour encouraged citizens to dissipate the anger and frustration that they otherwise might have directed against the established order. In 1843 one author admonished censorship and police authorities to leave the 'air-hole' (*Luftloch*) of Berlin wit open. Otherwise people 'would only brood about dark(er) things'. Three years later, in 1846, the communist littérateur Ernst Dronke sniffed that political humour was in fact a boon to the state. 'If the Berliner has laughed at something, then "it no longer exists" for him. He ignores it with equanimity.'[3]

The liberal author Theodor Mundt argued another point of view, claiming in 1844 that popular humour was 'the Robespierre of the Berliners, their charter, their constitution, their everything, their nothing'.[4] In his eyes Berlin wit could incite to rebellion, or it could soothe unruly spirits. In either case it was a force to be reckoned with.

This was a bold claim. In 1844 even more than today, Robespierre symbolized the danger – as well as the liberating dynamism – of the French Revolution. But contemporaries did not quibble with Mundt's characterization.[5] Nor did they balk at the seeming ambiguity of his claim that humour could function both as a revolutionary force and as a safety valve. On the contrary, they too recognized the many-faceted role of humour in German society.

Theodor Mundt's startling phrase and the intense contemporary debate about humour invite the curiosity of the twentieth-century reader. How are we to interpret the enthusiasm for – and fear of – popular humour? Sparkling wit and humour are not attributes conventionally associated with Germany, particularly not Germany in the staid nineteenth century. And the image of a 'Robespierre' in Berlin hardly fits our picture of the so-called unpolitical Germans. If this was an age of political repression, harsh censorship and moralistic prudery, how are we to explain the huge number of jokes and caricatures that defied, sometimes openly and sometimes surreptitiously, political and moral conventions? Also, one would like to know precisely: what role did popular humour play in nineteenth-century society? Was it used as a call to action, or did it function merely as a vent for letting off frustration? In other words, was humour truly a revolutionary force, or was it a subtle form of social control that served to pacify further an already docile population? Or is there some other reason that humour became so important at this moment in German history?

To answer these questions we must turn to the humour itself, looking

Figure 11.1 *Eckensteher*, by Franz Burchard Dörbeck, *Berliner Aus-rufer, Costüme und locale Ge-bräuche, c.*1830. Owner: Berlin, Stadtmuseum, Berlin. Photo: Stadtmuseum, Berlin

at the context and the content of individual jokes and caricatures. But we must also look at humour in the aggregate and at its larger, overall function in society.[6] Often, the simple act of sharing in laughter was more important than the specific content or immediate impact of any given joke or caricature. Laughing together meant participating in a common culture, communicating about an issue of mutual concern. In this way humour helped carve out a public space,[7] a field or arena within which all sorts of ideas could be discussed and debated, be they political, social or moral. The views expressed within this public space were never monolithic or uniform. Popular humour established a sense of community among participants, but at the same time it helped define and clarify the differences within that community. Laughter, whether trivial, subversive or something in between, formed part of an ongoing public debate, one in which nineteenth-century Germans defined themselves and their newly emerging national culture.

Bearing this in mind – that all individual examples of humour must be considered against the background of the whole – it is useful to focus on a single case study. His name is the *Eckensteher* Nante and he was the favourite comic figure of the pre-1848 period. Figure 11.1, a lithograph by Franz Burchard Dörbeck from *c*.1830, is the most famous portrait of this character who is part fact and part fiction.

Eckensteher were the real-life, rough-and-tumble day labourers familiar throughout Central Europe. The word translates literally as 'he who stands on the corner'. 'Nante', which is the nickname for Ferdinand, was the Christian name most often given to the literary and icono-graphic *Eckensteher*, and even today the name Nante suggests Dörbeck's stereotype of the bulky, impudent lower-class figure. (For the sake of convenience in this essay we can use the word *Eckensteher* to discuss the actual individuals, and the name Nante to indicate the fictional caricature created in art and literature.) For the historian's purposes Nante is ideal, because he illustrates the major features of humour in the nineteenth century: (1) the commercialization of humour for sale to a mass market; (2) the interplay of humorous stereotypes and the social reality upon which they were based; (3) the great variety in the content of humour, from innocent jesting to aggressive political criticism. Finally, (4) Nante allows us to say something about the overall function of humour.

In short, Nante demonstrates how humour played a crucial role in the creation of a public sphere in Central Europe. Commercialization made it possible for Nante to have a broad impact, and the ambiguities of humour allowed him to serve many functions, transgressing the bounda-ries of high and low culture, appealing to different audiences, and being interpreted in a multitude of ways. Sharing in laughter with Nante allowed Germans to shape a robust political culture beyond the limits of repression; but laughter directed at Nante helped predict the limits of rebellion in pre-revolutionary Germany.

NANTE ON GRUB STREET

Let us begin with the commercialization of humour. The *Eckensteher* Nante came of age during the Restoration, a time of great political uncertainty and repression. After decades of revolutionary wars and Napoleonic occupation, Europe's monarchs slept badly at night, haunted by the ghost of the French Revolution and the nightmare of a people beheading their king. At the Congress of Vienna in 1815 they tried to set back the clock by restoring the 'old order'.

In Germany this led to the Carlsbad Decrees of 1819, a series of harsh laws designed to suppress all forms of political dissent. Among its most important regulations were those on censorship. Prussia, as a member state of the German Confederation, enforced these measures and added some even stricter laws of its own.

This notorious censorship resulted in a certain blandness in German literature and art. Ironically, it also encouraged experimentation, as authors and artists sought ways to evade the ever-watchful eye of the state. One of the most successful tactics they found was the use of humour, which allowed them to veil their hidden meanings under the guise of 'innocent' entertainment. As a result, Germany gave birth to a new genre of publishing: commercial popular humour. Berlin quickly became the centre of this new publishing trend as enterprising young men seized upon traditional Berlin wit and adapted it to the needs of Germany's incipient mass press. Given its tremendous appeal, authors, artists and publishers experimented with many formats: humorous genre pictures, caricatures, posters and handbills; newspaper riddles, jokes and satire; calendars and almanacs with a humorous twist; and, most characteristic for the period, 'wit booklets' (*Witzhefte*), usually thirty to sixty pages in octavo format, often with a picture on the title-page. Works written in local dialect were particularly well received. Stock figures such as the *Eckensteher* Nante were used serially by individual humorists and often pirated by their competitors.

The success of this new genre was astonishing. Berlin had a seemingly endless supply of authors and artists willing to try their hand at humour. There was also a huge potential audience. In Central Europe in 1830 probably 40 per cent of the population over six years old could read. The Prussian census statistics of 1871 suggest that in 1840 85 to 90 per cent of the population of Berlin aged 29 or older could read or write.[8] Publishers were also well placed: the cylinder printing press, cheaper paper and the advent of lithography made it possible for them to print at ever lower prices. The railroad helped cut transportation costs and marketing innovations allowed booksellers to reach an expanding audience.

When contemporaries claimed that 'everyone' in Prussia read the new popular humorous literature, they were hardly exaggerating. We have concrete records of individuals from all social strata reading these booklets and looking at these caricatures. A short list would include a barber's helper, a hackney-cab driver, market women, errand boys, servants, apprentices, industrialists, a duchess and even members of the royal court in Berlin. Also, a textual analysis of the literature suggests that most (but not all) of this humour would be accessible to most potential readers. However, the price of these publications and the marketing needs of their creators – authors, artists and publishers – suggest that the actual purchasers of Berlin wit came from the broadest middle spectrum of society, from a handful of aristocrats down the social scale to wealthy industrialists, shopkeepers and prosperous artisans. Poorer Berliners would have known these publications from shop windows and pubs and would have acquired them through resale, as hand-me-downs and through lending libraries.[9]

The Prussian police were of two minds about this new commercial humour. On the one hand, government officials allowed humorous publications insofar as they provided an innocuous alternative to political agitation. But they also feared the other face of Berlin wit. Political humour could infect the populace with seditious notions, and humour that violated taboos could undermine the moral foundations of the state. Furthermore, because jokebooks and caricatures were so widely circulated, any dangerous ideas that slipped by the censors in the form of a 'harmless' joke were sure to reach all strata of society. The growth of mass-market humour thus documents a complex tug of war between an increasingly nervous Prussian regime, which recognized the explosive possibilities of ridicule, and writers and artists who tested the limits of state power.[10]

So where does this leave the fictional *Eckensteher* Nante? He was created by professionals, men who had to sell in order to earn their bread. And he was purchased by members of the broadest middle class, individuals who stood at some social and economic distance from the lowest classes, but who were familiar with ordinary *Eckensteher*. Finally, the Prussian police, who worried about his potential impact, kept a wary eye on Nante in all his literary and artistic manifestations. To a large extent then, the literary Nante presented a middle-class interpretation of a lower-class figure. But, as we shall see, Nante came to represent much more. Soon he became a symbol of the German *Volk* as a whole, embodying middle-class hopes, fears and fantasies about the 'common people'.

THE ECKENSTEHER IN FACT AND FICTION

The *Eckensteher* Nante began life modestly, as a day labourer in Berlin in the year 1832. By the time the revolution of 1848 broke out he was a major political figure, appearing regularly in the daily press, sometimes even mentioned as a candidate for emperor of a united Germany. The hero here is, of course, the literary and iconographic Nante, not his real-life, ruffian counterpart. However, the fictional *Eckensteher* did have deep roots in reality, and his life history has much to tell us – about his flesh-and-blood counterparts and about German society as a whole.

When the literary *Eckensteher* was born, he was a minor character in a local play by Karl von Holtei. Here Nante was a worker engaged to cut wood and eventually hired to help kidnap a child. His only dramatic moment came in a short scene before the police commissioner.

Figure 11.2 The actor Friedrich Beckmann in his most famous role as *The Eckensteher Nante Strumpf in Berlin*, by E. Dettmer, *c.*1833. Owner: Berlin, Stadtmuseum, Berlin. Photo: Stadtmuseum, Berlin

The actor who played the part, a gifted comedian named Friedrich Beckmann, grabbed the opportunity and, using a smattering of Berlin dialect, gave the character unexpected humour and life. In November of the same year Berlin's best-known humorist, Adolph Glaßbrenner, published his first *Eckensteher* pamphlet. Then, in December, Beckmann wrote a play entitled *Der Eckensteher Nante im Verhör*, which expanded on his scene in front of the commissioner in Holtei's piece. (Figure 11.2 shows Beckmann in this famous role.) Holtei and Glaßbrenner had both encouraged Beckmann to write the play, and Beckmann had stolen shamelessly from many of the jokes and a song in Glaßbrenner's pamphlet. Thus emerged a rivalry among the three for credit as creator of the *Eckensteher* Nante.[11] Nante's impact was so strong that even forty years later Glaßbrenner signed himself in a letter to an admirer as 'the humorist, the inventor of the *Eckensteher* Nante Strumpf'.[12]

By 1847 there were so many different types of literary *Eckensteher* that Glaßbrenner advised a fellow author not to use the figure in his writing:

What is Nante supposed to represent? Berlin? God forbid: Berlin is too eminent! The clever, witty and despite his criticism, warm-hearted Berlin burgher . . . ? Nante is too crude and too stupid.

No, said Glaßbrenner, Nante is 'the representative of the lowest *Volk*, in which [there is], I would like to say, an unconscious opposition against all the conditions which oppress him. . . . This is how I perceive Nante.' But, he lamented, his original conception of Nante had been corrupted. For the majority of readers Nante was no longer the lower-class savant nor even the dull-witted, timid German philistine. The comedian Beckmann and other imitators had debased Nante into a mere 'joker at all costs'.[13]

Glaßbrenner was right. In the vast *Eckensteher* literature published after 1832 Nante was usually a simple entertainer. This was true even of Glaßbrenner's own first *Eckensteher* pamphlet.[14] For most humorists Nante had become the symbol of Berlin, telling harmless jokes and commenting on the local scene. For some authors he was a literary device that allowed them to offer cautious comments about current events. Only the later Glaßbrenner and a few other humorists used Nante as a mouthpiece to encourage political awareness. Nevertheless, there was a common thread in all these versions of the *Eckensteher*. The character Nante consistently – though not always consciously – played upon Berliners' innermost feelings about the changing social structure of their city and the alarming growth of class tension.

It was no accident that Nante became so popular. Before 1840 *Eckensteher* were common on the streets of Berlin and the average Berliner would have seen them day in and day out. The young Karl Marx, for example, mentioned them in a letter to his father. Describing his manic high spirits after an outing in the country, he wrote, 'I . . . raced [back] to Berlin and wanted to embrace every *Eckensteher*.'[15]

By 1832, the year of Nante's birth, Germany's population explosion, massive migration to the city and severe economic crises had created a huge number of unemployed. They were highly visible, often loitering at busy intersections, passing the time or waiting for work. Among them was Nante. Today the word *Eckensteher* is often translated as 'loafer', and this comes close to the historical reality. Somewhere on the borderline between the lowest strata of respectable workers and the disreputable riff-raff and criminals of Berlin slouched the *Eckensteher*. Sometimes he accepted work on a day-to-day basis and thus might be called a day labourer. A Berlin encyclopedia published in 1834 describes him as a labourer who spent more time waiting on street corners than actually working. As the encyclopedia put it, this 'situation results not from lack of opportunity to work, but rather from a certain speculative indifference and a comfortable anticipation' of jobs that might come along offering more pay.[16] Franz Burchard Dörbeck's classic illustration (see fig. 11.1) reflects this view of the loafer and procrastinator. By 1840 cheap cabs had made town-porters obsolete; the police ended the registration of the *Eckensteher* and forbade their loitering on the streets.[17]

During his heyday the *Eckensteher* was known for his dry, cutting remarks to passers-by. In the words of one English traveller, 'They have a deal of sly cunning and drollery; a dry manner; will have the last word; and are sure to turn the laugh against their antagonists, be they high or low, educated or uneducated.'[18]

It is not clear how much of the legendary wit of the *Eckensteher* was native and how much was simply attributed to him by fanciful authors and artists.[19] In any event, his alleged talent for repartee became a useful literary tool. Even after the *Eckensteher* disappeared from the streets of the city, he lived on in the Berliners' imagination, ever popular in the theatre, caricatures and humorous literature.

NANTE AND THE LAST LAUGH

Now that we know something about his background, it is possible to analyse the jokes and caricatures that revolved around the *Eckensteher* Nante. Much of this humour was lighthearted prattle, silly turns of phrase and jokes about harmless topics. One *Eckensteher* writes a 'viel-o -sauf-ische' treatise, literally meaning 'much drinking', and earns the title 'Doctor of Worldly Wisdom'.[20] Often Nante vented frustrations about universal issues such as marriage. In one booklet he expresses vexation with strong-minded women. Displaying a picture of a woman made out of rubber, he explains to his audience: 'She will be invented in a hundred years. She will always give in, even when the man is irritable.'[21]

Sometimes humour about women was intertwined with contemporary observations. When Nante and his son stand in a crowd waiting to see the king and queen ride into town, they are jostled by a young girl behind them. 'Listen', says Nante, 'you are proving to be very forcible. ... Are you perhaps a daughter of the Parisian leader George Sand, that you ignore your feminine character?'[22]

These jokes about innocent and universal themes formed a large part of the literary *Eckensteher* humour, but its true sustenance came from reflective wit. A series of booklets about Nante on the newly built railroad is typical. In the first pamphlet Nante takes a train to Potsdam with his friend Blaubart (Bluebeard) and his wife Aspasia.[23] Blaubart is a coachman and the railroads threaten his profession. He reacts with both awe and annoyance to the new contraption. When the train stops unexpectedly Nante teases him, 'Blaubart, jump out and hold up a bundle of hay; perhaps that will help.' The conductor explains that the engine does not have enough water. Blaubart, who has been nipping schnapps all day, retorts, 'Aha, it wants a drink.'[24]

The early phases of railroad building in Prussia were marked by rampant speculation, so naturally Nante discusses this. When he does he creates a new word, *Akzionärsch*, slurring the word for stockholder, *Aktionär*, and combining it with the plural form of the word for buttocks, *Ärsche*:

BLAUBART: It goes dreadfully fast – the one-horse cabs will be ruined.
NANTE: The stockholders (*Akzionärsch*) also regard the railroad as the eighth wonder [of the world].
ASPASIA: What are they surprised at?
NANTE: What becomes of the money.[25]

The most pervasive theme in the *Eckensteher* literature was alcohol. In almost every booklet and caricature Nante or one of his companions

Figure 11.3 *Two Drunken Day Labourers (Eckensteher)*, by Franz Burchard Dörbeck, Folge ohne Titel, no. 22, *c*.1830. Owner: Berlin, Stadtmuseum, Berlin. Photo: Stadtmuseum, Berlin

drinks steadily from his schnapps bottle, and much of the humour revolves around bars and drunkenness, as illustrated by figure 11.3. When Nante dies in one story, the author blames his death on 'the temperance society and an overfilling of whisky and bitters'.[26] At the funeral, friends honour him by throwing their schnapps bottles on his grave. This humour was clearly rooted in reality. Between 1806 and 1831 the consumption of spirits in Prussia almost tripled.[27] In the early 1830s, just as Nante was gaining popularity, his real-life counterparts were drinking more. Many *Eckensteher* who could not, or would not, find regular employment filled their hours (and supplemented their diet) with cheap potato schnapps.

Jokes about the *Eckensteher* and his drinking reflect much more than this objective reality. They also reveal Berliners' subjective attitudes towards the changes going on around them. In literature and caricature the drunken *Eckensteher* was often comical, but seldom sympathetic.[28] In one story, a woman at a costume ball talks to an *Eckensteher* who is going to be evicted from his lodgings the next day because he is unable to pay the rent. She sympathizes but then asks where he found the money to come to the ball. He explains that he merely collected his ration of the firewood that was allotted to the poor as a form of charity. 'I sold it right away for a thaler, and used it to rent a costume.'[29] He then walks off in search of a drink.

Negative jokes about Nante sometimes portrayed him as a pretentious boor who spouts forth misinformation, usually drinking all the while. Often this meant confusing geographical areas or misusing foreign phrases and big words. For example, in one booklet acquaintances of an *Eckensteher* are watching a puppet show accompanied by music. One asks his neighbour: 'Can you perhaps insinuate to me what symphonanie the orchestra is playing?' The man replies: 'Nymphomanie? No, not this one, but my wife will recognize it; she's musical.'[30] The worldly reader who understood these mistakes could laugh at the uncouth, uneducated Nante and feel superior.[31]

Scenes where Nante appeared in court used a double-edged humour. Nante is amusing as he puts down the pompous bureaucrats with his clever simplicity. One chuckles as the underdog wins. Yet the underdog is not very attractive; he is silly and not particularly noble. In one story Nante must appear in court because he has ordered a coat made, and the tailor wants his money. Nante, who is drunk when he arrives, pulls a few coins out of his pocket and tells the judge that it is all he has in the world. He then inadvertently drops more money on the floor and hurries to explain that he has saved it to buy schnapps for his wife for her birthday. Of course it cannot be used towards the coat. Finally the court registrar is so sick of Nante's lame excuses that he agrees to pay the debt for him. Thus Nante is not one of the 'deserving poor'. He is merely lucky that his stubbornness and wit paid off by inducing the registrar to donate the necessary money. When the court usher brings him the coat and then asks for the customary tip, Nante tricks him out of it. He is treacherous, even to his social equals.[32]

Eckensteher humour of this sort helped create a sense of distance from the lowest classes, thereby filling a pressing subjective need in Restoration Germany. This humour could be interpreted differently by different readers. Anyone could laugh at Nante's slapstick antics or when he outsmarted bureaucrats and the law. But middle-class readers might well feel an extra frisson. Laughing at Nante reassured them that they were different: they were better educated, more industrious, more temperate, more upright. This humour also suggested that the *Eckensteher* did not deserve their sympathy. After all, Nante was lazy and dishonest. Jokes that laughed *at* Nante reinforced their sense of social cohesion and helped them feel more secure in their elevated social status.[33]

The gigantic social and economic dislocations of the Restoration period gave many Germans good reason to fear the lower classes. Some worried about the threat of revolution, while others, especially artisans, were anxious about sinking to the level of their social and economic inferiors. Times were hard, and many individuals could not adapt. Pauperism, one of the most widely discussed issues of the day, increased dramatically, with probably 50 to 60 per cent of the population in Prussia living in need by 1846.[34] Some observers feared that the unprecedented social mobility of the 1830s and 1840s was leading to social disintegration and polarization. 'The classes crumble apart ever faster', proclaimed the journalist and democrat Heinrich Bettziech in 1846. 'The disintegration of the earlier estates and classes has advanced so far that now there are only rich and poor, without the golden *Mittelstand*.'[35] Bettziech exaggerated, but the tone of his analysis reflects the all-pervasive sense of social upheaval in pre-revolutionary Berlin.

Although this uneasiness provoked a large number of negative jokes about *Eckensteher*, not all humorists responded in this way. Many of them portrayed Nante much more sympathetically. A significant portion of *Eckensteher* humour tried to bridge the gap between the day labourer and his social betters by fostering a sense of identity between Nante and the reader. Here Nante is not exactly a hero or a member of the deserving poor. Rather, he is a gadfly. He advocates political and social change that would benefit all society, including the lower classes. In some cases this meant that the *Eckensteher* character criticized the Prussian state; this Nante embodied the noble German *Volk* and its opposition to the repressive status quo. In other cases this humour took the form of poking fun at liberal do-gooders who theoretically sympathized with the poor, but in fact were arrogant, selfish and ineffectual.

When humorists used Nante to criticize the state, they did so in roundabout ways. In a typical scene two *Eckensteher* discuss the Wars of Liberation against Napoleon. When Nante boasts that he too was in Paris as a volunteer soldier, his friend Bummel reminisces: 'What surprised me was that in Paris the little children could speak such good French.' Nante does not laugh. Instead he inquires eagerly:

'Do you speak French too?'
'I speak [it] indeed, but no one understands me.'[36]

On the surface this seems to be a trivial joke. Everyone can laugh at it, and anyone who has tried to speak a foreign language can identify with poor Bummel. But, there is much more going on here. The key is the reference to the Wars of Liberation. The two speakers once fought bravely for their country, helping to free it from a foreign yoke. Their reward is unemployment and hopelessness. Also the two war heroes serve as a reminder that King Frederick William III never granted the constitution he had promised in 1815. The Prussian state's shabby treatment of its veterans is a theme that recurs in many pamphlets. In a joke booklet published in 1845, for example, an ex-soldier remarks to his friend, 'It is nice to die for the Fatherland . . . because then you don't have to live as a disabled veteran.'[37]

Another sympathetic *Eckensteher* who represents the oppressed German *Volk* is Nante Nantino. He comments on current affairs, encouraging the reader to laugh *with* him at the Prussian state. Nante describes a dream in which he encounters a police commissioner. In this dream the commissioner explains that someone had enquired about Nante the night before, so now Nante is officially under suspicion of having committed a crime. Nante protests, 'Now listen here, Mr Commissioner, maybe you were only dreaming?' The policeman responds, 'That doesn't matter, the dream of a police commissioner is sufficient [grounds for official] suspicion.'[38] By making the entire scene a dream sequence related by Nante, the author hoped to avoid having the pamphlet forbidden. In this classic literary ploy the reader is laughing at a dream about – not the reality of – the arbitrariness of the Prussian police. The police file on the booklet shows that the authorities were not fooled by this manoeuvre, but they decided the pamphlet would not appeal to the lower classes and thus was not dangerous enough to outlaw.[39]

In another booklet, published just before the revolution of 1848, a politically minded Nante has married a woman who owns a wax museum. The ex-*Eckensteher* is busy dusting the exhibits and talking to himself about the situation in France. When he comes to the figure of Louis-Philippe he remarks:

Soon I'll have to melt down old Ludwig-Philip; he already looks deathly pale. . . . But then what do I do with his Minister Goodso [Guizot]? If I take Philip away then he will fall down; he is already shaky. Well, let him fall; he has stood [there] long enough.[40]

When an *Eckensteher* lambasts liberal do-gooders, rather than the state, readers, even middle-class readers, can again feel solidarity with him. Albert Hopf was a master of this type of humour. In a booklet published in 1847, at the height of the potato famine and the industrial depression, he satirizes a group of wealthy individuals who have organized a club to discuss the plight of the poor. The charter members have telling names. The chairman is Dumkofsky (Dumbhead), and his friend the distillery owner is called Fusler (Fusel-Oiler). Other members include the master baker, Kleisack (Bran-Sack), and the grain speculator Sauger (Sucker, in the sense of 'to suck dry'). One of the most active participants is a man who lives off his revenues; his name is Schweißpresser (Sweatwringer). These men see their organization as a sort of miniature United Prussian Diet, and they use it as a place to practise parliamentary procedure in case they are ever elected to a political body. Naturally, their 'procedure' quickly degenerates into bombastic speeches and arguments. Early on Nante and his friend Brenneke force their way into the meeting, explaining that they have come 'to represent pauperism'. Schweißpresser protests the intrusion, wrinkling his nose: 'These are proletarians. We can't allow such creatures in an exclusive club like ours.' Remember, of course, that this is a charity club. Finally, after a heated debate the members allow Nante and Brenneke to stay.[41]

Each of the club members gives a speech followed by discussion. When someone suggests that the poor should be allowed to have only two children, the church sexton objects that this would cut into the money he makes on christenings. A factory owner describes his generosity and the ingratitude of the working classes:

I have treated the people like a father. I can assure you gentlemen, some of my workers have earned up to three thaler a week. . . . But when I saw that they became arrogant with this high wage, I made small deductions.[42]

Since an unmarried worker with no dependents needed more than two thaler a week for minimum living expenses, the satire in this remark was obvious.[43] Next, the baker argues that eliminating the mill tax would help the poor and, incidentally, the bakers as well. Schweißpresser vetoes this, because he fears an income tax would then be necessary. Finally, Nante lashes out at their insincerity. He pleads for work and

Figure 11.4 *Kaiser Nante*, anonymous illustration in broadside by Aujust Buddelmeyer, 1849. Owner: Berlin, Stadtmuseum, Berlin. Photo: Stadtmuseum, Berlin

fair wages. The would-be helpers of the poor are so shocked by his bluntness that they force him out and close the meeting.

NANTE AND THE PUBLIC SPHERE

Nante continued to thrive during and after the revolution of 1848. He starred in caricatures, broadsheets, posters and pamphlets, always agitating for political causes. These revolutionary publications featured the *Eckensteher* in all possible political roles, including, eventually, emperor of a united Germany (see fig. 11.4).[44] From his first appearance in 1832 through the revolution and beyond, Nante spanned the entire spectrum of humour in both art and literature: he indulged in innocent jests, laughed at universal problems, reflected upon social change and engaged in political commentary. Throughout he remained a privileged interpreter of the hopes and fears of all Germans.

After looking so closely at the *Eckensteher* Nante we are finally in a position to ask why he was such a commercial success. How was it possible that Nante appealed to such a wide audience – from hackney-cab drivers, market women and domestic servants to the highest reaches of the nobility?

The answer is threefold. First, Nante was based on a familiar phenom-enon, the day labourers who crowded the city streets of Central Europe, especially during the first half of the nineteenth century, with its dramatic social and economic developments. Second, the *Eckensteher*, slouching on the edge of respectable society, was uniquely poised to observe and comment on that society; he probed the ambiguities of humour and carried a multiplicity of messages to different audiences. As we have seen, literally anyone could laugh with Nante when he made fun of the newfangled railroads or outsmarted his inquisitors in a courtroom. But readers from the middle classes would notice other dimensions to this humour: they would also be laughing at Nante and his friends because of their ignorance, their laziness and their brutality.

For those who are willing to 'read' him in his many manifestations, Nante can act as a guide to the social and political realities of nineteenth-century Germany. Taken together, jokes and caricatures about the *Eckensteher* point to an ambivalent relationship between the two major social strata in pre-revolutionary society – the lowest class of unemployed and underemployed workers, and the broad middle class of successful tradesmen, professionals, businessmen and bureau-crats. Situated somewhere in between were Germany's hard-pressed artisans. Some skidded and fell into the lowest classes. Others, like those who frequented bookstores and libraries, managed to hold on, however tenuously, to their income and their self-esteem. Given the tremendous social mobility of the era, there was no clear split between well-defined classes. There were many groups, subgroups and unique individuals all nudging each other on their way up or down the socio-economic ladder. But, at the same time, there was a growing sense of 'us' versus 'them'. The 'us' were those who had a regular source of income and considered themselves respectable. The 'them' were the lowest classes, epitomized by the *Eckensteher* Nante.

The *Eckensteher* humour of the Restoration period reflects both the gulf between these two strata and middle-class ambivalence about that gulf. Jokes that laughed at Nante gave voice to the repugnance and the lightly masked fear that these people felt about the lower orders. On the other hand, jokes and caricatures that portrayed Nante as the embodiment of the oppressed German *Volk* revealed a different and not necessarily contradictory set of feelings. This humour reflected the desire of middle-class liberals to unite all the 'people' in opposition to the repressive Prussian state.

At first glance the ambiguity and the multiple meanings of jokes and caricatures about the *Eckensteher* might seem to thwart any hard conclusions about their ultimate social impact. This brings us to the third and final point: in order to understand the function of popular humour in nineteenth-century Germany, we must view it in the aggregate, as part of a larger public debate. This humour constituted an important part of the public sphere that Europeans were beginning to carve out for themselves, as they fought their way free from an absolutist past towards a more participatory form of public life.

This public debate was certainly diffuse and often ambiguous, but the fact that it existed at all was extremely important. This was especially true in Prussia, which was a repressive society with no parliamentary vehicle for political action and strong taboos against many forms of personal self-expression. In this setting, where public discourse was strictly regulated, often the simple act of speaking aloud was itself a political statement.[45] In the end, popular humour may have done little to focus the inchoate political consciousness of Germans in the early nineteenth century, but it did keep this consciousness alive, nurturing and strengthening the general level of critical awareness, and providing much of the rhetorical and emotional tinder that flared into revolution in 1848.[46]

NOTES

I am indebted to the University of Tulsa Faculty Research Grant Program for assistance in the preparation of this essay.
1 Given my focus on published, commercial examples of Berlin wit, it might

be more accurate to call this 'mass market' rather than popular humour. However, nineteenth-century Germans used the same term, *Volkswitz*, to describe both the 'native wit' (*Mutterwitz*) of Berlin's lowest classes and the humour created for sale by professional authors and artists. I prefer to use this term, too, which I translate as popular humour. One of the most striking things about this humour was that it occupied a middle ground between popular and high culture and provides an excellent example of how tenuous the distinction was between the two.

2 I use the word *class* in the general sense of social stratum, in keeping with contemporary usage; during the decades under discussion, *Klasse, Klassen, Schicht* and *Stand* were often used interchangeably.

3 F. Gustav Kühne, *Mein Carneval in Berlin 1843* (Braunschweig, 1843), p. 26, calls Berlin wit a *Luftloch*; E. Dronke, *Berlin* (Berlin, 1846), repr. ed. R. Nitsche (Darmstadt, 1974), p. 19.

4 T. Mundt, *Die Geschichte der Gesellschaft in ihren neueren Entwickelungen und Problemen* (Berlin, 1844), pp. 6–7.

5 Mundt's book was based on a series of public lectures he gave in 1844. In his *Berliner Stecknadeln*, Heft 2 (Berlin, 1844), p. 26, Feodor Wehl cites with approval Mundt's 'Robespierre' passage, directly from the lectures. The Berlin police do not mention the phrase in their reports on Mundt's lectures; see Brandenburgisches Landeshauptarchiv (Potsdam), Provinz Brandenburg, Rep. 30 Berlin, C Pol. Präs., Tit. 95 (14519), Acta des Königlichen Polizei-Präsidii zu Berlin betreffend das zu beobachtende Verfahren bei Ertheilung der Erlaubniß zur Haltung und Ankündigung von Privat-Vorlesungen, 1820–59, Bl. 21–22; and Brandenburgisches Landeshauptarchiv (Potsdam), Provinz Brandenburg, Rep. 30 Berlin, C Pol. Präs., Tit. 165 (20292), Acta collect. des Königlichen Polizei-Präsidii zu Berlin betreffend die von einzelnen Personen hier zuhaltenden [sic] Vorlesungen p.p., 1836–44, Bl. 151–6.

6 P. Burke, *Popular Culture in Early Modern Europe* (New York, 1978), prologue, makes a similar point, that he is 'concerned with the code of popular culture rather than the individual messages, and presenting a simplified description of the main constants and the principal trends.'

7 Here I am obviously indebted to Jürgen Habermas, *Strukturwandel der Öffentlichkeit: Untersuchungen zu einer Kategorie der bürgerlichen Gesellschaft* (Darmstadt, 1962); and Habermas, 'The public sphere', trans. Shierry Weber Nicholsen, in *Jürgen Habermas on Society and Politics: a reader*, ed. Steven Seidman (Boston, 1989), pp. 398–404.

8 R. Schenda, *Volk ohne Buch: Studien zur Sozialgeschichte der populären Lesestoffe 1770–1910* (Munich, 1977), pp. 444–5, estimates 40 per cent. Wolfram Fischer, Jochen Krengel, and Jutta Wietog, *Sozialgeschichtliches Arbeitsbuch I: Materialien zur Statistik des Deutschen Bundes, 1815–1870* (Munich, 1982), p. 234, give census statistics for Berlin that show that only 15.39 per cent of Berliners born in 1801 or earlier, and 8.60 per cent of those born between 1802 and 1811, could neither read nor write.

9 For an analysis of audience, text structure, distribution and purchase price, see Mary Lee Townsend, 'Lachen Verboten: zur Sozialgeschichte des Berliner Witzes im Vormärz, 1815–1848', in Norbert Dittmar and Peter

Schlobinski (eds), *Wandlungen einer Stadtsprache: Berlinisch in Vergangenheit und Gegenwart* (Berlin, 1988), pp. 183–210.

10 On the censorship of humour and Prussian state policy see Mary Lee Townsend, *Forbidden Laughter: popular humour and the limits of repression in nineteenth-century Prussia* (Ann Arbor, 1992), pp. 171–91.

11 V. Tennigkeit, 'Ein Mensch namens Nante: zur Geschichte der Nante-Darstellung', *Jahrbuch für brandenburgische Landesgeschichte*, 19 (1968), pp. 21–35.

12 Glaßbrenner in a letter to an unknown recipient, 5 November 1873, Landesarchiv Berlin, Rep. 241, Acc. 566, Nr. 28.

13 Glaßbrenner to A. Weinholz, 15 September 1847, Museum für Deutsche Geschichte, Abteilung Fundus, Autographen-Sammlung.

14 When courting a prospective publisher, Glaßbrenner declared that his early joke booklets, including the first *Eckensteher* pamphlet, 'crawl with tastelessness' and were 'written more for the publisher than for their own sake'. Glaßbrenner, letter to Veit and Co., 6 July 1837, Goethe- und Schiller-Archiv, Nationale Forschungs und Gedenkstätten der Klassischen Deutschen Literatur in Weimar, Abteilung II, Nr. 857; the letter is misfiled under 1857.

15 Letter dated Berlin, 10 November 1837, in Karl Marx and Friedrich Engels, *Werke*, ed. Institut für Marxismus-Leninismus beim ZK der SED (42 vols to date; Berlin/GDR, 1956–), vol. 40, p. 9. Robert Springer, *Berlin's Strassen, Kneipen und Clubs im Jahre 1848* (Berlin, 1850), p. 28, says of Glaßbrenner's pamphlets, 'Diese Typen eines Nante, . . . man hatte sie an der Poststraßen-Ecke gesehen.'

16 Modern definition, *New Cassell's German Dictionary*, ed. Karl Breul, rev. Harold T. Betteridge (New York, 1971), p. 115. Quotation, L. Zedlitz, *Neuestes Conversations-Handbuch für Berlin und Potsdam zum täglichen Gebrauch der einheimischen und Fremden aller Ständen* (Berlin, 1834), pp. 159–60.

17 On the banning of the *Eckensteher*, see Horst Denkler, 'Einleitung und Editionsbericht', in Horst Denkler et al. (eds), *Adolf Glaßbrenner: Unterrichtung der Nation. Ausgewählte Werke und Briefe* (3 vols; Cologne, 1981), vol. 1, p. 39.

18 W. Howitt, *The Rural and Domestic Life of Germany: with characteristic sketches of its cities and scenery* (London, 1842), p. 441.

19 Contemporaries extolled Dörbeck and Glaßbrenner for their accuracy; sometimes ostensibly objective books about Berlin sound as if they are a paraphrase of Glaßbrenner; see e.g. Zedlitz above, n. 16. We cannot know for certain how accurate Glaßbrenner's descriptions of the *Eckensteher* are, but we can see that his perceptions coincided with those of his peers.

20 Dr Nante, *Nante als Fremdenführer, oder Ganz Berlin für 7-1/2 Sgr.: ein Wegweiser* (Berlin, 1840), repr. ed. Herbert Sommerfeld, Sonderdruck aus den Berlinischen Blättern für Geschichte und Heimatkunde, vol. 7 (Berlin, 1936), p. 7, 'eine vielosaufische Abhandlung'; 'Doctor der Weltweisheit'; 'vielosaufisch' can also be translated as 'philo-sow-phical'.

21 Dr D., *Nante auf Reisen oder Schattenspiel an der Wand!* (2nd edn, Berlin, 1834), p. 12, '. . . 'ne Frauenperschon von Gummi-Elasticum, die man in

hundert Jahren erfinden wird. Die wird immer nachgeben, wenn och der Mann kriblich is.'

22 *Nante Strumpfs hinterlassene Papiere*, vol. 7, *Nante Strumpf bei der Einholung* (2nd edn, Berlin, 1842), p. 32, 'Heer'n Se, Sie Mamsell, Sie zeigen sich sehro indringlich. . . . Seind Sie villeicht eine Dochter von de Parisermacher George Sandten, daß Sie Ihr'n weublijen Kurrakter so entfremden?'

23 Educated readers would have recognized these names: Bluebeard, the wife killer in the well-known fairy tale, and Aspasia, Pericles's quick-witted consort.

24 L. Lenz, *Nante auf der Berlin-Potsdamer Eisenbahn* (5 vols, Berlin, 1839– 41), vol. 1, p. 40, 'Nante: Blaubart, springen se raus, un halten se ihr een Bund Heu vor; des helft vielleicht. Conducteur: Die Maschine hat nicht Wasser genug. Blaubart: Ach so, se will saufen.'

25 Lenz, *Nante auf der Berlin-Potsdamer Eisenbahn*, vol. 1, p. 13, 'Blaubart: Es jeht doch schändlich schnell – da müssn woll die Eenspänner zu Jrunde jehen. Nante: Ja, die Akzionärsch betrachten die Eisenbahn ooch als des achte Wunder. Aspasia: Worüber wundern se sich denn? Nante: Wo des Jeld bliebt.'

26 *Nante Strumpfs hinterlassene Papiere*, vol. 1, *Nante Strumpfs Weltgang* (Berlin, 1838), pt 1, [p. vii,] '. . . er starb am Mäßigkeitsverein und einer Überfüllung von Korn und Bittern.'

27 J. S. Roberts, *Drink, Temperance and the Working Class in Nineteenth-Century Germany* (Boston, 1984), p. 16.

28 Horst Denkler suggests in the introduction to his anthology of Glaßbrenner texts (see n. 17) that Glaßbrenner first used alcohol as an *object* of satire, but that in his works just before 1848 he used it as a *vehicle* of satire; thus Glaßbrenner moved from laughing at the *Eckensteher* to laughing with them. While this shift may be true in the case of Glaßbrenner, it is not true for the *Eckensteher* literature as a whole, as should become clear in the following paragraphs.

29 A. Hopf, *Lumpazi's Carneval*, vol. 1, *Die schöne Hulda* (Charlottenburg, 1846), p. 28, 'Ick habe heute Armenholz gekriegt, un det habe ick gleich vor'n Dhaler verkooft, un mir'ne Maskengarderobe davor geborgt.'

30 A. Bierglas, *Der ewige Jude: ein Berliner-Puppenspiel* (Demmin, 1844), p. 17, ' ". . . können Sie mir vielleicht insinuiren, was des vor'ne Symfomanie is, die des Orchester spielt?" "Nymfomanie? ne, die kenn' ick nich, aber meine Frau wird se woll kennen, die is musikalisch." '

31 For an introduction to the theoretical literature on superiority and disparagement humour see A. J. Chapman and H. C. Foot (eds), *Humour and Laughter: theory, research and applications* (London, 1976), esp. the first five essays; see also J. Morreall, *Taking Laughter Seriously* (Albany, 1983), pp. 1–37.

32 Jean P—r, *Der Eckensteher in anderm Costüm oder: Nante und sein Rock* (2nd edn, Zerbst, 1833), pp. 12–13.

33 Many other cultural phenomena of the period point to this desire for a sense of security and proof of the 'otherness' of the lower classes, for example the large number of clubs and the increasingly shrill discussion of poverty. On

clubs, e.g. P. H. Noyes, *Organization and Revolution: working class associations in the German revolutions of 1848–1849* (Princeton, 1966), p. 5; on poverty, W. Conze, 'Vom "Pöbel" zum "Proletariat": sozialgeschichtliche Voraussetzungen für den Sozialismus in Deutschland', in H.-U. Wehler (ed.), *Moderne deutsche Sozialgeschichte* (4th edn, Cologne, 1973 [1954]), *passim*. See also Dieter Richter's fascinating argument in *Das fremde Kind: zur Entstehung der Kindheitsbilder des bürgerlichen Zeitalters* (Frankfurt am Main, 1987) that during the nineteenth century the middle classes became fascinated with (and in part constructed) the 'otherness' of aborigines, the *Volk* and children.

34 Conze, 'Pöbel zum Proletariat', p. 122.

35 Beta [pseud. for Heinrich Bettziech], *Berlin und Potsdam: ihre Vergangenheit, Gegenwart und Zukunft* (Munich, 1846), pp. 65–6, 'die Klassen bröckeln immer rascher auseinander.' F. D. Marquardt, 'Sozialer Aufstieg, Sozialer Abstieg und die Entstehung der Berliner Arbeiterklasse, 1806–1848', *Geschichte und Gesellschaft*, 1 (1975), p. 75, notes that this social mobility took a psychological toll on the middle strata of society who experienced a new 'Angst vor ihrem Schicksal'.

36 *Nante Strumpfs hinterlassene Papiere*, vol. 4, *Nante Strumpf's [sic] Weltgang* (Berlin, 1839), pt 2, p. 14, '"Worüber ick mir blos gewundert habe, deß in Paris die kleene Kinder ganz gut franzesch sprechen konnten." "Sprechst du denn ooch franzesch?" "Ick sprechen woll, aber es versteht mir keener." '

37 L. Weyl, *Rebbenhagen auf dem Berliner Corso* (Berlin, 1845), p. 31, '. . . schön für's Vaterland zu sterben . . . weil man sonst als Invalide nich zu leben hat'; here the speaker is a baker.

38 Ad. Brennglas [pseud. for Adolph Glaßbrenner], *Berlin wie es ist und trinkt*, vol. 9, *Nante Nantino, der letzte Sonnenbruder, oder: die Entstehung der norddeutschen Volkspoesie* (Leipzig, 1843), p. 15, 'Hören Se mal, Herr Komzarius, vielleicht haben Sie ooch man blos jedrömt?' 'Des ist janz eingal, der Traum eines Polizeicommissarien is hinreichender Verdacht.'

39 Police report, Geheimes Staatsarchiv Preußischer Kulturbesitz, Abteilung Merseburg, Ministerium des Innern und der Polizei, Rep. 77, Tit. 2, Gen. Nr. 87, Acta betr. Die Censur und den Debit kleiner satyrischer Volksschriften, mit Berlinismen, verunglimpfenden Ausfällen auf Adel, Polizei p.p. Einzelne Schriften: 1, Nante Nantino, 1843, Bl. 1.

40 A. Hopf, *Nante's politisches Wachskabinet nebst einer sehr interessanten Unterhaltung zwischen Nante und Brenneke über das neue Strafgesetzbuch* (Berlin, 1848), p. 10, 'Den ollen Ludwig Philippen muß ick aber ooch bald umschmelzen lassen; er sieht schon so dodenfarbig aus. . . . Aber wat mach' ich denn mit seinem Minister Gütso? Nehme ick Philippen von'n Platz, denn fallt der um; wackelig steht er schon. Na laß ihm fallen, er hat lange genug gestanden.'

41 A. Hopf, *Der kleine Landtag und sein Schluß, oder Nante und Brenneke als Abgeordnete* (Berlin, 1847), p. 5, 'Des sind ja Proletarier. Wir können doch nich zugeben, daß sone Subjecte in eine noble Gesellschaft wie die unsrige.'

42 Hopf, *Der kleine Landtag*, p. 16, 'Ich habe wie een Vater an die Menschen gehandelt. Ick kann Ihn versichern, meine Herren, manche Arbeeter haben

et bei mir die Woche bis auf drei Dhaler Verdienst gebracht. . . . Als ick aber sah, daß sie bei den hohen Lohn übermüthig wurden, da machte ick kleene Abzüge.'

43 On living expenses in Berlin see Noyes, *Organization and Revolution*, p. 31; and F. D. Marquardt, 'A working class in Berlin in the 1840s?', in H.-U. Wehler (ed.), *Sozialgeschichte Heute* (Göttingen, 1974), p. 198.

44 The Märkisches Museum (Berlin) has an excellent collection of broadsheets from 1848 in Abteilung Geschichte, Flugblattsammlung; for Kaiser Nante, see IV 1249b S. See also Sigrid Weigel's eccentric but useful *Flugschriftenliteratur 1848 in Berlin: Geschichte und Öffentlichkeit einer volkstümlichen Gattung* (Stuttgart, 1979).

45 D. W. Sabean, *Power in the Blood: popular culture and village discourse in early modern Germany* (Cambridge, 1984), p. 84, makes a similar point in his discussion of a seventeenth-century village, that 'authorities grasped discourse as an act'.

46 Robert Darnton sees similar connections between the scandal sheets of the *ancien régime* and the French Revolution; see his *The Great Cat Massacre and Other Episodes in French Cultural History* (New York, 1984), p. 178, and *The Literary Underground of the Old Regime* (Cambridge, MA, 1982), *passim*.

12

Humour, Laughter and the Field: Reflections from Anthropology

HENK DRIESSEN

Ridendo dicere severum

Friedrich Nietzsche

Humour is both playful and serious, a vital quality of the human condition. What makes humour fascinating and relevant to anthropologists and historians is that it provides clues to what really matters in society and culture, academic subculture included. Humour often mirrors deeper cultural perceptions and offers us a powerful device to understand culturally shaped ways of thinking and feeling.

The title of this contribution expresses the two aims I would like to pursue. The first objective is to reveal some of the complexities of the comparative study of joking and to review briefly the anthropological work on humour. The second is to provide evidence of the functions and meanings of humour, this time not in alien communities, but rather in the tribe of ethnographic fieldworkers.

THE ANTHROPOLOGICAL STUDY OF HUMOUR

Humour is an elusive and difficult topic to explore cross-culturally and through time. The anthropological and historical study of the humoresque presupposes an awareness that reality is socially and culturally constituted. This relativist perspective is one of the issues on which anthropology and cultural history converge.[1] The first problem to be encountered by anthropologists and historians alike is a language problem, a problem of discourse, of *double* and even *triple entendre*. Let me just give you an example from my recent experience to illustrate this point.

In June 1993 I met Mimun, a young Berber activist from Morocco who studied in Granada. We liked each other, partly because I had visited his native village and we were both outsiders at a festival of

Moors and Christians in a small town in Southern Spain. During an evening hopping bars, Mimun told me of his aversion to the regime of King Hassan II, and, in order to stress his political attitude in the festive ambience, he made some jokes about the king, including this one:

> King Hassan was travelling to France in his private jet. Flying over the Rif region in the north he looked down on the mountains and mused aloud on the economic and political problems in this part of his kingdom. 'What can I do to make these people happy?' he sighed to his councillor. The latter, who actually originated from the Rif, replied: 'Well, your majesty, throw your gold watch out of the window and the person who finds it will be a happy man.' 'Hm, all that's very well, but then I will make only one Rifian happy', replied the king. The councillor thought for a moment and then answered: 'There is an easy solution to this problem, Sire.' 'Tell me what it is, my dear friend.' 'Well, beloved majesty, if *you* jump after your watch you'll not only make the Rifians happy but the entire nation!'

My companion told me this joke in Spanish. It circulates widely among Rifians. He first heard it told in the local language (*tamazight*), so he had to translate it for me into Spanish. The next day I noted it down in Dutch and for this paper I have translated it into English. This quadruple translation, interpretation, textualization and evocation is a delicate process in which the joke's expressivity is displaced at four removes. The first is the explicit one of the subject-matter, the second the elapse of time and distancing of space, and the third the remove of three languages all containing their own sets of referents. Equally problematic is the fourth remove, from oral to written, which affects the gist, tone, timbre, gestures, mimicry and postures that accompanied the actual telling of the joke and the setting in which it was performed. Part of the joke's grace is inevitably lost during this process. In this case, I had just taken a picture of Mimun in front of a group of mock Moorish soldiers who were holding a banner with nonsense Arabic script, a scene that was hilarious to all people involved, including myself.

The understanding of this particular joke is enhanced by background knowledge about the conflictive nature of Berber–Arab relations. In 1959 Hassan, then crown prince, commanded the army that cruelly repressed a Rifian uprising by bombing villages in the central Rif. It is equally enhanced by knowledge about the popular view of councillors as inherently untrustworthy. In sum, this example illustrates the problem of contextualization, which raises the issue of the relationship between joke and experience. It is well known that political humour flourishes under conditions of political repression and economic hardship. This was brought home to me when I did my first fieldwork in Franco's Spain, coming from a democratic country where political joking was and still is underdeveloped.

Huizinga, in *Homo ludens*, tried to capture play in its pure form, as a foundation of culture.[2] Although laughter, folly, jest and the comic are, according to Huizinga, in a sense opposed to seriousness, they are not necessarily linked to, or ingredients of, the ludic. These notions share their irreducibility, constituting realities on their own. Leaving pure essences aside, I would like to emphasize that humour and laughter, although intimately related, should not be considered inseparable. I agree with Mary Douglas, who is a good guide in matters of joking, that 'It would be wrong to suppose that the acid test of a joke is whether it provokes laughter or not. It is not necessary to go into the physiology and psychology of laughter, since it is generally recognised that one can appreciate a joke without actually laughing, and one can laugh for other reasons than from having perceived a joke.'[3]

Joking, in the anthropological sense, is a face-to-face discourse, a *performative* genre which includes plays, stories, folk tales, ritual forms, ritual clowning and ordinary conversation.[4] Jokes are acted out on a cultural stage by performers amidst an audience. Gestures, mimic, pantomime are central to much humour, since its effectiveness depends to a large degree on non-verbal behaviour.[5] We should, however, avoid taking the idea of the cultural stage too literally. It is the wider context that matters when identifying joke patterns and their meanings.

What did and does anthropology contribute to the understanding of humour? Early anthropologists, such as James Frazer and Edward Westermarck, studied humour mostly in an antiquarian way, rarely as a resource for cultural analysis. In the fieldwork guide to British social anthropology, humour, joking and laughter are not mentioned, although games, amusements, stories, sayings and songs are listed as separate categories of fieldwork interest.[6] Radcliffe-Brown's article on joking relationships was in a sense a breakthrough, though he studied the subject in a one-sided way, interested as he was in the structural implications rather than in the symbolic content of such relationships.[7] But, apart from attention to the joking relationship and to the role of the trickster figure in myths and rites, the comic was left largely to folklorists, philosophers and psychologists.

Mary Douglas's 'The social control of cognition: some factors in joke perception' was, I think, the most sophisticated essay on humour by an anthropologist until the early 1980s. Combining Bergson with Freud, she finds the essence of the joke in its attack on control: 'something formal is attacked by something informal, something organised and controlled, by something vital, energetic, an upsurge of life for Bergson, of libido for Freud.'[8] In other words, a joke is a play upon form.[9] She continues, 'It brings into relation disparate elements in such a way that one accepted pattern is challenged by the appearance of another which in some way was hidden in the first.'[10] She then distinguishes standardized jokes, which are set in a conventional context, from spontaneous ones. The joke pattern can easily be identified within the verbal form of standard jokes and puns. But the spontaneous joke organizes the total situation in its joke pattern. Douglas finally suggests that the achievement of consonance between different spheres of experience is a source of profound satisfaction for the people involved.[11]

In the late 1970s and early 1980s anthropologists became more interested in humour, thanks to the impact of symbolic analysis and a 'literary turn'. A minor rebellion against the positivist paradigm created room for new research topics and new modes of ethnographic writing.[12]

The first comprehensive and state-of-the-art-like study of the comic in anthropology appeared in 1985. It is a conventional yet useful book informed by a comparative and holistic perspective. Its author, Mahadev Apte, covers and discusses some 800 listed sources on the following topics: joking relationships, sexual inequality in humour, children's humour, ethnic humour, humour in language and religion, the trickster in folklore, and the biosocial and evolutionary aspects of laughter and smiling. Given the present state of the art, he rejects the possibility of a general theory of humour and instead focuses on a 'middle ground' in the form of theoretical propositions regarding each of the topics. There are some drawbacks to his approach, which does not deal with the symbolic aspects of humour and also excludes obscenity. Many of his propositions state the obvious.[13] Apte also neglects the problem of meaning involved in cross-cultural comparison. Mary Douglas, who is very much aware of this problem, cites the example of laughter, writing: 'In any of a number of social systems the idea of loud vociferous laughter may be unseemly in polite company. But what counts as loud and vociferous may vary greatly.'[14] Sensitivity to cultural variation grows with prolonged and diverse fieldwork experience.

A second landmark in the study of the comic is Christie Davies's comprehensive survey of ethnic humour, with more than 1600 bibliographical entries. Davies argues that 'ethnic jokes are a means by which the joke-tellers ascribe human deficiencies to other ethnic groups in an excessive or ludicrous fashion . . . the defects which are most frequently mocked can be arranged in pairs [e.g. the stupid and the canny, the stupid and the cowardly, militarism and cowardice] that relate to commonly experienced ambiguous and indeed contradictory situations, to dilemmas which seem likely to generate uncertainty and ambivalence.'[15] He deals mainly with the content of the jokes, and treats minimally form, structure and context. Davies introduces the notion of an 'ethnic script', which he distinguishes from ethnic stereotype. By this he means a conventional, fictional account of ethnic groups that forms the necessary backdrop for a joke. The author uses the notion to explain why the telling of an ethnic joke can be an expression of prejudice, but that this is not necessarily the case. Members of a group tell and enjoy jokes about themselves (for instance, self-disparagement is a well-known strategy in Jewish humour); and ethnic jokes can be told in mixed ethnic settings. The script demonstrates that the telling of jokes has a complex relationship to experience. From an ethnographic point of view I must stress that the evidence of this study differs in many respects from field evidence on the actual telling of jokes. Davies's interpretations must ultimately be checked against actual joking performances in multi-ethnic contexts.[16]

Davies and Apte are both members of the editorial board of *Humor: international journal of humor research*, an interdisciplinary journal that testifies to the increased interest in the topic also on the part of anthropologists and historians, who have published numerous case studies of humour since the mid-1980s. The relevance of anthropological studies of the comic for the cultural historian rests in their cross-cultural and holistic perspectives. Anthropologists document the richness of comic expression around the world, a task which requires meticulous contextual analysis. In doing so, anthropology may supply historians with viewpoints and concepts for discussing the symbolic meanings and functions of jocular behaviour in the past. Its value also lies in the awareness that matters of humour speak to large issues in the societies involved: to dominant interests, attitudes and values regarding identities (for instance, gender and ethnicity) and their counterpoints, contradictions and ambivalences.

The studies mentioned point out that humour creates a reality of its own. However, the degree of correspondence between joking and other domains of experience has to be assessed for each form, genre and context. For instance, many ethnic jokes bear only a vague resemblance to everyday reality (American jokes about Poles, Dutch jokes about the Flemish, urban Spanish jokes about the stupidity of the people of Lepe in rural Andalusia, and Canary Island jokes about the people from Gomera are cases in point). On the other hand, many political jokes are firmly rooted in the social and political reality of the societies involved. I now turn to a specific case: humour and laughter in anthropological fieldwork and writing.

HUMOUR AND LAUGHTER IN ANTHROPOLOGY

It has been claimed that sociology and humour have much in common, that they are congenial in their aim to relativize the taken-for-granted routines of everyday life by subjecting them to closer scrutiny.[17] But mainstream sociology lacks almost totally the qualities of playfulness, witticism, imagination and sense of cultural critique. In bad anthropological dreams sociologists often appear as dull, boorish, domineering bastards, explaining the obvious.

Humour as criticism is more characteristic of anthropology and arises from the very nature of traditional anthropological work, the result of the perspective gained by fieldwork in the periphery of the Western world. Anthropologists often revise categories in order to understand what in Western terms are exotic ways of life.[18] Anthropology shares with humour the basic strategy of defamiliarization: common sense is disrupted, the unexpected is evoked, familiar subjects are situated in unfamiliar, or even shocking, contexts in order to make the audience or readership conscious of their own cultural assumptions, prejudices and differences.[19] This is the task of cultural relativism, which is a basic, albeit contested, doctrine in anthropology aimed at combating intolerance and racism.[20] In this regard, anthropologists are akin to tricksters, clowns, jesters and comedians. Since the past which historians study is, to paraphrase David Lowenthal,[21] a foreign country with different customs, values and preoccupations, relativism and cultural critique also informs the work of cultural historians.

Perhaps one of the most famous examples of this ludic quality in anthropology is an article on body ritual by Horace Miner, published forty years ago in one of the most respected anthropological journals.[22] An excerpt follows:

[The Nacirema] are a North American group living in the territory between the Canadian Cree, the Yaqui and Tarahumare of Mexico, and the Carib and Arawak of the Antilles. Little is known of their origin, although tradition states that they came from the east. According to Nacirema mythology, their nation was originated by a culture hero, Notgnihsaw, who is otherwise known for two great feats of strength – the throwing of a piece of wampum across the river Pa-To-Mac and the chopping down of a cherry tree in which the Spirit of Truth resided. Nacirema culture is characterized by a highly developed market economy which has evolved in a rich natural habitat. While much of the people's time is devoted to economic pursuits, a large part of the fruits of these labors and a considerable portion of the day are spent in ritual activity. The focus of this activity is the human body, the appearance and health of which loom as a dominant concern in the ethos of the people ... The fundamental belief underlying the whole system appears to be that the human body is ugly and that its natural tendency is to debility and disease. Incarcerated in such a body, man's only hope is to avert these characteristics through the use of the powerful influences of ritual and ceremony. Every household has one or more shrines devoted to this purpose . . . The focal point of the shrine is a box or chest which is built into the wall. In this chest are kept the many charms and magical potions without which no native believes he could live. These preparations are secured from a variety of specialized practitioners. The most powerful of these are the medicine men, whose assistance must be rewarded with substantial gifts. However, the medicine men do not provide the curative potions for their clients, but decide what the ingredients should be and then write them down in an ancient and secret language. This writing is understood only by the medicine men and by the herbalists who, for another gift, provide the required charm . . . The daily body ritual performed by everyone includes a mouth-rite. Despite the fact that these people are so punctilious about care of the mouth, this rite involves a practice which strikes the uninitiated stranger as revolting. It was reported to me that the ritual consists of inserting a small bundle of hog hairs into the mouth, along with certain magical powders, and then moving the bundle in a highly formalized series of gestures . . . In addition to the private mouth-rite, the people seek out a holy-mouth-man once or twice a year. These practitioners have an impressive set of paraphernalia, consisting of a variety of augers, awls, probes, and prods . . . The medicine men have an imposing temple, or *latipso*, in every community of any size. The more elaborate ceremonies required to treat very sick patients can only be performed at this temple. These ceremonies involve not only the thaumaturge but a permanent group of vestal maidens who move sedately about the temple chambers in a distinctive costume and headdress.

The reader will have recognized in this quotation the health-cult of the Anglo-Americans (the 'tribe' is spelled backwards, as is its founding father and the temple of medicine). Using the 'neutral' language of behavioral science interspersed with common anthropological concepts, Miner defamiliarizes and criticizes a part of his own society and culture, making it seem exotic and even bizarre.

Miner's article was written at a time when few anthropologists did fieldwork in their own society. Since then an increasing number of fieldworkers have focused the anthropological lens – polished among the tribes of Africa, Asia and Latin America – on communities and problems 'at home'. This shift of interest has heightened the potential for debunking myths of Western uniqueness and superiority.[23] The trickster role of the anthropologist is perceived by scholars in other academic disciplines (sociologists in particular) and by readers in the wider audience with mixed feelings: some find it fanciful, sympathetic, pleasantly eccentric, while others react in an irritated way and tend to view this role as yet another proof of the not so scientific nature of the anthropological discipline.

To be sure, only a small number of publications by anthropologists are explicitly defamiliarizing and amusing. Most of the writings in mainstream anthropology lack this quality of humour, grace and satire. This, however, does not alter the fact that there is in anthropology a source of humorous potential not so readily available to other disciplines in the social and human sciences. This source is ethnographic fieldwork, the *fons et origo* of anthropology.

Fieldwork in not so familiar places is still the craft of anthropology, not only the main research strategy and most important source of evidence but also the major experience marking professional identity. It is one of the discipline's paradoxes that the fieldwork experience, in spite of its centrality, has long been shrouded in mystique.[24] Writing about fieldwork inevitably involves an unveiling of the self from which most anthropologists have recoiled unless in the form of travel books and novels separated from the 'real' ethnographies. The subjective dimension of fieldwork has been played down, ignored or hidden from public view under the pressure of the dominant scientific model, particularly in the formative stage of anthropology, when it had to prove itself as a fully-fledged member of the scientific community. But in the late 1960s growing scepticism about the positivist tenets of the research process and increased acknowledgement of the constructive dimension of ethnographic fieldwork have produced a number of publications on the personal experience of doing fieldwork.[25]

Yet in these confessional accounts anthropologists rarely acknowledge the vital role of humour and laughter in fieldwork and in the construction of ethnographic evidence.[26] It seems as if the humour has been edited out, leading a semi-secret life in fieldnotes. To be sure, there are some standing jokes. Everybody knows now that the average Pueblo family or typical Mexican family consists of a father, a mother, three children and an anthropologist. Several of these standard jokes revolve upon the lack of fieldwork training and the notion of fieldwork as a rite of passage, requiring the invention of one's own methods. Professors told their departing students such things as: 'You should take plenty of marmalade and cheap tennis shoes'; 'Take a big stick for the dogs'; 'Write down everything and keep away from the women.' The best advice Laura Bohannan received was, 'Always walk in cheap tennis shoes; the water runs out more quickly', and, 'You'll need more tables than you think.'[27] There are also anecdotes about the eccentricity of professors doing fieldwork: in order to protect his privacy when writing his notes in Dutch New Guinea, an anthropologist placed his dentures on a little table at the entrance of his tent. Such stories circulate among anthropologists during informal gatherings at the margins of conferences and seminars in corridors, at coffee and dinner tables and bars. But humorous tales of the field rarely enter into the external discourse of anthropology. Let me now try to illustrate the different forms humour and laughter may take in the field and discuss some of the few published descriptions.

<h2 style="text-align:center">Laughter without Joking</h2>

There seems to be a lot of laughter without joking during first contacts between the anthropologist and the host community to get over a situation that can be awkward, uncomfortable, and bewildering for both parties. Both parties find laughter a common ground of communication and a release to the tension inherent in the situation. Laughter makes the unbearable bearable.

The German ethnologist Hans Fischer describes his arrival among the Watut of Papua New Guinea in the late 1950s: 'I shook hands, laughed as much as I could and did not understand a word they said.'[28] This laughing is reciprocal. The unusual physical appearance of the anthropologist already sets the hosts off in fits of giggles. Often the first people who seek out anthropologists are the village fools and half-wits, not yet recognized by the fieldworker as such, who as marginal persons identify the newcomer as one of their sort. They parade the anthropologist about the community.

Much laughter also arises from the first clumsy attempts of the anthropologist to talk to the hosts in their language. I remember that when I established myself in an Andalusian agro-town to conduct fieldwork I asked the postman, who rented a house to me, for a bucket (*cubo*) but used the word *buco* (billy-goat), which obviously took his breath away for a moment (I could see him think: 'everything is to be expected from strangers'). With gestures I managed to indicate the object needed, which, when understood, triggered off a roar of laughter among the people who were witness to this scene. This incident was part of the circuit of local jokes for a long time.

Laughing and being laughed at also arise from the inevitable gaffes of the anthropologists, their tendency to bring to bear their own cultural assumptions about the investigated culture, and from the efforts to (over-)adapt to local life. Such situations abound particularly during the first weeks of fieldwork and although they usually tend to diminish as time elapses, they keep recurring. This is not always fun for the anthropologists, since they have to try to make sense of laughter among informants (whether polite, hysterical, cruel, mild) of which they are the butt. This may be experienced as embarrassing and frustrating as they do not always get the point. Figuring out the sense of humour is very much part of getting around in an alien culture.

Figure 12.1 *Anthropologist in the field,* by courtesy of Henk Driessen. Photo: W. H. M. Jansen, Andalusia, 1987.

Joking Relationships in the Field

Humour often becomes to a greater or lesser degree institutionalized in the interaction between anthropologist and investigated community. While there is a vast literature on the topic of joking relationships both in tribal and industrial societies, the concept has never been applied, as far as I know, to the relationships between anthropologists and their informants. Stretching the original definition of Radcliffe-Brown (who dealt only with the kin-based, formalized, standardized, obligatory type), a joking relationship may be defined as patterned playful behaviour between two persons (sometimes groups) in which one is by custom permitted (sometimes obliged) to tease or make fun of the other, who must take no offence. Such behaviour displays reciprocal or non-reciprocal verbal or non-verbal humour, including teasing, joking, banter, ridicule, insult, obscenity, the taking of property and horseplay, often in the presence of an audience.[29] The quality of kinship is by no means entirely absent in the relationship between anthropologist and the investigated communities/informants, as anthropologists are frequently adopted by a community or family and assigned quasi-kin roles of the joking type.

Generally speaking, joking relationships between anthropologists and informants are person-oriented, voluntary and based in friendship. They may become patterned and ritualistic over time. For instance, my height, considerable for Mediterranean societies, remained the object of joking and horseplay in male gatherings during the entire length of my stay in Spain. Men never tired of climbing on bar stools in order to outstrip me in height; putting very small men next to me; joking about the supposed symmetry between my height and penis length, and inventing theories to explain why I never got really drunk: 'It takes too much time for the alcohol to reach your brains', etc. Horseplay was not always pleasant, although I learned to do it in return (which was very much appreciated). The source of the recurrent banter was that my unusual stature touched a sensitive spot in the code of masculinity.

An American colleague had a similar experience among the Cakchiquel Indians in the mountains of Guatemala:

At get-togethers, I am frequently asked to tell jokes. Everyone likes jokes and stories (me too), which are told and retold. A great number of them make use of the double entendre, and, of course, there are the off-color jokes. Ernesto told me that it is we students who can screw and 'get it up' all the time but that he and the other *campesinos* (peasants) who work in the field are too tired to do much of anything in the evenings.[30]

One of the rare books that consistently deals with laughter in a fieldwork situation is the classic *Return to Laughter* by Laura Bohannan, first published in 1954 in the form of a novel and under a pseudonym in order to separate the subjective dimension (the joys and frustrations, stupidities, embarrassment and irrationalities, in fact shared by fieldworkers in many different field settings) from her scientific account based on fieldwork in Nigeria.[31]

The novel relates the rather painful process in which the anthropologist learned to accept the Tiv for what they were, rather than for what they should or might be. This acceptance inevitably involved a questioning of her own values. The Tiv frequently exploded into laughter ('. . . a people who laugh out loud . . . I also laughed'; 'At least, out here, people were not afraid to let go. There was always laughter'; 'they fight sorrow with laughter' (pp. 104, 180, 211). The author temporarily lost her ability to laugh with the Tiv when she was a witness of children poking fun at an old blind man, which provoked howling laughter among the adults. She wrote: 'Their laughter at suffering was merely one symbol of the gulf between their world and mine . . . where people laughed at human misery, our doctrine of kindness to animals, for the sake of mere kindness without intent to use or worship, seemed the wildest extravagance' (p. 231). After a devastating plague of smallpox, Bohannan returned to the field and was invited to an evening of storytelling, an occasion during which she regained her ability to laugh with the Tiv about herself. During that session one of the fabletellers began to play informant to another storyteller who played the role of the fieldworker: 'Accident in turn looked eager or baffled, scribbled in the air as though in a notebook, wiped imaginary glasses, adjusted imaginary skirts and took off my accent, gestures, errors of grammar and habits of phrase with such unmerciful accuracy that even as I laughed myself sore I resolved on improvement . . . Others took turns imitating Europeans' (pp. 291–2).

She reflected upon this liberating occasion as follows: 'Many of my moral dilemmas had sprung from the very nature of my work, which had made me a trickster: one who seems to be what he is not and who professes faith in what he does not believe . . . Only in a very sheltered life of the sort made possible by civilization can one maintain a fine and serious sense of the tragedy of misfortune. In an environment in which tragedy is genuine and frequent, laughter is essential to sanity' (pp. 290, 295).

Other instances of joking relationships can be gleaned from Chagnon's fieldwork among the Yanomamö in the rainforest of Venezuela and Brazil. In the first chapter of his famous monograph he discusses some of the problems that seem to be almost universal among fieldworkers, particularly those related to eating, bathing, sleeping, lack of privacy and loneliness. These problems are a source of both frustration and humour. Consider the following examples:

> Food sharing is important to the Yanomamö in the context of displaying friendship. 'I am hungry' is almost a form of greeting with them. I could not possibly have brought enough food with me to feed the entire village, yet they seemed not to understand this . . . I found peanut butter and crackers a very nourishing food, and a simple one to prepare on trips . . . More importantly, it was one of the few foods the Indians would let me eat in relative peace. It looked too much like animal feces to them to excite their appetites. I once referred to the peanut butter as the dung of cattle. They found this quite repugnant . . . Fieldworkers develop strange defense mechanisms, and this was one of my own forms of adaptation. On another occasion I was eating a can of frankfurters and growing very weary of the demands of one of my guests for a share in my meal. When he asked me what I was eating, I replied: 'Beef'. He then asked, 'What part of the animal are you eating?' to which I replied, 'Guess!' He stopped asking for a share . . .

In order to collect genealogies Chagnon had to resort to listing names. The Yanomamö, however, have very stringent name taboos:

> They enjoyed watching me learn these names. I assumed, wrongly, that I would get the truth to each question and that I would get the best information by working in public. This set the stage for converting a serious project into a farce. Each informant tried to outdo his peers by inventing a name even more ridiculous than what I had been given earlier, or by asserting that the individual about whom I inquired was married to his mother or daughter, and the like. I would have the informant whisper the name of the individual in my ear, noting that he was the father of such and such a child. Everybody would then insist that I repeat the name aloud, roaring in hysterics as I clumsily pronounced the name. I assumed that the laughter was in response to the violation of the name taboo or to my pronunciation. This was a reasonable interpretation, since the individual whose name I said aloud invariably became angry. After I learned what some of the names meant, I began to under-stand what the laughter was all about. A few of the more colorful examples are: 'hairy vagina', 'long penis', 'feces of the harpy eagle' and 'dirty rectum'. No wonder the victims were angry.[32]

That the relationships between anthropologists and informants display several characteristics of the joking relationship as depicted in the anthropological literature should not come as a surprise, given the many ambivalences inherent in the role of anthropological fieldworkers. They come as strangers to immerse themselves in the life of the investigated community and force themselves upon that community. They begin to participate as more or less innocent children yet hold university degrees and come from societies which are usually more powerful than those investigated. They neither become complete insiders nor remain complete outsiders. They have to strike a balance between participation and observation. Their mission is never entirely transparent to their hosts. They become familiar with many delicate aspects of local life yet keep a certain distance not only with regard to their hosts but also to their selves. They wish to get involved in local life and yet stay apart. After a period of extended and intensive participation, they return to their own societies where, sitting at their computers, they view the field from afar.[33] They seek both working relationships and friendship with their hosts within a veiled context of power differentials.[34] Both parties deal with so many ambivalences, tensions and dilemmas by resorting to humour and laughter. Humour and laughter help make communication possible, ease contact, reduce hostility, release tension and offer entertainment.

A Professional Jester out of the Box

As has been pointed out above, anthropological fieldworkers tend to celebrate and exchange jokes of and about the field in their backstage interactions, whereas their written accounts are almost completely devoid of humour and self-mockery. Anthropologists are thus hardly known as writers of humour. The British anthropologist Nigel Barley is an exception. He pokes fun at the profession in books widely read outside the discipline, and his popular writings about fieldwork are unprecedented in their persistently witty and humorous tone. His first and best book, *The Innocent Anthropologist: notes from a mud hut*,[35] relates Barley's first anthropological fieldwork in the late 1970s among the Dowayos of the Cameroons. Let me quote some passages.

On arrival at the national airport: 'First impressions count for a lot. The man whose knees are not brown will be marked down by all manner of people. At all events, my camera case was promptly seized by what looked to be an enthusiastic porter. I revised my ideas when he swiftly made off into the distance. I set off in pursuit, using all manner of phrases uncommon in everyday speech. "Au secours!" "Au voleur!"; I cried. Fortunately, he was delayed by traffic, I caught up, and we began to struggle. It ended with a swift blow that laid open the side of my face and the case was abandoned to me. A solicitous taxi-driver took me to my hotel for only five times the normal fare' (p. 20).

On arrival in the field: 'Villagers rushed out and shook hands with me jabbering in garbled Fulani. I had learned the rudiments of this tongue in London so I was able at least to say, "I am sorry, I do not speak Fulani." Since I had practised this sentence many times, it came out rather fluently and added to the incomprehension' (p. 38).

On learning a tonal language: 'My rather wobbly control of the language was also a grave danger. Obscenity is never very far away in Dowayo. A shift of tone changes the interrogative particle attached to a sentence to convert it into a question, into the lewdest word in the language, something like "cunt". I would therefore baffle and amuse Dowayos by greeting them, "Is the sky clear for you, cunt?" But my problems were not exclusively with interrogative vaginas; similar problems haunted eating and copulation' (p. 57).

The majority of these and other experiences (getting a research grant and permit, advice by professors, delay in the capital, vermin in the field, gaffes), both hilarious and/or frustrating, are familiar to fieldworkers in many different contexts.[36] Barley wrote down for a wider audience the oral lore of the fieldworking tribe with a sound sense of humour, wit and self-mockery and a sharp pencil. Making liberal use of understatement and overstatement, irony, satire and parody, he debunks much of the mystique surrounding fieldwork in exotic places. The book became rather popular among students, at least in the Netherlands, though the professional fieldworkers received it with less enthusiasm. Some colleagues felt that he poked too much fun at the profession, that he had washed its dirty linen in public. They were concerned about the public image of anthropology and felt that this book would reinforce public stereotypes about the triviality and irrelevance of the discipline. There is, indeed, some ground for concern here. As humour and irony work indirectly, there is a chance that the general reader will mistake the anthropologist for an upgraded rucksack tourist. Other colleagues simply refrained from discussing the book.[37] Were they touched in their professional pride, embarrassed by and suspicious of the popularizing tone of the book, did they suffer from *jalousie de métier*, or did they simply not share Barley's sense of humour?[38] However this may be, it is clear that Barley's critics would not regard Rabelais or Nietzsche as patrons of their profession.

CONCLUSION

What has been written about the functions of humour in tribal societies also applies to the social dynamics of the anthropological community, the occupational subculture, itself. In this sense, there is nothing distinctive about the fieldworkers' humour and laughter. They help to foster communication, create an ambiance of relaxation and strengthen cohesion.[39] We may recognize here a general social function of humour as marker of the boundaries of the group, consisting of symbols and performances that help to promote a kind of *esprit de corps*. That these humorous tales remain largely within the tribe finds its explanation in the fact that they also expose the emotions and vulnerability of the fieldworkers and informants. Nevertheless, they not only mark the professional identity of anthropology, they also seem to promote a sense of superiority *vis-à-vis* the neighbouring disciplines.

The content of many of the jokes relates to commonly experienced ambiguous situations in the field, to dilemmas which generate uncertainty. A basic dilemma is inherent in participant observation itself: when to get involved and when to maintain a distance. As is dramatically attested by Laura Bohannan's novel, fieldwork generates a 'double consciousness', a clash between perspectives from within the investigated community and those of the society to which the anthropologist belongs and between inner and outer experience. In this regard, the experience of fieldwork resembles the predicament of ethnic minorities in Western society. It has been noted that humour can draw on such a source of heightened sensitivity and that the best comedians have often been minority members.[40] Fieldwork, in fact, presupposes detachment and the ability to laugh at oneself. Humour buffers many difficulties inherent in the role of fieldworker. It is my contention that the potential of humour should also be used in writing, to make ethnography more vivid, accessible, playful and faithful.

It seems to me that the same applies to the work of cultural historians, who have to bridge the cultural gap between past and present, and, in doing so, deal with contradictions and ambiguities in the evidence. There is, of course, a major difference between the fieldworking anthropologist and the historian in the archive: the informants of the latter do not talk and joke back, at least not in the direct sense of the fieldworker's informants. Yet, both the historical and anthropological study of humour require a sense of humour and relativism on the part of the researcher and writer. I would guess that a similar essay could be written on the meanings and functions of humour in the professional community of historians with a focus on archives.

238   *Henk Driessen*

NOTES

Hearty thanks are due to William Christian Jr. for his suggestions, corrections and jest, and to Joy Clephart and Willy Jansen for sharing their wit with me.

1 See, for a recent discussion of the convergence between history and anthropology: P. Burke (ed.), *New Perspectives on Historical Writing* (Cambridge, 1991).

2 J. Huizinga, *Homo ludens: proeve eener bepaling van het spel-element der cultuur* (Groningen, 1938), pp. 5–6.

3 See M. Douglas, *Implicit Meanings: essays in anthropology* (London, 1975), p. 92.

4 See A. L. al-Sayyid Marsot, 'Humor: the two edged sword', in *Everyday Life in the Muslim Middle East*, ed. D. L. Bowen and E. A. Early (Bloomington, 1993), pp. 254–64. See also Roodenburg, Chapter 8 of this volume.

5 See M. L. Apte, *Humor and Laughter: an anthropological approach* (Ithaca, NY, 1985), p. 206.

6 *Notes and Queries on Anthropology* (6th edn, London, 1951[1874]). That colonial literature abounds with jokes *at the expense* of the natives (personal communication, Jean Kommers) is a point that I cannot elaborate upon in this article.

7 A. R. Radcliffe-Brown, 'On joking relationships', *Africa*, 13 (1940), pp. 195–210, repr. in his *Structure and Function in Primitive Society* (London, 1952), pp. 90–104.

8 Douglas, *Implicit Meanings*, pp. 90–114 (= *Man*, 3 (1968), pp. 361–76), especially p. 95. The quote that follows is on p. 96.

9 See A. C. Zijderveld, 'The sociology of humour and laughter', *Current Sociology*, special issue 31 (1983), who uses the phrase 'a play upon meanings' (p. 6).

10 See, for an early insight into this mechanism of humour, A. Schopenhauer, 'Zur Theorie des Lächerlichen', in his *Die Welt als Wille und Vorstellung*, vol. 2 (Darmstadt, 1990), p. 122.

11 See, however, Schopenhauer, 'Zur Theorie des Lächerlichen', who argues that such joy and satisfaction originate in the victory of empirical perception over thinking (p. 131).

12 It seems to me that this growing interest in humour is related to an increasing use of irony as a trope in ethnography, a point to which I will return below. See M. M. J. Fischer, 'Ethnicity and the post-modern arts of memory', in *Writing Culture: the poetics and politics of ethnography*, ed. J. Clifford and G. E. Marcus (Berkeley, 1986), pp. 194–234. He writes: 'Irony and humor are tactics that ethnographers have only slowly come to appreciate, albeit recently with increasing interest. A number of analyses now exist of previously unnoticed or misunderstood ironies (either intended or unintentionally revealing) in past ethnographic writing … Considerable potential still exists, however, to construct texts utilizing humor and other devices that draw attention to their own limitations and degree of accuracy, and that to do so with aesthetic elegance, and are pleasurable to read, rather than with pedantic laboredness' (p. 229).

Also see K.-P. Koeping, 'Lachen und Leib, Scham und Schweigen, Sprache und Spiel: die Ethnologie als feucht-fröhliche Wissenschaft', in *Der Wissenschaftler und das Irrationale*, vol. 2, ed. H. P. Duerr (Frankfurt am Main, 1985), pp. 119–52; G. A. Fine and D. D. Martin, 'A partisan view: sarcasm, satire, and irony as voices in Erving Goffman's *Asylums*', *Journal of Contemporary Ethnography*, 19 (1990), pp. 89–115, who focus on 'a small corner of emotion-laden writing: the use of humour in ethnographic description. As is widely known, humour contributes to rhetorical effectiveness; yet, this technique is infrequently employed in social scientific writing' (p. 90).

13 See, for instance, Apte, *Humor and Laughter*, p. 148: 'Ethnic humor is less likely to occur in highly homogeneous, small-scale societies than in heterogeneous, large-scale and complex ones'.

14 Douglas, *Natural Symbols: explorations in cosmology* (Harmondsworth, 1973), p. 14; idem, *Implicit Meanings*, p. 92: 'Now what is the difference between an insult and a joke? . . . Is the perception of a joke culturally determined so that the anthropologist must take it on trust when a joke has been made? Is no general culture-free analysis of joking possible? When people throw excrement at one another whenever they meet, either verbally or actually, can this be interpreted as a case of wit, or merely written down as a case of throwing excrement? This is the central problem of all interpretation.'

15 C. Davies, *Ethnic Humor around the World: a comparative analysis* (Bloomington, 1990), p. 307.

16 See J. Sherzer, review of *Ethnic Humor around the World*, *American Anthropologist*, 93 (1991), p. 721.

17 Zijderveld, 'The sociology of humour and laughter', pp. 3–4.

18 See G. M. Marcus and M. M. J. Fischer, *Anthropology as Cultural Critique: an experimental moment in the human sciences* (Chicago, 1986), pp. 137–8.

19 See Marcus and Fischer, *Anthropology as Cultural Critique*, for further discussion of techniques of cultural critique in anthropology.

20 See, for two influential recent contributions to the perennial debate on cultural relativism, C. Geertz, 'Distinguished lecture: anti anti-relativism', *American Anthropologist*, 86 (1984), pp. 263–78; M. E. Spiro, 'Cultural relativism and the future of anthropology', *Cultural Anthropology*, 1 (1986), pp. 259–86. Geertz, one of the most gifted and wittiest anthropological authors, described the gist of the profession as follows: 'We have, with no little success, sought to keep the world off balance; pulling out rugs, upsetting tea tables, setting off firecrackers. It has been the office of others to reassure; ours to unsettle. Australopithicenes, Tricksters, Clicks, Megaliths – we hawk the anomalous, peddle the strange. Merchants of astonishment' (p. 275).

21 Cf. D. Lowenthal, *The Past is a Foreign Country* (Cambridge, 1985).

22 H. Miner, 'Body ritual among the Nacirema', *American Anthropologist*, 58 (1956), pp. 503–7.

23 This shift has met with considerable resistance, not least among anthropologists themselves. See J. W. Cole, 'Anthropology comes part-way home: community studies in Europe', *Annual Review of Anthropology*, 6 (1977),

240   Henk Driessen

pp. 349–78. Also see H. Driessen (ed.), *The Politics of Ethnographic Reading and Writing: confrontations of Western and indigenous views* (Saarbrücken and Fort Lauderdale, FL, 1993), for a discussion of views resulting from different insider–outsider positions.

24 See G. D. Berreman, *Behind Many Masks: ethnography and impression management in a Himalayan hill village* (Ithaca, NY, 1962), who characterized this atmosphere as a 'conspiracy of silence'; see also R. F. Ellen (ed.), *Ethnographic Research: a guide to general conduct* (London, 1984).

25 See, among many others, J. Van Maanen, *Tales of the Field: on writing ethnography* (Chicago, 1988).

26 Again in this paper I limit myself to humour and laughter in fieldwork (accounts). Apart from the examples discussed here, I would like to mention J. Vansina, 'Initiation Rituals of the Bushong', *Africa*, 25 (1955), pp. 138–52; R. B. Lee, 'Eating Christmas in the Kalahari', in *The Human Way: readings in anthropology*, ed. H. R. Bernard (New York, 1975), pp. 131–8. There are many more uses and functions of humour, wit and irony in anthropological writing, i.e. as rhetorical, educational and polemic devices. One of the rare published views about anthropologists by a 'native' is J. Salinas, 'On the clan of anthropologists', in *The Human Way*, pp. 71–7.

27 L. Bohannan (pseud., Elenore Smith Bowen), *Return to Laughter: an anthropological novel* (1954; repr. New York, 1964), p. 4.

28 H. Fischer, 'Erste Kontakte: Neuguinea 1958', in *Feldforschungen: Berichte zur Einführung in Probleme und Methoden*, ed. H. Fischer (Berlin, 1985), p. 29.

29 See Radcliffe-Brown, 'On joking relationships'; J. Middleton, 'Joking relationship', in *A Dictionary of the Social Sciences*, ed. J. Gould and W. L. Kolb (New York, 1964), p. 358; Apte, *Humor and Laughter*, pp. 30–1.

30 K. Heggenhoughen, 'The inseparability of reason and emotion in the anthropological perspective', in *The Naked Anthropologist*, p. 248. Joking in male homosocial gatherings frequently revolves on women and sexuality: see T. Gregor, *Anxious Pleasures: the sexual lives of an Amazonian people* (Chicago, 1985), pp. 206–7: 'Men's clubs, whether Mehinaku or American, encourage boisterous comradery among the members and promote a hostile yet anxious image of women. Jokes and banter, which are inevitable in all-male settings, effectively serve both of these ends'. See also H. Driessen, 'Gestured masculinity in rural Andalusia', in *A Cultural History of Gesture*, ed. J. Bremmer and H. Roodenburg (Cambridge, 1991), pp. 237–53.

31 E. Smith Bowen, *Return to Laughter*. Her professor, Meyer Fortes, seems to have been furious and is reported to have said that he would not have sent her out if he had known she was going to write such a book.

32 N. A. Chagnon, *Yanomamö: the fierce people* (New York, 1968), pp. 7, 8, 11. Anthropologists frequently get involved in joking relationships among their informants. For instance, among the male Maroons of Suriname the highly developed forms of etiquette often bear the brunt of joking by exaggeration. The fieldworker is expected to play along with his informants (personal communication, Bonno Thoden van Velzen).

33 A similar ambiguity marks the attitude of anthropologists towards their

fieldnotes. It has been noted that anthropologists tend to avoid talking about fieldnotes or only joke about them. See J. E. Jackson, '"I am a fieldnote": fieldnotes as a symbol of professional identity', in *Fieldnotes: the making of anthropology*, ed. R. Sanjek (Ithaca, NY, 1990), pp. 3–33. Jackson writes: 'While in our "corridor talk" we anthropologists celebrate and harvest anecdotes about the adventure and art of fieldwork, playing down and poking fun at our attempts to be objective and scientific in the deep bush, the tensions remain – because at other times we use our fieldnotes as evidence of objectivity and rigor' (p. 26).

34 The vast literature of confessional tales of the field testify to the fact that fieldwork is fraught with emotion, ambivalence and dilemma. Some recent examples of reflective work are C. Geertz, *Works and Lives: the anthropologist as author* (Oxford, 1988); J. Clifford, *The Predicament of Culture: twentieth-century ethnography, literature, and art* (Cambridge, MA, 1988); P. Stoller, *The Taste of Ethnographic Things: the senses in anthropology* (Philadelphia, 1989); M. Hammersley, *What's Wrong with Ethnography? Methodological explorations* (London, 1992); A. Krupat, *Ethnocriticism: ethnography, history, literature* (Berkeley, 1992); J. P. Dumont, *Visayan Vignettes: ethnographic traces of a Philippine island* (Chicago, 1992). Oddly enough, none of these authors refer to the issue of humour and laughter in the field, although several of them point at the use of irony as a trope of ethnographic writing.

35 N. Barley, *The Innocent Anthropologist: notes from a mud hut* (London, 1983), which was translated into many languages. Also see his *A Plague of Caterpillars: a return to the African bush* (Harmondsworth, 1987) and *Not a Hazardous Sport* (Harmondsworth, 1989). His monograph based on his fieldwork among the Dowayos, *Symbolic Structures: an exploration of the culture of the Dowayos* (Cambridge, 1983), lacks the witty, humorous and hilarious tone of his popular writings.

36 There is, for instance, great and more subtle humour on similar themes in A. Gottlieb and P. Graham, *Parallel Worlds: an anthropologist and a writer encounter Africa* (New York, 1993).

37 *The Innocent Anthropologist* is rarely referred to in the professional literature. For one of the few reviews I could find in anthropological journals, see W. Arens, *American Anthropologist*, 87 (1985), p. 170.

38 There was much open controversy regarding the posthumous publication of Malinowski's diary. This book contrasts sharply with Barley's account. Here no humour or self-mocking at all but rather ponderousness and self-pity. Another genre of writing, which I can only mention in passing, is the novel in which anthropologists figure in humorous, ironic or satirical ways. One of the best examples is Barbara Pym's *Less than Angels* (1955). This book offers sharp and entertaining miniatures of the anthropological community.

39 See, among others, F. C. Miller, 'Humor in a Chippewa tribal council', *Ethnology*, 6 (1967), pp. 263–71.

40 See U. Hannerz, *Cultural Complexity: studies in the social organization of meaning* (New York, 1992), pp. 132–3. Moreover, anthropology is betwixt and between the humanities and the social sciences.

Humour and History:
A Research Bibliography

JOHAN VERBERCKMOES

This bibliography lists a selection of books and articles on the history of laughter and humour. Its aim is to inform about the variety of ongoing and past research, taking into account the relative confusion about the exact boundaries of the topic. It is definitely not a complete bibliography. Studies on irony, satire, theatre and comedy have been left out, as well as anthologies and studies on individual authors. On caricature only some general introductions with good bibliographies have been retained, as well as some older surveys. Section VII contains a personal selection of some of the main theoretical studies. The recent bibliography on *Humor Scholarship* by Don Nilsen contains very little on history and humour and concentrates moreover on US studies. I thank Jan Bremmer and Herman Roodenburg for various suggestions.

I BIBLIOGRAPHIES OF HUMOUR STUDIES

Chapman, A. J. and Foot, H. C. (eds), *It's a Funny Thing, Humour: international conference on humour and laughter* (Oxford, 1977), pp. 469–504.
Nilsen, D. L. F., *Humor Scholarship: a research bibliography* (Westport, CT, and London, 1993).

II GENERAL STUDIES

Alexandre, A., *L'art du rire et de la caricature* (Paris, 1892).
Bennett, G., *Spoken in Jest* (Sheffield, 1991).
Billington, S., *A Social History of the Fool* (Brighton and New York, 1984).
Bouza, F., *Locos, enanos y hombres de placer en la corte de los Austrias. Oficio de burlas* (Madrid, 1991).
Cameron, K. (ed.), *Humour and History* (Oxford, 1993).
Cazamian, L., *The Development of English Humor* (Durham, NC, 1952).
Davies, C., *Ethnic Humor around the World: a comparative analysis* (Bloomington, 1990).
Duvignaud, J., *Le propre de l'homme. Histoires du comique et de la dérision* (Paris, 1985).

Escarpit, R., *L'humour* (6th edn, Paris, 1976).

Flögel, K. F., *Geschichte der komischen Literatur* (4 vols, Liegnitz and Leipzig, 1784–7).

——, *Geschichte des Grotesk-Komischen. Ein Beitrag zur Geschichte der Menschheit* (Liegnitz and Leipzig 1788); reissued by M. Bauer (2 vols, Munich, 1914).

——, *Geschichte der Hofnarren* (Liegnitz and Leipzig 1789).

——, *Geschichte des Burlesken* (Leipzig, 1794).

Gilman, S. L., *The Parodic Sermon in European Perspective: aspects of liturgical parody from the Middle Ages to the twentieth century* (Wiesbaden, 1974).

Gombrich, E. H., 'The experiment of caricature', in *Art and Illusion: a study in the psychology of pictorial representation* (London, 1962), pp. 279–303.

Humor, special issue of *Yale French Studies*, 23 (1959).

L'humour et la médaille à la Monnaie de Paris (Paris, 1981), exhibition catalogue.

L'Humour Européen: les formes du rire, du risible et de la dérision dans le patrimoine multiculturel de l'Europe (Lublin and Sèvres, 1993).

Jahn, F., *Das Problem des Komischen in seiner geschichtlichen Entwicklung* (Potsdam, 1904).

Kuhlmann, W. and Röhrich, L., *Witz, Humor und Komik im Volksmärchen* (Regensburg, 1993).

Langemeyer, G. et al. (eds), *Bild als Waffe. Mittel und Motive der Karikatur in fünf Jahrhunderten* (Munich, 1984).

L'Estrange, A. G., *History of English Humour: with an introduction upon ancient humour* (New York, 1970).

Lever, M., *Le sceptre et la marotte: histoire de fous de cour* (Paris, 1983).

Lipovetsky, G., *L'ère du vide: essais sur l'individualisme contemporain* (Paris, 1983), pp. 153–93.

Malcolm, J. P., *An Historical Sketch of the Art of Caricaturing* (London, 1813).

Melot, M., *Die Karikatur: das Komische in der Kunst* (Fribourg, 1975).

Nohain, J., *Histoire du rire à travers le monde* (Paris, 1965).

Piddington, R., *From Plato to Freud: the psychology of laughter* (New York, 1963).

Piltz, G., *Geschichte der europäischen Karikatur* (Berlin, 1976).

Posthumus Meyjes, G. H. M., *Geloven en lachen in de historie* (Leiden, 1992).

Rütten, T., *Demokrit – lachender Philosoph und sanguinischer Melancholiker. Eine pseudohippokratische Geschichte* (Leiden, 1992).

Sauvy, A., *Aux sources de l'humour* (Paris, 1988).

Schneegans, H., *Geschichte der grotesken Satire* (Strasbourg, 1894).

Smadja, É., *Le rire* (Paris 1993).

Stollmann, R., 'Lachen, Freiheit und Geschichte', *Jahrbuch für internationale Germanistik*, 20–2 (1988), pp. 25–43.

Welsford, E., *The Fool: his social and literary history* (London, 1935, repr. Gloucester, MA, 1968).

Wendland, V., *Ostermärchen und Ostergelächter: brauchtümliche Kanzelrhetorik und ihre kulturkritische Würdigung seit dem ausgehenden Mittelalter* (Frankfurt am Main, Bern and Cirencester, 1980).

Wright, T., *A History of Caricature and Grotesque in Literature and Art* (London, 1865).

Zuno, J. G., *Historia general de la caricatura* (Guadalajara, 1959).

III ANTIQUITY

Adkin, N., 'The fathers on laughter', *Orpheus*, n.s. 6 (1985), pp. 149–52.

Arnould, D., *Le rire et les larmes dans la littérature grecque: d'Homère à Platon* (Paris, 1990).

Cataudella, Q., *La facezia in Grecia e a Roma* (Florence, 1971).

Cebe, J.-P., *La caricature et la parodie dans le monde romain antique des origines à Juvénal* (Paris, 1966).

De Saint-Denis, E., *Essais sur le rire et le sourire des latins* (Paris, 1965).

Ephraim, D., 'Laughter in Spartan society', in A. Powell (ed.), *Classical Sparta: techniques behind her success* (London, 1989).

Grant, M. A., *The Ancient Rhetorical Theories of the Laughable: the Greek rhetoricians and Cicero* (Madison, 1924).

Gribaudi, P., *Bons mots et facéties des Pères du désert* (Paris, 1987).

Halliwell, S., 'The uses of laughter in Greek culture', *Classical Quarterly*, 41 (1991), pp. 276–96.

Horst, P. W. van der, 'Is wittiness unchristian? A note on *eutrapelía* in Eph. V.4', in T. Baarda et al. (eds), *Miscellanea Neotestamentica* II (Leiden, 1977), pp. 163–77, repr. in P. W. van der Horst and G. Mussies, *Studies on the Hellenistic Background of the New Testament* (Utrecht, 1990), pp. 223–37.

Jäkel, S. and Timonen, A. (eds), *Laughter down the Centuries* (2 vols, Turku, 1994–5).

Jonson, J., *Humour and Irony in the New Testament* (Leiden, 1985).

Kenner, H., *Weinen und Lachen in der Griechischen Kunst* (Vienna, 1960).

Lateiner, D., 'No laughing matter: a literary tactic in Herodotus', *Transactions of the American Philological Association*, 107 (1977), pp. 173–82.

Milanezi, S., 'Le rire d'Hadès', *Dialogues d'histoire ancienne*, 21 (1995), pp. 231–45.

Monaco, G., 'Quintino Cataudella e l'umorismo antico', in G. Basta Donzelli et al. (eds), *Quintino Cataudella* (Catania, 1992), pp. 79–87.

Radday, Y. T. and Brenner, A. (eds), *On Humour and the Comic in the Hebrew Bible* (Sheffield, 1990).

Reinhardt, U. and Sallman, K. (eds), *Musa Iocosa. Arbeiten über Humor und Witz, Komik und Komödie der Antike, Andreas Thierfelder zum siebzigsten Geburtstag am 15 juni 1973* (Hildesheim and New York, 1974).

Richlin, A., *The Garden of Priapus: sexuality and aggression in Roman humor* (New Haven and London, 1983).

Steidle, B., 'Das Lachen im alten Mönchtum', *Benediktinische Monatschrift zur Pflege religiösen und geistigen Lebens*, 20 (1938), pp. 271–80, repr. in his *Beiträge zum alten Mönchtum und zur Benediktusregel* (Sigmaringen, 1986), pp. 30–9.

Süss, W., *Lachen, Komik und Witz in der Antike* (Zürich and Stuttgart, 1969).

Van de Walle, B., *L'Humour dans la littérature et dans l'art de l'ancienne*

Egypte (Leiden, 1969).
Voeltzel, R., *Le rire du Seigneur: enquêtes et remarques sur la signification théologique et pratique de l'ironie biblique* (Strasbourg, 1955).
Woodbury, L., *Quo modo risu ridiculoque Graeci usi sunt* (Diss., Harvard, 1944).

IV MIDDLE AGES AND RENAISSANCE

Adolf, H., 'On mediaeval laughter', *Speculum*, 22 (1947), pp. 251–3.
Amman, L., *Vorbild und Vernunft: die Regelung von Lachen und Scherzen im mittelalterlichen Islam* (Hildesheim, 1993).
Aubailly, J.-C., 'Le fabliau et les sources inconscientes du rire médiéval', *Cahiers de civilisation médiévale (Xe–XIIe siècles)*, 30 (1987), pp. 105–17.
Bakhtin, M., *Rabelais and his World*, trans. H. Iswolsky (Cambridge, 1968).
Barolsky, P., *Infinite Jest: wit and humor in Italian Renaissance art* (Columbia, MO, and London, 1978).
Billington, S., *Mock Kings in Medieval Society and Renaissance Drama* (Oxford, 1991).
Blaicher, G., 'Über das Lachen im englischen Mittelalter', *Deutsche Vierteljahrsschrift für Literaturwissenschaft und Geistesgeschichte*, 44 (1970), pp. 508–29.
Blanke, F., *Luthers Humor. Scherz und Schalk in Luthers Seelsorge* (Hamburg, 1954).
Bloch, R. H., 'The fabliaux, fetishism, and Freud's Jewish jokes', *Representations*, 4 (1983), pp. 1–26.
Bouché, T. and Charpentier, H. (eds), *Le rire au Moyen Âge dans la littérature et dans les arts* (Bordeaux, 1990).
Bowen, B. C., 'Renaissance collections of facetiae, 1344–1528', *Renaissance Quarterly*, 39 (1986), pp. 1–15, 263–75.
——, 'Rire est le propre de l'homme', in J. Céard and J.-C. Margolin (eds), *Rabelais en son demi-millénaire: actes du colloque international du C.N.R.S., Université Fr. Rabelais de Tours, 24–29 sept. 1984* (Geneva, 1988), pp. 185–90.
Bristol, M. D., *Carnival and Theater: plebeian culture and the structure of authority in Renaissance England* (New York and London, 1985).
Ciappelli, G. 'Ridere nel Medioevo', *Quaderni medievali*, 28 (1989), pp. 120–8.
Le comique au moyen âge, special issue of the *Cahiers de l'association internationale des études françaises*, 37 (Paris, 1985).
Cooke, T. D. and Honeycutt, B. L. (eds), *The Humor of the Fabliaux: a collection of critical essays* (Columbia, MO, 1974).
Curtius, E. R., 'Excursus IV: Scherz und Ernst in Mittelalterlicher Literatur', *Europäische Literatur und Lateinisches Mittelalter* (6th edn, Bern and Munich, 1967).
Delattre, F., 'La naissance de l'humour dans la vieille Angleterre', *Revue anglo-américaine* (1927), pp. 289–307.
Delègue, Y., 'La signification du rire dans l'*Heptaméron*', in S. Perrier (ed.), *L'Heptaméron de Marguerite de Navarre: actes de la journée d'étude*

Marguerite de Navarre 19 octobre 1991 (Paris, 1992), pp. 35–49.

Demerson, G., *Humanisme et facétie* (Caen, 1994).

De Rocher, G., *Rabelais' Laughers and Joubert's 'Traité du Ris'* (Tuscaloosa, AL, 1979).

Facétie et littérature facétieuse à l'époque de la renaissance. Actes du colloque de Goutelas, 29 septembre – 1er octobre 1977, special issue of *Réforme, Humanisme, Renaissance. Bulletin de l'Association d'Études sur l'Humanisme, la Réforme et la Renaissance*, 7 (1978), pp. 1–150.

Gourevitch, A., 'On heroes, things, gods and laughter in Germanic poetry', *Studies in Medieval and Renaissance History*, 5 (1982), pp. 107–72.

——, *Medieval Popular Culture: problems of belief and perception*, trans. J. M. Bak and P. A. Hollingsworth (Cambridge and Paris, 1988), pp. 176–210.

Haug, W., 'Das Komische und das Heilige: zur Komische in der religiösen Literatur des Mittelalters', *Wolfram-Studien*, 7 (1982), pp. 8–32.

Heers, J., *Fêtes des fous et carnavals* (Paris, 1983).

Herrick, M. T., *Comic Theory in the Sixteenth Century* (Urbana, 1964).

Horowitz, J. and Menache, S., *L'humour en chaire: le rire dans l'église médiévale* (Geneva, 1994).

Kremer, K. R., *Das Lachen in der deutschen Sprache und Literatur des Mittelalters* (Diss., Bonn, 1961).

Lazard, M., 'La thérapeutique par le rire dans la médecine du XVIe siècle', in M. Milner (ed.), *Littérature et pathologie* (Paris, 1989), pp. 13–27.

Le Goff, J., 'Le rire dans les règles monastiques du haut moyen âge', in C. Lepelley et al. (eds), *Haut moyen-âge: culture, éducation et société. Études offertes à Pierre Riché* (La Garenne-Colombes, 1990), pp. 93–103.

——, 'Jésus a-t-il ri?', *L'histoire*, 158 (1992), pp. 72–4.

Lehmann, P., *Die Parodie im Mittelalter* (Stuttgart, 1963).

Luck, G., 'Vir facetus: a Renaissance ideal', *Studies in Philology*, 55 (1958), pp. 107–21.

Marzolph, U., *Arabia ridens: die humoristische Kurzprosa der frühen adab-Literatur im internationalen Traditionsgeflecht* (2 vols, Frankfurt am Main, 1992).

Ménager, D., *La Renaissance et le rire* (Paris, 1995).

Ménard, P., *Le rire et le sourire dans le roman courtois en France au Moyen Âge (1150–1250)* (Geneva, 1969).

——, *Les fabliaux: contes à rire du moyen âge* (Paris, 1983).

Mezger, W., *Hofnarren im Mittelalter: vom tieferen Sinn eines seltsamen Amts* (Konstanz, 1981).

Nédoncelle, M., 'L'humour d'Érasme et l'humour de Thomas More', in J. Coppens (ed.), *Scrinium Erasmianum*, vol. II (Leiden, 1969), pp. 547–67.

Pleij, H., 'De sociale functie van humor en trivialiteit op het rederijkerstoneel', *Spectator*, 5 (1975–6), pp. 108–27.

Porter, L. C., 'Le rire au moyen âge', *L'esprit créateur*, 16 (1976), pp. 5–15.

Resnick, I. M., '"Risus monasticus": laughter and medieval monastic culture', *Revue bénédictine*, 97 (1987), pp. 90–100.

Rosenthal, F., *Humor in Early Islam* (Westport, CT, 1976).

Schindler, N., 'Karneval, Kirche und die verkehrte Welt: zur Funktion der Lachkultur im 16. Jahrhundert', *Jahrbuch für Volkskunde*, 7 (1984), pp. 9–

57, in expanded version repr. in his *Widerspenstige Leute. Studien zur Volkskultur in der frühen Neuzeit* (Frankfurt am Main, 1992), pp. 121–74.

Schmitz, G., '... quod rident homines, plorandum est. Der "Unwert" des Lachens in monastisch geprägten Vorstellungen der Spätantike und des frühen Mittelalters', in F. Quarthal and W. Setzler (eds), *Stadtverfassung – Verfassungsstaat – Pressepolitik* (Sigmaringen, 1980), pp. 3–15.

Schmitz, H. G., *Physiologie des Scherzes. Bedeutung und Rechtfertigung der Ars Iocandi im 16. Jahrhundert* (Hildesheim and New York, 1972).

Screech, M. A. and Calder, R., 'Some Renaissance attitudes to laughter', in A. M. T. Levi (ed.), *Humanism in France at the End of the Middle Ages and in the Early Renaissance* (New York, 1970), pp. 216–28.

Suchomski, J., *'Delectatio' und 'Utilitas': ein Beitrag zur Verständnis mittelalterlicher komischer Literatur* (Bern, 1975).

Swain, B., *Fools and Folly during the Middle Ages and the Renaissance* (New York, 1932).

Tatlock, J. S. P., 'Mediaeval laughter', *Speculum*, 21 (1946), pp. 289–94.

Tschipper, M., *Lachen und Komik in England vom späten Mittelalter bis zur Elisabethanischen Zeit: Studien zu conduct books, mystery plays and jestbooks* (Bamberg, 1969).

Van Nierop, H. F. K., 'Edelman, bedelman: de verkeerde wereld van het Compromis der Edelen', *Bijdragen en Mededelingen betreffende de Geschiedenis der Nederlanden*, 107 (1992), pp. 1–27 (English version in *European History Quarterly*, 21 (1991), pp. 419–43).

Walser, E., *Die Theorie des Witzes und der Novelle nach dem 'De sermone' des Jovianus Pontanus: ein gesellschaftliches Ideal vom Ende des XV. Jahrhunderts* (Strasbourg, 1908).

Wehrli, M., 'Christliches Lachen, christliche Komik?', in D. H. Green, L. P. Johnson and D. Wuttke (eds), *From Wolfram and Petrarch to Goethe and Grass: studies in literature in honour of Leonard Forster* (Baden-Baden, 1982), pp. 17–31.

Zuber, R., 'Les éléments populaires de la culture savante: les humanistes et le comique', in *Histoire sociale, sensibilités collectives et mentalités: mélanges Robert Mandrou* (Paris, 1985), pp. 283–90.

V EARLY MODERN PERIOD

Alpers, S., 'Realism as a comic mode: low-life painting seen through Bredero's eyes', *Simiolus*, 8 (1975–6), pp. 115–44.

Appelberg, B., *Teorierna om det komiska under 1600- och 1700-talet* (Helsingfors, 1944).

Bertrand Brunet, D., *Histoire du rire à l'âge classique* (Diss., Paris VII, 1985).

——, 'Le siècle de Louis XIV en quête d'un rire à la française', *Papers on French Seventeenth Century Literature*, 19 (1992), pp. 55–69.

——, *Dire le rire à l'âge classique: représenter pour mieux contrôler* (Aix-en-Provence, 1995).

Brewer, J., 'Theater and counter-theater in Georgian politics: the mock elections at Garrat', *Radical History Review*, 22 (1979–80), pp. 7–40.

Brunner, S., *Der Humor in der Diplomatie und der Regierungskunde des 18. Jahrhunderts* (2 vols, Vienna, 1872).

Castle, T., *Masquerade and Civilisation: the carnivalesque in eighteenth-century English culture and fiction* (Stanford, CA, 1986).

De Baecque, A., *Le corps de l'histoire: métaphores et politique (1770–1800)* (Paris, 1993).

Dekker, R. and Roodenburg, H., 'Humor in de zeventiende eeuw: opvoeding, huwelijk en seksualiteit in de moppen van Aernout van Overbeke (1632–1674)', *Tijdschrift voor sociale geschiedenis*, 10 (1984), pp. 243–66.

De la Sagrada Familia, S. and de la Visitacion, I. (eds), *Humor y espiritualidad en la escuela teresiana primitiva* (Burgos, 1966).

Delumeau, J. (ed.), *Injures et blasphèmes*, issue of *Mentalités: histoire des cultures et des sociétés* (Paris, 1989).

De Man, J., 'De etiquette van het schertsen: opvattingen over de lach in Nederlandse etiquetteboeken en spectators uit de achttiende eeuw', *De Achttiende Eeuw*, 25 (1993), pp. 93–136.

Findlen, P., 'Jokes of nature and jokes of knowledge: the playfulness of scientific discourse in early modern Europe', *Renaissance Quarterly*, 43 (1990), pp. 292–331.

Goldzink, J., *Les lumières et l'idée du comique* (Fontenay-aux-Roses, 1992).

Granger, B. I., *Political Satire in the American Revolution, 1763–1783* (Ithaca and New York, 1980).

Hansen, J., *'The Philosophers of Laughter': Velazquez' portraits of jesters at the court of Philip IV* (Diss., U. of Arizona, 1990).

Isherwood, R., *Farce and Fantasy: popular entertainment in eighteenth-century Paris* (New York and Oxford, 1986).

Jacques, É., 'Humeur et humour jansénistes: sur un curieux manuscrit de la bibliothèque du Musée Puissant, à Mons', in his *Jansénisme, antijansénisme: acteurs, auteurs et témoins* (Brussels, 1988) [separate numbering: 17pp.].

Kenney, W. H. (ed), *Laughter in the Wilderness: early American humor up to 1783* (Kent, OH, 1976).

Koopmans, J. and Verhuyck, P., *Een kijk op anekdotencollecties in de zeventiende eeuw. Jan Zoet, 'Het Leven en Bedrijf van Clément Marot'* (Amsterdam and Atlanta, 1991).

Miedema, H., 'Realism and the comic mode: the peasant', *Simiolus*, 9 (1977), pp. 205–19.

Moser-Rath, E., *'Lustige Gesellschaft': Schwank und Witz des 17. und 18. Jahrhunderts in kultur- und sozialgeschichtlichem Kontext* (Stuttgart, 1984).

Neumann, N., *Vom Schwank zum Witz: zum Wandel der Pointe seit dem 16. Jahrhundert* (Frankfurt am Main and New York, 1986).

Popoff-Böcker, E., 'Laughter in 17th century Russia', in *To Honour Frans Vyncke, Slavica Gandensia*, 13 (Ghent, 1986), pp. 415–21.

Porteman, K., 'The emblem as "genus jocosum": theory and practice. Jacob Cats and Roemer Visscher', *Emblematica*, 8-2 (Dutch version in *De zeventiende eeuw*, 11 (1995), pp. 184–97).

Ramondt, M., 'De evolutie van de "gros rire" in de 17e eeuw', *De nieuwe taalgids*, 47 (1954), pp. 190–8.

Risa y sociedad en el teatro español del Siglo de Oro: rire et société dans le

Humour and History: A Research Bibliography   249

théâtre espagnol du Siècle d'Or. Actes du 3ième colloque du groupe d'études sur le théâtre espagnol, Toulouse, 31 janvier–2 février 1980 (Paris, 1980).

Stipriaan, René van, *Leugens en vermaak. Boccaccio's novellen in de kluchtcultuur van de Nederlandse renaissance* (Amsterdam, 1996).

Tave, S. M., *The Amiable Humorist: a study in the comic theory and criticism of the 18th and 19th centuries* (Chicago, 1960).

Thomas, K., 'The place of laughter in Tudor and Stuart England', *Times Literary Supplement*, 21 January 1977, pp. 77–81.

Vandenbroeck, P., *Over wilden en narren, boeren en bedelaars: beeld van de andere, vertoog over het zelf* (Antwerp, 1987) [exhibition catalogue].

Van Overbeke, A., *Anecdota sive historiae jocosae: een zeventiende-eeuwse verzameling moppen en anekdotes*, ed. R. Dekker and H. Roodenburg (Amsterdam, 1991).

Verberckmoes, J., 'The emperor and the peasant. The Spanish Habsburgs in Low Countries' jests', in W. Thomas and B. De Groof (eds), *Rebelión y resistencia en el mundo Hispánico del siglo XVII: actas del Coloquio Internacional Lovaina, 20–23 de Noviembre de 1991* (Louvain, 1992), pp. 67–78.

——, *Schertsen, schimpen, schaterlachen: het komische in de cultuur van de Spaanse Nederlanden (16de–17de eeuw)* (Diss., Louvain, 1993).

Woodruff, P., 'Rousseau, Molière, and the ethics of laughter', *Philosophy and Literature*, 1 (1977), pp. 325–36.

VI NINETEENTH AND TWENTIETH CENTURIES

Baum, G., *Humor und Satire in der bürgerlichen Ästhetik* (Berlin, 1959).

Boskin, J., *Humor and Social Change in Twentieth-Century America* (Boston, 1979).

——, *Sambo: the rise and demise of an American jester* (New York, 1986).

Bricker, V. R., *Ritual Humor in Highland Chiapas* (Austin, 1973).

Cohen, S. B., *Jewish Wry: essays on Jewish humor* (Bloomington, 1987).

Drozdzynski, A., *Der politische Witz im Ostblock* (Munich, 1978).

Dundes, A., *Cracking Jokes: studies of sick humor cycles and stereotypes* (Berkeley, CA, 1987).

Feuerhahn, N., *Traits d'impertinence: histoire et chefs-d'oeuvre du dessin d'humour de 1914 à nos jours* (Paris, 1993).

Gamm, H.-J., *Der Flüsterwitz im Dritten Reich* (Munich, 1979).

Glettler, M., 'Totalitarismus und politischen Witz: zur Analyse des Totalitarismusbegriffes an beispielen des politischen Witzes', *Österreich in Geschichte und Literatur*, 23 (1979), pp. 26–42.

Grojnowski, D., 'Le rire "moderne" à la fin du XIXe siècle', *Poétique. Revue de théorie et d'analyse littéraires*, 21 (1990), pp. 453–69.

Hamamoto, D. Y., *Nervous Laughter: television situation comedy and liberal democratic ideology* (New York, 1989).

Hillenbrand, F. K. M., *Underground Humour in Nazi Germany, 1933–1945* (London, 1995).

Jongejan, E., *De humor-'cultus' der romantiek in Nederland* (Zutphen, 1933).

Lahue, K. C., *World of Laughter: the motion picture comedy short, 1910–1930* (Norman, OK, 1972).

Lipp, C., 'Die Frau in der Karikatur und Witz der 48er Revolution', *Fabula: Zeitschrift für Erzählforschung*, 32 (1991), pp. 132–64.

Mintz, L. E. (ed.), *Humor in America: a research guide to genres and topics* (New York, 1988).

Nysenholc, A., *Charles Chaplin: ou la légende des images* (Paris, 1987).

Pelton, R. D., *The Trickster in West Africa: a study of mythic irony and sacred delight* (Berkeley, CA, 1980).

Les petits maîtres du rire, special issue of *Romantisme: revue du dix-neuvième siècle*, 75 (1992).

Radin, P., *The Trickster: a study in American Indian mythology* (Westport, CT, 1956).

Rankin, A. M. and Philip, P. J., 'An epidemic of laughing in the Buboka district of Tanganyika', *Central African Journal of Medecine*, 9 (1963), pp. 167–70.

Rire et rires, special issue of *Romantisme: revue du dix-neuvième siècle*, 74 (1992).

Rosaldo, R., 'Politics, patriarchs, and laughter', *Cultural Critique*, 6 (1987), pp. 65–86.

Schechter, W., *The History of Negro Humor in America* (New York, 1970).

Streip, K., '"Just a cérébrale": Jean Rhys, women's humor, and ressentiment', *Representations*, 45 (1994), pp. 117–44.

Thompson, R., 'Popular reading and humour in Restoration England', *Journal of Popular Culture* (1976), pp. 653–71.

Townsend, M. L., *Forbidden Laughter: popular humor and the limits of repression in nineteenth-century Prussia* (Ann Arbor, 1992).

Unterbrink, M., *Funny Women: American comediennes, 1860–1985* (Jefferson, NC, 1987).

Vázquez Lucio, O. E., *Historia del humor grafico y escrito en la Argentina* (2 vols, Buenos Aires, 1985–6).

Vieira, N., 'The Luso-Brazilian joke', *Western Folklore*, 30 (1980), pp. 51–6.

Walker, N. A., *A Very Serious Thing: women's humor and American culture* (Minneapolis, 1988).

Wechsler, J., *A Human Comedy: physiognomy and caricature in 19th century Paris* (London, 1982).

Zeldin, T., *France, 1848–1945*, vol. 2: *Intellect, Taste and Anxiety* (Oxford, 1977), pp. 646–724.

Ziv, A. (ed.), *National Styles of Humor* (New York, 1988).

VII Anthropology, Sociology, Philosophy, Language, etc.

Apte, M. L., *Humor and Laughter: an anthropological approach* (Ithaca, NY, and London, 1985).

Attardo, S., *Linguistic Theories of Humor* (Berlin, 1994).

Bergson, H., *Le rire: essai sur la signification du comique* (Paris, 1900).

Chapman, A. J. and Foot, H. C. (eds), *Humour and Laughter: theory, research and applications* (London, 1976).

Davies, C., 'Commentary on Anton C. Zijderveld's trend report on "the sociology of humour and laughter"', *Current Sociology: la sociologie contemporaine*, 32–1 (1984), pp. 142–57.

Douglas, M., 'Jokes', in her *Implicit Meanings: essays in anthropology* (London and Boston, 1975), pp. 90–114.

——, 'Do dogs laugh? A cross-cultural approach to body symbolism', in T. Polhemus (ed.), *Social Aspects of the Human Body: a reader of key texts* (Harmondsworth, 1978), pp. 295–301 (repr. in *Implicit Meanings*, pp. 83–9).

Durant, J. and Miller, J. (eds), *Laughing Matters: a serious look at humour* (London, 1988).

Freud, S., *Der Witz und seine Beziehung zum Unbewussten* (Leipzig and Vienna, 1905).

Grimm, R. and Hermand, J. (eds), *Laughter Unlimited: essays on humor, satire and the comic* (Madison, 1991).

Janitschek, R. and Naafs, J., 'Uitingsvormen van humor in romantische literatuur in Holland en Duitsland. Een literatuursociologisch en cultuurhistorisch onderzoek', *Sociale Wetenschappen*, 27 (1984), pp. 65–98.

Johnson, R., 'Jokes, theories, anthropology', *Semiotica*, 22 (1978), pp. 309–34.

Jurzik, R., *Der Stoff des Lachens. Studien über Komik* (Frankfurt am Main and New York, 1985).

Koller, M. R., *Humor and Society: explorations in the sociology of humor* (Houston, 1988).

Language and Humor, special issue of the *International Journal of the Sociology of Language*, 65 (1987).

Legman, G., *Rationale of the Dirty Joke: an analysis of sexual humor* (London, 1969).

Lixfeld, H., 'Witz und soziale Wirklichkeit: Bemerkungen zur interdisziplinären Witzforschung', *Fabula: Zeitschrift für Erzählforschung*, 25 (1984), pp. 183–213.

McGhee, P.E. (ed.), *Humor and Children's Development* (New York, 1989).

McGhee, P. E. and Goldstein, J. H. (eds), *Handbook of Humor Research* (2 vols, New York, Berlin, Heidelberg and Tokyo, 1983).

Morreall, J. (ed.), *The Philosophy of Laughter and Humor* (Albany and New York, 1987).

Palmer, J., *Taking Humour Seriously* (London and New York, 1994).

Philosophy and Humor, special issue of *Philosophy East and West*, 39–2 (1989).

Powell, C. and Paton, G. E. C. (eds), *Humour in Society: resistance and control* (London, 1988).

Preisendanz, W. and Warning, R. (eds), *Das Komische* (Munich, 1976).

Raskin, V., *Semantic Mechanisms of Humor* (Dordrecht, Boston and Lancaster, 1985).

Röhrich, L., *Der Witz: Figuren, Formen, Funktionen* (Stuttgart, 1977).

Santarcangeli, P., *Homo ridens: estetica, filologia, psicologia, storia del comico* (Florence, 1989).

Stora-Sandor, J., *Le monde du rire et le rire du monde* (Paris, 1992).

Zijderveld, A. C., *Reality in a Looking-Glass: rationality through an analysis of traditional folly* (London, 1982).
——, 'The sociology of humour and laughter', *Current Sociology: la sociologie contemporaine*, 31–3 (1983), pp. 1–103.
Ziv, A., *Personality and Sense of Humor* (New York, 1984).

VIII Periodicals

Humor: international journal of humor research, 1 (1988–).
Humoresques, 1 (1988–).
Journal of Popular Culture, 1 (1967–).
L.I.G.H.T.: laughter in God, history and theology, 1 (1984–).
Maledicta: the international journal of verbal aggression, 1 (1978–).
Thalia: studies in literary humor, 1 (1978–).

Index of Names

Index of Subjects

Lightning Source UK Ltd.
Milton Keynes UK
14 September 2010

159840UK00002B/25/P

9 780745 618807